THE AMERICAN EXPRESS POCKET GUIDE TO NEW YORK

Herbert Bailey Livesey

PRENTICE HALL PRESS
NEW YORK

The Author
A native New Yorker, Herbert Bailey Livesey is a novelist and travel writer who contributes regularly to *Travel & Leisure* magazine. He is also the author of *Toronto, Montréal and Québec City, Spain* and the forthcoming *Madrid and Barcelona* in this series.

Acknowledgments

The publishers would like to thank the following for their help and/or advice during the preparation of this book: Chris and Mike Cowie, Muriel and Alf Jackson, and Mike De Mello of Triptych Systems Ltd.

The *American Express Pocket Travel Guide Series* was conceived under the direction of Susannah Read, Douglas Wilson, Hal Robinson and Eric Drewery. Diana Grant edited the original edition.

For the series
General Editor	David Townsend Jones
Managing Art Editor	Nigel O'Gorman
Art Editor	Christopher Howson
Map Editor	David Haslam
Indexer	Hilary Bird
Gazetteer	Sharon Charity

For this edition
Edited on desktop by	Eileen Townsend Jones
Illustrators	Illustrated Arts, Coral Mula, Karen Cochrane
Jacket illustration	Christian Broutin

Edited and designed by Mitchell Beazley International Limited, Artists House, 14-15 Manette Street, London W1V 5LB for the American Express (R) Pocket Travel Guide Series

New edition © American Express Publishing Corporation Inc. 1991
Previous editions © American Express Publishing Corporation Inc. 1983, 1986 (reprinted 1987), 1988

Published by Prentice Hall Trade Division
A Division of Simon & Schuster, Inc.
Gulf & Western Building
One Gulf & Western Plaza
New York, New York 10023

PRENTICE HALL is a trademark of Simon & Schuster, Inc.

Library of Congress Cataloging-in-Publication Data
Livesey, Herbert B.
   The American Express pocket guide to New York / Herbert B. Livesey. — Rev. ed.
      p. cm.
   Includes index.
   ISBN 0-13-025677-3 : $10.95
   1. New York (N.Y.)—Description—1981-   —Guide-books.
   I. Title.
F128.18.L57 1991
917.47'104928—dc20   90-43642
                                 CIP

Maps in 2-color and 4-color by Lovell Johns, Oxford, England.
Desktop layout in Ventura Publisher by Castle House Press, Llantrisant, Wales.
Typeset in Garamond and Univers.
Linotronic output through Microstar DTP Studio, Cardiff, Wales.
Produced by Mandarin Offset. Printed and bound in Malaysia.

Contents

How to use this book

The American Express Pocket Guide to New York is an encyclopedia of travel information, organized in the sections listed on the previous page. There is also a comprehensive *Index* (pages 207-214), a *List of street names* (pages 215-216), and full-color *Maps* of New York and environs at the end of the book.

For easy reference, all major sections (*Sights and places of interest*, *Hotels*, *Restaurants*), and other sections where possible, are arranged alphabetically. For the organization of the book as a whole, see *Contents*. For individual places that do not have separate entries in *Sights and places of interest*, see the *Index*.

Abbreviations　　As a rule, only standard abbreviations are used, such as days of the week and months, points of the compass (N, S, E and W), street names (Ave., Pl., Rd., Sq. and St.), St (Saint), rms (rooms), C (century), and measurements.

Bold type　　**Bold type** is used mainly for emphasis, to draw attention to something of special interest or importance. It also picks out places — shops or minor museums, for example — that do not have full entries of their own. In such cases, it is usually followed in brackets by the address, telephone number, details of opening times, etc., which are printed in *italics*.

Cross-references　　A special typeface, *sans serif italics*, is used for cross-references. Each time you see a place name, such as *Frick Collection*, printed in this way, expect to find a full entry under that heading in the alphabetical *Sights and places of interest* (pages 57-121). Similarly, when you see the title of a section of the book, such as *Hotels* or *Shopping*, printed in this way, you can turn to that section for further information. (You will find a complete section-by-section breakdown of the book on the *Contents* page.)

How entries are organized

Hood House

1411 Lincoln Ave., Lincoln Green, Sherwood Forest
☎ *426-5960 (house), 426-5961 (group tour reservations).*
Map 8J11 🖅 ✗ *Open Apr-Sept 9am-5pm, rest of year 9am-4pm. Closed Christmas, New Year's Day. Metro: Bow & Arrow.*

Robin Hood (?1149-1205) was the leading spokesman for the poor and downtrodden in their struggle for freedom and justice under the Plantagenets. He lectured and wrote books about his own early life as a serf, campaigned endlessly for human rights, helped recruit peasants to the Civil Service, and finally settled down to a distinguished old age in Sherwood Forest. He lived first in A St. (see *National Museum of Outlawed Art*), then bought Sheriff Villa, which he renamed Hood House, a handsome white dwelling on a height overlooking the Trent Valley. All the furnishings, except for curtains and wallpaper, are original. Hood's library and other belongings are still *in situ*, and the whole house is redolent of the spirit of a very remarkable man. In the **Visitors' Centre** at the foot of the hill you can see a film about Hood's life.

For easy reference, use the headers printed at the top corner of each page (for example, **Staten Island Zoo** on page 114, or **Architecture** on page 25).

Floors   To conform with American usage, "first floor" is used throughout the book to refer to the floor at ground level, "second floor" to the floor above that, and so on.

Map references   Each full-color map at the end of the book is divided into a grid of squares, identified vertically by letters (A, B, C, D, etc.) and horizontally by numbers (1, 2, 3, 4, etc.). A map reference pinpoints the page (the first **bold** number) and position — thus *Lincoln Center* is located in Map **6**M3.

Price categories   Price categories for hotels and restaurants are represented by the symbols ▭ ▮▭ ▮▮▭ ▮▮▮▮ and ▮▮▮▮, which signify cheap, inexpensive, moderately priced, expensive and very expensive, respectively. These correspond approximately with the following actual prices, which give a guideline at the time of printing.

Although actual prices will inevitably increase, as a rule the relative price category — for example, expensive or cheap — is likely to remain more or less the same.

Price categories	Corresponding to approximate prices	
	for **hotels** *double room with bath; single slightly cheaper*	for **restaurants** *meal for one with service, taxes and house wine*
▭ cheap	under $100	under $20
▮▭ inexpensive	$100-125	$20-30
▮▮▭ moderate	$125-170	$30-50
▮▮▮▮ expensive	$170-200	$50-90
▮▮▮▮ very expensive	over $200	over $90

—— Bold blue type for entry headings.

—— Blue italics for address, practical information and symbols.
For list of symbols see page 6 or back flap of jacket.

—— Black text for description.

—— Sans serif italics used for cross-references to other entries or sections.

—— Bold type used for emphasis.

Entries for hotels, restaurants, shops, etc. follow the same organization, and are usually printed across a half column.

In hotels, symbols indicating special facilities appear at the end of the entry, in black. ——

Pullman
2600 Express Ave., Orient City 20037 ☎ *299-4450* ✆ *299-4460.* *Map* **2**F4 ▮▮▮▮ *238 rms* ➡ ⚍ ⒜Ⓔ ⒸⒷ ⒪ ⒸⒹ ⒱ⓈⒶ *Metro: High Standard.*
Location: On a height overlooking the Universal Trade Center. Part of a large conglomeration overlooking the seafront, this luxurious hotel is set in attractively landscaped grounds and is run with clockwork precision. Its restaurant, the **Simplon**, is highly regarded.
& ♥ 《 ☎ ♈

5

Key to symbols

- ☎ Telephone
- ⊕ Telex
- ⊛ Facsimile (fax)
- ★ Recommended sight
- 🚗 Parking
- 🏛 Building of architectural interest
- 🔲 Free entrance
- 🔳 Entrance fee payable
- 🔳 Entrance expensive
- ♿ Facilities for disabled people
- 📷 Photography forbidden
- ✗ Guided tour
- 🍽 Cafeteria
- ✱ Special interest for children
- 🏠 Simple hotel
- 🏨 Luxury hotel
- ♣ Good value
- ▱ Cheap
- ▱ Inexpensive
- ▱ Moderately priced
- ▥ Expensive
- ▥ Very expensive
- ▤ Air conditioning

- AE American Express
- ⊡ Diners Club
- ⊡ MasterCard
- VISA Visa
- 🖼 Secure garage
- 🏠 Quiet hotel
- ⬍ Elevator
- 🐕 Dogs not allowed
- 〰 Swimming pool
- ᵞ Gym/fitness facilities
- Ⴤ Bar
- ℘ Tennis
- ▭ Restaurant
- ◆ Simple restaurant
- △ Luxury restaurant
- ⌐ A la carte available
- ▆ Set (fixed-price) menu available
- ➤ Good wines
- 🍷 Open-air dining
- ⊙ Disco dancing
- ♫ Nightclub
- ♪ Live music
- ⚬ Dancing
- ⬎ Revue

A note from the General Editor

No travel book can be completely free of errors or be totally up to date. Telephone numbers and opening hours change without warning, and hotels and restaurants come under new management, which can affect standards. We make every effort to ensure that all information is accurate at the time we go to press, but are always delighted to receive corrections or suggestions for improvements from our readers, which if warranted will be incorporated in a future edition. We are indebted to readers who wrote to us during the preparation of this edition.

The publishers regret that they cannot accept any consequences arising from the use of the book or from the information it contains.

An introduction to New York

New York is not America. A world city — *the* world city, by any reasonable measure — it cannot be contained within geopolitical boundaries. Every language is spoken in New York, every cuisine prepared, every nation and race represented, every dream conjured, every depredation performed. If an idea, an object, a hope, a taste, a scent, a sin cannot be found here, the likely conclusion is that it does not exist. The only emotion New York cannot arouse is indifference. No other place created by man provokes such adoration and abhorrence, often at the same time, in the same individual. Few words applied to this city can be dismissed as hyperbole. It is an entity of exhilarating, numbing, horrifying, glorious excess.

Ethnic diversity

Although among the greatest of cities, it can no longer claim to be the largest. New York covers nearly 300 square miles and has a population of more than 7 million people, only a third that of Mexico City. A recent census recorded 4,293,695 whites, 1,784,124 blacks, 11,824 Native Americans, 231,505 Asians, with a further 749,882 regarded as racially unclassifiable.

The largest ethnic minority is probably that of Hispanic origin, but there is no ethnic majority. People of Italian, Irish and Eastern European origins are present in enormously influential numbers. Germans and other Northern Europeans were among the earliest immigrants and were quickly assimilated. Puerto Ricans and others of Caribbean background continue as largely unified groups, as do the Chinese. Refugees from Southeast Asia, Haiti, Central America, Greece, and the Indian subcontinent, are increasingly apparent.

City of villages

Water-girt New York is comprised of five distinct divisions called boroughs, only one of which — The Bronx — is situated on the North American continent. The island of Manhattan is, of course, the central borough. Brooklyn (largest in population) and Queens (largest in area) take up the western tip of Long Island, which itself stretches 125 miles east into the Atlantic. Staten Island, to the south of its sisters, snuggles up to New Jersey. When approached from the east through the outlying industrial dross, the famous Manhattan skyline appears somehow diminutive. At the southern tip of the island, the concrete spires and glass slabs of the Financial District are dominated by the twin pillars of the World Trade Center. The profile then dips to the lower heights of converted warehouses ("loft" buildings) and tenements, lifting gradually once more to midtown and the peak of the instantly recognizable Empire State Building. After another two miles, the skyline dips again, nearly meeting the rising ground that continues for another six miles, terminating at the lip of the inky tidal course known as the Spuyten Duyvil.

Once you plunge into the street canyons, warring stimuli battle for attention. The noise of endless construction and millions of lurching vehicles is trapped between the rearing phalanxes of stone and steel and glass. In winter, clouds of steam billow from manholes as if from an inferno just below. Rivers of people press forward, set on apparently urgent tasks. Traffic jerks and clogs along congested arteries. All the senses are staggered, and continue to be bombarded even when the newcomer has begun to adapt to the pace.

But there are quiet places, too. Side streets end in shaded cul-de-sacs, more than 50 museums muffle the clamor beyond their thick walls, and there are nearly 37,000 acres of parks. The most important of these is Central Park, in the heart of Manhattan. Two Monacos could be contained within its borders, with room left over for a chunk of Nice.

A brief history

The broad protected harbor was first discovered in 1524, but permanent settlement did not take place until a century later. The English took New Amsterdam from the Dutch in 1664, and the city was renamed New York. Resentment against British rule culminated in the War of Independence in 1775, and New York was for a time the capital of the infant nation.

The population was then slightly more than 30,000. It multiplied dramatically with the mass immigrations of the 19thC, and those who prospered moved uptown. In the 40 years following the Civil War (1861-65), Central Park was finished and the first skyscrapers erected. In 1898, the four outer boroughs were annexed to Manhattan, instantly fashioning the largest city in the world. The population was now more than 3 million. ˜

Despite the Wall Street Crash of 1929, construction of the Empire State Building began. Twenty years later, the city's population reached 8 million, and the United Nations moved into its new headquarters on the East River. The city was at its zenith — the capital of the world, untouched by war.

Since then, the pattern has been of decline followed by resurgences, which are in turn punctured by sharp descents into fiscal crises, deteriorating public services, accelerating crime rates and loss of industry and workers. At the moment, despair mounts over the hydra-headed pandemic of rampant crack cocaine use, the AIDS tragedy, and poverty brought to the doorstep by growing legions of homeless people. History insists that these problems will be solved or at least made tolerable, to be replaced by others as yet unimagined. And visitors inclined to sigh in relief that such painful occurrences don't happen where they live are wise to remember that things have a way of happening first in New York... before they move on.

Turn the coin and realize that tourism continues to grow, as new generations of Americans and foreigners rediscover the pleasures that never left New York. The demise of Broadway has been proclaimed with tedious regularity since the Depression, and with the arrival of the Talkies, yet it still continues to flourish. Despite two decades of unprecedented construction, hotels fill up as soon as they open their doors. Every newly-shuttered restaurant is replaced by another, frisky and eager to please. New York remains the white-hot center of activity for those intent on careers in publishing, finance, advertising, ballet, opera and the visual arts. There are still free concerts and Shakespeare in the Park. And inviting new neighborhoods. And jazz in the subway. And Miss Liberty is in her rightful place in the harbor, as bright and inviting as a new penny.

Safety first

To avoid a visit to New York on the basis of out-of-proportion stories of crime is akin to denying oneself Venice because of rubbish in the canals. Several US cities are statistically more dangerous, but the presence of the national news media focuses attention on New York, doing perhaps unnecessary harm to its international image. Still, prudence is in order. After dark, women and older people are wise to travel in groups, or with escorts. Although the odds are that a nightly walk across the nearest park or along deserted streets would be uneventful, there is no reason to tempt fate. Expensive-looking jewelry and clothing should be avoided when traveling by foot. Grip handbags firmly, even inside stores, and keep wallets in a safe place (not the left rear pants pocket). When in the subways at night, ride in the crowded central cars, not the empty ones at front and back.

New Yorkers

The reputation New Yorkers have earned for rudeness and pugnacity is not without foundation. Yet beneath their often brusque exterior lies an enviable openness to new experiences and relationships. There is no fad, art form, life-style or ideology that they will not sample, or at least tolerate. Outside of working hours — and, in a 24-hour city, that means any time — they can be seen jogging, cycling, flipping Frisbees, roller- or ice-skating, dancing in nightclubs, demonstrating at the UN, taking the sun on Hudson piers or watching it set from Riverside Park. Of all the surprises of a first visit to this city, one of the most agreeable can be New Yorkers themselves.

Before you go

Documents required

To rent a car, you need a valid **driver's license**. If you are arriving by private car from other states and countries, you should bring the **car registration** and **certificate of insurance** with you. It is also wise to take out short-term extra coverage, as the accident rate in New York City is higher than average.

Senior citizens are eligible for a discount in some hotels but must be able to show **identification** in order to claim it.

Travel and medical insurance

Medical care is good to excellent, but costly. Theft is also more common than average. Extra medical and baggage insurance is therefore strongly recommended. If you are a member of an automobile association, this can be arranged through them. Larger hotels have doctors on call, but visits are expensive.

Money

It is wise to carry cash in small amounts only, keeping the remainder in travelers checks. **Travelers checks** issued by American Express, Bank of America, Barclays, Citibank and Thomas Cook are widely recognized, and Mastercard and Visa have also introduced them. Make sure you read the instructions included with your travelers checks. It is important to note separately the serial numbers of your checks and the telephone number to call in case of loss. Specialist travelers check companies such as American Express provide extensive local refund facilities through their own offices or agents. Many shops accept dollar travelers checks.

A worldwide instant money-transfer system has been introduced by American Express. The **MoneyGram (R)** service is available from any American Express Travel Office (*for details of locations* ☎ *800-543-4080 in US or Canada*), and is open to all customers, whether or not they hold an American Express card.

Before you go

Credit cards are welcomed by nearly all hotels, airlines and car rental agencies, most restaurants and garages, and many stores. American Express, Diners Club, Mastercard and Visa are the major cards in common use. While **personal checks** drawn on out-of-town banks are not normally accepted, many hotels will cash small amounts in conjunction with a credit card.

Getting there

John F. Kennedy is the largest of New York's three **airports**, but as it deals mainly with international flights it is best avoided if you have a choice. Most national and some international airlines serve both the other airports — **LaGuardia**, which is the smallest and closest to the center (30mins), and **Newark**, which is on the other side of the Hudson River in New Jersey (45mins). Private planes can land at **Teterboro** in NE New Jersey.

Long-distance and commuter **trains** arrive at **Pennsylvania Station** (*7th Ave. and 32nd St.*) or **Grand Central Terminal** (*Park Ave. and 42nd St.*).

All **buses**, both long-distance and local, arrive at the **Port Authority Bus Terminal** (*8th Ave. and 41st St.*). The long-distance buses have their platforms below street level; passengers from local buses arrive at the upper stories.

From the W and S, **Interstate Highways I-78**, **I-80** and **I-95** connect with Manhattan via the **George Washington Bridge** (for upper Manhattan), the **Lincoln Tunnel** (for mid-Manhattan) and the **Holland Tunnel** (for lower Manhattan). From the N, **I-87** (Governor Thomas E. Dewey Thruway) and **I-95** (New England Thruway) lead to the **Triborough Bridge** and other Harlem River and East River crossings. Most of these funnel into the FDR Drive, which parallels the East River. Tolls across the Hudson River are paid when entering the city, but not when leaving. Automobile clubs will suggest the best route from your point of departure.

Climate

May, June, Sept and Oct are agreeable, incorporating the best days of the short and unpredictable spring and fall seasons. Extended periods of oppressive humidity and temperatures of 90°F (32°C) and more are characteristic in July and Aug. Dec through Feb feature cold rains, occasional snow, and readings at or near freezing point. True extremes are rare, however. Temperatures infrequently drop below freezing point or exceed 100°F (38°C), and a snowfall of more than four inches is unusual.

Clothes

A raincoat with a zip-out lining is a good investment for an Oct-Apr visit, as are collapsible rubber boots and a waterproof hat. The winds that accompany rain often turn umbrellas inside-out. High settings of interior heating and air conditioning mean that layering of clothes is advisable.

New Yorkers have grown less formal in dress in recent years. Men feel most comfortable with a jacket at medium-priced and luxury restaurants, but a tie is mandatory at only relatively few establishments. Pants may be worn by women at all but a handful of the same places. Denim clothing is sometimes barred by smarter discos and clubs.

General Delivery

A letter marked "General Delivery," addressed to a specific post office, will be held there until collected. Identification is usually required when you collect your mail, and a fee may be charged. Some commercial firms also provide this service for their customers. The following are centrally located: **American Express** (*150 E 42nd St., New York, NY 10017*), **Central Post Office** (*42 8th Ave., New York, NY 10001*), **Thomas Cook** (*18 E 48th St., New York, NY 10017*).

Getting around

From the airport to the city

Carey Airport Express **buses** depart Kennedy and LaGuardia every 20-30mins between early morning and midnight, less frequently at other times. They stop at Grand Central Terminal. Fares from Kennedy and LaGuardia are similar, and neither is expensive. Similar service is provided by the Olympia Trails company from Newark to the Port Authority Bus Terminal at 8th Ave. and 42nd St, the World Trade Center, Pennsylvania Station, and Grand Central Terminal. New Jersey Transit buses operate 24hrs a day every 15-30 minutes, from the AirTrans Center of the Port Authority Terminal (*for further information ☎ 800-247-7433*). Some hotels provide transportation from the airports, if advance arrangements are made.

Taxis from Kennedy (45-60mins) and LaGuardia (30-40mins) to destinations within the city are metered. From Newark (30-60mins), however, the fare is twice the meter toll. From New York *to* Newark, the fare is the amount on the meter plus $10. In all cases bridge and tunnel tolls are extra, and traveling in the rush hour can double the fare and time taken. Non-metered car services provide transportation *to* the airports at lower rates than regular taxis. Two that have proved reliable in the past are **Aviv** (☎ 505-0555) and **Sabra** (☎ 410-7600).

Helicopters fly between the three airports and between Kennedy and the heliport at 34th St. and the East River. The flights between Kennedy and the Heliport take 10mins and leave every 30mins between 1.30-7.30pm, but cost twice as much as a taxi. Operations are sometimes suspended due to bad weather.

Private limousines are clean, comfortable and often cost little more than taxis, as they charge a flat rate and can be shared. You can arrange in advance to have one waiting for you (see *Other transportation* on page 14).

Cars can be rented at all airports (see *Renting a car* on page 13).

Public transportation

Subways and buses have improved significantly in recent years. Delays are less common, graffiti has been largely eliminated and a majority of subway cars are air conditioned. Stations, however, are still dirty, littered, and often populated by large numbers of homeless people, especially in winter. For information on subways and buses ☎ 330-1234. Free maps are theoretically available at most token booths. Trains operate 24hrs a day, with reduced frequency between midnight-6am. A single fare lets you journey as far as you like along any one line. Peak rush hours, to be avoided if possible, are 8-9am and 5-7pm.

Subways

The system began as three privately-owned lines that went pretty much where they wished. They are still known unofficially as the **IRT** (running from N to S on the E and W sides of Manhattan),

IND (running along 6th and 8th Aves.), and **BMT** (running roughly from lower Manhattan to Brooklyn and Queens). To use the subway, buy a token at the booth near the entrance. Free transfers can be made at 25 intersections with other lines. In order to get on the right train going in the right direction, first note whether you must go uptown, downtown or crosstown, and whether your final station is a local or express stop (see Maps **14**&**15**). Insert the token into the turnstile, then follow directional signs to the correct platform. Once there, look for signs to indicate whether express and local trains stop on the same or on opposite sides of the platform. The front and sides of a train have signs indicating the route number, whether the train is express or local, and the last station on the route.

Buses
Upon boarding, deposit a subway token or the equivalent in coins in the box next to the driver. He cannot give change, but can sell "Add-a-ride" transfers to intersecting lines. Routes roughly follow the major N-S avenues (see Map **16**). E-W crosstown routes serve as connections between subway lines, which are primarily N-S. "Culture Bus Loops" stop at major attractions in Manhattan and downtown Brooklyn, at 20-30min intervals on weekends and most holidays. The inclusive fare permits passengers to embark and disembark as often as they wish. Descriptive pamphlets are usually available on the bus.

Taxis
Licensed taxis are painted yellow; they have electronic digital meters that print out receipts if required. There are nearly 12,000 in operation and they can be hailed anywhere if the sign on the roof is illuminated. Cabstands are also found outside major hotels. Drivers are required to take passengers to any destination in the city. Within the five boroughs there is a set rate for the first ninth of a mile and for every additional ninth. Bridge and tunnel tolls are extra.

If you are going to an unusual destination, it is wise to give the full address and the nearest cross street — orientation examinations for drivers are lax, and some drivers speak little English. Tip 20 percent of the total fare.

For lost articles ☎ 825-0416.

Getting around by car
Using a car in the city borders on irrationality. Street parking is often nonexistent, and garage parking is very expensive. One alternative is to drive to a municipal garage (*8th Ave. and W 52nd St.; Leonard St. at Lafayette St.; Delancey St. at Essex St.; Park Row and Pearl St.; or Washington St. and Greenwich Ave.*), then use public transportation. Most large hotels have garages, but these are often expensive and a fee is usually charged every time a car is taken out and returned. If you must bring a car to New York, at least try to confine its use to evenings after 9pm and weekends, or to touring the countryside. When parking, do not exceed the time limit in a metered parking space, or your car could be towed away to a pound.

Most cross streets and many avenues are one-way, the direction alternating from one street or avenue to the next. In New York City, unlike the rest of the state, right turns are not permitted at red traffic lights unless stated. Speed limits are signposted, usually 35mph (55mph in New York State) or less.

For further details and information, contact the American

Automobile Association, or seek advice from your own automobile club.

Renting a car

Car rental agencies are located at airline terminals and at offices throughout the city. See also Yellow Pages under *Automobile Renting* and *Leasing*. Most vehicles are equipped with radios and air conditioning at no extra charge. A credit card can be presented in lieu of a deposit, in which case the driver is allowed to be as young as 18. Otherwise, a cash deposit is required, and the driver must be over 21. Rent-it-here-leave-it-there, weekend, and unlimited-mileage packages are available.

Getting around on foot

See Maps **2-11**.

The best, and most agreeable, way to cover short distances in Manhattan is on foot. Above 14th St., it is difficult to lose your way. Streets are laid out in a straight grid. Named and numbered avenues run N-S, from **1st Ave.** in the E to **11th Ave.** in the W. **5th Ave.** is the dividing line between E and W. Cross streets run E-W from **14th St.** in the S to **225th St.** in the N. Building numbers mount from one to the mid-hundreds to the E, and in the same way to the W. On the avenues, numbers increase as they proceed N. Because the avenues and Broadway are so long, the nearest cross street is often mentioned when asking for a main avenue address. **Avenue of the Americas** is always spoken of as **6th Ave.**, although the grander name is still used for addresses.

The Manhattan grid is not perfect, of course. **Broadway** cuts diagonally across the island from **Park Ave.** and **14th St.** to the W of Central Park. Below **14th St.**, in the older part of the city, the grid goes awry. Down there a map is essential.

Railroad services

Both long-distance and commuter trains arrive at **Grand Central Terminal** (*Park Ave. and 42nd St.*) and **Pennsylvania (Penn) Station** (*7th Ave. and 32nd St.*). The Harlem, Hudson and New Haven commuter lines feed into Grand Central from up to 100 miles N, while the Long Island and New Jersey commuter lines use Penn Station. Amtrak trains from Canada, Boston, Chicago, Washington, Florida and intermediate points use both terminals.
Amtrak   ☎736-3967 (Metroliners) ☎736-4545 (all others)
Metro North (commuter)   ☎532-4900 (Westchester County and Connecticut)

Domestic airlines

Domestic flights leave all three airports. The Trump Shuttle and the Pan Am Shuttle to Washington and Boston have separate terminals at LaGuardia. The two services have hourly flights during the day and early evening. The addresses below are for main Manhattan ticket offices, while the telephone numbers are for central reservation networks. The several offices listed at 100 E 42nd St. are opposite Grand Central Terminal.
Air Canada   488 Madison Ave. ☎869-1900
American   100 E 42nd St. ☎431-1132
Continental   1 World Trade Center ☎718-565-1100
Delta   100 E 42nd St. ☎239-0700
Northwest   299 Park Ave. (49th St.) ☎736-1220
Pan Am   100 E 42nd St. ☎687-2600
TWA   100 E 42nd St. ☎290-2121

| **United** | 100 E 42nd St. ☎ 800-241-6522 |
| **US Air** | 108 E 42nd St. ☎ 489-1460 |

Ferry services

America's favorite boat ride — the **Staten Island ferry** — is still the biggest bargain in town, serving up spectacular views and bracing breezes. It departs from the Whitehall St. pier at downtown Battery Park every 20-30mins, 24hrs a day, 7 days a week. The **Statue of Liberty ferry** also leaves from Battery Park. Ferry service to *Ellis Island* has resumed now that the monument's extensive restoration is nearly complete. The price of the ride includes a guided tour of the museum.

Other transportation

Hourly rates for **private limousines** are high, but there are special airport and theater/dinner flat rates that can total little more than taxi fares. Among the reputable firms:

A-Marquis   70-28 45th Ave. (Queens) ☎ 718-639-2338
Dave-El   219 W 77th St. ☎ 645-4242
Manhattan International   13-05 43rd Ave. (Long Island City) ☎ 718-729-4200
Silver Screen Limo   P.O. Box 4283, Sunnyside, NY 11104 ☎ 718-937-3808 or 937-3321

Rent a **rowboat** or **bicycle** at the 72nd St. boathouse in Central Park. Bicycles and mopeds can be rented from the following:
Metro Bicycles   1311 Lexington Ave. (88th St.) ☎ 427-4450
6th Ave. Bicycles   546 Ave. of the Americas (15th St.) ☎ 255-5100
West Side Bicycle   231 W 96th St. ☎ 663-7531

Rides in **horse-drawn hansom cabs** begin from near the 5th Ave. and 59th St. corner of Central Park, day or night. Most rides take 30mins and are expensive. Establish the rate in advance.

On-the-spot information

Public holidays

Jan 1; Martin Luther King Day, third Mon in Jan; President's Day, celebrated on a 3-day weekend in mid-Feb; Memorial Day, a 3-day weekend at the end of May; Independence Day, July 4; Labor Day, first Mon in Sept; Columbus Day, second Mon in Oct; Election Day, first Tues in Nov; Veterans Day, Nov 11; Thanksgiving, last Thurs in Nov; Dec 25.

As in the rest of the country, shops, schools, banks, post offices and most public services are usually closed on these days, although some shops stay open on the 3-day weekends.

A number of other special days are observed with religious services, parades, gift-giving, or other celebrations. These include: Chinese New Year, Jan/Feb; St Patrick's Day, Mar 17; Easter and Passover, Apr; Mother's Day, May; Puerto Rican Day, June; Rosh Hashanah, Sept; Halloween, Oct 31; Chanukah, Dec.

Time zones

New York is in the US Eastern Time Zone, 1hr ahead of Central Time Zone, 2hrs ahead of Mountain Time Zone and 3hrs ahead of Pacific Time Zone. All zones on Daylight Saving Time put their clocks forward 1hr Apr-Oct to benefit from extra daylight.

Banks

Customary banking hours are Mon-Fri 9am-3pm; some close at

4pm and some are open Thurs evenings or Sat mornings.
Travelers checks can be cashed at all banks.

Shopping hours

Department stores, clothes and sports equipment shops usually
open between 9-10am and close at 6pm. Late-night shopping is
on Mon and Thurs, usually until 9pm. Although many fast-food
stands, coffee shops and delicatessens open by 8am and don't
close until 10pm or later, more formal restaurants confine
themselves to noon-3pm and 6-11pm, with slight variations. Bars
and discos do not have to close until 4am. In sections of the city
where merchants are predominantly Jewish, stores often close
from mid-afternoon Fri through Sat and are open on Sun. In
Greenwich Village and SoHo, boutiques and galleries often do
not get going until noon.

Rush hours

Driving, or using public transportation between 8-9am and
5-6.30pm, could be considered an exercise in masochism, and
the situation is almost as bad for an hour before and after these
times. Avoiding lunch between noon and 2pm is canny, as is
making dinner reservations before 7.30pm or after 8.30pm.

Postal and telephone services

Post offices are open Mon-Fri 8am-5pm, Sat 8am-noon. The main
post office at 8th Ave. and 33rd St. is open 24hrs.

Telephones are everywhere. Try to use those in shops or public
buildings — the ones installed on street corners are often out of
order. Manhattan and The Bronx are in area code **212**. Local calls
need only their 7-digit number. When calling an out-of-town
number, or Brooklyn, Queens or Staten Island, dial **1**, then the
area code, and finally the 7-digit number. Direct dialing to all US
numbers and many foreign countries is available, but calls are
best made from hotel rooms, considering the amount of coins
required for a pay phone. But remember that hotels typically add
surcharges. Cheaper rates apply after 5pm and on weekends.

There are independent shops specializing in fax, telex and
postal services; larger hotels also offer these services. Money can
be wired from one Western Union office to another, and a
mailgram might arrive sooner than a letter; see also **MoneyGram**
in *Money* on page 9. **ITT** is the primary international cable
service (☎ 797-3311).

Public rest rooms

These are to be avoided at all times in subway stations. Those in
museums and public buildings are usually satisfactory. *In
extremis*, duck into the nearest hotel.

Tipping

In restaurants tip the waiter at least 15 percent of the check
before tax; 20 percent is more usual in luxury establishments, or
if the service warrants it. An easy way to compute the minimum
is to double the 8¾ percent sales tax. Some restaurants have
taken to adding a service charge, so don't tip twice. Bellmen
expect a dollar per bag. Doormen get 50¢-$1 for hailing a taxi; tip
chambermaids a similar amount for each night of a stay, too. Rest
room attendants should be given 50¢, to be left on the
conspicuous plate. When there is a stated fee for checking coats
and parcels, that is sufficient. Otherwise give $1 per item. Tour
guides expect $2-5, depending upon the length of the tour.

Disabled travelers

Federal regulations have brought about improvements in access
to most places. Many rest rooms provide special facilities for the
disabled, and certain buses are equipped with motorized
platforms. Most hotels have specially converted rooms. Subways
offer reduced fares for disabled passengers but are nearly
impossible to negotiate without help. Seeing-eye dogs are
permitted everywhere in New York. For further information,
contact **Rehabilitation International USA** (*1123 Broadway,
NY 10010 ☎ 420-1500*).

Local publications

Special arts and leisure sections appear Fri and Sun in the *New
York Times* and in the weekly magazines *New York* and *The New
Yorker*. They provide useful reviews and listings of current plays,
concerts, films, exhibitions, ballets and operas; The *New York
Times* includes ticket availability. *The Village Voice* is a weekly
that emphasizes the offbeat arts and presentations. The *Daily
News* and *New York Post* have extensive sports coverage.

Useful addresses

Tourist information
American Express Travel Service   150 E 42nd St.
☎ 687-3700; a valuable source of information for any traveler in
need of help, advice or emergency services
NY Convention and Visitors Bureau   2 Columbus Circle
☎ 397-8222

Main post offices
8th Ave. (33rd St.) or Lexington Ave. (45th St.)

Telephone services
Daily events   ☎ 360-1333
International calls   Dial operator
Sportsphone   ☎ 976-1313 or ☎ 976-2525
Telephone information   ☎ 555-1212
Time and temperature   ☎ 976-1616
Traffic report (during rush hours)   ☎ 976-2323

Tour operators
Adventure on a Shoestring   300 W 53rd St. ☎ 265-2663
American Sightseeing International/Short Line Tours
166 W 46th St. ☎ 354-4740. 2-8hr bus tours
Circle Line   Pier 83, end of W 42nd St. ☎ 563-3200. 3hr boat
cruises around Manhattan, Apr-Nov.
Gray Line Tours   254 W 54th St. ☎ 247-6956
Harlem, Your Way! Tours Unlimited   129 W 130th St.
☎ 690-1687
Landmark Tours   151 1st Ave. ☎ 979-5263. Walking tours
Apr-Oct.
Island Helicopter   Heliport at end of E 34th St. ☎ 683-4575
Manhattan Sightseeing Bus Tours   150 W 49th St.
☎ 869-7866
New York Big Apple Tours   203 E 94th St. ☎ 410-4190

Major places of worship
Baptist   Calvary Baptist, 123 W 57th St.
Catholic   St Patrick's Cathedral, 5th Ave. (51st St.)

Emergency information

Emergency services

For **Police**, **Ambulance** or **Fire** ☎ **911**. You will need a coin if using a call box.

Hospitals with emergency rooms

Ambulances called on 911 carry the patient to the nearest municipal hospital. Private hospitals are preferable, however, so if possible take a taxi to one of these:
Financial District: Beekman Downtown Hosp., 170 William St., ☎ 312-5000. **Greenwich Village**: St Vincent's Hosp., 7th Ave. (11th St.) ☎ 790-7000. **Midtown East**: New York University Medical Center, 1st Ave. (30th St.) ☎ 340-7300. **Midtown West**: Roosevelt-St. Luke's Hosp., 9th Ave. (58th St.) ☎ 523-4000. **Upper East Side**: New York Hosp., York Ave. (68th St.) ☎ 746-5454. **Upper East Side and East Harlem**: Mount Sinai Hosp., 5th Ave. (100th St.) ☎ 241-6500. **West Harlem**: Columbia Presbyterian Medical Center, 622 W 168th St. ☎ 305-2500.

Other emergencies

Doctors Emergency Service ☎ 570-2600
Dentists Emergency Service ☎ 679-3966 (9am-8pm)
☎ 679-4172 (8pm-9am)

Late-night drugstore (pharmacy)

Kaufman 557 Lexington Ave. (50th St.) ☎ 755-2266

Help lines

Alcoholics Anonymous   ☎ 473-6200
Battered Women   ☎ 433-7297
Child Abuse   ☎ 800-342-3720
Crime Victim Hotline   ☎ 577-7777
Drug problems   ☎ 800-538-4840
Help line (personal counseling)   ☎ 481-1070
Poison   ☎ 340-4494 or 764-7667
Rape Help Line   ☎ 777-4000
Suicide Prevention   ☎ 532-2400
Traveler's Aid Society   ☎ 944-0013

Automobile accidents

- Call the police immediately
- If car is rented, call number in rental agreement
- Do not admit liability or incriminate yourself
- Ask witnesses to stay and give statements
- Exchange names, addresses, car details, insurance companies and 3-digit insurance company codes
- Remain to give your statement to the police

Car breakdowns

Call one of the following from nearest telephone:
- Number indicated in car rental agreement
- Local office of AAA (if you are a member)
- Nearest garage or towing service.

Lost travelers checks

Notify the local police immediately, then follow the instructions provided with your travelers checks, or contact the issuing company's nearest office. Contact **American Express** (☎ 323-2000) if you are stranded with no money.

CULTURE, HISTORY AND BACKGROUND

Episcopal   St Thomas' Church, 1 W 53rd St. (Entrance on 5th Ave.)
Jewish   Temple Emanu-El, 5th Ave. (65th St.)
Lutheran   Holy Trinity, Central Park West (65th St.)
Methodist   Lexington United Methodist Church, 150 E 62nd St.
Presbyterian   Presbyterian Church, 5th Ave. (55th St.)

Libraries
American Bible Society   1865 Broadway ☎581-7400
Donnell Library Center   20 W 53rd St. ☎790-6463
Library for the Blind and Physically Handicapped   166 Ave. of the Americas ☎925-1011
Lincoln Center Library (music, theater)   11 Amsterdam Ave. ☎799-2200
Mercantile Library (contemporary books)   17 E 47th St. ☎755-6710
New York Public Library   5th Ave. (42nd St.) ☎790-6262
Schomburg Center (black studies)   103 W 135th St. ☎862-4000

Time chart

1524	Italian explorer Giovanni da Verrazano discovered New York Bay while searching for a NW passage.
1609	Henry Hudson sailed his *Half Moon* up the river that was eventually given his name.
1623	New Netherland became a province of the Dutch West India Company, and the cluster of huts at the s tip of Manhattan was called New Amsterdam.
1626	Provincial Director-General Peter Minuit bought the island from the Algonquin Indians.
1643	Population grew to about 500 people speaking 18 different languages. During the tenure of Governor Peter Stuyvesant, settlements were established in the areas eventually known as The Bronx, Queens, Brooklyn and Staten Island.
1664	The Duke of York sent a fleet into the harbor. Abandoned by the burgomasters who chafed under his authoritarian rule, Stuyvesant surrendered the city to the English. It was renamed New York.
1674	After extended hostilities between the English and Dutch — and one brief reoccupation by the Dutch — the city and province were ceded by treaty to the English.
1689	A German merchant, Jacob Leisler, led a revolt against oligarchic trade monopolies when he learned of the overthrow of James II. He was hanged for treason.
1712	Slaves now constituted a substantial segment of the population. Despite ordinances denying them weapons and the right of assembly, a number of blacks set fire to a building near Maiden Lane and killed nine whites who attempted to stop the blaze. When soldiers arrived, six of the blacks committed suicide; 21 others were captured and executed.
1725	The *New-York Gazette* was founded.
1734	John Peter Zenger, publisher of the *New York Weekly Journal*, was charged with libeling the Government.

	He was acquitted in the first test of the principle of freedom of the press in the colonies.
1754-63	Population now 16,000. King's College founded. Benjamin Franklin proposed union of the colonies for common defense during the French and Indian War, but was rejected. A force led by George Washington was defeated by the French at Fort Necessity in Pennsylvania. The conflict, which was part of the worldwide Seven Years War, ended with the Treaty of Paris. English sovereignty over the major part of explored North America was thereby conceded.
1764-70	Colonial grumbling over British rule escalated into sporadic demonstrations and protests, with the passage of the punitive Sugar, Stamp, and Colonial Currency Acts. The Quartering Act permitted British troops to requisition private dwellings and inns, their rent to be paid by the colonies. At the Stamp Act Congress held in Manhattan, delegates of nine colonies passed a Declaration of Rights and Liberties. Skirmishes between soldiers and the insurrectionist Sons of Liberty culminated in Jan 1770 in the killing of a colonial and the wounding of a number of others. The Boston Massacre, in which British troops fired upon taunting protesters, occurred 7wks later.
1775-83	The American Revolution. The Continental Congress appointed Washington as Commander-in-Chief and, on July 4, 1776, adopted the Declaration of Independence. After early battles ranging from Manhattan to Long Island, most of which he lost, Washington withdrew. New York was occupied by the British for the remainder of the War. With the Treaty of Versailles in September 1783, the British troops left the city.
1789	Washington was sworn in as first President at Federal Hall in New York, the first capital of the Federal Government.
1790	An official census recorded the population at 33,000.
1807-09	Robert Fulton made a round trip from New York to Albany in his steamboat *Clermont*. In reaction to British and French seizure of American ships at sea, Congress prohibited export of most goods. This Act did more harm to New York and New England agriculture and commerce than to the other side, and was repealed.
1812	War declared against Britain. New York blockaded.
1814	Peace treaty signed at Ghent.
1825	Erie Canal opened, enhancing New York's role as a port.
1832	New York and Harlem railroad completed.
1830-60	The influx of immigrants — largely German and Irish — rose to flood proportions. Epidemics of yellow fever and cholera followed, made worse by poor water supplies, insanitary conditions and the poverty of most of the newcomers. Yet on the eve of the Civil War, the population neared 750,000.
1861-65	Civil War, caused by growing differences between northern and southern states, notably the slavery issue. New York on the side of the Union (North) against the Confederates (South).
1863	Draft Riots, following a conscription law that

	permitted the rich to buy deferment. New Yorkers set fire to buildings, and looted shops and homes. More than 1,000 people died.
1868-98	The first waves of Italian and Eastern European immigrants arrived, many of them working on the new elevated railroad, Brooklyn Bridge and early skyscrapers. The Statue of Liberty, a Franco-American project, was inaugurated in 1886. At the culmination of a period of annexation and expansion, New York assumed its present boundaries. There were now more than 3 million inhabitants, and New York was already the world's largest city.
1900-29	Immigration continued unabated, despite growing pressure for its curtailment. The railroad system was extended, now underground as well as above. The decade after World War I brought Prohibition, women's suffrage, economic prosperity, and a Federal Act cutting immigration (1924).
1929-39	The Wall Street Crash and the start of the Great Depression. The worst of the Depression was over by 1936, but it did not end until 1939, when the country began to prepare for war.
1941-45	Apart from rationing, blackouts and shortages, New York was not greatly affected by World War II. It grew more prosperous, as did the rest of the country.
1948	Idlewild Airport opened in Queens (renamed after John F. Kennedy in 1963).
1952	United Nations headquarters complex opened.
1973	World Trade Center opened.
1975-76	American Bicentennial celebrations.
1989	World Financial Center opened at Battery Park City.

Biographies

One of the most cosmopolitan of cities, New York has a history rich in memorable characters. The following are a representative selection.

Allen, Woody *(born 1935)*

The writer-actor-comedian-satirist-director is said to get the bends whenever he ventures beyond the city limits of New York. Nevertheless, by his own account, a Brooklyn childhood and an aborted career at New York University gave him little joy but much material for his *New Yorker* magazine essays and his many memorable movies, which include *Annie Hall* and *Hannah and Her Sisters*.

Beecher, Henry Ward *(1813-87)*

A minister, lecturer, author and firebrand abolitionist, he was also the older brother of Harriet Beecher Stowe, who wrote *Uncle Tom's Cabin*. His pulpit was the Plymouth Church on Orange St. in Brooklyn Heights.

Booth, Edwin *(1833-93)*

Often cited as the first important American actor, Booth made his permanent home in New York. His career was blighted after his brother, John Wilkes, killed Abraham Lincoln.

Bryant, William Cullen *(1794-1878)*

Best known as a poet, Bryant made his living as a reform-minded editor of the *Evening Post* (1826-78). He is credited with prodding the city into the development of Central Park.

Burr, Aaron *(1756-1836)*
In a checkered political career that saw him lose as many
elections as he won, Burr's highest position was as Vice-
President to Thomas Jefferson. The image of Burr as an amoral
schemer gained strength from his shooting of Alexander
Hamilton in a duel, and from the plan, attributed to him, to
establish an independent republic in the southwest. He was tried
for treason and acquitted, but never re-entered public life.

Dinkins, David N. *(born 1927)*
The first black mayor of New York worked his way quietly and
diligently up through the ranks of the powerful local Democrat
Party, finally assuming the City's highest office in in 1990.

Fulton, Robert *(1765-1815)*
Talented and energetic, Fulton's curiosity led him to careers in
painting, gunsmithing, civil engineering, and the invention of
ambitious mechanical devices. Although he was not, as is widely
believed, the creator of the steamboat, his *Clermont* (1807) was
the first profitable version.

Greeley, Horace *(1811-72)*
After his arrival in New York at the age of 21, Greeley worked as
a printer, editor and newspaper columnist. He founded *The New
Yorker* (1834) and the *Tribune* (1841), and edited them, in
various combinations, for more than 30yrs.

 Although initially considered a conservative, he advocated
women's suffrage, the abolition of slavery, labor unions and
experiments in communal living. These were all remarkably
daring stands at that time.

Hamilton, Alexander *(1755-1804)*
Born out of wedlock in the West Indies, Hamilton came to New
York to study at King's College in 1773. His anonymous writings
on behalf of the Revolutionary cause drew much attention, as did
his service on the battlefield and as General Washington's aide.
An influential delegate to the Continental Congress at 25, he was
one of the leading proponents of the Constitution drafted by
Jefferson. Undeniably brilliant, he nevertheless made many
enemies. One of them, Aaron Burr, mortally wounded him in a
duel in 1804.

Henry, O. *(1862-1910)*
The pen name of William S. Porter, a short-story writer noted for
his tight plots and surprise endings, exemplified in *Gift of the
Magi*. He began writing in prison, to which he was sentenced for
embezzlement.

 Most of his literary production took place in the last 10yrs of his
life, which he spent in New York.

Hopper, Edward *(1882-1973)*
Born in a small town on the Hudson River, Hopper moved in
young adulthood to Greenwich Village. The muted, melancholy
cityscapes of this Realist painter began to gain favor in the 1920s,
although they ran against Modernist trends. In later years, his
studio was at 3 Washington Sq. North.

Irving, Washington *(1783-1859)*
Diplomat, biographer, satirist and author — of *Rip Van Winkle*
and *The Legend of Sleepy Hollow* among other tales — Irving was
born in New York. His estate in nearby Tarrytown is open to the
public.

Koch, Edward *(born 1924)*
Child of immigrant parents, Koch narrowly won election as
mayor of New York in 1977. Known for speaking his mind, he
early on established himself as the most popular mayor since
LaGuardia. He was elected to three terms, and although his later

Biographies

years in office were dogged by scandal, none of this attached directly to him.

LaGuardia, Fiorello Henry *(1882-1947)*
Probably the most beloved mayor in the city's history — serving from 1935-45 for an until-then unprecedented three terms — the "Little Flower" gave luster and color to an office that had become celebrated for both the flamboyance and the corruptibility of its previous incumbents.

Millay, Edna St Vincent *(1892-1950)*
The popular lyric poet was a leader of the Greenwich Village Bohemian group that founded the Provincetown Players.

Minuit, Peter *(1580-1638).*
The famous $24 purchase of Manhattan was negotiated by Minuit, who was then appointed Director General (1626-31) of the new colony by the Dutch West India Company.

Morgan, John Pierpont *(1837-1913)*
Beginning with the fortune accumulated by his father, J.P. used it as seed money to build a financial empire that is said to have exceeded even that of the first Rockefeller. Along the way, he bought out industrialists Andrew Carnegie and Henry Frick. All three of them spent their declining years in New York, where they engaged in a variety of good works and acts of philanthropy, and thereby formed New York's strong cultural foundation.

Morse, Samuel F.B. *(1791-1872)*
While a member of the arts faculty at New York University, Morse perfected his telegraph device and the code to be used with it. A demonstration was given at Castle Clinton in 1842. Morse was also a pioneer in the development of photography.

Olmsted, Frederick Law *(1822-1903)*
Travel writer and prolific landscape architect in the US and in Canada, Olmsted designed Central Park, Prospect Park (Brooklyn) and Riverside Park, all in collaboration with Calvert Vaux.

O'Neill, Eugene *(1888-1953)*
The work of the playwright who fashioned *The Iceman Cometh* and *Mourning Becomes Electra* is the standard against which all American dramatists must be measured. One of his finest plays, *Long Day's Journey into Night*, was discovered among his papers after his death. O'Neill was awarded the Nobel Prize in 1936.

Parker, Dorothy *(1893-1967)*
Renowned for the razor-sharp wit she directed as readily at herself as at others, Parker employed that gift in verse, plays, movies, essays and short stories. Much of her work appeared in *The New Yorker* magazine.

Perelman, S.J. *(1904-79)*
Brooklyn-born Perelman wrote for *The New Yorker* magazine from 1934 almost until his death. Essentially a humorist and satirist, his interests focused on the inanities of advertising and Hollywood. He also wrote movie scripts and plays in the 1930s and 1940s, often in association with such luminaries as the Marx Brothers, Ogden Nash and George S. Kaufman.

Poe, Edgar Allen *(1809-49)*
Impoverished for most of his adult life, having alienated his wealthy foster father through his alcoholism and gambling, Poe moved to New York with his child bride in 1844. Their cottage in the Fordham section of The Bronx is now a museum. He finally achieved recognition for his poetry with *The Raven*, which led to fame for such mystery stories as *The Gold Bug* and *The Murders in the Rue Morgue*.

22

Pollock, Jackson (1912-56)
Although contemporaries were working in similar directions, the seminal work of this innovative artist heralded the explosion of postwar creativity known as the New York School. Inspired by Picasso and impatient with the academic techniques he mastered in his early years, he applied paint to vast canvases by splashing, dribbling, thrusting and pouring, in a method later labeled "action painting."

Porter, Cole (1893-1964)
The enduring sophistication of Porter's lyrics is remarkable. He penned both words and music of more than 400 songs, for such stage musicals as *Can-Can, Silk Stockings* and *Kiss Me, Kate.*

Pulitzer, Joseph (1847-1911)
Hungarian-born Pulitzer emigrated to the US in 1864 and became a journalist, editor, and publisher in short order. He bought the *New York World* in 1883, and in competition with William Randolph Hearst permitted it to plummet to the nadir of "yellow journalism." After the Spanish-American War (1898), his newspapers altered course to become relatively dignified. His will bequeathed money for the establishment of the Columbia University School of Journalism.

Rauschenberg, Robert (born 1925)
Rauschenberg first attracted attention with an exhibition of entirely black canvases, but then moved on to "combine-paintings" — assemblages of pigment, collage and such three-dimensional objects as stuffed goats and rubber tires. Born in Texas, he is nonetheless an exemplar of the New York School of painting.

Rockefeller, John D. Jr. (1874-1960)
The son of the incalculably wealthy oil magnate and financier was granted control of his father's interests at the age of 37. To a large extent, this involved philanthropic activities, many of which benefited New York. Among the projects he inspired or helped underwrite were Riverside Church, the Cloisters of the Metropolitan Museum of Art and the Rockefeller Center.

Rockefeller, Nelson Alrich (1908-79)
After able participation in both Democrat and Republican federal administrations during World War II and after, Nelson defeated W. Averell Harriman for the governorship of the State of New York in 1958. His subsequent bids for the Republican presidential nomination were unsuccessful, but he was re-elected governor three times and was appointed Vice-President for the brief term of Gerald Ford (1974-77). He made substantial contributions to New York's cultural and educational institutions, as did his siblings.

Roosevelt, Theodore (1858-1919)
The 28th and youngest President passed the first 15yrs of his extraordinarily active life at 28 E 20th St., near Gramercy Park. Hunter and environmentalist, rancher and author, statesman and chauvinist, peacemaker and militarist, explorer and politician, he pursued these contradictory interests vigorously until his death.

Runyon, Damon (1884-1946)
Born in Manhattan (the one in the state of Kansas), this popular journalist came to New York, where he quickly mastered the patois of the criminal fringe and transferred that knowledge to a long string of evocative and humorous short stories, which provided the basis of the hit musical *Guys and Dolls.*

Ruth, George Hermon (1895-1948)
A near-legendary athlete, "Babe" Ruth played for the New York Yankees professional baseball team from 1920-35. Most of his

pitching and batting records went unchallenged for decades, and some still stand.

Stuyvesant, Peter *(1610-72)*
A harshly autocratic man intolerant of religious and political dissent, this Director General of New Amsterdam held power from 1647-64. In 1664 he surrendered the colony to an English naval force and retired to his farm, near the present Lower East Side.

Tweed, William Marcy *(1823-78)*
The undisputed leader of Tammany Hall, which controlled the city and state Democrat Party, "Boss" Tweed ruled the city from 1857 until the early 1870s. He died in prison, having defrauded taxpayers and contractors of unaccounted millions, in bribes, kickbacks and related schemes.

Warhol, Andy *(c.1930-1986)*
No one is certain when he was born (about 1930), or where (probably Philadelphia), but there is no question of his primacy in the Pop Art movement of the 1960s. Through repeated prints of commonplace objects — cows, soup cans, movie stars — he endeavored to elevate the mundane and overexposed into subjects worthy of serious consideration. He went on to found a "factory" that produced films of elusive intent, and a magazine of celebrity interviews.

White, Stanford *(1853-1906)*
As the most celebrated partner of the architectural firm of McKim, Mead & White, he probably received more credit than his due for their collective achievements. Many of their buildings have been lost, but a rich heritage remains. These include Washington Arch, the Villard Houses, the portico of St Bartholomew's Church, three buildings at Columbia University and three more at the former Bronx campus of New York University, in all of which White had a hand.

Whitman, Walt *(1819-92)*
The innovative free verse of *Leaves of Grass* drew mostly negative reaction on its first appearance in 1855, but many 20thC scholars regard Whitman as America's finest poet.

Wolfe, Thomas Clayton *(1900-38)*
The haunted author of *Look Homeward, Angel* and *You Can't Go Home Again* joined the English faculty at New York University in 1924 and spent most of the last years of his life in the city.

The arts

Creativity found a foothold as soon as the city emerged from the early settlement period. The first theater opened its doors on Maiden Lane in 1732, to be followed by dozens more. But New York was chiefly a commercial center, and artists who achieved prominence — painters Benjamin West and John Singleton Copley, for example — went off to Europe, setting a pattern that was to prevail for nearly two centuries.

Impressionism and the other "isms" that reverberated around Europe in the later 19thC had little influence across the Atlantic. The esthetic ferment did not spill over to the United States until the New York Armory Show of 1913, when Duchamp's *Nude Descending a Staircase* scandalized public opinion. By then, however, most of the men who were to form the first generation of post-World War II Radical Abstractionists were already alive. Encouraged by such artist-teachers as Hans Hofmann, who fled the gathering European tragedy in the 1930s, these artists champed under the restraints of the Depression and War, exploding after 1945 into what seemed to be a movement already mature at the instant of birth.

The controlled "splash-and-dribble" canvases of Jackson Pollock were no less shocking than the earlier Cubist fantasies, which now seemed sedate by comparison. Pollock died young, but compatriots Robert Motherwell, Clyfford Still, Mark Rothko, Willem de Kooning, Philip Guston, James Brooks, Jack Tworkov, Franz Kline and Sam Francis all contributed to the importance of the movement. All were associated with the city, and together they became known as the "New York School." They gathered in the same bars, summered on Long Island, and inspired a new row of galleries along E 10th St. It was a zesty era, enhanced, not inhibited, by its coexistence with the conformist Eisenhower-McCarthy period.

Art, like life, should be free, since both are experimental.
George Santayana

New York, which had long regarded itself as an oasis on the edge of a cultural wasteland, was the natural wellspring of what proved to be a surge to international pre-eminence in the arts. As the only major city to emerge unscathed from the 1939-45 global conflict, it could indulge its artists with almost unlimited support. The Guggenheim Museum, Frank Lloyd Wright's only commission in the city, was intended to serve as a repository for modern painting and sculpture. It was completed in 1959.

The Lincoln Center for the Performing Arts was conceived in 1955 to house the Metropolitan Opera, the Philharmonic Orchestra, the City Opera and Ballet companies, a repertory theater, a concert hall for small classical and popular groups, and the Juilliard School for actors, musicians and dancers. The five principal buildings were finished between 1962 and 1966. Additions to the Metropolitan Museum and the Museum of Modern Art, and the erection of a new home for the Whitney, maintained the pace.

During the last decade, creative endeavor in the visual arts has been highly experimental: Conceptual, Minimal, Neo-Constructivist, Optical — all executed in wildly mixed media: neon, ferro-concrete, forged metal, shaped canvas, boxes and heaps of earth.... The descendants of Pollock are as unrestrained as he, and every bit as provocative.

Architecture

Were the existing 18thC structures of New York grouped together, they would constitute a sizeable and quite handsome village. As it is, they are scattered throughout the city, largely neglected survivors of the Great Fires of 1776 and 1835. Most are Georgian Colonial or Federal, corresponding to the style prevalent in England during the successive reigns of the four Georges.

Although the Georgian style was itself imitative of Classical Greco-Roman themes, the first half of the 19thC saw a heightened enthusiasm for Greek and Gothic Revival. These overlapping modes dominated from 1830-55, manifest in the Athenian "temple" that is the Federal Hall National Memorial (1842), and that homage to medieval workmanship, Trinity Church (1846). In the increasingly popular attached town houses,

Architecture

Greek Revival was largely confined to decorative facades.

After the Civil War, an unabashed enthusiasm for virtually all European styles took hold. Motifs ranged from Venetian Renaissance to French Second Empire to Tudor to Romanesque, not infrequently all on the same building. The result was often called "Kitchen Sink." The fashionable architectural firm of the time was McKim, Mead and White, whose fondness for the Italian Renaissance is best seen in the Villard Houses (1886).

Technology was prompting fresh looks at old design assumptions. The Brooklyn Bridge (1883) employed Gothic granite towers, but also spidery cables of woven steel. No longer limited by the weight of masonry, and able to use steel and reinforced concrete, architects capitalized on the presence of a sturdy bedrock known as "Manhattan schist." Skyscrapers became a growing reality very rapidly. Fortunately, the hydraulic elevator was invented at the same time. By 1900, commercial buildings of 20 floors and higher were routine.

At first, architectural styles changed remarkably little, despite the new horizons that had been opened up by the introduction

St Paul's Chapel (1766). The only Colonial church left in New York. The interior is noted for its fluted Corinthian columns and Palladian window.

Morris-Jumel Mansion (1768). Georgian Colonial, remodeled in Federal style in 1810. Tuscan-columned portico and wooden quoins are typical Federal features.

Trinity Church (1846). A landmark at the end of Wall Street, Richard Upjohn's church is the city's best-known example of Gothic Revivalism.

Federal Hall National Memorial (1842). This Neo-Greek temple is perhaps the purest example of Greek Revival architecture in New York.

of *caisson* (steel pile) foundations. The Flatiron Building (1902), although constructed around a steel frame, was decked out with cornices reminiscent of the Florentine Renaissance style. The Woolworth Building (1913) has all the detail of a Gothic cathedral, complete with gargoyles.

Row houses persisted as the favored residential mode, however, now embellished with Italianate carving around arched doors and pediments. The wide use of red sandstone as a facing material gave this style the generic name "brownstone". Blocks of brownstones remain throughout Manhattan and Brooklyn, lending a Parisian flavor to their neighborhoods.

Luxury high-rise apartments made their appearance with the Chelsea and the Dakota in 1884, but the wealthy resisted that innovation for decades. The turn of the century brought a flirtation with the voluptuous Beaux Arts style and related neo-chateau fancies, which is best demonstrated in the Metropolitan Museum of Art (1902).

Sense prevailed in 1916, when the zoning law created a regulation of the height of buildings in relation to the width of

Washington Square North (c.1832). Ionic porticos reflect the mid-19thC rage for Greek Revivalism.

Villard Houses (1886). Now incorporated into the Palace Hotel, a complex of six houses inspired by the Palazzo della Cancelleria in Rome.

Flatiron Building (1902). The revolutionary steel frame is disguised by rusticated stone facades.

Metropolitan Museum of Art (1902). Rich, Neo-Classical decoration typical of the Beaux Arts movement.

the street below. One side effect of this was the development of buildings that were tiered, and a number of "wedding cakes" emerged.

Meanwhile, commercial architecture was entering the Modernist phase with the form-follows-function theories of Louis Sullivan, who proved to his successors that tall structures need not simulate stacked neo-Georgian or Romanesque tiers.

The next major influence was Art Deco, applied to spectacular effect in the steel-arched tower of the Chrysler Building (1930). With the Empire State Building (1931) and RCA Building (1932; now renamed the GE Building), the Chrysler represents the apogee of the first phase of the skyscraper phenomenon. Many feel that this period has never been surpassed.

Further developments were delayed until peacetime economic recovery in the late 1940s. A technique was developed in which walls of glass without a weight-bearing function were literally hung on the sides of steel skeletons. Among the first and most enduring realizations of this International Style were Lever House (1952) and the Seagram Building (1958).

More recently, sculptural planes and masses have shaped both small and large buildings, such as the Whitney Museum (1966) and the Waterside Houses (1974). The latest, Post-Modernist trend shows a revival in decorative interest.

Chrysler Building (1930). The world's tallest building until overtaken by the Empire State in 1931.

Whitney Museum (1966). A return to sculptural solidity.

Lever House (1952). One of the earliest glass-and-steel curtain wall constructions.

AT & T Building (1978-82). The Chippendale cornice shows a Post-Modernist trend.

Guide to the galleries

In this vibrant and volatile playground of creativity, gallery-hopping is a cherished pastime of culturally aware New Yorkers. Although the galleries are in the business of selling art, browsers are welcome. Most galleries are open Tues-Sat; a few are open on Mon as well, usually 10am-5pm or 6pm. Summer is the slow season, with various closing periods, often July or Aug, or both.

The galleries cluster in three principal areas: Madison Ave. and 57th St. are still very active, but the focus has shifted dramatically to SoHo in recent years. The art boom has stimulated spillover into adjacent neighborhoods as well, notably TriBeCa and the East Village. Galleries move and close with the unpredictability of discotheques, so the listings below should be regarded as a guide, not gospel. Furthermore, the list is selective, not comprehensive, but takes the walker past many buildings that house additional dealers.

Walking tours are the practical way to get to know the galleries, and the suggested routes below are laid out in that manner. Dealers gather in substantial numbers under single roofs, and the galleries are grouped by sequential street addresses. Many buildings are de facto mini-museums.

Pricing artworks

The New York City Department of Consumer Affairs caused an uproar among art gallery owners a few years ago, simply by demanding that firm prices be made available to potential buyers of works of art. In the past, few dealers voluntarily committed themselves to this matter, either on tags or inventory lists. Their distress over the new regulation was predictable. The galleries' traditional pricing policies bore striking resemblances (and still do!) to those of Middle Eastern rug merchants, unchartably amalgamating artists' reputations, previous sales, what the market might bear, the state of the economy in general and the gallery in particular, overhead costs and informed and/or wishful thinking. Bargaining is expected, even on very expensive artworks.

Caveat emptor

The best way for those of limited means to begin a collection of fine art is by purchasing graphic art prints. The pitfalls, although avoidable, are many. A true print is made by several methods: silk-screen, lithography, and engraving or etching on wood or metal are the principal methods. Most of these leave slight elevations or depressions on the paper surface, if only by overlapping layers of ink.

Prints are run in editions, usually under the supervision of the artist who created the original stones, blocks or screens. Editions might have as few as one or two copies or as many as 200-300. Typically, the artist signs each print, often adding a title. This increases the value of the print and indicates his or her approval of the result. A notation such as "14/120" (denoting the 14th print of an edition of 120) is normally added, and the original is destroyed at the end of the print run, thereby ensuring the limit of the edition.

Excellent photographic reproductions, sometimes with faked artists' signatures, are hard to detect, and unscrupulous or ignorant dealers might term these "artists' prints." Exercise caution by patronizing only reputable, well-established galleries. Avoid at all costs those shop fronts and "galleries" blazoned with

Guide to the galleries

such signs as "Fine Art Liquidations — 50 percent off!" Obtain both a receipt of sale and a certificate of authenticity on gallery notepaper, signed by the dealer.

57th St.

Start on the W side of Fifth Ave., walking N toward 57th St.

---

724 Fifth Ave. **Grace Borgenicht** ☎ 247-2111, influential in promotion of the New York School and the movements that followed. **Krausharr** ☎ 307-5730, recent sculpture. **Merrin** ☎ 757-2884, ancient sculpture and artifacts from Egyptian to pre-Columbian. **Helen Drutt** ☎ 974-7700, living artists. **Holly Solomon** ☎ 757-7777, Moderns. **Zabriskie** ☎ 307-7430, international artists, post-World War II onward.

Continue N on 5th Ave. and turn W (left) on 57th St., walking along the S side.

---

20 W 57th St. **Associated American Artists** ☎ 399-5510, drawings and prints. **Blumhelman** ☎ 245-2888, contemporary artists. **Galerie Lelong** ☎ 315-047, contemporary paintings, sculpture.
24 W 57th St. **Arras** ☎ 265-2222, multimedia works by living artists, with a branch in Trump Tower. **Fishbach** ☎ 759-2345, primarily American painters of the last 40yrs. **Galeria Joan Prats/Poligrafa** ☎ 315-3680, modern Americans and Europeans. **Galerie St Etienne** ☎ 245-6734, lithographs, drawings, etchings, graphics. **Marian Goodman** ☎ 977-7160, living Americans. **Grand Central Galleries** ☎ 867-3344, realists. **Multiples Inc.** ☎ 977-7160, serigraphs, lithographs, prints etc. **Reece** ☎ 333-5830, international contemporary sculptures and paintings. **Suzuki** ☎ 582-0373, drawings and graphic arts. **Jack Tilton** ☎ 247-7480, new paintings and sculpture.
29 W 57th St. **Sid Deutsch** ☎ 754-6660, all manner of quality 20thC work.
40 W 57th St. **Kennedy** ☎ 541-9600, American graphics and figurative paintings since 18thC. **Marlborough** ☎ 541-4900, 19th and 20thC works in many styles and media.
50 W 57th St. **Terry Dintenfass** ☎ 581-2268, recent representational work. **Allan Frumpkin** ☎ 757-6655, active East and West Coast figurative artists. **Carlo Lamagna** ☎ 245-6006, landscapes. **Douglas Drake** ☎ 582-5930, emphasis on modernists of last 40yrs. **Lillian Heidenberg** ☎ 586-3808, Impressionists and Post-Impressionists. **Luise Ross** ☎ 307-0400, recent paintings and sculpture. **Robert Schoelkopf** ☎ 765-3540, contemporary painting and sculpture. **Tatistcheff** ☎ 664-0907, young Americans.
110 W 57th St. **Sidney Janis** ☎ 581-0110, influential dealer in Abstract Expressionists and those who followed.

Cross to the N side of 57th St. and walk E.

---

41 W 57th St. **Tibor de Nagy** ☎ 421-3780, non-objective and representational paintings and sculpture. **Sherry French** ☎ 308-6440, recent landscapes and figurative paintings. **Schmidt Bingham** ☎ 888-1122, landscapes and representational images. **Brewster** ☎ 980-1975, modern masters, American, European and Mexican.
33 W 57th St. **Hammer** ☎ 644-4400, mainstream 19th and 20thC Europeans and Americans.

11 E 57th St.   **Midtown** ☎758-1900, 20thC representational works.

17 E 57th St.   **Wally Findlay** ☎421-5390 (one of a chain), French Impressionists, contemporary Europeans and Americans.

41 E 57th St.   The Fuller Building has 25 galleries, including: **ACA** ☎644-830, contemporary American and European painting and sculpture. **Andre Emmerich** ☎752-0124, cutting-edge paintings and sculpture since the 1950s. **David Findlay Jr** ☎486-7660, American 19th and 20thC painting and sculpture. **James Goodman** ☎593-3737, Calder, Léger, Hepworth and other 20thC masters. **Jan Krugier** ☎755-7288, Picasso and other European masters since 1890. **Marisa del Re** ☎688-1843, postwar Europeans.

Madison Ave.

Many of these galleries are on side streets, but near Madison. Start at 63rd St. and walk N on the W side of Madison. Return to the Ave. after each short detour, continuing N.

---

19 E 64th St.   **Wildenstein** ☎879-0500, 17th-20thC paintings, sculpture and furniture.

21 E 65th St.   **Richard York** ☎772-9155, American art of last two centuries.

23 E 67th St.   **Blumka II** ☎879-5611, eclectic holdings of largely European antique art. **L'Ibis** ☎734-9229, ancient Egyptian and Coptic artifacts.

822 Madison Ave.   **Schlesinger-Boisante** ☎734-3600, European and American modern artists.

19 E 70th St.   **Knoedler** ☎794-0550, prominent dealer in American vanguardists.

21 E 70th St.   **Hirschl & Adler** ☎535-8810, British and American 20thC art. Two more galleries on opposite side of Madison.

19 E 71st St.   **Martina Hamilton** ☎744-8976, paintings by contemporary Americans. **Kovedsy** ☎628-6886, Eastern European 20thC artists. **Kurland-Zabar** ☎517-8576, 19th and 20thC decorative arts. **Prakapas** ☎737-6066, photography.

23 E 73rd St.   **Kouros** ☎288-5888, abstractionists. **Mary-Anne Martin** ☎288-2213, Rivera, Tamayo and other Latin American painters.

922 Madison Ave.   **Jane Kahan** ☎744-1490, prints, drawings, paintings, sculptures by very important 20thC Americans and Europeans.

13 E 75th St.   **CDS** ☎772-9555, sculpture, drawings and other works by Latin and North American artists. **Thompson** ☎249-0242, American and European paintings and sculptures.

956 Madison Ave.   **Avanti** ☎772-6606, works by Larry Rivers, Franz Kline, Jim Dine, and other Americans who first gained attention in the 1960s.

982 Madison Ave.   **Galerie Tamexnaga** ☎734-6789, Japanese-owned, but representing mostly French and American contemporary artists.

984 Madison Ave.   **David Findlay** ☎249-2909, primarily figurative paintings.

988 Madison Ave.   **Weintraub** ☎879-1195, mostly sculpture, by Henry Moore, Alexander Calder, Giacometti *et al.*

1014 Madison Ave.   **Graham** ☎535-5767, diverse works, 19th and 20thC. **Graham Modern** ☎535-5767, works by living modernists.

Guide to the galleries

1018 Madison Ave.   **Rachel Adler** ☎517-4005, early 20thC European progressives. **Forum** ☎772-7666, contemporary American realists.
18 E 79th St.   **Acquavella** ☎734-6300, Chagall, Braque, Cézanne and Léger, supplemented by important American abstractionists. **Salander-O'Reilly** ☎879-6606, early 20thC modernists plus contemporary painters of considerable reputation.
1044 Madison Ave.   **Jay Johnson** ☎628-7280, American folk artists.
1046 Madison Ave.   **Hubert** ☎628-2922, prints by Picasso, Warhol, Chagall, others.

Return to Madison, cross to E side, walk S.

1045 Madison Ave.   **Denise Cadex** ☎734-3670, 20thC Europeans.
1035 Madison Ave.   **Sindin** ☎288-7902, European, Latin, and North American masters since 1900.
959 Madison Ave.   **Solomon & Co.** ☎737-8200, sculpture and paintings by Noguchi, Calder, de Kooning, Dubuffet and others of that lofty ilk.
851 Madison Ave.   **Hirschl & Adler Folk** ☎988-3655, American folk artists. **Hirschl & Adler Modern** ☎744-6700, living artists. **Barbara Mathes** ☎249-3600, paintings and drawings by the likes of Matisse, Vuillard, Picasso.

SoHo

Once the exclusive arena of wildly avant-garde artists working beyond esthetic and ideological boundaries, SoHo is now the principal art marketplace in New York. Established painters and sculptors from the postwar boom onward now mingle with young turks in galleries that are often merely new outlets of pre-eminent uptown dealers.

Anticipate the unimaginable mingled with the familiar, the reason little effort is made below to delineate specialties. Galleries are listed in sequential order, on both sides of each street. Those mentioned are frankly only an arbitrary sampling. Many others are located on side streets and at the edges of the district.

Walk S on West Broadway (not to be confused with Broadway, fours blocks E) from Houston St.

---

465 West Broadway   **Access** ☎353-2080.
457 West Broadway   **Martin Lawrence** ☎995-8865.

Detour W to 130 Prince St, where nine new galleries reside, then return to West Broadway and turn S.

---

429 West Broadway   **Nancy Hoffman** ☎966-6678.
420 West Broadway   **Leo Castelli** ☎431-5160. **Charles Cowles** ☎925-3500. **Sonnabend** ☎966-6160. **Marilyn Pearl** ☎966-5506. **49th Parallel** ☎924-8349.
417 West Broadway   **Mary Boone** ☎431-1818.
415 West Broadway   **Scott Hanson** ☎334-0041. **Stephen Haller** ☎219-2500. **Witkin** ☎925-5510, photographs. **Gimpel/Weitzenhoffer** ☎925-6090.

Turn E on Spring St.

155 Spring St.　　**Laurie Rubin** ☎226-2161. **Lieberman & Saul** ☎431-0747.
134 Spring St.　　**Jeffrey Ruesch** ☎925-1137.
128 Spring St.　　**Multiple Impressions** ☎925-1313.
121 Spring St.　　**Gallery 121** ☎925-4331.
114 Spring St.　　**Jacques Carcanagues** ☎925-8110, Third World handicrafts.
109 Spring St.　　**Carolyn Hill** ☎226-4611.
96 Spring St.　　**Gallery Revel** ☎925-0600.

Turn N on Broadway.

---

560 Broadway
Among many:　　**Wolff** ☎431-7833. **Jack Shainman** ☎966-3866. **Max Protetch** ☎966-5454. **David Nolan** ☎925-6190. **Diane Brown** ☎219-1060. **Paula Allen** ☎334-9710.
568 Broadway　　A total of 22 galleries, including: **Damon Brandt** ☎431-1444. **Phoenix** ☎226-8711. **Crown Point Press** ☎226-5476. **Fawbush** ☎966-6650. **John Gibson** ☎925-1192. **Lang & O'Hara** ☎226-2121.
583 Broadway　　**New Museum of Contemporary Art** ☎219-1222, multiple simultaneous exhibitions.
584 Broadway　　**Mocha** ☎966-6699, contemporary Hispanic artists.
591 Broadway　　**Vera Engelhorn** ☎966-6882.

Turn W on Houston St., then S on Mercer St.

---

168 Mercer St.　　**NoHo** ☎219-2210. **Ledel** ☎966-7659.
164 Mercer St.　　**Morningstar** ☎334-9330. **Pleiades** ☎226-9093, 14 sculptors ☎966-5790. **John Szoke Graphics** ☎219-8300. **Amos Eno** ☎226-5342.

Turn W on Prince St., then N on Greene St.

---

142 Greene St.　　**Massimo Audiello** ☎475-4241. **Sperone Westwater** ☎431-3685. **John Weber** ☎966-6115.
133 Greene St.　　**Littlejohn-Smith** ☎420-6069. **Moos** ☎982-0411.

When and where to go

Not long ago, the conventional advice was to avoid New York in its relentlessly humid summer. Probably for that reason, the theater and concert season did not begin until Oct, when most of the new plays opened. That is still one of the best months to visit, when the gathering energy of the city is palpable. But the widespread adoption of air conditioning in the last three decades now makes July bearable, and major new musicals and dramas hold their premieres throughout the year.

While affluent New Yorkers still flee to summer cottages by the sea or in the New England hills, there is never that impression of an abandoned city given by, say, Paris in Aug. Some of the deluxe restaurants lock up for 2-3wks, but most remain open for business, as do the museums and landmark buildings. Concerted efforts under the "New York is a Summer Festival" rubric have brought about a full schedule of established cultural events, as a glance at the *Calendar of events* below reveals. Many of these events feature front-rank performing groups at little or no cost — which is decidedly not the case from Oct-May. There is a marked shirt-sleeved looseness in New Yorkers themselves in the hot months, a departure from their inclination toward dressier formality during the rest of the year. Visitors devoted to art should avoid July and Aug, when most galleries are closed.

Apr-May, Sept-Oct are the best months in terms of weather. For that reason, hotels are heavily booked then. Demand slackens in Jan-Feb, but although there will be some bone-chilling days, winters are usually not too severe and snowfalls of more than four inches are rare.

Those intent on a shopping vacation will encounter large crowds and frayed tempers in the weeks between Thanksgiving and Christmas. The biggest sales are in Jan-Feb. Sports enthusiasts find that the seasons of the eight major professional teams overlap in early fall. Allowing for these few caveats, little will be missed no matter what time of year is chosen.

New York is an island city, with four of its five administrative units, called boroughs, separated by water from the North American continent. They are linked with each other, and the mainland, by 65 bridges and 19 tunnels. Every likely tourist destination is within reach of the extensive public transportation system — by subway, bus, or a combination of the two. Many out-of-town locations can be reached by rail or bus as well, although a car is often preferable.

At the spiritual and geographical center is **Manhattan**. Even residents of the other boroughs refer to it as "The City," a reality made official by the Postal Service: all addresses in Manhattan are given as "New York, NY," while the others are designated **Brooklyn**, **Queens**, **The Bronx** and **Staten Island**. Nearly all visitors to New York stay in Manhattan. The major hotels are there, as are approximately 15,000 restaurants and most of the theaters, concert halls, art galleries, landmarks, corporation headquarters, libraries, universities and best-known churches and department stores.

The outer boroughs, although largely residential and industrial, are by no means bereft, however. The Bronx has its *Zoo* and **Yankee Stadium**; Queens has **Shea Stadium** and the **Aqueduct Racetrack**; Brooklyn has its beaches and a fine museum; and Staten Island has a *Tibetan temple*, and two complexes of restored architectural treasures.

Calendar of events

See also *Sports and activities* and *Public holidays* in *Basic information*.

January

‡ Early Jan: one-day **Winter Festival in Central Park**, on the Great Lawn, near 81st St. Festivities include snow sculpture contest, cross-country skiing demonstrations and winter fashions. Snow is provided by machine if nature is uncooperative (☎ 408-0100 for exact date and information).

‡ Mid-Jan for 2wks: **Boat Show**. Javits Convention Center. Same motives and same lavish display as the Auto Show, but the subject is pleasure craft, both power and sail.

‡ Between mid-Jan and early Feb: **Chinese New Year**. Chinatown, lower Manhattan. Ten days of

fireworks and celebrations feature silk lions and a fearsome dragon that snakes and dances along Mott St. to frighten evil spirits (☎ 397-8222 for details). ‡ Late Jan: **Winter Antiques Show**. 7th Regiment Armory, Park Ave. and E 67th St. This exhibition of superior antiques is also an excuse to see the grand interiors by Stanford White and Louis Comfort Tiffany, usually closed to the public.

February

‡ Feb is designated **Black History month**: Libraries, schools, universities, TV stations and neighborhood associations sponsor a wide range of events highlighting the contributions of African-Americans to American history and culture. Newspapers carry daily specifics (☎ 397-8222 for information). ‡ Feb 12-22: **Lincoln and Washington Birthday Sales**. On the days around these national holidays, the large department stores mount enormous sales. ‡ Mid-Feb: **Westminster Dog Show**. Madison Square Garden, 7th Ave. and 33rd St. Two days of intense competition. ‡ Mid-Feb for 1wk: **National Antiques Show**. Madison Square Garden, 8th Ave. and 32nd St. Perhaps the largest show of antiques and related objects in the world (☎ 564-4400 for dates). ‡ Late Feb: **Lantern Day**. Chinatown and City Hall, lower Manhattan. On the night of the 15th day of the Chinese Lunar New Year, children form a parade to present paper lanterns to the Mayor. There are martial arts demonstrations, dancing and singing (☎ 397-8222 for details).

March

‡ For **Easter** events, see *April*. ‡ Mar 17: **St Patrick's Day Parade**. 5th Ave. from 44th St. to 86th St. All New Yorkers are Irish on this day. Beer is green, clothing is green, even the line down the middle of 5th Ave. is green. Irish taverns and St Patrick's Cathedral are the centers of activity. ‡ Late Mar for 2mths: **Ringling Brothers and Barnum & Bailey Circus**. Madison Square Garden, 7th.Ave. and 33rd St. A small parade of elephants and wagons heralds the opening.

April

‡ 2wks preceding Easter: **Easter Egg Exhibition**. Ukrainian Museum, 2nd Ave. (12th St.). A specially mounted display of hand-painted eggs, a staple of this small museum (☎ 228-0110 for details). ‡ Week before Easter: **Easter Flower Show**. Macy's Department Store, Herald Sq. The nation's largest department store blooms on several floors. ‡ Mid-Apr: **International Auto Show**. Javits Convention Center. A vast glittery exhibition of foreign and American-made cars: antique, classic, custom and brand new. ‡ Week before Easter: **Easter Lilies display**. Channel Gardens, Rockefeller Center. ‡ Easter Sunday: **Easter Parade**. 5th Ave., from 49th St. to 59th St. Not an organized parade at all, but a promenade of celebrants showing off their new spring finery, some of it extraordinary.

May

‡ Weekend in mid-May: **Ninth Avenue International Festival**. 9th Ave. from 36th St. to 59th St. Once known as "Paddy's Market," this stretch of 9th Ave. specializes in prosaic and exotic foods. The festival is a gustatory orgy of *kielbasa*, quiche, *falafel*, *knishes*, *tacos*, Belgian waffles, *zeppoli*, *baklava*, *souvlaki* and every fast food conceived by man. Crafts, merchandise and entertainment. ‡ May 20: **Martin Luther King Jr. Memorial Parade**. 5th Ave. above 59th St. ‡ Around mid-May: **Greek Independence Day Parade**. 5th Ave. above 59th St. Less widely celebrated than St Patrick's Day. The growing Greek population nevertheless provides a substantial parade each year, with floats and bands. ‡ Last weekend in May: **Memorial Day Weekend**; **official opening of city beaches**; **antiques show** at 7th Regiment Armory; **women's 10,000m L'Eggs Marathon**. ‡ Late May-early June: **Washington Square Outdoor Art Exhibition**. Washington Sq. and adjacent streets. Artists, amateur and otherwise, fill walls and fences with paintings (landscapes, tigers on velvet, sedate nudes), metalwork, tooled leather and wire jewelry. Everything is for sale, and bargaining is expected. The event is repeated in early Sept.

June

‡ All month: **music and other cultural events**, many of them free. There is dance, Shakespeare, opera, jazz, pop and folk music. Leading groups and companies perform outdoors, in Central Park, at the

Calendar of events

Rockefeller Center, in the Sculpture Garden of the Museum of Modern Art, at the South Street Seaport and at the World Trade Center (☎ 755-4100 *for a daily recorded announcement*). ‡ Sun in early June: **Puerto Rican Day Parade**. 5th Ave. above 59th St. Colorful, well-attended, sprightly celebration associated with the patron saint of the Puerto Rican capital, San Juan. ‡ Early June for 2wks: **Festival of St Anthony**. Little Italy, lower Manhattan. Sullivan St. below Houston St. is lined with booths selling games of chance, sizzling sausages, *calzone*, pizza and flavored ices. Religious observances dominate during the day; secular entertainments take over after dusk. Go hungry, for the aromas are irresistible. ‡ Early June: **Rose Day Weekend**. New York Botanical Garden, The Bronx. Stunning demonstration of the horticulturist's craft, with tours and lectures. ‡ Mid-June: **Salute to Israel Parade**. 5th Ave. above 59th St. ‡ Late June-early July: **JVC Jazz Festival**. Concert halls and outdoor locations around Manhattan. Jazz in all its permutations, from Dixieland to atonal, takes over from noon-midnight. Some events are free. Check newspapers for details.

July

‡ July 4th: **Independence Day Festivities**. Battery Park, lower Manhattan. **Old New York Harbor Festival** takes place in the afternoon and evening, with patriotic ceremonies, food, music and performers. **Richmondtown Restoration, Staten Island: celebrations** matching the Colonial and Federalist ambience. South Street Seaport, downtown Manhattan. This is one of the best vantages for the spectacular **fireworks over the East River**, sponsored by Macy's Department Store. The display starts around 9.30pm, but check newspapers. **Tall ships and sailing vessels** from other nations and ports often visit. **Street festival** has music, crafts and food. ‡ July-Aug: **Summer Festival**. Snug Harbor Cultural Center, Staten Island. Music and art exhibitions on weekends throughout the summer. ‡ Mid-July through Aug: **Mostly Mozart Festival**. Lincoln Center, West Side Manhattan. This treasured event commences with a free outdoor concert, then proceeds through the rest of the summer indoors,

primarily in Avery Fisher Hall. Ticket prices are unusually low (☎ 874-2424 *for details*). ‡ July-Aug: **Washington Square Music Festival**. Washington Square Park, Greenwich Village. Chamber music by the fountain on Tues evenings (☎ 431-1088). ‡ Late July to mid-Aug: **New York Philharmonic Parks Concerts**. Various park locations in all boroughs. The famed symphony orchestra performs beneath the stars, for free (☎ 755-4100 *for details*).

August

‡ Aug: **Greenwich Village Jazz Festival**. ‡ Mid-Aug to early Sept: **Lincoln Center Out-of-Doors**. Lincoln Center, West Side Manhattan. Free live entertainment on the plaza from noon-sunset (☎ 877-1800 *for details*).

September

‡ Early Sept for 2wks: **Washington Square Outdoor Art Exhibition**. Washington Sq. and adjacent streets. A duplicate of the spring event (see *May*). ‡ Sun in mid-Sept: **"New York is Book Country"** street fair. 5th Ave. from 47th St. to 57th St. and adjacent blocks. ‡ Mid-Sept: **Steuben Day Parade**. 5th Ave. from 59th St. to Yorkville. Exuberant small-scale commemoration of the German officer who aided the Revolutionary cause. ‡ Late Sept: **Festa di San Gennaro**. Little Italy, lower Manhattan. Blocks of gaming- and eating-booths tempt with the possibility of sudden modest riches and the certainty of excessive calorie consumption. It is becoming an increasingly intercultural event, Sicilian sausages being augmented by Cantonese egg rolls. ‡ Sun in late Sept: **Atlantic Avenue Antic**. Southern edge of Brooklyn Heights. This predominantly Syrian neighborhood asserts its individuality with displays of crafts, foods and Middle Eastern dancing (☎ (718)875-8993 *for details*). ‡ Mid-Sept to early Oct: **New York Film Festival**. Alice Tully Hall, Lincoln Center. Serious film buffs revel in 3wks of afternoon and evening showings, with no need of questionable awards and overheated publicity.

October

‡ On or about Oct 5: **Pulaski Day Parade**. 5th Ave. The Polish community takes its turn. ‡ Weekend in early Oct: **Brooklyn Heights Art Show**. The

Promenade. Arts and crafts from scores of local artists, compete with spectacular vistas of lower Manhattan. From about noon-6pm.
‡ Early Oct: **Columbus Day Parade**. 5th Ave. Second only to the St Patrick's Day Parade in intensity and numbers, and along the same route. ‡ Early Oct for 1wk: **Fall Antiques Show**. W 54th St. and Pier 90 (☎ 777-5218). ‡ 3rd Sun in Oct: **Old Home Day**. Richmondtown Restoration, Staten Island. Crafts demonstrations, dancing and entertainment in this re-created old-time village. ‡ Oct 31: late afternoon. **Halloween Parade**. Greenwich Village, lower Manhattan. Villagers in outlandish costumes wind through the streets of their district, with ghoulish happenings along the route, and a party at Washington Sq.

November

‡ First Sun in Nov: **New York City Marathon**. From Staten Island to Central Park. Not the oldest, but the biggest marathon, with more than 24,000 runners following a route from the w end of the Verrazano Narrows Bridge through all five boroughs. ‡ Early Nov for 6 days: **National Horse Show**. Madison Square Garden. Equestrian competition of jumping and dressage. ‡ Last Thurs in Nov: **Macy's Thanksgiving Day Parade**. Broadway, 77th St. to 34th St. Traditional 3hr morning event with bands, celebrities and huge helium-filled balloons in the shapes of such folk as Bugs Bunny, Snoopy, Superman and Mickey Mouse. ‡ Nov 26-Jan 6: **Star of Wonder Show**. Hayden Planetarium. The night sky of Bethlehem is vividly reproduced, with music and commentary (☎ 873-8828). ‡ Thanksgiving-New Year's Day: **Lord & Taylor Christmas Windows**. 424 5th Ave. (39th St.). All the big stores vie with

each other in Christmas decorations, but this one is the perennial champion, managing to outdo itself every year.

December

‡ Late afternoon in early Dec: **Rockefeller Center Tree-Lighting Ceremony**. 5th Ave. between 50th St. and 51st St. The huge tree that rises above the ice-skating rink and the gilded statue of *Prometheus* is illuminated, by dignitaries and celebrities, to the accompaniment of Christmas carols. Extravagantly **decorated trees** are also set up in the American Museum of Natural History and the Metropolitan Museum of Art. ‡ First Sun in Dec: **Christmas in Richmondtown**. Richmondtown Restoration, Staten Island. Period Christmas celebration in the restored village, complete with costumed guides (☎ (718) 351-1611). ‡ First night of Chanukah: **Lighting of Chanukah Candles**. City Hall, lower Manhattan. 92nd St. YM-YWHA, 1395 Lexington Ave. ‡ Dec: **Nutcracker Ballet**. Lincoln Center. Traditional performance by the New York City Ballet (☎ 870-5500 for details). ‡ The two Suns before Christmas: 11am-3pm. **Fifth Avenue** Holiday Mall. 5th Ave., 34th St. to 57th St. The Ave. is **closed to traffic**, and public entertainments draw shoppers past sublime and gaudy windows. ‡ Dec 31: **New Year's Eve**. All over the city. A "Big Apple" slides down a flag pole above Times Sq., reaching the bottom at the first second of the New Year to the cheers of thousands of witnesses. Cars sound their horns, boats in the harbor blow their whistles, and celebrants kiss each other in the ballrooms of dozens of hotels. There is also a 5-mile run in Central Park, which commences at midnight and is accompanied by fireworks.

Area planners

Manhattan

Manhattan is 12 miles along its N-S axis and about 3 miles across at its widest point. The roll of history and fashion flows northward, for development started with a Dutch settlement at the s tip and spread in the only direction available. **Financial District** (Map 2U4). This neighborhood long ago assumed the role evident in its present name, and now bristles with concrete and glass monuments to capitalism, among which are a few public buildings surviving from the

Orientation map

Major places of interest

1 American Museum of Immigration
2 American Museum of Natural History
3 Audubon Terrace
4 Bronx Zoo and New York Botanical Garden
5 Carnegie Hall
6 Cathedral Church of St John the Divine
7 Chrysler Building
8 City Hall
9 Cloisters
10 Cooper-Hewitt Museum
11 Empire State Building
12 Federal Hall National Memorial
13 Flatiron Building
14 Fraunces Tavern Museum
15 Frick Collection
16 Guggenheim Museum
17 Hall of Fame for Great Americans
18 Lincoln Center
19 Madison Square Garden
20 Metropolitan Museum of Art
21 Morris-Jumel Mansion
22 Museum of Modern Art
23 New York Public Library
24 Pan Am Building
25 Pierpont Morgan Library
26 Rockefeller Center
27 St Patrick's Cathedral
28 South Street Seaport Museum
29 Statue of Liberty
30 Trinity Church
31 Union Square
32 United Nations Headquarters
33 Washington Square
34 Whitney Museum of American Art
35 Woolworth Building
36 World Financial Center

US Highway
Interstate Highway
State Highway

N

George Washington Br.
9A
3
Broadway
Harlem
NEW JERSEY
Hudson River
6
Riverside Park
Upper West Side
Yorkville
9A
2
Central Park
20
10
16
34
East Side
15
18
Broadway
MANHATTAN
5
Roosevelt Is.
Lincoln Tunn.
Queensboro Br.
26
22
27
Theater District
23
Grand Central Term.
24
32
Garment Center
25
Penn. Station
19
11
Murray Hill
Queens–Midtown Tunn.
13
Chelsea
33
Greenwich Village
Lower East Side
East River
SoHo
Little Italy
Williamsburg Br.
Holland Tunn.
35
Chinatown
8
Battery Park City
36
Financial District
30
12
14
28
Manhattan Br.
Ellis Is.
Battery Pk.
Brooklyn Br.
Brooklyn Heights
Brooklyn–Battery Tunn.
29
Governors Is.
Liberty Is.
BROOKLYN
Hudson River
Henry Hudson Parkway
F. D. Roosevelt Dr.
Brooklyn Queens Expressway

late Colonial and early Federalist periods. They constitute a captivating history lesson, enhanced by vistas of New York's rivers and harbor. Despite the frenetic business activity, however, there is, to date, still only one hotel of consequence and few first-class restaurants.

Chinatown and Little Italy (Maps 2&3). When space began to run out in the Financial District, corporation rulers transferred their building mania to midtown. In doing so, they leapfrogged a band of small residential communities, former villages that still cling to very specific identities. While neither Chinatown, s of Canal St., nor Little Italy, a block or two to the N, are postcard-pretty, their ethnic vitality persists.

Lower East Side (Map 3R5). This lies to the E, and historically was the first land-fall of impoverished immigrants. A dreary area of rubbish-filled streets and sagging tenements — then and now — its only touristic significance is the frenetic Sunday shopping along Orchard St., when startling bargains in high-style apparel can be plucked from heaps of used and poorly-made clothing and shoes.

SoHo and TriBeCa (Map 2S4). In the 1960s, the warehouses and lofts of SoHo were "discovered" by artists seeking larger spaces at lower rents. Inevitably, they drew gallery owners and restaurateurs, until boutiques and stockbrokers began to supplant the painters and sculptors. So the artists moved on to nearby TriBeCa, where a similar transformation is under way.

Greenwich Village (Map 2R4). This area also knows the cycle well. After a time as an upper-middle-class suburb, it too became an artist's enclave. Experimental theaters, art galleries and the new Bohemia flourished here in the early 20thC, and many of the theaters remain. Rows of brownstones and carriage-house mews alternate with tacky commercial streets. The restaurants of SoHo and Greenwich Village blanket the entire field of price and achievement.

Chelsea, Gramercy Park and Murray Hill (Maps 4&5P4, Q3-4). North of 14th St., the planned gridwork of streets and avenues takes hold. On the w is Chelsea, at an early stage of gentrification, as growing numbers of antique stores and trendy bars and eateries show. East of Park Ave. and N of 42nd St. are the contiguous neighborhoods of Gramercy Park and Murray Hill, where pockets of 19thC elegance persist. Quiet and relatively small hotels provide alternatives to the flashy behemoths farther N, and the restaurants and nightspots give fair value without sacrifice of elbow room.

Midtown district (Map 5). This area, from 42nd St. to 59th St. and Hudson River to East River, and particularly *Midtown East* , contains a disproportionate share of the attractions for which New York is known. Most of the major hotels, theaters, stores and world-class restaurants are within its elastic boundaries, as well as the *United Nations Headquarters* , **Times Square**, *Rockefeller Center, St Patrick's Cathedral*, the *Museum of Modern Art, Grand Central Terminal*, and dozens of examples of New York's most renowned contribution to architecture, the skyscraper. The pace is swifter here, crowds thicker, rooms and meals more costly, aggravations greater.

Upper East Side (Map 7). By comparison, this is relatively tranquil. Along 5th Ave., its western border, are most of the major museums of art and history, dominated by the *Metropolitan Museum of Art*. Mingled with the private townhouses of the side blocks are eclectic galleries and stores; and toward the East River, upwardly mobile young married couples and single people, who favor the postwar highrises, keep the many pubs and discos full.

Upper West Side (Map 6J-K2-3). This is an area in transition. It is not as sleek as the Upper East Side, and has large concentrations of low-income families, but is enjoyed by professionals who find the area and its people less superficial. The *Lincoln Center* for the Performing Arts and the *American Museum of Natural History* are the centerpieces. Between the Upper East and Upper West Side is *Central Park* .

Harlem (Maps 8&9H3-4). The area stretches river to river immediately to the N of the preceding two neighborhoods. Despite its substandard housing, poverty, and attendant ills, it boasts a number of important cultural institutions, especially the four specialized museums of *Audubon Terrace*.

The high, narrow neck of land at the NW corner of Manhattan Island has the sanctuary of *Fort Tryon Park*, and a remarkable assemblage of medieval chapels and gardens from European monasteries, known as *The Cloisters*.

Even in combination, the other four boroughs cannot match this panoply, although each has its charms.

The Bronx

The only borough on the mainland. A full day can be profitably spent at the *Bronx Zoo and New York Botanical Garden* , with a side trip to the *Van Cortlandt Mansion and Museum*.

Brooklyn

Had it resisted annexation in 1898, Brooklyn would now be the fourth largest city in the United States. It is still self-contained, with its own civic and cultural centers, concert halls, downtown shopping district, beaches, colleges, and residential neighborhoods both elite and prosaic. Among its inducements are the *Brooklyn Museum*, *New York Aquarium*, *Brooklyn Heights* and the promenade that overlooks an extraordinary panorama of the Manhattan skyline from the *Statue of Liberty* to the *Empire State Building*.

Queens

This borough has both **LaGuardia** and **JFK airports**. Sports fans take the subway to the **Aqueduct Racetrack** for thoroughbred racing, and to **Shea Stadium** for Mets baseball games. (See *Sports and activities*.)

Staten Island

Despite the 1964 *Verrazano Narrows Bridge*, which connects it with Brooklyn, Staten Island remains somewhat isolated from the other boroughs. Those who take the time to look around, however, will discover pockets of bucolic solitude, notably: *Richmondtown Restoration*, a village of Colonial and 19thC homes and stores; *Snug Harbor Cultural Center*, a living museum of buildings in every 19thC style; the re-created temple that is the *Tibetan Museum* ; and the small but remarkable *Staten Island Zoo*.

Walks in New York

Many parts of Manhattan, and Brooklyn Heights across the East River, have a surprisingly intimate character, which can be best appreciated on foot. The following walks serve as samples.

Walks

Walk 1: An introduction to New York

Tourists and natives alike find themselves passing through the *Rockefeller Center* and its immediate surroundings repeatedly. They come for the shopping along 5th Ave., to watch the iceskaters, for shows at Radio City Music Hall, to see the city's tallest Christmas tree, and to join the Easter Parade.

Begin at the **Channel Garden** entrance on the w side of 5th Ave. between 49th St. and 50th St., perhaps after a visit to *St Patrick's Cathedral*, one block N. The Channel itself, with, appropriately, **La Maison Française** on the s and the **British Empire Building** on the N, has long, raised flower beds, where the plantings are changed with seasons. At the end of this walkway, a golden statue of Prometheus hovers above a sunken rectangular plaza, which is an outdoor café from Apr-Sept and an ice-skating rink from Oct-Mar.

Circle around, glancing up at the narrow limestone slab that is the **GE (RCA) Building**, with Art Deco details over and around the high portals. Inside, heroic murals in sepia tones depict muscular workers striding across walls and ceilings. Unhappily, the rooftop observation deck that once drew thousands of visitors every day is now closed to the public. Part of that space, however, is taken up by the lounge of the revamped **Rainbow Room**, so much of the panoramic vista can be seen from inside. Drinks and snacks in the lounge are not too expensive, but men must be dressed in jacket and tie, which are not the usual sightseeing garb. Alternatively, descend to the subterranean concourse, one floor beneath ground level. A village of small shops thrives down there, along arcades that connect buildings from 6th Ave. to 5th Ave., and from 48th St. to 53rd St.

Return to Rockefeller Plaza at the front of the GE Building and turn right, s, then right again, w, into 48th St. The mock-Dublin pub **Charlie O's Bar & Grill** (*#33*) is a good place to stop for a hamburger or a platter of fried calamari. Continue w to Ave. of the Americas (known to all as 6th Ave.). The wall of intimidating skyscrapers on the opposite side is technically part of the Rockefeller Center, although the buildings were erected in the 1960s. Cross the Ave. and walk N. Note the gray 19thC building at the NE corner of 49th St., a defiant hold-out against the monoliths that surround it. Its ground floor is a bar-restaurant, **Hurley's**. There are usually several food carts at the next corner. If they tempt, take your snack to the marble bench around the fountain in front of the **Time-Life Building** at the corner of 6th St. and 50th St. Directly opposite is the **Radio City Music Hall**. For 50yrs it featured big Hollywood "family" movies interspersed with stage shows that focused on the precision dance troupe known as The Rockettes. Business fell off in the 1970s and the hall nearly closed, but was saved by a new policy of special events, rock and pop concerts, and limited-run revues. The ornate vaulted interior must be seen to be believed.

NBC maintains studios in Rockefeller Center, in which are produced such popular TV shows as *Saturday Night Live*, *Donahue* and *Late Night with David Letterman*. Tickets for guided tours of the studios (*about every 15mins, Mon-Sat 9.30am-4.30pm*) may be purchased at the GE Building. Tours of Radio City Music Hall are also available (☎ *632-4041 for information*).

Walk 2: Financial District

From the day the first Dutch settlers crept into hastily constructed bark shelters, the foremost business of New York was commerce.

Gradually, merchants became financiers, ever more distant from the commodities they bartered, and as ever greater space was needed to contain the people who administered the system, so the present thicket of skyscrapers emerged, a 20thC metropolis built to the edges of a 17thC street plan.

By 1850, few people actually lived below Chambers St. and the *Brooklyn Bridge*, the approximate northern border of what was "Little Old New York" and is now the *Financial District*. From Mon-Fri 8am-6pm the streets teemed with millions of workers, then at dusk and on weekends the dark canyons heard only the sigh of winds and the rustle of blown refuse. That is less true today, for New Yorkers are starting to move back, and restaurateurs and retailers are following close behind them. So whether a Fri or a Sat is chosen for a look around depends on the tastes of the visitor. Most buildings of note are open both days, but most eating places lock up as soon as the last commuter has downed his Martini and headed for home.

A walking tour logically begins with the observation deck of the south (*#2*) tower of the *World Trade Center*, the easiest structure to find in New York City. Exit onto Liberty St. Turn left, to the E, then right, S, on Broadway. Three blocks down is *Trinity Church*. The Gothic Revival third version (1846) of a 1696 original, it stands out from its towering neighbors by virtue of a layer of city grime so black it (almost) glistens. After a stroll through the surrounding graveyard, continue S on Broadway to *Bowling Green*. Directly beyond that fenced pocket park is the **Custom House**, usually cited as one of the city's best examples of the florid Beaux Arts style popular at the turn of the century. The four sculptures in front are by Daniel Chester French, best known for his monumental renderings of Abraham Lincoln. They represent the continents of Africa, America, Asia and Europe.

Bear right, SW, into *Battery Park*, following the main path to the semicircular *Castle Clinton National Monument*. An 1807 fortress that never fired on an enemy ship, it served instead as a concert and exposition hall, an immigrant processing center, and

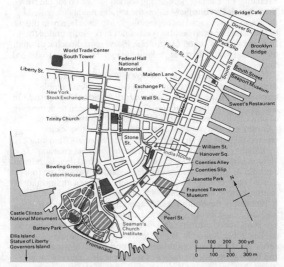

43

an aquarium. There are historical exhibits inside, and booths sell tickets for the Statue of Liberty and Ellis Island ferries. Walk through the castle onto the promenade at the water's edge, for a panorama that includes *Ellis Island*, the *Statue of Liberty*, **Governors Island** (a military base) and, to the E, *Brooklyn Heights*.

Passing the ferry docks, turn inland opposite the sign that reads "Gangway 1," keeping the park on the left. There is a refreshment stand on the right. Walk straight ahead, to the opposite side of the park. Directly across State St. is a **Georgian-Federal mansion** (#7), with an inset columned porch. It is the last of a row of such homes that once bordered this avenue. Turn left (N) and cross over at the next intersection, Pearl St. The narrow byway is now hemmed in by looming glass towers, but continue on, and three short blocks later, at the corner of Broad St., is the *Fraunces Tavern Museum*, a re-creation of a Colonial Georgian residence. It has a museum of Revolutionary War artifacts upstairs, a pleasant restaurant down. Breakfast is the best meal served, but there is also afternoon tea.

Proceed along Pearl St. The next corner is Coenties Slip, so named because it was once a docking bay for merchant ships, but long ago filled in. Cross the street into what looks to be a small plaza with herringbone brick paving, flanked by a block of convenience stores and the upstairs **Grazio's Ristorante**. The "plaza" is actually the refurbished Coenties Alley. Pass the stores and turn right, into narrow Stone St. This was the first paved pathway in the Dutch colony. It isn't much to look at now, but ends shortly in Hanover Sq. To the right is the 1854 **India House**, Italian Renaissance in style to serve the merchant princes that were its earlier occupants. It is now a private club, but members of the public are welcome to use the restaurant, **Harry's at Hanover Square**. Its food is relatively inexpensive, if unremarkable, and the bar is packed with brash young brokers and office workers at the end of the working day.

Turn left, curving N along William St., then left, to the W, into Exchange Pl. Turning right, N, into Broad St., watch for the **New York Stock Exchange** (#8) on the left. It's readily identified by the Neo-Grecian facade. The seemingly inchoate frenzy in the pit of the main floor can be observed, if not necessarily understood, from the visitor's center (*Mon-Fri 9.30am-4pm*). Reach it through the building at 20 Broad St., taking the express elevator to the 3rd floor.

At the next corner, glance left down Wall St., its concrete canyon framing Trinity Church. The Greek Revival "temple" directly across the street is *Federal Hall National Memorial*. On that site, in an earlier structure, George Washington took the oath of office as the first president of the United States.

Continue E down Wall St., named for the wood stockade erected there in 1653 to protect the Dutch colonists from attack by Indians or the British. Turn left, N, on Water St., crossing Maiden Lane, where young women once washed their laundry in a brook. At John St., glance right for a startling view of the four-masted bark *Peking*, one of the floating exhibits of an unusual maritime museum. Continue to Fulton St., and turn right, E. This is the heart of the South Street Seaport restoration district, a fetching amalgam of early 19thC architecture and artifacts and late 20thC merchandising and recycling techniques. From here to the East River, Fulton St. is a pedestrian mall, the buildings to either side filled with boutiques, fast food stalls, informal cafés and restaurants, and branches of such upscale chains as Laura

Ashley, Ann Taylor and Abercrombie & Fitch. On sunny days, every weekend, and most evenings, it is awash with locals and out-of-towners alike. The row of buildings on the right, one block E, is Schermerhorn Row. Built around 1812 as a block of warehouses, it has now been restored to its Federalist origins. At #12 is the museum's visitor center (*open daily 10am-5pm*). Upstairs at #2 is **Sweet's** seafood restaurant, opened in 1842 and, by some accounts, resting on its laurels since 1900. That doesn't stop the files of customers who dutifully line up for unadorned seafood lunches every weekday. At the end is the much newer **North Star Pub**, which serves Guinness and Watney's brews. Just round the corner is the entrance to **Sloppie Louie's**, another historic spot that treats its patrons as cavalierly as its competitors but produces somewhat better fish. Sailing vessels of a more romantic era are moored at the piers of the *South Street Seaport* across the way. In good weather, there are concerts, puppet shows, street musicians, and chairs in which to sit and admire the view of the Brooklyn Bridge.

Leave along the N side of Fulton St., turning right, N, into Water St. A restored stationer's store is followed by the **Seaport Gallery**, with maritime exhibits and helpful maps of the neighborhood. New stores open (and close) frequently with the ongoing development of the area. At the corner with Peck Slip, look toward the river at the amusing *trompe-l'oeil* mural that covers the entire side wall of a brick building, complete with a reproduction of a bridge tower duplicating the real one just beyond. At the end of these last shabby blocks of Water St. is a forerunner of the sprightly new bar-restaurants springing up in the district, the **Bridge Café**. It now serves breakfast as well as lunch, dinner and Sun brunch.

Walk 3: Civic Center-Chinatown-Little Italy
Contrasts are endemic to New York, sometimes jarring, sometimes poignant. They tumble over each other, person by person, structure by structure; overweening power and grinding need, harsh modernity and mellowed history, optimism and despair, cosmopolitanism and parochialism. This walk is an illustration.

Start at the junction of Broadway, Park Row and Vesey St., at *St Paul's Chapel*. Completed in 1766, it is the oldest church and public building in Manhattan. Back on Broadway, turn left, to the N. Two blocks up is the *Woolworth Building*, whose cathedral-like lobby deserves a detour.

Cross Broadway to **City Hall Park**, with the approaches to the *Brooklyn Bridge* in the background. Municipal architecture is more often dreary than inspired, but the 1811 *City Hall* is exceptional. Its elegant facade faces S, an evocation of the palaces of the Sun King. Pass City Hall on the right, continuing to the NE corner of the park. Across Chambers St. is the marvelously Baroque **Hall of Records** (the sign above the door reads "Surrogate's Court"), and to the right is the towering **Municipal Building**. An agglomeration style that was the hallmark of the McKim, Mead & White firm, it employs a concave facade, a forest of Corinthian columns before a triumphal arch that pierces the base, and 34 stories of statues, carvings and embellishment that owe debts to every European architectural fancy of the last 600yrs. Glimpsed through the arch is a monumental steel sculpture that announces the entrance of the aggressively contemporary **Police Headquarters**. Cross Chambers St., keeping right of the Hall of Records. The street opens into Foley

Walks

Sq. On the E is an odd structure that can be said to signal the end of the Classical vogue in Federal architecture. Somber and intimidating, the 1936 **United States Courthouse** has a "temple" base, but an incongruous tower looming overhead. It is on the National Register of Historic Sites, for some reason. Pass in front of it and its marginally more graceful sister, the **New York County Courthouse**, still bearing right, then walk E along Worth St. to the small Columbus Park on the opposite side. Cross over and turn N, on Mulberry St., bordering the far side of the park.

This, it will be instantly apparent, is *Chinatown*. A Cantonese enclave for more than 100yrs, it is home to as many as 150,000 Chinese, and spiritual center for ten times as many relatives who have scattered along the East Coast. Evenings and weekends, they all seem to have returned. The musty sterility of the Civic Center is instantly replaced by a barrage of visual and olfactory stimuli (most of them agreeable or at least intriguing).

Stroll along Mulberry until it intersects with Bayard St. Turn right, then right again on Mott St., where shades of crimson and yellow flare against the dark backdrop of the upper stories of grimy brick. In just these short blocks, window displays and maddening aromas inspire an irresistible urge to eat. At #22, for example, is the well-regarded **Peking Duck House**. But before snatching up the nearest egg roll, look for the **Chinatown Fair** game arcade (*8 Mott St.*). Inside, among bleeping and clanging pinball and video machines, are two of Chinatown's longest-running attractions. First is "Birdbrain," a live chicken that plays tick-tack-toe with all comers. He will win. Second, at the end of the room, is another cage, with a chicken that dances on command.

Returning to Mott St., continue to the corner and turn left into Chatham Sq., which soon blends into The Bowery. The building at the corner of Pell St. is a restored brick house of the Revolutionary War era.

But Chinatown is not about landmarks. First, to eat. That can be bewildering, for there are more than 200 restaurants in these few streets. To surmount the language and gastronomic barrier, try a *dim sum* parlor, where you will be served a limitless variety of tasty oddments, each nestling in a small dish. Just look and point and eat, as often as required. At the end, the check is calculated by the number of empty dishes. **Hee Seung Fung** (*46 Bowery, open 7.30am-5pm daily*) is one such place.

Afterward, double back to Pell St. and turn right, w. In the midst of all the Far Eastern turmoil, near the corner of Pell St. and Mott St., is the Georgian-Gothic *Church of the Transfiguration*. Turn right, N, into Mott St., shortly passing a Buddhist temple on the right. Tucked between grocery stores and restaurants are stores offering satin shoes, kites, jade, fans, woks, kimonos, medicinal herbs, paper lanterns, embroidered silks, chopsticks, candles, cricket cages and Buddha figurines — often all together. Narrow staircases lead up to clubrooms, whence can be heard gongs and drums and the clack of *mah-jong* tiles. Telephone booths have pagoda roofs, and banners flutter overhead.

At Canal St., turn left, w, one block, crossing over, N, at Mulberry St. For many years, Canal St. was an unofficial *cordon sanitaire* between Chinatown and *Little Italy*, but the former community is expanding N and E, the latter shrinking. Little Italy persists, however, despite the advancing age of its remaining inhabitants, still a Neapolitan-Sicilian bubble of trattorias and cafés and scrupulously fervent allegiances to church and family.

As in Chinatown, uptown and suburban relatives stream back for every native celebration and holiday. There, the big one is Chinese New Year (*mid-Jan to early Feb*); here, it's the *Festa di San Gennaro* (*Sept*). Try to be there, for floats, parades, dancing, and miles of sizzling sausage and *calzone*. During the rest of the year the preservation of ethnicity is the draw, largely as regards food, although neighborhood *ristoranti* rarely surpass Italian eateries in other parts of the city. Nevertheless, fair value is given by **Fratelli** (*115 Mulberry St.*), **Il Cortile** (*125 Mulberry St.*), **Puglia** (*corner of Hester St. and Mulberry St.*), **Angelo's** (*146 Mulberry St.*) and **Grotta Azzurra** (*corner of Broome St.*). All are open for lunch and dinner, Tues-Sun. After, or instead, turn right, E, along Grand St., for a *cappuccino* and a pastry at **Ferrara's** (*#195*). It has sidewalk tables in summer. Alternatively, a similar treat can be had at **Cafe Roma**, on the corner of Mulberry and Broome St. From here, it is only a few blocks w on Broome St. into the creative ferment of SoHo. See *Guide to the galleries* on page 32 for a tour that doubles as a walk in this district.

Walk 4: Greenwich Village

"The Village isn't the same," say those who prospered, matured and moved away. They are correct, but it doesn't matter. The neighborhoods of New York are not static. They shrink, or expand, or divide, or deteriorate, or adjust, or rally. Next year, or tomorrow, The Village will have changed again, but the past and provocative present remain.

Begin a tour at the University Pl. end of Washington Mews, one-half block N of the NE corner of *Washington Square*. To the left is **La Maison Française**, to the right, **Deutsches Haus**. Both are units of *New York University*, which owns much of the property in this area. Proceed down the cobblestoned Mews. Once servant quarters and stables for the grand houses on Washington Sq. North and 8th St., most of the buildings are now private homes.

Turn left into 5th Ave., toward **Washington Arch**. A wooden version of the monument was first erected in 1886 to commemorate the centennial of George Washington's inauguration. It became an instant landmark, so the architect Stanford White designed this marble rendition, completed in 1892. Washington's statue on the left was carved by A. Stirling Calder, father of Alexander Calder.

Turn left along Washington Sq. North. This block of Greek Revival row houses was built in the 1830s, and #16 was the site of Henry James's novel, *Washington Square*. Note the bronze lions bracketing the steps of #6, which now houses university offices and seminar rooms. Painter Edward Hopper maintained a studio at #3, but the upper floors burned away in the early 1970s. Continue along as the street becomes Waverly Pl., turning right into Greene St.

At the foot of Greene St. is **Tisch Hall**, with its flower- and tree-filled plaza. It is the second of Philip Johnson's commissions for the university. Turn right into W 4th St., which soon becomes Washington Sq. South. On the left is a one-block mall dubbed "Bobkin Lane" by one wag, after the bordering buildings, the **Bobst Library** and **Shimkin Hall**. The once-controversial library was Johnson's first design for N.Y.U. Step inside to see the 12-story balconied atrium. Outside, turn left, then left again on LaGuardia Pl., and walk S as far as Bleecker St. Turn left, E, to see the three high-rise apartment houses on the right, which are the university-owned **Silver Towers**. In the plaza at their base is a monumental rendering of Picasso's *Silvette*, one of only two exterior sculptures by the influential artist in North America. Return to Bleecker St., now heading W, and continue to Sullivan St. This intersection is the center of the long-established Italian community of the South Village. Walk N, on Sullivan. Once a block of poultry stores and dim cafés, it is now undistinguished. Press on to the next intersection and turn left on W 3rd St. for a short block, then left again into MacDougal St. The **Cafe Reggio** (*119 MacDougal St.*) is an authentic throwback to the legendary Bohemian and beatnik days of The Village, dark and smoky, with

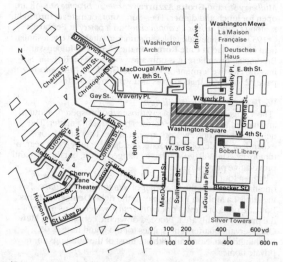

a well-used espresso machine hissing at one side. Continue s. At the next corner, across the street, is another famous old coffee house, **Le Figaro**. Turn right into Bleecker St., crossing 6th Ave. and picking up Bleecker St. again on the other side.

Turn left into Leroy St., which becomes St Luke's Pl. on the other side of 7th Ave. The houses on the right-hand side of this peaceful tree-shaded block date from the 1860s. Turn right into Hudson St., right again into Morton St., then left into Bedford St. (#75½), where Edna St Vincent Millay, the poet and actress, resided for a time. Only 8ft wide, it is the narrowest house in The Village. The oldest is probably #77, next door, built in 1799.

Just beyond, turn left into Commerce St. At the end of the short block is the **Cherry Lane Theater**, one of several in which the energetic Ms. Millay had a hand. Turn right into Barrow St., bearing right again until you are back on Bedford St. Turn left. After one more block on Bedford, at the corner of Grove St., is a squarish wooden clapboard house of obvious age. It dates back to 1820, as does the much smaller frame house behind it, which was probably the kitchen and servant quarters for its larger neighbor. And behind the cookhouse are the double-gabled houses known as the "Twin Sisters," reputedly built by a seafaring father whose daughters would not live under the same roof. Turn left into Grove St. In a few paces, look for the iron gate marked "private." Peer into the courtyard beyond. Among the bordering houses, built in the 1840s, are some of the few surviving wood houses in Manhattan.

Turn around, walk back along Grove St. and turn right into Bleecker St., a commercial artery, dominated by abundant displays of foodstuffs. Turn left into Cornelia St., and left again into W 4th St. for more stores of even greater diversity. Make a right turn at 7th Ave. and continue as far as Charles St., then turn right again and walk to Greenwich Ave. Turn left, window-gazing, then cut across and backtrack down the other side. The triangular garden between 10th St. and 6th Ave. was made possible by the demolition of the unlamented Women's House of Detention. The adjacent structure with the fanciful brick tower is the **Jefferson Market Courthouse Library**, a mouthful that describes its sequential uses.

Turn right into Christopher St., walking away from 6th Ave., then left into Gay St., which was home (*at #14*) to two sisters from Ohio, one of whom wrote *My Sister Eileen*. In a classic case of cultural recycling, her novel begat a play that was transformed into a musical that started the whole thing over again, complete with remakes and a television series. At the end of this crooked street, turn left into Waverly Pl. and follow it to the NW corner of Washington Square. Make one last detour — a half-block to the left. On the right is **MacDougal Alley**, a quaint relic of the privileged past. It is a deceptively ramshackle variation of Washington Mews, its former carriagehouses now serving as expensive residences.

Return to the square. Two blocks s, chess and domino players and *kibitzers* form knots around the cement games tables installed there. At the central fountain, which is used more for splashing than beauty, and functions on an unpredictable schedule, several musical groups are bound to be performing, at least on fine days. Farther E is a statue of Garibaldi. Consistent with campus legends everywhere, *Il Signore* is said to unsheathe his sword whenever a virgin passes. Finally, stroll over to the *Gray Art Gallery* on the E side; this is another university facility, featuring exhibitions more lively than the name suggests.

Walk 5: Central Park

An amenity without which life in New York is unimaginable, the park is a product of mid-19thC vision and expediency. At that time, the land N of 59th St. was a place of mosquito-infested swamps, malodorous meat-rendering factories, and the festering hovels of thieves and the homeless. Prompted by poet-journalist William Cullen Bryant and his supporters, the city authorities launched a design competition that was won by landscapist Frederick Law Olmsted and the British architect Calvert Vaux. The squatters were evicted, the swamps drained or reshaped into lakes, 100,000 trees planted, tons of rock and earth pushed about, to supplement existing topographical features and create new ones. After 20yrs it was complete, with gravel carriageways, bridle paths, secluded glades, lakes for boating and fishing, and playing fields. Most of these remain, despite the trampings of generations of New Yorkers, periods of neglect, vandalism, and intrusions both well-intentioned and profane.

Olmsted and Vaux envisioned a people's park, a place of refuge for poor and privileged citizens alike, not an enclosed chunk of ersatz wilderness. To enhance circulation and fantasy, they incorporated bridges, fountains, promenades, and even a castle. Ever since they completed their commission, however, would-be benefactors and entrepreneurs have proposed "improvements." Most are turned away before the predictable firestorms of protest, but over the decades a number of projects both grand and irrelevant have squeezed through the screen. As a result, there are more structures and monuments within the park than even natives can enumerate, constituting an agreeable walking tour of surprising diversity. One reluctant caveat, however: the stories about Central Park at night are true. Apart from on those frequent evening occasions — concerts and plays — that provide the security of large crowds, it is statistically unwise to visit after dusk.

Enter the park at 79th St. and 5th Ave., walking W along the path to the N of the Transverse Rd. This hugs the S wing of the **Metropolitan Museum of Art**, continues over a low rise and heads down under an arched stone bridge. Go through, bearing right, N. A few steps farther on is *Cleopatra's Needle*, an Egyptian obelisk given to the city and erected in 1881. Turn about, taking the first footpath to the right. It soon bears left. The level green to the N called **The Great Lawn** was once a reservoir, drained and filled in the 1930s and now busy much of the year with softball and football players. Above the small lake on the left, S, is **Belvedere Castle**. At the end of the lake is the open-air **Delacorte Theater** (*check newspapers for current performances or* ☎ *861-7277*). Bear left around the back of the theater and up the hill to the castle. Paths at the back cross over the Transverse Rd. Take the one on the left, down the stone stairs, proceeding SW, then SE. Eventually, it winds past the Loeb Boat House. Bicycles and rowboats are available for rent. There is a fast-food counter with a patio. Follow the same pathway due E, crossing the nearby East Drive, until it soon reaches the concrete oval of **Conservatory Pond**. At its N end is a statue of *Alice in Wonderland*, and on the W, one of Hans Christian Andersen. Children clamber all over them, especially when stories are told at the Andersen monument on Sat mornings (*May–Sept*).

Take the walkway that goes W from the S end of the pond, under the Park Drive, up the stairs, and along the bank of the lake. **Bethesda Fountain** is just ahead, the most grandiose element of the Vaux contributions. A winged angel surmounts a

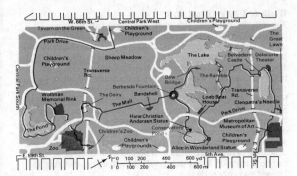

gaggle of cherubim and, when New York is not having a water crisis, there is pretty splashing in the pool at the base.

Take the exit path leading W along the lake shore to the lovely cast-iron **Bow Bridge**. Another Vaux design, it was restored in 1974, and crosses the lake into **The Ramble**, a cat's cradle of footpaths that curl through low trees, patches of grass and plantings of bush and flower. The section is favored by serious birdwatchers. Return across the bridge to the Bethesda Fountain, go up the stairs and cross the roadway. Walk S along The Mall. On the left, E, is a band shell, site of summer evening concerts.

Continue S on The Mall, a wide straight walk beneath a canopy of ancient trees. Off to the right, runners, skate-boarders, eaters and musicians compete for space on a parallel road. At the end of the mall are bronze statues of Walter Scott, Robbie Burns, Shakespeare and Christopher Columbus. Continue past Columbus, crossing the road. After about 20yds, there is a walk on the right down to **The Dairy** (*open Tues-Thurs and Sat, Sun 11am-5pm, Fri 1-5pm, closed Mon*). Recent restoration of the building was faithful to its Victorian Gothic origins, and a loggia that was removed in the 1950s has been re-created. The vaulted interior is now an information center, with exhibitions and a slide show, and walking tours depart from there.

Return to the nearby road and turn right, S. An entrance to *Central Park Zoo* is about 100yds down on the left, E, and it might be time to have a snack in one of its cafeterias, near the front gate. The **Children's Zoo** is to the N. That can be the end of a tour, but if energy and curiosity remain, leave the zoo through the S gate, emerging briefly from the park into Doris C. Freedman Plaza. Turn right (W), cross the road, turn right again, then go down the path on the left. Bear left at the lake encountered there. At the road that enters the park from Central Park South, head W, following the Park Drive as it curves N along the W side of the park. This is the final leg of the New York Marathon in Nov, with the finish line at about 66th St. The expanse of lawn to the right, E, is the Sheep Meadow. A road to the left, W, passes the **Tavern On The Green** restaurant (which until the 1930s was the barn for the sheep that grazed on the Meadow) and exits on Central Park West.

Children's playgrounds are located at intervals along the E and W borders of the park (see *New York for children*). From May-Oct, park roads are closed to vehicular traffic, Mon-Fri 10am-3pm, Mon-Thurs 7-10pm, Fri 8pm until Mon 6am, holidays 7pm until 6am in the morning of the next working day. From Nov-Apr only the weekend closings apply.

51

Walk 6: Upper East Side

The wealthy and super-rich made the Upper East Side their
habitat in the late 19thC, pushing aside the squatters and farmers
then in residence. They erected Italo-Franco-Anglo châteaux and
palazzi one after the other, each grander than its neighbor.
Those were the last decades before enactment of income tax,
however, and even these privileged folk couldn't maintain their
50-room retreats long after that blow. But the rest of us profited,
for many of those mansions now serve the public as schools and
museums. The result is "Museum Mile," along 5th Ave., bordering
Central Park, a string of public repositories of arts and antiquities
of astonishing diversity, stretching from 70th St. to 103rd St. This
suggested walk links many of those museums, which are
described in detail in *Sights and places of interest*. The walk
can be broken off at any point and returned to, another day, as
interest and energy dictate.

Start at the headquarters of the *Asia Society*, at the NE corner
of Park Ave. and 70th St. Opened in 1981, the handsome red
granite structure houses galleries of Far Eastern artifacts. Exhibits
are changed 2-3 times a year. Cross Park Ave. continuing W on
70th St. Several buildings along the next two blocks are
interesting. The **Explorer's Club** (*at #46*) reflects the waning
Gothic Revival enthusiasm of the pre-World War I years, and #32
has Florentine detailing of the same period.

This district is home to at least a third of the city's important art
galleries, and **Knoedler & Co.** (*#19*), dealing in 20thC moderns
and some earlier masters, is one of the most influential. Keeping
to the N side of the street, watch for the entrance to the *Frick
Collection* on the right. Industrialist Henry Clay Frick intended to
have his 1914 mansion converted to a museum upon his death,
and with that prospect in mind, he filled it with Renaissance and
French and English 18thC paintings.

After completing your visit, exit by the front door and turn
right, W, into 70th St., then right, N, into 5th Ave., where it forms
one of the grand boulevards of the city, the green of *Central
Park* to the left and placid apartment blocks to the right. At 75th
St., turn right, E. On the N side is a Romanesque mansion
surrounded by an unusual iron fence, formerly the Harkness
House, now a foundation headquarters. Continue to Madison
Ave. The striking cantilevered structure on the SE corner is the
Whitney Museum of American Art, suggesting a fortress,
complete with moat and fixed bridge. The leafy restaurant on the
glassed-in sub-street level provides a welcome place to sit down
and relax, in full view of an outdoor sculpture garden.

Walk N on Madison Ave., intimate by contrast with Park Ave.
and 5th Ave., with shoulder-to-shoulder art and antiques galleries
and compact, idiosyncratic stores. Along 76th St. is the exclusive
Carlyle hotel, choice of John F. Kennedy when he was in town.
Opposite the hotel is the famed auction house, **Sotheby's**
(*#980*), where estate treasures and fabulous artworks routinely
fetch millions of dollars. Go on to 78th St. and walk W to 5th Ave.
to the family home that tobacco heiress Doris Duke bequeathed
to New York University. It now houses the highly regarded
Institute of Fine Arts. At 5th Ave., turn right, N, once again. A
cultural annex of the French Embassy is housed within the
building at #972, which was designed by McKim, Mead & White
(see Stanford White, in *Biographies*). Note the vigilant iron owl
perched atop the second door.

The Gothic Revival house (1899) at the next corner is the
Ukrainian Institute of America (*open Tues-Fri 2-6pm*), which

shelters a collection of contemporary Ukrainian paintings and folk art and costumes. The choices here are to spend the next 2-3hrs in the *Metropolitan Museum of Art*, just across 5th Ave.; to pick up the Central Park walk (see *Walk 5*) along the pathway at the s end of the Met; or to continue N along 5th Ave. to visit, in sequence, the *Guggenheim Museum*, the *Jewish Museum*, the *International Center of Photography* and the *Museum of the City of New York*.

Should those alternatives seem daunting, have a coffee at the sidewalk café (*summer only*) of the **Stanhope Hotel** (*81st St.*), then go to 82nd St. and turn right. This tree-lined, unblemished block of town houses serves as a fitting approach to the Met, seen to good advantage from Madison Ave. Turn left, N, into Madison, then right, E, into 86th St. The casual **Summerhouse** (*#50*) is an agreeable possibility for lunch, dinner or weekend brunch. Across Lexington Ave. you are in *Yorkville*. Once a village of Germans and Slavic immigrants, little is now left to lend

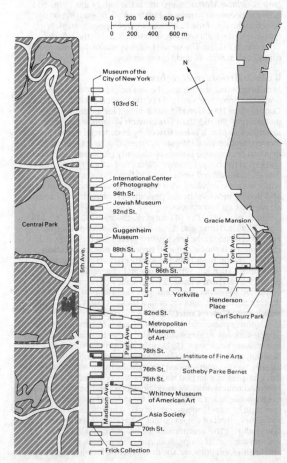

any middle-European distinction, apart from a *bierstube* or two, with the exception of the **Cafe Geiger** and **Kleine Konditorei** on the S side of 86th St. between 3rd and 2nd Ave., which evoke something of the atmosphere of Viennese pastry shops.

For the most part, this welter of fruit stands, fast food shops, fifth-rate hotels and banal apartment buildings is in stark contrast to the relative serenity of 5th Ave. that preceded them. Appreciate its liveliness instead, and continue E on 86th St. After York Ave., cross to the N side. Near the end of the block is **Henderson Place**, a rear-entry mews for a block of 1882 row houses that has thus far survived encroaching development. Continue to the corner of East End Ave. and turn left, N. This provides a close look at the red-brick and black-trimmed structures. They would look more at home in London than here, and this has now been declared an official historic district. At the next corner, cross East End Ave. and walk through the entrance to *Carl Schurz Park*. Strolling E, the building at the N end of the park is *Gracie Mansion*, erected at the turn of the 19thC and now the home of the mayor. End the walk by pausing on a bench at the lip of the East River. On the opposite bank is Queens; to the right is Roosevelt Island; and to the left, the Triborough Bridge. The nearest subway station for your round trip is back at 86th St. and Lexington Ave.

Walk 7: Brooklyn Heights

Manhattan's first suburb and the first neighborhood to come under the protection (in 1965) of the Landmarks Preservation Commission, Brooklyn Heights is meant for leisurely meandering. Smaller than *Greenwich Village*, which it resembles in part, it is less flawed by commercial shabbiness and modern architectural intrusions. Street after street is lined with restored brownstone houses, with hardy plane trees in front and gardens at the back. Lovingly maintained details of cast-iron fences, chandeliered vestibules and flower boxes on the windows are contrasted with the spectacular panorama of harbor and skyline provided by the pedestrian esplanade that hangs above the East River docks.

Start from the BMT or IRT subway stations on Court St., walking S one block to turn right, W, on Remsen St. After passing St. Francis College on the left, the first prominent building encountered is the brick-faced **Brooklyn Bar Association** (*#123*). Dating from 1855, it recently enjoyed an elegant restoration. Turn left, S, into Henry St. In the middle of the block, on the left, is **Hunt's Lane**, a forlorn alley of carriage houses converted to residences. Continue along Henry St. to Joralemon St., turn right, then right again into Hicks St. After a few steps, wander into **Grace Court Alley** on the right. It is far more handsomely preserved than Hunt's Lane, a true mews with upper-story hay cranes still in place, above the stables where horses were once kept. Go N again along Hicks, then left, W, into Remsen, and right, N, into Montague Terrace. Unlike the houses already seen, commissioned individually by their first owners, this grouping of attached residences was designed as a set in 1886 and retains much of its original look. Author Thomas Wolfe lived a while at #5, a fact attested by a bronze plaque. At the end, turn right, E, into Montague St. proper. This, the main commercial and eating street of the community, has known its ups and downs during the gentrification of Brooklyn Heights. Once abloom with crafts shops, boutiques, bookstores and gourmet and health food emporia, the direction in which it is now headed is uncertain. Franchised fast-food stands now intrude, and a number of buildings are slated for demolition or remodeling. None of the eating places is likely to attract the attention of highbrow Manhattan restaurant critics, but they cover a range of ethnic proclivities; some have sidewalk tables. Consider **Teresa's** (*#80*), **FujiSan** (*#130*), **La Traviata** (*#139*) or **Foffe** (*#155*).

After three blocks along Montague St. turn left, N, into Clinton St., then left, W, again into Pierrepont St. **The Brooklyn Historical Society** building on the corner, erected in 1880, shows the Classical influences in vogue at the time. Exhibits of books, paintings and artifacts related to the heritage of Long Island and New York are open to the public. Continue W along Pierrepont St. The **Unitarian Church** at the corner of Monroe Place was designed by the influential early 19thC architect Minard Lafever. Look up at the imposing turret on #114. It is hard to believe that the Renaissance Revival pile beneath it was once the duplicate of the Greek Revival mansion at #108.

Follow Pierrepont St. to the end. Until 1950, it ran downhill to the river's edge. A plan to run the Brooklyn-Queens Expressway through the heart of the Heights was resisted by residents, and the compromise that evolved was to stack the highway in two tiers and divert it along the westerly edge of the neighborhood. As a final fillip, it was roofed over, smothering traffic noises and exhaust fumes, and providing a 5-block promenade that bestows a glorious, unobstructed vista from the *Statue of Liberty* northward past the spires of lower Manhattan, to the *Brooklyn Bridge* and Manhattan Bridge and all the way to the *Empire State Building*. Take it all in while strolling N, noting the trellised gardens and balconies of the narrow houses along the promenade. Sunset is a good time, for the heavens blaze behind that famous skyline in a manner that cannot be duplicated on film. The masted tall ships just S of the Manhattan end of the Brooklyn Bridge are exhibits of the South Street Seaport Museum.

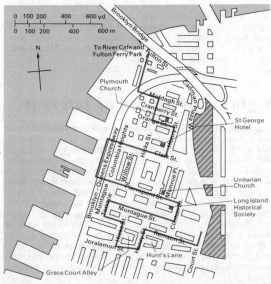

Take the next exit right, E, into Clark St., glancing both ways as you cross Columbia Heights and then Willow St., for you might be drawn to explore them further. Down on the right on Columbia Heights, for example, is a rare clapboard house of considerable age. Beyond Hicks St., pass the former (1885) **St George Hotel**, turning left, N, on Henry St., then left again, W, into Orange St. **Plymouth Church** is in mid-block, a chunky 1847 edifice. Its importance lies with its founder and first preacher, Henry Ward Beecher. An ardent opponent of slavery, he attracted the attention of Abraham Lincoln, who worshiped here, as did Charles Dickens and Mark Twain. His sister, Harriet Beecher Stowe, was the author of *Uncle Tom's Cabin*.

Proceed to Hicks St. and turn right, N. At Middagh St., named after a local burgher of the early 18thC, turn left, W. Most of the buildings along this block have been altered beyond recognition, but the splendid 1829 Federalist clapboard house at #24 is an exception, its streetside fence enclosing a garden with a willow tree and connecting with a former servants' cottage. Step up to examine the carvings and leaded windows around the main door.

Continue to Columbia Heights. From here, you may wish to turn left (S), down to Clark St., and left again to reach the subway station at Clark and Henry Sts. Or, turn right, N, on Columbia Heights, as it dips toward the base of the Brooklyn Bridge, framed beneath a walkway connecting two sections of the Watchtower Building. This passage leads down to Old Fulton St. From 1814-1924 this Fulton St. was linked to the one in Manhattan by ferry.

Turn toward the river. A former fireboat house stands on the site of the old ferry terminal. For a short time, it was a modest maritime museum, now closed and falling into disrepair. Opposite it is the **Harbor View** restaurant (*1 Old Fulton St.*), an agreeable possibility for lunch or a drink.

But for a truly grand finale, walk N past the fireboat house to the **River Café**, in the white building at water's edge. Its staples are good-to-memorable food and an unimprovable vista. Reservations are usually necessary, but there might be a free table on the outside terrace in good weather. They'll call a taxi for the return to your hotel.

Sights and places of interest

Few major cities can rival New York for its sheer diversity — at every level of consciousness. Its museums and art galleries, whose reputation resounds throughout the civilized world, offer visitors and residents an endless choice of cultural experiences. More than three hundred years of American history are charted at such places as Staten Island's *Richmondtown Restoration* and the *Museum of the City of New York*. The centers of science and technology, and the monuments and historic buildings, display the phenomenal diversity of the city's makeup. For a balanced picture, be sure to try to see some of the more specialized centers as well as the star attractions.

Many galleries and museums are expanding their collections, and some are modernizing their halls. These frequent reorganizations can mean that rooms — entire wings even —

can be closed, their contents moved to other floors or into storage. Individual artworks can be withdrawn from display — perhaps to be lent to traveling exhibitions, for restoration, or even to be sold. For all these reasons, detailed cataloguing here is impossible, and our descriptions are intended to convey a general impression. Fortunately, organization in most museums and galleries is excellent, with clear labeling and helpful floor plans.

Our admiration of the antique is not admiration of the old but of the natural.

Emerson, *Essays, First Series: History*

If you wish to find a quiet retreat from the madding crowds of Manhattan, consult *Oases*, for some suggestions of free resting places. Comprehensive lists are given overleaf, which will allow you an at-a-glance view of the number and type of sights, and districts, that are described in detail on the following 65 pages.

Look for the ★ symbol against the most important sights and 🏛 for buildings of great architectural interest. Good views (◀€) and places of special interest for children (✱) are also indicated.

Abigail Adams Smith Museum 🏛
421 E 61st St.(1st Ave.), NY 10021 ☎ 838-6878. Map 5N5 ▨ ✗ open Mon-Fri 10am-4pm. Closed Sat, Sun, Aug. Discounts for senior citizens; free entry for under 12s.
An unexpected retreat amid the feverish pace of the East Side, this 1799 carriage house sits on a slope behind stone retaining walls, a fetching remnant of the Federalist era. The estate it served was owned by William Stephens Smith, but the titular tenant was his wife, the daughter of the eventual second President of the United States. She didn't stay long. After dismemberment of the property, it became a residence in 1826. It remained in private hands until its purchase in the early 20thC by the Colonial Dames of America. That organization is still headquartered here, and maintains several exhibition rooms. Most of the furnishings are of the early 19thC, although they are not traced to the original owners.

American Academy and Institute of Arts and Letters
Part of the *Audubon Terrace* museum complex, this is primarily a society of prominent artists and thinkers. Exhibitions of an eclectic nature are laid on at certain times.

American Craft Museum
40 W 53rd St. (6th Ave.), NY 10019 ☎ 956-3535. Map 5N4 ▨ Open Wed-Sun 10am-5pm, Tues 10am-8pm. Closed Mon. Half-price entry for senior citizens and students ▨ under 12s.
Wit, panache, and impeccable workmanship mark the ever-changing displays of antique and contemporary works, the latter often blurring the line that once separated crafts from pure art. The handsome new three-level building is opposite the *Museum of Modern Art*. There is a library branch at 77 W 45th St.

American Museum of the Moving Image
35th Ave. and 36th St., Astoria (Queens), NY 10006 ☎ 718-784-0077 ▨ ✱ open Wed, Thurs 1-5pm, Fri

American Museum of the Moving Image

1-7.30pm, Sat 11am-7.30pm, Sun 11am-6pm. Closed Mon, Tues. Subway R or G train to Steinway St.

Film-making in America began not in the Hollywood Hills but in and around New York City. Much of it took place here in Astoria, continuing from the earliest days of the silents to the first talkies. The Marx Brothers, Gary Cooper, and Claudette Colbert were only a few of the stars who appeared before the cameras of the Astoria studios. The old sound stages have now been refurbished, and a three-floor studio building has been set aside for this fascinating museum.

Movies, television shows, and videos are the featured attractions, but are by no means the extent of the collection. Memorabilia and artifacts are as ephemeral as old fan magazines, tin lunch boxes with inept portraits of actors, Disney toys, posters, costumes, and Cher dolls; as nostalgic as bulky models of 1940s TV receivers, and complete stage sets. A wide net is cast, including an amusing send-up by artist Red

---

Main sights classified by type

Bridges and tunnels
Brooklyn-Battery Tunnel
Brooklyn Bridge 🏛 ★ 📢
George Washington Bridge
Holland Tunnel
Queensboro Bridge
Queens-Midtown Tunnel
Verrazano Narrows Bridge

Churches and synagogues
Cathedral Church of St John The Divine 🏛
Church of the Ascension 🏛
Church of the Transfiguration
Grace Church 🏛
Judson Memorial Baptist Church 🏛
Marble Collegiate Church 🏛
Riverside Church 🏛
St Bartholomew's Church 🏛
St Mark's-In-The-Bowery 🏛
St Patrick's Cathedral 🏛 ★
St Paul's Chapel 🏛
Temple Emanu-El
Trinity Church 🏛

Colleges and universities
Columbia University 🏛
Cooper Union
New York University 🏛
Yeshiva University

Districts
The Bowery
Brooklyn Heights 🏛 📢
Chelsea
Chinatown
Coney Island
East Side ★
Financial District ★
Garment Center
Gramercy Park 🏛
Greenwich Village 🏛 ★
Harlem
Little Italy
Lower East Side
Midtown East
Murray Hill
SoHo ★
Theater District
TriBeCa
Upper West Side
Yorkville

Exhibition halls
AT&T InfoQuest Center ♣
Forbes Magazine Galleries ♣
Guinness World Records Exhibit Hall ♣
Jacob K. Javits Convention Center

Historic buildings
Abigail Adams Smith Museum 🏛
Castle Clinton Monument 🏛
City Hall 🏛
Dakota Apartments
Dyckman House 🏛
Ellis Island ★
Federal Hall National Memorial 🏛
Gracie Mansion 🏛

Grand Central Terminal 🏛
Morris-Jumel Mansion 🏛
Old Merchant's House
Richmondtown Restoration 🏛 ★
Snug Harbor Cultural Center 🏛
Theodore Roosevelt Birthplace
Van Cortlandt Mansion and Museum 🏛
Villard Houses 🏛

Libraries
Bible House
New York Public Library
Pierpont Morgan Library 🏛

Monuments
Cleopatra's Needle
General Grant National Memorial
Hall of Fame for Great Americans
Statue of Liberty ★ 📢

Museums of art
American Academy and Institute of Arts and Letters
American Craft Museum
Asia Society
Audubon Terrace
Center for Inter-American Relations
The Cloisters 🏛 ★ 📢
Cooper-Hewitt Museum

...continued

Grooms of extravagantly ornate old-time movie palaces, and a high-tech theater capable of screening both ancient nitrate prints and the latest 70-millimeter spectacles.

American Museum of Natural History ▥ ★
Central Park W (79th St.), NY 10024 ☎ *769-5100. Map 6-7*
▩ ▣ *Fri, Sat 5-9pm* ✗ ⬛ ✻ *Open Mon, Tues, Thurs, Sun 10am-5.45pm, Wed, Fri, Sat 10am-9pm.*

Beloved by generations of schoolchildren for its realistic animal dioramas and models of Indian villages, the museum interprets its mission in the broadest sense. Appealing as the exhibits of mounted Alaskan bears and African lions unquestionably are, adults are drawn to the halls highlighting the crafts, costumes, jewelry, masks, and artifacts of the peoples of Asia, Mexico, and pre-colonial North America. The collections, begun in 1874, include 34 million items, from a 29m (94ft) model of a blue whale to the fabled Star of India.

Calvert Vaux, who shared credit for Central Park, worked with Jacob Wrey Mould on the first building (1877). So many additions were made from then until 1933, however, that only a portion of it is still visible, and that from the rear. Critics cite the southern red granite facade as a superior example of the Romanesque Revival. Perhaps so, if one's notion of romantic architecture derives from ponderous Teutonic fortresses. The main entrance, dominated by a 1939 equestrian statue of President Theodore Roosevelt, is even less graceful. Yet in spite of the forbidding exterior, this great museum qualifies as an obligatory stop.

For maximum impact, choose the W 77th St. entrance rather than the one on Central Park W. Directly beyond the door leading to the first (ground) floor is an impressively scaled ocean-going canoe of a British Columbian tribe. (Adjoining rooms are devoted to North American mammals, birds and invertebrates, meteorites and gems.) The prow of the canoe points at a staircase, which you should ascend to the second (main) floor. On the left is the **Hall of Asian Peoples**, one of the most ambitious sections of the museum. In a masterful mix of scholarship and showmanship, its displays chart the progress of Eurasian cultures from prehistory to the recent past, employing every imaginable device to delineate the evolutionary stages of religion, commerce, language, art and science.

Returning to the main hall, pass beneath the sign for the **Birds of the World** hall and you soon come to the **Man in Africa** galleries, on the right. Covering societies of desert and bush, veldt and jungle, the museum uses models of irrigation systems, examples of fishing techniques, dance and worship, and tribal government, all to the strains of appropriate recorded music. Make a counter-clockwise loop of the rooms, returning to the "Birds" hall. Turn right, and walk straight ahead into an area of exhibits concerned with the arts and histories of the pre-Columbian Indian societies of Mexico and Central America. The first space is dominated by a huge Olmec head, carved from a single stone and weighing 20 tons. Along the walls are examples of pottery, ceramic sculptures and ornaments from specific cultures, primarily Mayan, Aztec and Olmec.

At the far end is the museum's newest addition, opened in 1988: the **Hall of South American Peoples**. Children are certain to take grisly delight in the assembled shrunken heads and blowpipes of the Amazon rainforest. Their parents may prefer to veer toward the archeological artifacts of the Andes. Layout and display methods are similar to those used in the preceding African and Asian halls.

After visiting these rooms, return again to the main hall and ascend the staircase immediately on the left, to the third floor. At the top of the stairs, bear right. The first rooms are concerned with Indians of the American woodlands and plains, followed by a gallery of aboriginal cultures of the Pacific, where homage is paid to the work of anthropologist Margaret Mead. Returning to the main hall, you will find the rest of this floor is devoted to primates, North American birds, African mammals, and reptiles and amphibians. Most exhibits are mounted in large glass cases, with replicas of their habitats, executed with considerable ingenuity and artistry. Walking around these galleries in turn, the visitor will eventually arrive in a space allocated for temporary exhibitions, followed by the museum shop. The stairs just beyond lead up to the top floor, the arena for reassembled **dinosaur skeletons**. The awesome *Tyrannosaurus Rex*, which figures in so many Grade B fantasy movies, is a particular star.

In addition to the basement cafeteria, there is a cocktail lounge in the lobby on certain days, and tables set around hot-dog carts on the front steps in summer. **Nature Max** (☎ 769-5650) is a theater with the largest screen in New York, for the showing of relevant films. Traveling shows, lectures, and music and dance programs augment the permanent exhibitions.

Hayden Planetarium
Central Park W (81st St.), NY 10024 ☎ 769-5100 ▧ ✿ *Open Mon-Fri 12.30-4.45pm, laser show (extra ▧) Fri, Sat 7.30pm, 9pm and 10pm. Special shows Mon-Fri 1.30pm and 3.30pm, Sat, Sun 1pm, 2pm, 3pm and 4pm. Admission includes American Museum of Natural History.*

Since 1935, the artful technology of the Hayden Planetarium has reproduced on its domed ceiling the movements of constellations, planets, and meteor showers. Seasonal shows focus on the "Star of Wonder," nebulae and stellar formations, and the projected end of the world through astronomical accident. Music and commentary supplement the 1hr presentations, and there are "cosmic laser concerts" (☎ 769-5921 *for times and prices*). Just observing the 2½-ton projector in action is worth the admission.

American Numismatic Society
Housing a large collection of coins and medals, this is part of the *Audubon Terrace* complex.

Asia Society
725 Park Ave. (E 70th St.), NY 10021 ☎ 288-6400. Map 7M4 ▧ ✗ Open Tues-Sat 11am-6pm, Sun noon-5pm. Closed Mon.

A striking addition to a bland stretch of Park Ave., the 1981 headquarters of the Asia Society echoes imperial palaces of India, with its facing of alternately polished and textured red granite. The gallery floors house one of the many benefactions of the Rockefeller family: in this case, the collection of Nepalese and Chinese artifacts assembled by John D. III. That is not the extent of the holdings, however, and there are supplementary loan exhibitions 3-4 times a year, as well as films, lectures and recitals. As this is not a formal museum operating within the strictures of scholarship, objects on display reflect the tastes of the contributors. Fortunately, those predilections are disciplined and educated. Sculptured metal and polychromed ceramics mingle with ancient many-armed buddhas from Kampuchea and fierce feline temple guardians.

Audubon Terrace
Broadway at 155th St. Map 8F2. Subway 1 to 157th St; AA, B to 155th St.

Gathered around a Neo-Classical plaza in a NW precinct of Harlem is a remarkable complex of four museums and associated societies. While they are not all individually of great importance, as a group they rival all but a handful of the city's cultural repositories. Only their location denies them the recognition they deserve.

Ornithologist John James Audubon owned this property at the crest of the slope above the Hudson River and intermittently lived here from 1825 until his death in 1851. It was purchased by a speculator, who was convinced that the steady northward thrust of the city would eventually make him rich. When it became clear that growth had stabilized at a point 5 miles s, the tract changed hands. A master plan was drawn up in 1908, and the present buildings were completed by 1926. They can be characterized as of the Beaux Arts mode, with a typical Greco-Renaissance mix. All the buildings are clustered in the block abutting Broadway between W 155th St. and W 156th St.

Museum of the American Indian

☎ 283-2420 ▣ Open Tues-Sat 10am-5pm, Sun 1-5pm. Closed Mon.

The largest repository of Native American artifacts anywhere, with more than one million items on display and in storage, this museum is of particular interest to overseas visitors who plan to go no farther w than Manhattan. Even three large, crammed (if skillfully organized) floors can contain no more than a small portion of the acquisitions. These are rotated from a storage annex in seemingly inexhaustible numbers. "American" here refers to the entire Western Hemisphere, with Eskimo carvings. Hopi kachina dolls, Chilean silverwork, and tools, funeral urns, tomahawks, jewelry, pottery, beadwork, feather head-dresses and costumes, and fetishes from many Indian tribes and empires. The shrunken bodies (not mere heads) of captives of the Ecuadorean Jivaros are a macabre revelation. This museum deserves to be ranked among the best in the city, at least in terms of comprehensiveness. Discussions are continuing about the possible relocation of all or part of the collection to other sites in the city, or even to Washington, DC, so call ahead before making a special visit.

Hispanic Society of America

☎ 926-2234 ▣ Open Tues-Sat 10am-4.30pm, Sun 1-4pm. Closed Mon.

The entrance is marked by an equestrian bronze of *El Cid*, the 11thC Spanish hero — a fitting choice for a museum that concerns itself with Iberian rather than Latin American culture and history. At the very minimum, step into the splendid main hall and savor the rosy blush of terra-cotta Renaissance arches and ornamentation. During certain hours, light through the two-story skylight heightens the play of intricate shadow on carved scrollwork and panels.

Of conventional interest are the canvases and drawings of El Greco, Velázquez and Goya. But the Spain of the Catholic kings is upstaged by that of the earlier Moors, with tiled chambers and relics of exquisite workmanship. The Roman and Visigothic occupations are represented as well, and there is a substantial library of pre-1700 books.

American Numismatic Society

☎ 234-3130 ▣ Open Tues-Sat 9am-4.30pm, Sun 1-4pm. Closed Mon. Ring bell for entry.

The first floor is given over to a large display of coins, medals and banknotes, the second floor to a specialist library.

American Academy and Institute of Arts and Letters

☎ 368-5900 ▣ Open Mon-Sat 9.30am-4.30pm, Sun 1-6pm. *Telephone first to confirm hours and exhibitions.*

Primarily an association of celebrated artists and intellectuals, not unlike its French counterpart, this institution mounts periodic exhibitions covering a wide range of subjects, from ancient manuscripts to architectural themes.

AT&T InfoQuest Center

550 Madison Ave. (56th St.), NY 10022 ☎ *605-5555. Map 5N4* ▣ ✴ *Open Tues 10am-9pm, Wed-Sun 10am-6pm. Closed Mon.*

A glass elevator zips to the 4th floor, where each visitor receives a specially-programed "access card" to the exhibits. As might be expected of the corporate sponsor, these are concerned with all aspects of telecommunications. The presentations demonstrate the workings of photonics, video, fiberoptics, microelectronics, and computer software, but are hardly dry or stuffy. They are slick displays, blinking, chattering, beeping, gleaming. Children, who understand these things better than their elders, gleefully punch messages into keyboards, manipulate robot arms, and talk to computers.

Aunt Len's Doll and Toy Museum
6 Hamilton Terrace (W 141st St.), NY 10031 ☎ 281-4143. Map 8G3 ▥ ✗ ✻ Open Tues-Sun. Closed Mon. An advance appointment is essential. Subway 1 to 137th St.
An enthusiasm for collecting has a way of getting out of hand — in this case, to the delight of parents and children alike. "Aunt Len" was a local schoolteacher who gathered more than 5,000 dolls, miniature houses with scale furniture, mechanical and clockwork toys, dolls' carriages and accessories. When she saw what she had done, she decided to give everyone else a chance to share it. Every corner and surface is crowded with her acquisitions, and the effect is magical. A visit might be combined with a trip to the several museums of *Audubon Terrace*, some 14 blocks to the N.

Battery Park
Battery Pl. and State St. (foot of Broadway). Map 2V4.
Named for a rank of cannon that defended the old town from uncertain foes — presumably British — after the Revolution, the present 21 acres occupy the western rim of the extreme southern tip of Manhattan. Financial District workers eat their packed lunches in view of the *Statue of Liberty* and the now diminished but no less beguiling harbor traffic. Other attractions are the **Verrazano Memorial**, commemorating the Italian explorer who first saw New York Bay in 1524, and the *Castle Clinton National Monument*, once an islet but later joined by landfill to what is now the park. The ferry taking passengers to the Statue of Liberty departs from a pier at the edge of the park, and the one to Staten Island is nearby.

Bible House
1865 Broadway (61st St.), NY 10023 ☎ 581-7400. Map 4N3 ▨ ✗ for groups. Open Mon-Fri 9.30am-4.30pm. Closed Sat, Sun.
More than 38,000 volumes are on permanent display, including scraps of the Dead Sea Scrolls, pages from the 15thC Gutenberg Bible, and Braille editions once owned by Helen Keller.

The Bowery
Map 3S5.
A country road from the time of the original Dutch colony, the "Bouwerie" retained its bucolic status into the 19thC. It went downhill from there — apart from a brief revival in the 1890s as a place for bawdy music halls — and rapidly slid into utter despair. Now it is a grimy concentration of dosshouses and bars, the last stop for derelict men and women made homeless by alcoholism, drug addiction, madness and misfortune. There are, to be sure, a handful of useful discount kitchenware and home furnishing stores, but the persistence of The Bowery as a tourist attraction is a mystery.

Bowling Green
Battery Pl. (foot of Broadway). Map 2U4.

This oval green once hosted early Colonial bowlers, under the eyes of a statue of George III. It was the city's first park, leased in 1733 at a rental of one peppercorn a year. True to revolutionary tradition, the monument was pulled down in 1776. The fence that still encloses the green dates from then. For a long time, it was the only lingering element of even minor historical or visual interest, but a recent restoration has repaired the green and its benches, and added a fountain and circular pool.

Bronx Zoo and New York Botanical Garden
These adjacent and spectacular sights constitute two of the best reasons for venturing over the Harlem River.
Bronx Zoo ★

Southern Blvd. (185th St.), Bronx, NY 10460 ☎ 220-5100. Map 13B-C4 ▣ Tues-Thurs ▩ Fri-Mon in winter ▩ Fri-Mon in summer. Modest extra charges for a few special sections; also tractor train, aerial tram and monorail ✗ free by appointment ☎ 220-5141 ▣ ♿ ➡ Open Mon-Sat 10am-5pm (4.30pm in winter). Most outdoor exhibits closed in winter (roughly Oct-Apr). Subway 2,5 to Pelham Parkway.

Many New York attractions are as engaging as ever, others are in decline, but few have actually improved in recent years. The Bronx Zoo falls into this last felicitous category. Known officially, in those days, as the New York Zoological Park, it was inaugurated in 1899 and now has more than 3,000 animals of 800 species, deployed in imaginative settings carved out of the hills and meadows of the original 252 acres. Because such diversity can cause indecision, the management have provided the means to obtain overviews and thereby make choices. The **Safari Tour tractor train** with guide makes a complete circuit of the grounds, the **Skyfari aerial tram** glides over the African Plains section, and the **Bengali Express monorail** meanders about Wild Asia, where tigers and elephants roam free.

To proceed in an orderly manner on foot, begin at the **Pelham Parkway** entrance. This leads to the earliest part of the zoo, the formal Baird Court, centering on the **Seal Pool**, around which are arranged the **Aquatic Birds**, **Carnivores**, **Monkeys**, **Elephants**, and a giant bird enclosure called the **Flying Cage**. Pause by the 3-acre **Bison Range** for a look at the beasts that once roamed over thousands of square miles of the Old West. Beyond that is the 1972 **World of Birds**, through which you can pass in the company of more than 500 birds, with no interceding screens. South of the Elephant House is a popular group of buildings sheltering the **Reptiles**, **Penguins** and **Gorillas**. Nearby is the fascinating **World of Darkness**, where a variety of nocturnal creatures are fooled by artificial lighting into believing that day is night.

Apart from these necessary structures, animals are at liberty in much of the park, in simulated habitats. Cleverly camouflaged moats keep them apart and protect the public. The Skyfari aerial tram carries observers above the remarkably convincing veldt of the **African Plains**, and you can look down on moving lion prides, antelope and deer.

The park embraces a stretch of the Bronx River, wide enough here to be called a lake. Most exhibits are to the w, but **Wild Asia** takes up the E bank. The concept is similar to the African Plains area, but the Bengali Express monorail follows a looping route around the perimeter and across the river. Fences separating

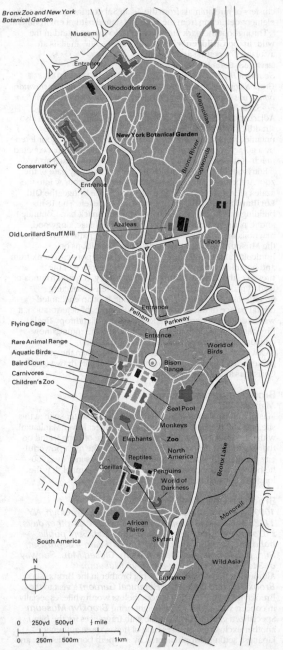

Bronx Zoo and New York
Botanical Garden

Museum

Entrance

Rhododendrons

New York Botanical Garden

Magnolias

Bronx River

Dogwoods

Conservatory

Entrance

Old Lorillard Snuff Mill

Azaleas

Lilacs

Pelham

Parkway

Entrance

Flying Cage

Entrance

Rare Animal Range

World of
Birds

Aquatic Birds

Baird Court

Bison
Range

Carnivores

Children's Zoo

Seal Pool

Monkeys

Zoo

Elephants

North
America

Bronx Lake

Reptiles

Gorillas

Penguins

World of
Darkness

Monorail

African Plains

South America

Skyfari

Wild Asia

N

0   250yd 500yd   ½ mile

0   250m   500m   1km

clusters of rare animals from the Asian Subcontinent are the only element detracting from the carefully staged natural environment.

Throughout the park are specimens no longer found in the wild. In the **Children's Zoo**, young and gentle animals are available for petting and feeding.

New York Botanical Garden
Southern Blvd. (200th St.), Bronx, NY 10460 ☎ 220-8700 ▨ ✗ ▣
Grounds open Apr-Oct 8am-7pm, Nov-Mar 8am-6pm. Conservatory
open Tues-Sun 10am-4pm. Museum open Mon-Thurs 9.30am-6pm,
Fri-Sat 9.30am-4pm.

Adjacent to the zoo on its northern border, these 250 acres also straddle the Bronx River, but here the river is narrow and untamed, tumbling through a deep gorge. Its course is bordered by a 40-acre preserve of virgin hemlock — the trees that covered much of the metropolitan region before the Europeans arrived.

Entry can be made opposite the Pelham Parkway gate of the zoo. At the first main pedestrian intersection, detour W into the azalea glen, then retrace the route E. After the bridge, the **Old Lorillard Snuff Mill** becomes visible on the left. The 1840s building is restored and used as a summer snack bar. Continue E and N, pausing along the way for displays of lilac, dogwood, magnolia and rhododendron. Eventually the paths converge on the **Museum**, which mounts changing exhibitions on horticultural and ecological themes and incorporates a herbarium and botanical library. To the SW is the centerpiece of the preserve, the **Enid A. Haupt Conservatory**. A grand rotunda of leaded glass is the focus of a complex of ten connecting greenhouses. The effect, inside and out, is of an enchanted crystal palace of the Victorian era. After years of deterioration, it was in danger of demolition. Reason and philanthropy finally prevailed in this glorious rejuvenation, and the rotunda now contains topiary, desert plants and tropical flora.

Obviously the best time to go is Apr-Aug, when the groves and gardens are ablaze with color, but special events draw visitors at Christmas and Easter.

Brooklyn-Battery Tunnel
Map 2V4 ▨
Master builder Robert Moses intended an overwater span at this site, just S of the *Brooklyn Bridge*, to connect lower Manhattan with the Belt Parkway, which skirts the edge of Long Island on the way to JFK Airport. Despite his clout as the most powerful city planner of his time — from the early 1930s into the 1960s — he bowed to public pressure and settled for a tunnel. It is the longest vehicular tunnel in the US — nearly 2 miles.

Brooklyn Botanic Garden
1000 Washington Ave. (Eastern Parkway), Brooklyn, NY
11225 ☎ 622-4433. Map 12E3 ▣ Tues, Fri ▨ other days
✗ Open Apr-Sept Tues-Fri 8am-6pm, Sat, Sun, public
holidays 10am-6pm; Oct-Mar Tues-Fri 8am-4.30pm, Sat,
Sun, public holidays 10am-4.30pm. Closed Mon. Subway 2
or 3 to Eastern Parkway-Brooklyn Museum.

Although much smaller than its big brother in the Bronx (see *Bronx Zoo and New York Botanical Garden*) a visit to the Brooklyn Botanic Garden is nonetheless worthwhile, especially in concert with a visit to the neighboring *Brooklyn Museum*. Specialized gardens include one with fragrances for the blind, another exclusively of roses, one of herbs, three authentic Japanese settings supplemented by a superb bonsai display, and an ebullient horticultural tribute to Shakespeare, incorporating 80 plant species mentioned in his plays. The restrained Victorian conservatory was designed by the ubiquitous McKim, Mead & White in 1918, and was restored in 1989 and incorporated into the new **Steinhardt Conservatory**. That grand 55,000sq.ft facility has three octagonal pavilions that echo but improve upon the designs of their forerunners and are devoted to collections from tropical, temperate, and desert zones. They make the Garden a more compelling attraction than ever.

Brooklyn Bridge 🏛 ★
Map 3U5 ▣ 🚇

Perhaps the most spectacular engineering achievement of its time, the enduring grace of the 486m (1,595ft) span has inspired paeans by painters and poets. John Roebling conceived it in 1857, but construction did not begin until 1869. There was skepticism about its feasibility, the need for a bridge across a river well-served by ferry lines, and the projected expense. In the manner of public projects, those costs routinely multiplied, eventually totaling the then-stunning sum of nearly $16 million. Since construction paralleled the reign of one of New York's most corrupt political regimes, undetermined portions of the budgeted funds were diverted to the accounts of the notorious Boss Tweed and his cronies.

Roebling died in the first year of construction, contracting tetanus after his foot was crushed by a docking ferry. His son Washington took over. While rising from an underwater chamber, he suffered an attack of the bends and was permanently disabled. Although confined to a wheelchair, he oversaw the project to its conclusion, employing his wife Emily as a go-between. Thousands of new immigrants, largely Irish and Italian, labored 14yrs on the project. Uncounted numbers died, many of them victims of the hazards associated with the nascent technology.

Six days after the opening on May 24, 1883, a rumor that the bridge was collapsing raced through the festive crowd of sightseers. There were 12 fatalities in the ensuing panic. Since then, the 40m (133ft) height of the span has proved tempting to the foolhardy and suicidal. At least 34 jumpers have not survived the fall.

Despite early doubts about its stability, there is every reason to believe that the grande dame of New York bridges will be there when today's youngest pedestrians bring their grandchildren. There are incomparable **vistas** of East River traffic and the lower Manhattan skyline from the elevated walkway.

Brooklyn Heights 🏛
Map 3U6.

In 1646, a handful of Dutch families decided to give official status to their settlement on the bluffs overlooking the juncture of the Hudson and East rivers and the larger village at the toe of Manhattan Island. They called their new home "Breuckelen" ("broken land"). The establishment of a regular steam ferry service in 1820 transformed the rural community into a suburb. Shipping magnates and wealthy merchants chose to move in, insulated from the traumas of the troubled city and yet in a position to monitor river traffic. Their terraced row houses and mansions competed in harbor vistas and luxury of appointments. A substantial number persisted into the 20thC, but by the 1950s, Brooklyn Heights was in decline.

A plan to ram a highway through the neighborhood was narrowly averted, and the resulting community spirit signaled its renaissance. Now designated an Historic District, it is the most desirable residential enclave in the borough. (See *Walk 7* on pages 54-56.)

Brooklyn Museum

188 Eastern Parkway (Washington Ave.), Brooklyn, NY 11238 ☎ 638-5000 📠 🖵 Open Wed-Fri 10am-5pm, Sat 11am-6pm, Sun 1-6pm, public holidays 1-5pm. Closed Mon, Tues. Subway 2,3,4 to Eastern Parkway-Brooklyn Museum.

Despite a history of fiscal uncertainty, this fine institution has launched a massive expansion project that probably won't be completed until the year 2030. This ambitious undertaking will double the size of what is already one of the largest museums in the US. It has long been the keystone of the borough's cultural and recreational complex, which includes the adjacent *Brooklyn Botanic Garden*, *Prospect Park* and zoo, and the **Brooklyn Public Library**. The museum must be ranked among the most important in the city and might have challenged even the nonpareil *Metropolitan Museum of Art*, had the initial plans of the architectural firm of McKim, Mead & White been carried out. As it is, the scaled-down scheme that was erected at the turn of the century is an imposing Neo-Classical pile, flawed only by a misguided 1930s modernization that removed the noble exterior staircase. Some compensation for that desecration is provided by the two 1916 Daniel Chester French statues that were moved outside onto pedestals in 1963.

Inside are five floors of arts and antiquities spanning centuries and continents from Egypt to Oceania. Exhibits are grouped essentially along geographical or societal lines. The planned expansion, when it finally begins, will bring with it many upheavals, and the precise location of some parts of the collection may not always be as given below. However, for the lifetime of this edition, what follows is likely to remain true.

The first floor is devoted to the **arts and crafts of the primitive** (or at least pre-colonial) **peoples of the Americas, Africa and the South Pacific**. Totem poles of the NW tribes loom over cases of New Guinean ceremonial masks, Columbian ritual urns, Inca jewelry, Hopi and Zuni dolls, African fetishes and weapons. Adjacent rooms house a gallery reserved for art shows drawn from the Brooklyn community, a cafeteria, and a museum shop that purveys a remarkable array of crafts from around the world at reasonable prices.

On the second floor are **arts of Asia and Islam**, spotlighting ceramics, rugs, textiles, paintings, metal and jade secular and religious objects from India, China, Persia, Japan, Tibet and Indochina. A separate print room encompasses European and American graphic arts from the 14th-20thC.

The pride of the museum is the collection of **relics of Dynastic and Coptic Egypt** on the third floor, with sarcophagi mingling with alabaster figurines and an ebony sphinx. Of particular interest are the **Assyrian reliefs** in the Kevorkian Gallery, just beyond the elevator vestibule. The wall sculptures, some from the Palace of Ashurnasirpal II, depict winged deities and griffin-headed genies. With them are ceremonial vessels, partly animal-shaped, and engraved silver bowls.

Enter, then, into an unexpectedly dramatic inner court ringed with shallow cases of exquisite objects ranging from Egyptian to

Cypriot and Greek: amulets, amphoras, glass bottles as fragile as paper, beakers, fragments of textiles, busts of monarchs. Additional rooms are given to still more jewelry, pottery and funerary pieces.

The fourth floor is devoted to **furniture and decorative arts**, largely of the 17th and 18thC, but also including the early Colonial period and some Manhattan Art Deco. The **Jan Martense Schenck House**, a Dutch 2-room dwelling of New York c.1675, is reconstructed and fully furnished with authentic pieces. There is also a costume institute. Near the fifth floor entrance is a lush **landscape** by the 19thC American Albert Bierstadt, startlingly overpowering the viewer with its rolling thunderclouds, shafts of light, alpine cascades and snowy peaks. The smaller canvases of the Hudson River School that follow are pale by comparison, but are momentarily diverting. The first doorway leads into the East Galleries, reserved for **European painting**. After the glories of the first and third floors, these are disappointingly minor works by important artists. The supposed highlight is *Mlle. Fiorre in the Ballet La Source*, a very early (1866) Degas that looks merely half-finished and gives barely a hint of the off-center composition that was to become his hallmark. Next to it are two minor Corots. The rest of the room holds portraits of modest distinction and some bucolic scenes by Millet. A small room of preliminary studies in pastels and gouache includes an appealing Toulouse-Lautrec, alongside drawings by Manet, Gauguin, Degas and Pissarro. They and their compatriots Renoir, Monet and Cézanne are represented in the last room by larger oils that demand little attention. On the way out of this section, note the 15th and 16thC Italian religious paintings on wood. The rest of the floor is normally used for special exhibitions, often of an Americana theme.

An unusual outdoor court at the rear of the building preserves ornamental fragments scavenged from such lamented buildings as the razed Penn Station. Lectures, films, concerts and gallery talks are regular features in the museum's program.

Bryant Park
Ave. of the Americas and 42nd St. Map 5O4.
Most midtown blocks have supported disparate functions over the last 150yrs of development, but few as profound as this site. In the early 19thC, it was a potter's field. Two decades later, a fortress-like reservoir was completed, and in 1853, an imitation of London's Crystal Palace was erected on an adjacent strip of land. That was destroyed by fire in 1858, and the scorched earth was designated a park, dedicated to poet and journalist William Cullen Bryant (1794-1878).

At the turn of the century, the reservoir was drained and filled and the *New York Public Library* and park extension took its place. Office workers drop by to enjoy the sun, and concerts of live and recorded music. Lolling among them are a number of drug dealers of placid mien and suspect merchandise. Renovations are underway.

Carl Schurz Park
Map 7L5.
Schurz was a German-born immigrant who became a US senator. The park in his name is at the eastern end of 86th St., the central artery of the German community known as *Yorkville*. The official residence of the mayor, *Gracie Mansion*, is at the northern edge of the green.

Carnegie Hall
154 W 57th St. (7th Ave.), NY 10019 ☎ 247-7459. Map 4N3.
It was feared that the 1891 hall would be demolished along with
the old Metropolitan Opera House after the completion of the
Lincoln Center. Preservationists scored a too-infrequent victory,
however, and funds were raised to renovate the interior. The
acoustics are still superb and the concert schedule is full, with
artists and groups clamoring for dates.

Castle Clinton National Monument ▥
*Battery Park (foot of Broadway), NY 10004 ☎ 344-7220.
Map 2V4 ▣ ✗ Open 8.30am-5pm.*
Concern over a possible second conflict with the English
prompted initial plans for the battery of 28 cannon on the rocky
outcrop 60m (200ft) off the sw tip of Manhattan. The eventual
reality of British impressment of crews of American merchant
ships lent credence to the fear, and additional fortifications were
thrown up. The intention was to discourage hostile ships
attempting to enter the East River, in concert with crossfire from a
similar installation on nearby Governor's Island (still a military
post). Perhaps it worked, for the fort never loosed a volley.
  When the lingering hatreds of the 1812 War faded, the circular
sandstone structure was given to New York City. It was
transformed into an entertainment center, hosting concerts and
recitals. By the middle of the century, it had been joined with
Manhattan, and in 1855 it became an immigrant processing
center. By 1892, that function was assumed by *Ellis Island*, and
the fort was converted into a public aquarium, a role it held until
1941. After World War II, it was restored to its original status, and
is now a Federal landmark run by the National Park Service.
Tickets for the ferries to the *Statue of Liberty* and *Ellis Island*
are sold at booths inside. The boats leave from docks on the
promenade to the w of the Castle.

Cathedral Church of St John The Divine ▥
*1047 Amsterdam Ave. (112th St.), NY 10025 ☎ 678-6888.
Map 8I3 ▣ ✗ Open 7am-5pm. Occasionally closed during
special events.*
Work on the cathedral started in 1892. By the year 2000, they
hope to have the two towers completed. That will still leave the
transepts and other additions to be undertaken — perhaps
somewhere around 2050? Even now, the interior space is second
only to St Peter's in Rome, and the combined floor space of
Chartres and Notre-Dame de Paris would fit within the 44x183m
(146x601ft) area. The measured pace of construction is due to the
determination to use methods that reach back to the Middle
Ages. English master masons instruct American apprentices in the
stonecutting yard (*open to the public Mon-Fri 8.45am-
3.45pm*). Religious and secular works have been donated to the
cathedral over the last 100yrs and offhandedly stored for future
display. A recent inventory revealed the surprising scope of the
collection, which includes 13th-16thC tapestries and paintings of
the Italian Renaissance. They are on view on a circulating basis in
the **Museum** (▣ *Mon-Sat 11am-4pm, Sun noon-5pm ✗ Mon-
Sat 11am, 2pm, Sun 12.30pm*).

Center for Inter-American Relations
*680 Park Ave. (68th St.), NY 10021 ☎ 249-8950. Map 7M4
▣ ✗ by appointment. Open Tues-Sun noon-6pm. Closed
Mon.*

The architectural firm of McKim, Mead & White was responsible for many notable buildings of the late 19th and early 20thC in New York, and a substantial number still exist. Perhaps because the third and most famous partner, Stanford White, died at the hands of a jealous husband in 1906, this 1909 structure is a Neo-Georgian departure from the Italianate preferences of their earlier projects. After a period as home for the Russian Delegation to the UN, one of the many Rockefellers bought it and gave it to the Center. Although arts and crafts of every country and age of the Western Hemisphere are exhibited, the emphasis is on Latin America.

Central Park ★
Maps 6&7.
Throughout its history, pragmatic visionaries have tempered the city's headlong rush to squeeze every penny of profit from the limited available land. In 1844, most of Manhattan N of 50th St. was a wasteland, supporting only squatters. Poet William Cullen Bryant prodded City Hall into acquiring 840 acres between what were to become 5th Ave. and 8th Ave. and 59th St. and 110th St. Frederick Law Olmsted and Calvert Vaux submitted the winning landscaping scheme in 1857. Its execution required 20yrs, but the results are cherished by every New Yorker, whether cyclist, jogger, stroller, lover, picnicker or baseball player. There are lakes, bridges, ponds, glades, hillocks, meadows, fountains, zoos, boat houses, playgrounds, bandstands, bridle paths, sculptures, terraces, a skating rink and an outdoor theater for summer Shakespeare. In a real sense, it is New York's greatest single achievement. (See *Walk 5* on pages 50-51.)

Central Park Zoo
5th Ave. and 64th St., NY 10021 ☎ 360-8213. Map 7M4 ☒
Children's Zoo ☒ ■ ♣ Open 11am-5pm; Children's Zoo open 10am-4.30pm.
Relatively small and always crowded, the zoo is a handy alternative for those without the time or inclination to travel to the far superior *Bronx Zoo*. Mid-afternoon feeding time for the seals is a major draw, but the red pandas, monkeys, penguins, and polar bears are nearly as diverting. The zoo was closed in 1983 for desperately needed renovation. The grand reopening didn't take place until 1988, three years late and at triple the original estimated cost.

It was worth the wait. The former prison-like atmosphere was modified to provide more space and natural habitats for the animals, and more gardens and plantings were introduced, to help integrate the zoo into the surrounding park. A minor disappointment is the absence of such larger animals as elephants, too big to be comfortably housed on the 5½-acre property. The separate **Children's Zoo**, where farm animals come forward to be fed and scratched behind the ears, is a short stroll to the N. Cross the Transverse Rd. to reach it.

Chelsea
Map 4Q3.
The genesis of the neighborhood known as Chelsea is attributed to an unlikely creator. Writer Clement Clark Moore inherited the land and drew up plans for its streets and buildings. Many of his blocks of brownstone row houses remain, albeit often scarred by 20thC so-called improvements, but all too frequently they have been displaced by uninspired residential and industrial buildings.

There are now signs of gentrification, however, with antique stores, off-off Broadway experimental theaters, music pubs, art galleries, and nightclubs sufficiently chic to entice uptowners into long taxi rides. The principal landmark is the **Chelsea Hotel**. Constructed in 1884 as one of the first luxury apartment houses, it failed to attract the wealthy tenants for which it was intended, and became a hotel in 1905. Writers, artists, and composers found it irresistible, and Thomas Wolfe, Sarah Bernhardt, Tennessee Williams and Jackson Pollock are but a few of those who lived there. Less well known is the **General Theological Seminary**: enter the door at 175 9th Ave. and emerge in an unexpected square of trees and lawns. Boundaries of the district are 14th St. to 23rd St., and 7th Ave. to the Hudson River.

Children's Museum of Manhattan

212 W 83rd St. (near Broadway), NY 10024 ☎ 721-1234. Map 6L3 ▨ ✳ *Open Tues-Sun 10am-5pm.*

The new home of a museum that occupied cramped quarters on 54th St for 12yrs is four stories high, with a total of 36,000sq.ft of exhibition space. It endeavors, successfully, to walk the narrow line between instruction and play, with interactive exhibits full of sound, light, and color. The **Brainatarium**, for one, is a 20ft-high domed theater, a kind of cerebral planetarium that glories in the wonders of the human mind, with a short film and a rap song describing its functions. A **communications center** on the 2nd floor has a television studio where children can pretend to be news reporters, camera operators and actors; the more serious **"Magical Patterns"** exhibition zone explains by demonstration the types of patterns that inform nature and the arts. In the course of a visit, each child's photo and fingerprints are taken, presented at the end in a one-page "newspaper," with the picture and an account of the day's activities.

China Institute

125 E 65th St. (Park Ave.), NY 10021 ☎ 744-8181. Map 7M4 ▨ *Open Mon-Sat 10am-5pm.*

Ferocious carved dogs at the entrance, twice-yearly exhibitions of art from the mother country (usually held in spring and late fall), and cooking and language classes, help satisfy (and arouse) the current Occidental curiosity about things Chinese. But the China Institute has had a longer life and different sponsorship than might be expected. The parent institute was created in 1926 to aid Chinese-Americans and foster cultural relations with the West. In 1945, a grand East Side house was donated by publisher Henry Luce to serve as headquarters. Luce was co-founder of the Time-Life empire and had been born in China of missionary parents. A range of educational and cultural offerings is available to citizens of Chinese origin and the larger public, including films, lectures, courses in calligraphy, opera, and vocational training for newly-arrived immigrants.

Chinatown

Map 2T4.

Traditionally defined as eight square blocks between *The Bowery* and Mulberry, Worth, and Canal Sts., Chinatown long ago spilled over those boundaries. From 1882, when a Federal law specifically excluded Chinese immigrants, until the 1960s, when such clearly racial restrictions were raised, the population of the community was relatively stable. Since then, it has grown dramatically, threatening to swallow up Little Italy, to the N. The core of the neighborhood is gratifyingly exotic, the air heavy with dialects and enticing aromas. Every other restaurant is hung with golden ducks, and even the telephone booths have pagoda roofs. (See *Walk 3* on pages 45-47.)

Chrysler Building 血
405 Lexington Ave. (42nd St.), NY 10017 ☎ 682-3070. Map 5O4 ⊡ Open Mon-Fri 9am-5pm. Closed Sat, Sun.
For a flicker of time after its completion in 1930, this was the highest structure in the world at 320m (1,048ft), the first to surpass the Eiffel Tower. But that was a period of intense speculative competition, and the *Empire State Building* soon took the title. More than 60yrs later, however, the Chrysler is still in the top ten, and it remains the most satisfying esthetic result of the skyscraper mania. Art Deco arches of stainless steel surmount the tower, flaring in the sun and illuminated at night, base for a slender spire that thrusts 37m (123ft) into the clouds. Abstract representations of automobile parts inform friezes and other decorative details, in deference to the first owner's business. There is no observation floor, but step inside for a look at the Cubistic assemblages of grained marble and chrome in the lobby.

Church of the Ascension 血
36 5th Ave. (10th St.), NY 10003 ☎ 254-8620. Map 2R4. Open Mon-Sat noon-2pm, 5-7pm.
The first church on lower 5th Ave. (when upper 5th was still country), this was also the first to be executed in the Gothic Revival mode then sweeping through Europe. Brownstone was used for the facing, a material that was to become a favorite of the well-to-do for their row houses. In 1889, McKim, Mead & White remodeled parts of the interior and the parish house, hiring Louis Comfort Tiffany for the design of some of the stained glass.

Church of the Transfiguration
1 E 29th St. (5th Ave.), NY 10016 ☎ 684-6770. Map 5P4. Open 8am-6pm.
It is said that when an actor asked to be married, he was firmly dispatched to this "Little Church Around the Corner," an institution presumably not overly concerned about the dubious professions and social status of its parishioners. The church was built around 1850, and has a long association with show folk.

Citicorp Center
153 E 53rd St. (Lexington Ave.), NY 10022 ☎ 559-4259. Map 5N4 ⊡ Open 8am-midnight.
Posterity has yet to render its verdict on this building. Its distinctive sloping roofline moves it into the Post-Modernist category of skyscraper design, away from the rectangular glass boxes of the Bauhaus school. The roof was intended to house solar energy collectors, a good intention sacrificed to the gods of cost accounting. Quibbles aside, the 1978 building brought life to a dreary block, and accommodated into its design the modest but striking **St Peter's Lutheran Church**. Office floors begin at 39m (127ft), clearing the church steeple and providing a public atrium embracing 22 stores and restaurants. The interior plaza is filled with trees and tables, and live music is sometimes played there.

City Hall 血
City Hall Park (Broadway and Murray St.), NY 10007

Cleopatra's Needle

☎ 566-5200. Map 2T4 ⊡ Open Mon-Fri 10am-4pm. Closed
Sat, Sun.
Both dwarfed and enhanced by the taller buildings that enclose it
on three sides, the third and present City Hall (1811) is a
Georgian-Federal-Renaissance gem that even the Sun King might
have accepted (at least as a summer cottage). (See *Walk 3* on
page 45.)

Cleopatra's Needle
Central Park. Map 7L4.
One of only four obelisks outside Egypt, it was erected in
Central Park in 1881, behind the *Metropolitan Museum of
Art*. The red granite spire is covered with hieroglyphics from the
time of Thutmose III (c.1600BC). Regrettably, the change in
climate, plus air pollution, has worn them down.

The Cloisters 🏛
*Fort Tryon Park, NY 10040 ☎ 923-3700. Map 10B2 ▨
Half-price entry for senior citizens and students ⊡ children
under 12. Ticket includes same-day admission to
Metropolitan Museum of Art ✗ ➳ Open Mar-Oct 9.30am-
5.15pm, Nov-Feb 9.30am-4.45pm. Closed Mon, some
holidays. Subway A to 190th St.*
Save The Cloisters for a day when the freneticism of the Big
Apple becomes overbearing. This far-uptown unit of the
Metropolitan Museum of Art is a wondrous sanctuary in *Fort
Tryon Park*, overlooking the Hudson River from the northern
heights of the island. On the crest of a hill banked by woodland
and meadows, parts of several European monasteries and
chapels have been blended in a unified edifice of blissful
serenity. The collection was founded by George Grey Barnard,
who gathered vast amounts of superb medieval sculpture on his
many visits to Europe. It was first opened to the public in 1914,
and moved to its present home in 1938, following a donation by
the Rockefeller family.
Main floor (N and W)   Approach is made up a curving
driveway from the bus stop and parking lot, and entry is past
nine arches from the **15thC Benedictine friary of Froville**.
Walk through the French 12thC archway into the **Romanesque
Hall** and turn right into the **Fuentidueña Chapel**. The low black
stone baptismal font just inside is from Belgium, the
barrel-vaulted apse from Segovia, the fresco above the altar from
Catalonia. All are believed to be of the 12thC. On the left is a
16thC painted limestone sculpture from Zamora. The grinning
hyena-like creature was meant to be a lion, and is surmounted by
a headless Christ figure placing a crown on Mary's head. Return
to the Romanesque Hall and turn into the **St Guilhem Cloister**.
Perhaps because of the delicacy of the ornamentation on the
ancient pillars, this is the only indoor cloister. A glass ceiling
permits boxed plants to grow in winter. Paired capitals and
columns feature stylized leaves, flowers, and human figures. No
two pairs are the same. As in the other rooms, a plan on the wall
shows which portions are authentic.
Return to the Romanesque Hall once more and turn into the
Langon Chapel. Note the thick oak doors banded with
ironwork that serves both decorative and support functions.
Much of the stonework is from an 11thC church in Langon, near
Bordeaux, and the carved faces of the capital high on the right of
the nave are often alleged to be Henry II and Eleanor of
Aquitaine. The centerpiece of the chapel is the marble ciborium

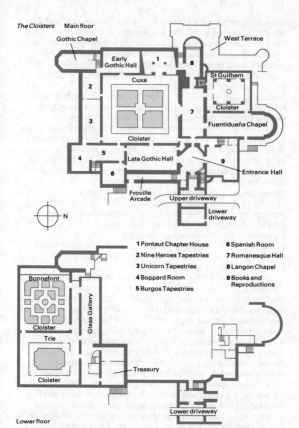

The Cloisters Main floor

Gothic Chapel

West Terrace

Early Gothic Hall

1

8

Cuxa

St Guilhem

2

Cloister

7

Fuentidueña Chapel

3

Cloister

5

4

Late Gothic Hall

9

6

Entrance Hall

Froville Arcade

Upper driveway

Lower driveway

N

1 Pontaut Chapter House
2 Nine Heroes Tapestries
3 Unicorn Tapestries
4 Boppard Room
5 Burgos Tapestries

6 Spanish Room
7 Romanesque Hall
8 Langon Chapel
9 Books and Reproductions

Bonnefont

Cloister

Glass Gallery

Trie

Cloister

Treasury

Lower driveway

Lower floor

or tabernacle, a roofed structure on four pillars that shelters an altar and a 12thC Burgundian *Virgin and Child* carved from birch. Leave the chapel through the door on the left and turn sharply right to the **West Terrace**, a belvedere overlooking the usually placid Hudson and the high bluffs on the opposite shore called the Palisades. Apart from the *George Washington Bridge* to the s, there is little to detract from the impression that this was the way the riverscape looked when the first European settlers arrived. Go back inside, turning right at the end of the short corridor.

The Pontaut Chapter House is from a Benedictine abbey in Gascony, probably dating from the late 12thC. Because the room is nearly all original, it conveys the strongest sense of place of anywhere in The Cloisters. Ribbed, vaulted ceilings hint at early Gothic influences, but the rounded arches, somber capitals, and massive walls are clearly Romanesque. Bands of brick alternate with crudely shaped stone, all of which was once covered in plaster. Walk out in the **Cuxa Cloister**, in which the monastic mood is usually enhanced by recorded Gregorian chants and other sacred music of the Middle Ages and Renaissance. This is the largest of the cloisters, open to the sky, its four-sided

75

colonnade enclosing a garden. It covers approximately half the area of its original 12thC site, a monastery in the French Pyrénées. Look closely at the capitals of the rose-streaked marble columns, for each is different, depicting simple leaf motifs, lions, complex hunting scenes and mythical animals. Circle the courtyard, looking for the mermaid capital in the E arcade, the best decorative work in the group.

Continue past the Chapter House and enter the **Early Gothic Hall** to examine the ecclesiastical figures, then move on to the **Gothic Chapel**. Distinctions from the Romanesque style predominating to this point are evident in the pointed arches and ribbed vaulting, the 14thC stained glass, and the greater delicacy of the stonework, especially at the tops of the window openings. Large effigies and sarcophagi are dotted about. Their origins are French and Catalan, while most of the glass is Austrian. Take the stairs down to the lower floor.

Lower floor   In the **Glass Gallery**, pause to study the 15th-16thC stained glass from which it takes its name. At the end is a large section of intricately carved woodwork, which once enclosed the staircase of a house in Abbeville, France. Although holy figures are duly depicted, the effect is of secular Gothic exuberance. The room straight ahead houses 37 carved wood panels, again from Abbeville, but this time they convey a distinctly religious impression.

Turn left into the **Treasury**, which features liturgical fans and combs, a silver reliquary in the shape of an arm, and exquisite chalices of silver and gold, one from the 4thC. This route leads back past the Abbeville woodwork to a door opening into the **Trie Cloister**. Off the main traffic lanes of the museum, this secluded spot encourages the contemplative frame of mind for which it was intended. Each capital varies from the others, the scenes more literal than those so far encountered, and the slender double pillars are of differently colored marble. The plants surrounding the fountain are examples of those found in the Unicorn Tapestries (see below). Leave by the doorway at the NW corner, walking along the arcade modeled on the cloister of the abbey at Bonnefont-en-Comminges. Here, the attraction is not the architecture but the **garden**, which is heady with lemon thyme, marjoram, mace and woodruff. Brick paths separate beds of violets and forget-me-nots, dominated by four quince trees. A low wall affords views of the park to the S, and birdwatchers are often surprised by the variety of species attracted to the garden. When ready, re-enter the Glass Gallery and return upstairs.

Main floor (s and E)   From the Gothic Chapel, turn into the **Nine Heroes Tapestries** room. The late 14thC hangings show five of the heroes who featured in this popular theme, among them Alexander the Great, Charlemagne and Julius Caesar. Understandably faded and fragmented, the tapestries provide a foretaste of the splendid 16thC **Unicorn Tapestries** in the next hall. Scholarly consensus ranks this set of seven superbly executed panels among the finest in existence. That assessment may be restrained, for in concept, detailing and craftsmanship, they are peerless. The remarkable petal-by-leaf renderings of plants and flowers make it possible to identify many of the live specimens seen in the Trie Cloister (see above). Beyond such surface delights is the telling of a tale with deep symbolic undercurrents. Christ is seen as a Unicorn, Gabriel as a hunter with a horn, Satan as a snake; pagan beliefs mingle with Christian convictions; fruits and blossoms represent purity, lust, fertility. Baronial German furnishings and a flamboyant French Gothic

fireplace suggest the surroundings in which the tapestries were
for a long time viewed.

The **Boppard Room** is named after the German town where
its six 15thC stained-glass panels originated. Go past the late
15thC **Burgos Tapestries**, executed to the glorification of
Charles VIII of France, and turn into the **Spanish Room** to see
Robert Campin's *Annunciation* triptych (c.1425). The altarpiece
is remarkable for the choice of setting: a simple Flemish interior
rather than the traditional ecclesiastical or historical environment.
The painted Gothic red pine ceiling in this room is also worthy of
attention. Leave the museum through the **Late Gothic Hall**,
noting the fine 15thC Spanish retable on your way out.

Columbia University 🏛

Broadway (116th St.), NY 10027 ☎ 280-1754. Map 8I2 ═
*Campus open 24hrs. Subway 1 to 116th St.-Columbia
University.*
Established in 1754 as King's College, and fueled by more than
two centuries of alumni bequests and gifts, Columbia is one of
the wealthiest universities in the US. As a member of the
prestigious Ivy League, which includes Harvard, Yale and
Princeton, it is also one of the most distinguished. With the end
of the Revolution, "King's" College became "Columbia," and after
an intermediate move to Madison Ave. and 49th St., settled here
at Morningside Heights in 1897. Over the years, the original
men's college has joined with a teacher's college and Barnard
College for women, and courses now include business
administration, law, medicine, dentistry, librarianship, journalism,
social work and public health. Founding father Alexander
Hamilton graduated from here, and Dwight Eisenhower was the
university's president after World War II before moving on to a
somewhat higher office.

The original layout of the campus and two of the first buildings
were products of McKim, Mead & White. Fortunately, their
design was opened up to permit larger pedestrian plazas, which
in turn lent greater drama to the most prominent building, **Low
Library**. Its style is Neo-Classical, with a surmounting dome and
a portico with ten columns and coffered ceiling. The elevated site
makes the most of the building's monumentality. Halfway up the
wide front steps is a statue of *Alma Mater* by Daniel Chester
French, best known for his sculptures of Abraham Lincoln. Low
Library is essentially an administration building. **Butler Library**,
to the s, is the main repository of the university's 5-million-
volume collection.

The **Terrace Restaurant** on the top floor is open to the public.
Given its situation, the food and service are quite good, and it
affords excellent views of Manhattan.

Coney Island

*Brooklyn. Map 12F3. Subway B, D, F, M, N, QB to Stillwell
Ave.-Coney Island.*
For generations of working-class New Yorkers, Coney Island was
Riviera-on-the-Subway, a wide strip of powdery sand that gave
surcease from the steaming streets and tenements of the city. It
has fallen on hard times, the shattered and burned-out housing
inland occupied primarily by pensioners and the poor, the
Steeplechase Park amusement center a wasteland. Still, the beach
has been cleaned up, the boardwalk repaired, the original
Nathan's Famous grills hundreds of incomparable hot dogs
daily, teenagers squeal through roller coaster dips at **Astroland**,

and families gape at the sharks and dolphins of the *New York Aquarium*. The district is on the Atlantic Ocean in S Brooklyn, along Surf Ave. between W 37th St. and Ocean Parkway. Thousands of Soviet immigrants have made nearby Brighton Beach a virtual Little Odessa.

Cooper-Hewitt Museum

2 E 91st St. (5th Ave.) ☎ *860-6868. Map 7K4* ▨ ▣ *Tues 5-9pm* ✗ *Open Tues 10am-9pm, Wed-Sat 10am-5pm, Sun noon-5pm. Closed Mon.*

In this pricey venue at the top of the 5th Ave. "Museum Mile," even millionaires built their mansions flush with their property boundaries, foregoing lawns and gardens. But in that lamented time before the imposition of income taxes, Scottish-born Andrew Carnegie was more than simply rich. He had just sold his steel company (1901) for more than $250 million. When he built this 64-room house in the same year, he left himself a green buffer all around and transplanted mature trees from upstate. Only a friend and business associate such as Henry C. Frick could indulge himself in a similar fashion (see the *Frick Collection*).

If pressed, an art historian might describe the Carnegie house as Georgian, but the design was carried out with such an elephantine hand that this label is hardly appropriate. Despite the unfortunate facade, there is a pleasant garden behind the cast-iron fence and a marvelous stained-glass canopy over the entrance. Within are the decorative art acquisitions of Peter Cooper (founder of *Cooper Union*) and his granddaughters Eleanor and Sarah Hewitt. The only New York branch of the **Smithsonian Institution**, its subtitle is the **National Museum of Design**. That objective is broadly defined, to incorporate wallpapers, furniture, glassware, metalwork, lace and ceramics, with superb examples of each. The dual strengths of the museum are its textiles and more than 30,000 drawings. The drawings include works by Dürer, Rembrandt and Winslow Homer. Fabrics and embroidery come from as far afield as Persia, France, India, Egypt and Italy, and span 14 centuries.

Cooper Union

Cooper Sq., NY 10003 ☎ *254-6300. Map 2R4. Open 8am-10pm.*

Peter Cooper became a millionaire through participation in the key 19thC industries of railroads and iron-making. In the benevolent if paternalistic manner of his fellows, he founded this college for the training of artists and engineers, and built the somber pile (1859) that still houses part of the institution. The Foundation Building rather resembles a railroad station of the time — dark, brooding, ponderous.

Still, Cooper made provision for a free-tuition curriculum for talented persons of any race, sex, creed or economic status, at a time when such notions were deemed dangerous to the natural order of things. That policy persists, and has profited tens of thousands of Americans who might not otherwise have had the chance of higher education. The Great Hall within hosted many celebrated 19thC speakers, among them suffragette Susan B. Anthony, abolitionist Henry Ward Beecher, Mark Twain and, in a rare New York appearance, Abraham Lincoln.

Dakota Apartments ⅏

1 W 72nd St., NY 10023. Map 6M3.

Until 1884, members of New York's establishment would not

consider living in anything but a private house. This luxury 10-floor apartment building changed their minds, even though it was so far uptown that wags said it was in Dakota Indian territory. Its capacious rooms, high ceilings, thick-walled quiet, and offbeat Bavarian fortress exterior ensure its continued cachet with celebrities and other privileged folk. *Rosemary's Baby* was filmed here. John Lennon, who lived here, was murdered outside the entrance in 1980.

Downtown Whitney Museum
33 Maiden Lane, Nassau St. NY 10005 ☎ 943-5655 ⊡ Open Mon-Fri 11am-6pm. Closed Sat, Sun.
A child of the uptown *Whitney Museum of American Art*, this branch caters to the mostly nonresidential population of the *Financial District*. After a decade of migrations around lower Manhattan, it has found a permanent home at Federal Reserve Plaza on the concourse level of a 26-story skyscraper. Rotating shows from the permanent collection and other sources are augmented by art appreciation classes and concerts. Gallery talks are offered Mon, Wed, and Fri at 12.30pm.

Dyckman House ▥
4881 Broadway (204th St.), NY 10543 ☎ 923-8008 (Morris-Jumel Mansion) for information. Map 10B2 ▨ Open Tues-Sun 11am-4pm. Closed Mon. Subway 1 to 217th St.
The original owner of the property was Jan Dyckman. He came to New Amsterdam in 1661 and swiftly assembled the substantial estate he was to pass on to his descendants. For no recorded tactical reason, the house built here in 1748 was burned to the ground by British troops, toward the end of the Revolutionary War. The existing replacement was erected in 1783, before they left Manhattan. The estate was once thick with fruit trees and was tilled by tenant farmers well into the 19thC. Parts of the orchard still bloomed past 1900. Brick and flagstone form portions of the lower sections of the house, with weatherboarding rising to a low gambrel roof. The effect is appropriately Dutch Colonial, and some of the furnishings are authentic not only to the period but to the original family.

 Although it is a long subway ride N to the Inwood district, the tranquil setting and park-like grounds smooth nerve ends frayed by the clamor of midtown.

East Side ★
Map 7L4.
From 5th Ave. to the East River and 59th St. to 92nd St., this chic precinct (also known as the Upper East Side) harbors most of the city's major museums, upscale single people, and resident millionaires, foreign and domestic. Tree-shaded cross streets near 5th Ave. are lined with attractive townhouses, the owners of which have succeeded in fending off the blandishments of developers. Commercial interlopers tend to be low-profile boutiques and art and antique galleries. Near the river are the luxury enclaves of **Beekman Place** and **Sutton Place**. Along the avenues, beautiful people swirl in a fickle flow from this month's bistro to the bar-of-the-moment and meet each other in lines for the latest movie. (See *Walk 6* on pages 52-54.)

Ellis Island ★
New York Harbor, NY 10004 ☎ 269-5755. Map 12D3 ▨ X Open daily. Ferry from Battery Park.

The echoing, gloomy halls must have seemed forbidding to the 12 million immigrants who passed through this bureaucratic purgatory between 1892-1954. Some were held for weeks and months before being permitted entry to the tantalizing city in sight across the bay. Restoration of the principal buildings — of more than 30 on the island — was completed in 1990, at a cost nearing $150 million. Chandeliers were rehung in the Great Hall of the Beaux Arts **Main Building**, and its four copper domes were laboriously cleaned to their original condition. Rubble was cleared, and the grime of decades of neglect was scoured away. Graffiti left by the immigrants has been preserved, however. The effort took more than 5yrs, so public interest in the reopening has been high. As a result, the ferry schedule from Battery Park continues to be adjusted according to visitor traffic. Call ahead for information about hours and ferry departures, or inquire at the ticket booth inside *Castle Clinton National Monument*.

Empire State Building 🏛 ★
350 5th Ave. (34th St.), NY 10001 ☎ 736-3100. Map 5P4 ▧
✗ ▣ ✳ Observatory floors open 9.30am-midnight. Check
visibility notice before buying tickets.

From its inception, the Empire State Building attracted superlatives — in achievement and in tragedy. Now only the third highest building in the world, after the Sears Building in Chicago and the downtown *World Trade Center*, it nevertheless remains the foremost symbol of New York. And it does, after all, stand 448m (1,472ft) high, including TV mast. By comparison, the Eiffel Tower is 300m (984ft).

King Kong swatted at biplanes from his perch in the 1931 movie classic, a plane crashed into the 79th floor in 1945, and at least 17 people have flung themselves to their deaths off parapets and down elevator shafts. The distinctive stepped cap was sketched in during one of the later design stages. It was to have been a mooring mast for airships. One attempt to bring that fanciful notion to reality resulted in some celebrated citizens nearly being blown away, and the idea was discarded. Without the rounded cap, the original 86 stories were only 61cm (2ft) higher than the *Chrysler Building*. With it, another 61m (200ft) and a second public observatory were added. Perhaps as remarkable as its height was the fact that the Empire State came in under schedule and under budget.

Twice a month, 6,500 windows must be washed. There are 60 miles of water pipes within the walls and 60,000 tons of structural steel. For reasons best known to the participants, an annual foot race is run *up* the 1,575 steps to the 86th floor. The facing is limestone, fashioned in modified Art Deco. The observatory on the 86th floor is wide open, the one on the 102nd floor enclosed with glass. Go during the day or at night, and save the other time for another of Manhattan's aeries.

Equitable Center
787 7th Ave. (between 51st and 52nd Sts.), NY 10010. Map
4N3 ▧ ➾ Open Mon-Sat 9am-6pm.

A continuation of the post-modernist trend in skyscraper architecture that began with the *AT&T Building*, the Center incorporates the Equitable Tower and the Paine Webber Building. While attractive enough by those standards, with its arches and cream-and-brown exterior, it is more notable for what it contains than the visage it presents to the street. Within its walls are several good-to-excellent restaurants, including **Le**

Bernardin and Palio, both described in *Restaurants*. And, to the left and right of the impressive 7th Ave. lobby are two art galleries, one a branch of the *Whitney Museum* (☎ *554-1113, open Mon-Fri 11am-6pm, Sat noon-5pm*), the other sponsored by the Paine Webber group (☎ *713-2885, open Mon-Fri 8am-6pm*). In the lobby itself is a mural by Roy Lichtenstein, nearly four stories high, and down one corridor is a panoramic vision of America executed by Thomas Hart Benton.

Federal Hall National Memorial 🏛

26 Wall St. (Nassau St.), NY 10005 ☎ 264-8711. Map 2U4
🔲 𝒦 *by appointment. Open Mon-Fri 9am-5pm. Closed Sat, Sun.*

Paradigm of the early 19thC enthusiasm for the Greeks, Federal Hall is not the building in which Washington took his oath of office in 1789, as is inferred by many. The **statue of George Washington**, outside, stands where the first President did indeed make those vows, but the building behind was not completed until 1842. It housed government offices from then until 1955, when it was converted to its present use as a museum. Now grandly labeled the **Museum of American Constitutional Government**, a newly installed permanent exhibit employs interactive video terminals to inform visitors on a variety of historical and contemporary issues. There are also artifacts of the Revolutionary War period, including a railing from the porch on which Washington repeated those famous words, and the clothes he wore that day.

Architects Town & Davis resisted the impulse to slap on sculptured friezes and ornate capitals, opting for fluted Doric columns and an unadorned pediment, all of marble quarried a few miles N of the city. Their only major deviation from their Greek inspiration was the interior rotunda, but the dramatic space works, which is ample justification. All in all, it is a trimlined Parthenon of disciplined stolidity and the finest example of Greek Revival in Manhattan.

Financial District ★

Map 2U4.

Bits and scraps of "Little Old New York" remain, but the southern end of Manhattan has long shuddered beneath the thrusting monoliths of international commerce and the machinations taking place within. The world eavesdrops on every whisper at the Stock Exchange, and conglomerates eye each other from their steel and concrete aeries.

Not long ago, the restaurants closed in this district in the evenings and on weekends, and Sun afternoons drew only a few strollers down ghostly windswept canyons. Now people are moving back to live in rehabilitated warehouses and middle-aged skyscrapers, and visitors come for sun and nautical history to the *South Street Seaport*. (See *Walk 2* on pages 42-45.)

Firefighting Museum   See *New York City Fire Museum*.

Flatiron Building 🏛

175 5th Ave. (23rd St.), NY 10010. Map 5Q4.

There are two reasons to seek out the Flatiron Building; its status as the first true skyscraper (a disputed claim), and its odd triangular shape (dictated by its plot at the confluence of 5th Ave. and Broadway). In the earliest tall buildings, made possible by the invention of the electric elevator, metal cages supported floors while masonry facings bore their own weight. In the decade before the Flatiron, new techniques allowed riveted steel frames to bear both floors *and* facing. That sort of steel skeleton was employed here, 87m (286ft) high and only 2m (6ft) wide at its narrow end. To calm the conservative citizenry, a rusticated limestone facade imitated a stacked Italianate palace. Nevertheless, many were convinced that the building would collapse in the high winds characteristic of the area. It didn't. You can enter the lobby during business hours, but there is no compelling reason to do so.

Forbes Magazine Galleries
62 5th Ave. (12th St.), NY 10011 ☎ 206-5548. Map 5R4 ▣ ✳
Open Tues, Wed, Fri, Sat 10am-4pm.
The late Malcolm Forbes was America's favorite millionaire. Many saw the immensely successful publisher as an ebullient man who enjoyed every dollar of his vast wealth, from his motorcycling tours and hot-air ballooning to his sumptuous yachts and lavish parties. He was also an inveterate collector, most noticeably of bejeweled Fabergé Eggs. There were 12 in his possession, of only 54 ever made. They are on view here, along with flotillas of model warships and ocean liners, legions of toy soldiers (more than 12,000), and a gallery of presidential papers and memorabilia. They are a delightfully playful array, the joyous accumulations of a man who must have left this mortal coil with a smile on his face.

Ford Foundation Building �
320 E 43rd St. (2nd Ave.), NY 10016 ☎ 573-5000. Map 5O5 ▣ Open Mon-Fri 9am-5pm. Closed Sat, Sun.
Atriums have become a cliché as pervasive as sunken plazas, in contemporary New York commercial architecture — sops to planning boards and environmental groups. Resulting spaces are often bleak and inhuman. The Ford Foundation presented a gift to the city, however, not a burden, with its 1967 headquarters. The interior contains a third of an acre of mature trees and shrubs. A brook, hushed and clear, curls through the garden. Passers-by are welcome to step inside for a moment's respite. The offices above the greenery are for the staff of the Foundation, which was created by Henry and Edsel Ford. It is the largest philanthropic trust in the world, concerning itself with a broad spectrum of human welfare issues, although it is best known for its contributions to education and the arts.

Fort Tryon Park
Map 10C2 ◁≡ ⬛ ⬟ Subway A to 190th St.
While *The Cloisters* museum is the prime motive for the long subway ride to this pastoral far-north Manhattan sanctuary, also tendered are hills, woodlands, meadows, a small but fascinating botanical garden, a children's playground with wading pool, and staggering Hudson River vistas from the site of the namesake fortification. During the week, only an occasional cyclist or jogger interrupts the solitude.

Fraunces Tavern Museum
54 Pearl St. (Broad St.), NY 10004 ☎ 425-1778. Map 2U4 ▣ ✗ by appointment ⬛ Open Mon-Fri 10am-4pm, Sun noon-5pm (Oct-May only). Closed Sat, Sun from June-Sept.
Tourist literature routinely implies that this is the tavern where

George Washington bade farewell to his troops. It isn't. Rather, it is a 20thC approximation, of debatable accuracy, constructed on the site of the original and incorporating parts of the remaining walls. The first building was a three-story mansion, converted into a tavern in 1762 by Samuel Fraunces. A West Indian, he became steward to Washington when the English took New York in 1776. The General returned on December 4, 1783 for lunch with his officers and delivered the famous address. Downstairs is now a restaurant; upstairs and in adjacent buildings there is a collection of Revolutionary musketry and mementoes, and two period rooms.

French Institute

22 E 60th St, (Madison Ave.), NY 10022 ☎ 355-6100. Map 5N4◻ Open Mon-Thurs 10am-8pm, Fri 10am-6pm, Sat (Sept-June) 10am-1.30pm. Closed Sun.

In a spectrum of activities to gladden the heart of every Francophile, the institute offers language and cooking classes, recent and venerable films, concerts, recitals, lectures — all relating to the mother country. Students and homesick expatriates can find French magazines and newspapers, and perhaps a new friend, in the small gallery and library.

Frick Collection ★

1 E 70th St. (5th Ave.), NY 10021 ☎ 288-0700. Map 7M4 ◫ ▨ Open Tues-Sat 10am-6pm, Sun 1-6pm. Closed Mon, major holidays. Children under 10 not admitted; 10-16s only with adult.

From the 1890s onward the part of 5th Ave. facing lower Central Park has been a millionaires' row. Now the privileged live in duplex penthouses, for not even the very wealthy can afford to maintain the palatial residences built by their antecedents. Most of those mansions have been demolished, a few converted to institutional use. The Andrew Carnegie residence, for example, is now the *Cooper-Hewitt Museum*. All this makes the Frick Collection even more special, for the house is much the way that it was left by the first and only owner — filled with paintings, furniture, clocks and Persian carpets.

Carnegie and industrialist Henry C. Frick were business associates who parted company over policy disputes. Frick chose to build his house (in 1914) only 20 blocks s of his former friend's 64-room residence. Although bearing allegiance to no particular style, its low roofline and front lawn are a welcome visual break in the prevailing wall of high-rises. And there is no more gracious oasis in the city than the interior court with its splashing fountain and flowering plants. After Frick's death, a harmonious addition doubled the floor space. The house was opened to the public in 1935.

Entrance is made from E 70th St. The first important room on your left is the **Boucher Room**, with eight panels representing the Arts and Sciences that François Boucher painted for one of Madame de Pompadour's legendary Rococo bedrooms. Next is the corner **Dining Room**, which is perhaps the most striking room in the mansion, with its French furniture and 18thC paintings by Hogarth, Gainsborough and Reynolds. To the N is the **Fragonard Room**, where four paintings known as *The Progress of Love*, once owned by Madame du Barry, celebrate the different stages of love. The other seven panels were also executed by Jean-Honoré Fragonard, a disciple of Boucher and a favorite at the court of Louis XV. Furnishings in the room are

Frick Collection

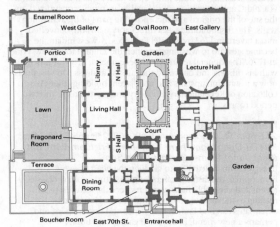

consistent with the period. The high point of the **Living Hall** is
the El Greco portrait of *St Jerome* over the fireplace. It is flanked
by two Hans Holbein paintings, and there are also works by
Titian and Bellini. On the center table is a bronze by Pollaiuolo.
Leading off from this room are the **South Hall**, notable for
Vermeer's *Officer and Laughing Girl*, and **North Hall**, which has
Ingres' portrait of *La Comtesse d'Haussonville*. The **Library**
concentrates on English painting, with a George Romney portrait
of *Lady Hamilton* and a luminous early Turner. Priceless
Chinese vases add to the authentic appeal of this paneled room.

Largest of the chambers is the **West Gallery**, its imposing
chilliness offset by the splendor of the masterpieces within. They
deserve a methodical clockwise examination. (On the way, make
sure you turn into the small **Enamel Room** for a look at Limoges
painted enamels of the 15th-17thC.) Among the treasures of this
trove are a trio of Rembrandts, two works by Van Dyck, a
Velázquez, a Goya and an El Greco. Turner was a progenitor of
the Impressionist revolution that followed his death in 1851, and
his vivid cityscape of Dieppe is particularly significant in this
respect.

Pass through the **Oval Room**, with its Whistlers and terra-cotta
Diana, into the **East Gallery**, where Goya, Gainsborough and
Van Dyck are featured. Finally, there is the **Garden Court**, with
its glass roof and fountain. Chamber music concerts take place
on occasional Sundays. Inquire at the entrance desk for detailed
information.

Garment Center
Map 4P3.

Neither steel nor automobiles nor their ilk are fabricated in New
York so, by default, people in suits conjuring advertising jingles
and peddling stocks describe themselves as "industries." As that
word is commonly understood, however, the primary
manufacturing enterprise of the city is clothing. Somewhere
between 80,000 and 300,000 citizens are employed in the rag
trade, depending upon how a statistician tots up the cutters,
shippers, salesmen, suppliers, designers, messengers, models,

packers, deliverymen, buyers, union organizers and sewing machine operators. Between breakfast and dinner, all of them seem to pour through the streets of this scruffy district along 7th Ave. between 34th and 40th Sts., dodging handcarts, gulping coffee from paper containers, grabbing lapels, scuttling to appointments, making deals. The fashions they produce often rival the best of Paris and Milan.

GE Building *(formerly RCA Building)* 🏛

30 Rockefeller Plaza (between 5th Ave. and Ave. of the Americas and 49th and 50th Sts.), NY 10017. Map 504.
Long known as the RCA Building, the new owners, General Electric, have imposed this name. As fast as Manhattan real estate changes hands, there is no certainty it won't soon be changed again. By whatever label, it remains the centerpiece of the 19-building *Rockefeller Center* complex, at 850ft (259m) and 70 stories. Completed in the Depression years, its first-floor murals are in the heroic Social Realist mode. Unfortunately, the observation deck is now closed.

General Grant National Memorial

Riverside Drive (122nd St.), NY 10027 ☎ 666-1640. Map 8H2 🔾 ✗ Open Wed-Sun 9am-5pm. Closed Mon, Tues.
Popularly known as Grant's Tomb, it is no accident that the official designation honors the Civil War service of Ulysses S. Grant rather than his scandal-ridden tenure as the 18th US President. The mausoleum is fashioned after the style of a 4thC Greek tomb, and was financed by private contributions rather than by Congress. After its completion in 1897, both Grant and his wife were interred within, behind impressive bronze doors. A gallery shows photographs and memorabilia from both careers. The Gaudíesque mosaic benches around the plaza outside are more interesting.

George Washington Bridge

Map 10D1.
Dreamers of the 19thC insisted that the broad Hudson River could be spanned, but it took the capitalistic euphoria of the late 1920s to bring together the necessary funds and determination. The bridge was completed in 1931, within months of the *Empire State, Chrysler* and *GE (formerly RCA) Buildings*, and, like them, was defiant of the economic desolation of the Great Depression. For a time, the 1,067m (3,500ft) between its main towers made it the longest suspension bridge in the world. Budgetary considerations and public opinion fortunately prevented plans to sheath the open steel framework in concrete and granite, as envisioned by architect Cass Gilbert. A second deck for trams and trains was planned by engineer Othmar H. Ammann, but was not added until 1962, when it was given over to general road traffic. There are eight lanes on the upper deck, six below.

Goethe House

1014 5th Ave. (82nd St.), NY 10028 ☎ 744-8310. Map 7L4 🔾 Open Wed, Fri, Sat noon-5pm, Tues, Thurs 11am-7pm. Closed Sun, Mon.
Films, lectures, art exhibitions and research materials fill this cultural repository, one of dozens sponsored by the Federal Republic of Germany around the world.

Grace Church 🏛

802 Broadway (10th St.), NY 10003 ☎ 254-2000. Map 2R4.
Open Mon-Fri 9am-5.45pm, Sat noon-4pm, Sun for
services.

Although a practicing engineer, James Renwick took advantage
of the mid-19thC tolerance for professional generalism, to design
this fine Episcopal church. Its success led to commissions for *St
Patrick's Cathedral* and the Smithsonian Institution in
Washington, all in the Gothic Revival style then in favor. The
wealthy congregation already had a church downtown, but
opened a competition in 1843 for a new one closer to their
homes. Renwick won, although he was only 25, and construction
began in the same year. The marble steeple, with its delicate
filigrees and curls, replaced the wooden original in 1884. There is
a lovely **English garden** to the N, in front of the rectory, a later
Renwick accomplishment. Although the parishioners were
virtually all from fashionable society, propriety was briefly cast
aside when circus promoter P.T. Barnum wangled a wedding of
his stellar attraction, Tom Thumb, to a lady midget who was also
in his employ.

Gracie Mansion 🏛

East End Ave. (E 88th St.), NY 10028. Map 7K5 🚌
✗ compulsory, 10am-4pm Wed. Visit by appointment only
(write to: Tour Program, Gracie Mansion, East End Ave.,
NY 10128).

Now the residence of the mayor, the mansion is named after the
merchant who built it in 1799. Prominent details are the
encompassing veranda and lattice railings at porch and roof
levels. It is hard to believe that the house once served as a public
rest room in *Carl Schurz Park*, in which it is still located. The
wealth that permitted Archibald Gracie to erect this stately
Federalist house evaporated when two of his ships were seized
by the French in 1807. His family was forced to sell in 1823, and it
went neglected for a century, even though the city purchased it
in 1887. Popular Fiorello LaGuardia was the first mayor to move
in, during World War II. Tours are difficult to arrange and tourists
without reservations are fenced off at some distance, so the best
way to view it is from the deck of a Circle Line tour boat (see
Useful addresses on page 17).

Gramercy Park 🏛 ★

Map 5Q4.

A small community forever battling against the dreary
commercial encroachments nibbling at its edges, these few
square blocks evoke 19thC residential elegance as no other area
in Manhattan can. The focal point is the rectangular park from
which the district takes its name. The park is protected by a high
fence, and only people living in the surrounding houses have
keys to the gate. Edwin Booth is represented by a statue inside;
by all accounts, he was a better actor than his brother John
Wilkes Booth, the assassin of Lincoln. Another president,
Theodore Roosevelt, lived nearby. Gramercy Park is part of an
official Historic District, a designation which has been awarded
to many areas of the five boroughs by the city's Landmarks
Preservation Commission.

Grand Central Terminal 🏛

Park Ave. and 42nd St., NY 10017. Map 5O4 🚇 🚃 ☕ Open
6am-2am.

An attempt to level the terminal to make way for yet another speculative office tower was thwarted in the late 1970s. Grand Central was therefore saved from the fate of Penn Station, over on the West Side. The conservationist effort was worthwhile. Straddling Park Ave., the main facade looks s, toward what was in 1913 the center of population and commerce. Its Beaux Arts adornment includes a heroic sculpture group comprised of Mercury, Athena and Hercules draped around a clock, but this is masked from street level by the second-story flyovers that encircle the terminal and join lower and upper Park Ave.

Inside, a vast vaulted space 38m (125ft) wide, and more than twice as long, arcs over rush-hour throngs of 120,000 daily commuters. Despite their headlong rush, not even those who have accumulated 20yrs of workday arrivals and departures are unaware of the grandeur of this main concourse. Line paintings depict the celestial constellations against the pale blue ceiling, and light streams through high arched windows. The latest in a series of renovations has removed the famous giant Kodak photograph at the E end to make room for another grand staircase. Take it all in from the open bar inside the Vanderbilt Ave. entrance, or wend down to the **Oyster Bar and Restaurant** (see *Restaurants*) between the main and lower levels. Despite the unlikely location, this is one of the top seafood restaurants in town.

Grant's Tomb   See *General Grant National Memorial.*

Greenacre Park
51st St. (2nd Ave.). Map 5N5.
Private benefactors have contributed a number of public "pocket" parks that bestow touches of grace and greenery in otherwise congested neighborhoods. This is a somewhat ostentatious example, its open space cluttered up with a semisculptural arrangement of rough-hewn sentinels, but it is nevertheless an agreeable retreat from exhaust fumes and noise.

Greenwich Village ⅲ ★
Map 2R3.
Those who could afford it fled the disease, fires and squalor of the city in the s to build homes in this rural village of the late 18thC. Pastoral serenity was short-lived, for the northward sprawl of the metropolis soon swamped it. The rich moved farther uptown, and artists took their places, turning brownstone row houses into apartments and studios. Henry James, Winslow Homer, Edgar Allen Poe and, later, Edna St Vincent Millay and Edward Hopper lived here, and "The Village" became America's Left Bank. Although present-day rents are beyond the means of most poets and painters, *laissez-faire* life-styles pertain, and eccentricity remains in evidence. *Washington Square* is the focal point of the neighborhood, which is usually delineated by Houston St., 14th St., 4th Ave. and the Hudson River (see *Walk 4* on pages 47-49.)

Guggenheim Museum ⅲ ★
1071 5th Ave. (89th St.), NY 10028 ☎ 860-1313. Map 7K4 ▨
⚐ ▣ Closed until late 1991. Call ahead for times.
Curmudgeonly genius Frank Lloyd Wright detested New York — he suggested that it be razed and begun again — and the Solomon R. Guggenheim Museum was his only completed commission in the city.

To say that the result was controversial falls short of the truth. Along a boulevard characterized by conservative apartment houses and Neo-Classical public buildings, the exterior of the Guggenheim resembles a flower pot teetering on the edge of a coffee table. The circular central gallery with its spiral stripe of glass is smaller at the base than at the top and squats off-center on a floating horizontal slab. Wright wanted a marble facing, but the concrete used instead had an unfortunate yellow cast. Reaction was predictably divided, even before the 1959 opening. Scornful perplexity was perhaps the most common response, not unlike that accorded to the nonobjective and abstract works of art displayed inside. By then, however, Wright was unable to counter-attack, as he was dead.

However one feels about the exterior, there can be little argument over the effectiveness of the interior design, at least in the core structure. Simple logic insists that the best way to view a museum's exhibits is to begin at the top and work down, not exhausting yourself with thoughts of missing rooms and finding elevators. That's how it is here. Take the elevator to the top and slowly descend along the spiral ramp, past bays of paintings and sculptures. Illumination comes from the glass dome and continuous window band, supplemented when necessary by artificial lighting.

The collections and loan exhibitions tread a line between the modern art establishment — represented by Picasso, Mondrian, Braque, Klee, Chagall and Kandinsky — and exponents of the New York School of Abstract Expressionism and their successors. Younger experimental artists provide spice. The adjacent horizontal gallery is given to the Thannhauser collection of Impressionists and their descendants: Manet, Pissarro, Gauguin, Van Gogh, Cézanne. Once out of the door, the question persists as to whether the architecture serves to enhance or overwhelm the art it is intended to set off.

Whatever you decide in the end, it certainly sharpens the experience. A new wing is under construction, and the entire museum is consequently closed. From the expected time of reopening in late 1991, new works go on view, and the Guggenheim will be reassessed in a new light.

Guinness World Records Exhibit Hall
Empire State Building (350 5th Ave.-34th St.) ☎ *947-2335. Map 5P4* 🖼 ✳ *Open daily 9am-10pm.*
Trafficking in predictable astonishments presented through video, film and replicas, the hall is an understandable favorite with those suffering a surfeit of profundity from other exhibitions. Compare yourself with life-sized photographs of the tallest, fattest, fastest humans, all under the rubric of the famous encyclopedia of trivia published by the Anglo-Irish brewer. It's fun, for a quick circuit.

Hall of Fame for Great Americans
Bronx Community College, 181st St., Bronx, NY 10453 ☎ *220-6187. Map 10B3* 🖼 *Open daily 10am-5pm.*
This neglected national monument was designed by Stanford White and dedicated in 1901, when the land it stood on was part of the new uptown campus of *New York University*. To attract the prestige coveted by its administration, the university decided to invent a memorial to Americans who had made substantial contributions to the arts, sciences, statesmanship and pedagogy. White conceived a semicircular Neo-Classical loggia, with busts

of national heroes such as Lincoln, Benjamin Franklin, Edison,
Thomas Paine and Alexander Graham Bell. To be considered for
inclusion, candidates must have been dead for at least 25yrs. The
campus is now Bronx Community College, part of the City
University of New York.

Harlem
Map 8H3.
At the turn of the century, Harlem was still a semirural district,
shrinking farms alternating with the summer homes of residents
of the city to the s. Blocks of tenements were spreading out from
the main streets, however, and shortly before World War I, they
began to fill with American blacks migrating from the harshly
segregationist South. Their lot improved little, but despite
unspeakable poverty, there existed a number of lively music halls
and nightclubs. During the 1920s and early 1930s, whites from
downtown engaged in the social ritual of dancing to jazz and
drinking bathtub gin at such places as the Cotton Club (in which
blacks worked and entertained but could not be patrons). Many
foreigners still cherish that romantic image, as unreal today as
that of cowboys pushing cattle herds through downtown Dallas.
    It is necessary to stress, therefore, that much of Harlem is
uninviting, its addicts and desperate unemployed posing a
constant threat to residents and outsiders alike. With notable
exceptions, it is emblematic of the failures of American society,
and is of interest primarily to visiting sociologists. That said, there
are isolated streets and institutions that deserve the attention
even of casual tourists. Among these are the museums of the
Audubon Terrace complex, the *Museo del Barrio, Aunt Len's
Doll and Toy Museum*, the **Schomburg Center for Research
in Black Culture** (*515 Lenox Ave. near 135th St.* ☎ *862-4000*),
the restored **Apollo Theater** (*253 W 125th St.* ☎ *749-5838*),
and the **Studio Museum** (*144 W 125th St. (5th Ave.)* ☎ *864-
4500*). Architectural restorations of note include the Victorian
cottage row of **Sylvan Terrace** near the *Morris-Jumel
Mansion* and the 1890s **St Nicholas Historic District**,
popularly known as Strivers' Row. The safest ways to see these
are by taxi, chauffeured car, or as part of conducted tours such as
those offered by the **Penny Sightseeing Co** (☎ *410-0800*).
    The district is bounded, roughly, by 96th St., 165th St.,
Broadway and the East and Harlem rivers. Spanish Harlem, called
El Barrio by its largely Puerto Rican residents, is the subdivision
from 5th Ave. to the East River and N to 125th St. Remnants of
Italian Harlem are found in the vicinity of the intersection of
116th St. and 2nd Ave.

Hayden Planetarium   Part of the *American Museum
of Natural History* complex, the Planetarium features "cosmic
laser concerts," as well as the more usual heavenly explorations.

Hispanic Society of America   Part of the complex
known as *Audubon Terrace*, this museum focuses on the
culture and history of the Iberian Peninsula rather than the
Spanish and Portuguese colonies of America.

Historical Society   See *New-York Historical Society*.

Holland Tunnel
Map 2S2 🚗
The first road tunnel (1927) under the Hudson River, and

therefore something of a technological feat, it links Jersey City and Canal St. in Manhattan. The longer, westbound tube is more than 1½ miles in length. Even though the air is changed by giant fans every 1½mins, few drivers envy the guards who take turns inside. The tunnel is named after the chief engineer.

International Center of Photography

1130 5th Ave. (94th St.), NY 10028 ☎ 860-1778. Map 7K4 ☒ ✗ Open Tues noon-8pm, Wed-Fri noon-5pm, Sat, Sun 11am-6pm.

One of New York's younger (1974) museums is housed in a 1914 Georgian-Federal house, its brick face and shutters made more attractive by contrast with the grandiose mansions that are customary along this stretch of 5th Ave. The expanding collection focuses on 20thC luminaries Ansel Adams, Irving Penn, Henri Cartier-Bresson, Weegee, and Robert Capa, and is supplemented by as many as 15 special-theme and one-person shows every year. Lectures, audiovisual presentations, workshops, and a book-and-print store contribute to the generally lively atmosphere. There is a smaller midtown branch (*77 W 45th St.* ☎ *536-6443* ☒).

Intrepid Sea-Air-Space Museum

Pier 86 Hudson River, end of W 46th St. ☎ 245-0072. Map 4O2 ☒ ✱ Open Wed-Sun 10am-5pm. Closed Mon-Tues.

The *Intrepid* is an aircraft carrier that first saw active service in the Pacific in World War II, with subsequent duty off Vietnam and as a recovery ship for space vehicles. Now decommissioned and permanently moored in the Hudson, it displays weaponry, warplanes and space hardware. Short films show the ship in action, and tours include the impressive control room and bridge.

Jacques Marchais Center of Tibetan Art

338 Lighthouse Ave., Staten Island, NY 10306 ☎ 718-987-3500. Map 12F2 ☒ ✗ by appointment. Open Apr-Nov Wed-Sun 1-5pm, other months by appointment. Closed Mon, Tues. Staten Island Ferry from Manhattan. Near Richmondtown Restoration. Take a taxi or S113 bus from ferry terminal.

The Staten Island Ferry is worth taking just for the breathtaking views it affords. But if an additional excuse is required, this museum should head the list. Within the relatively accurate replica of a Buddhist temple (1947) are exquisite bronzes, scrolls, painted silks, and religious books. Some objects are carved from human bones. Many are Tibetan in origin, but China, Nepal, and adjacent regions are also represented. Linger afterwards in the terraced gardens dotted with Oriental deities and animal sculptures. Jacques Marchais, the founder, was in fact a female (and American) art dealer, but in the 1940s a male (and French) name was a business asset.

Japan House

333 E 47th St. (1st Ave.), NY 10017 ☎ 832-1155. Map 5O5 ☒ ✗ by appointment. Open Tues-Sun 11am-5pm. Closed Mon. Longer hrs during exhibitions.

The contemplative and ordered *shibui* tradition flourishes in this otherwise electric neighborhood, with frequent loan exhibitions of such delicacies as *Noh* masks, decorated paper screens, scrolls, and diverse Shinto and Buddhist objects. Founded in 1907 to promote understanding between the two countries, the parent Japan Society has grown even more relevant with the influx of Japanese businessmen and their families, and the attendant adjustment problems. While symposiums, lectures and counseling programs are major features of the society's agenda, the art gallery is of greater interest to tourists. Frequently changed shows focus on everything from ceremonial swords and kimonos to contemporary photography and art films.

Jacob K. Javits Convention Center
655 W 34th St. (12th Ave.), NY 10001 ☎ 216-2000. Map 4P2.
A center for extra-large meetings and expositions was sorely needed by the city, and this contemporary crystal palace facing the Hudson was the solution. Designed by the noted I.M. Pei firm, its two main halls are the size of 15 football fields, and the lobby is high enough to shelter the Statue of Liberty. It is the venue of choice for such events as political conventions and auto shows. The only deficiency is its somewhat isolated location and the resultant difficulty in finding transportation.

Jewish Museum
*1109 5th Ave. (92nd St.), NY 10028 ☎ 860-1888. Map 7K4
▨ ▣ Tues 5-8pm ✗ Open Mon, Wed, Thurs noon-5pm, Tues noon-8pm, Sun 11am-6pm. Closed Fri, Sat.*
Within this conventional 1908 *château*, with its bland 1963 wing, is an important collection of Judaica that is of interest to people of all faiths. Special exhibitions of contemporary painting and sculpture are mounted on the first floor, beyond a vestibule that reproduces a section of a Persian synagogue, with lighted niches for Torah containers. The second floor is devoted to ceremonial objects, both intricately wrought and stunningly simple: wedding rings, Torah headpieces and crowns, circumcision instruments, 8-candle *menorahs*, prayer-holding *mezuzahs*, spice boxes, and amulets.

On the third floor is a mixture of folk arts, coins, medals, Torah arks, and artifacts of the Jewish experience in Colonial America and the Middle East. Especially poignant are reminders of the poverty of Lower East Side immigrants and the incomprehensible tragedy of the Holocaust. The 4th-floor exhibit, a diorama of Israel, created by schoolchildren, is both charming and enlightening.

Judson Memorial Baptist Church 🏛
55 Washington Sq. S (Sullivan St.), NY 10012 ☎ 477-0351. Map 2R4. Open Mon-Fri 9am-5pm. Closed Sat, Sun except for service at 11am; July-Aug closed Mon.
More than merely supportive of the cultural and political concerns of its **Greenwich Village** constituency, Judson initiates. Parishioners and ministers carry forth energetic programs in the arts and community affairs. Architects McKim, Mead & White elected a Venetian variation on their customary predilection for the Romanesque, and the 1892 facade continues to brighten the hodgepodge of Washington Sq. South. The adjacent campanile is now part of a **New York University** residence hall. A fundraising campaign is underway to enable urgently needed repairs of the roof, plumbing, and marble exterior.

Lever House 🏛
390 Park Ave. (53rd St.), NY 10022. Map 5N4.
In its way as difficult to miss as **St Bartholomew's Church** two blocks s, Lever House was in the forefront of the Bauhaus-

influenced third phase of skyscraper fever that seized the imagination of developers in the post-World War II years. The builders embraced the new glass-and-steel curtain wall technology, but with important variations. For one, they broke the unvarying high-rise canyon of Park Ave. by the astonishing decision not to use every bit of available air space. The wide side of the unadorned slab tower is turned s, at a right angle to the avenue, permitting air and sun to circulate. For another, the color is an unusual blue-emerald. In its totality, Lever House is the promise of the International Style that was to be denied by its descendants. Even architects Skidmore, Owings & Merrill infrequently matched their achievement in subsequent efforts.

Liberty Island   See *Statue of Liberty*.

Lincoln Center 𝍐
140 W 65th St. (Columbus Ave.), NY 10023. Map 6M3 ⊡ ✗
▆ ⇌ ☕ Open 10am-5pm; theaters various times and prices.

An ambitious conglomeration of six concert halls and theaters, the Lincoln Center for the Performing Arts is the home of the **Metropolitan Opera Company**, **New York Philharmonic Orchestra** and **New York City Opera and Ballet**. It also hosts a variety of visiting ballet and repertory companies, symphony orchestras, and popular and classical performing artists and events. No project of such magnitude, especially one concerned with the arts, could hope to sail from conception to realization without conflict. The Lincoln Center provoked dismay, outrage, and a chain reaction of second-guessing that persists to this day, all on a scale consistent with its monumentality.

It happened that in the post-World War II years, several of the city's premier performing arts organizations were seeking new premises. This need coincided with planners casting about for ways to arrest the decline of various Manhattan neighborhoods. The new United Nations Headquarters accomplished that on the *East Side*, helping to establish New York as a world capital of statesmanship. It seemed that the proposed Lincoln Center might do the same for the arts. On balance it has, allowing for quibbles over decor and acoustics. Admittedly, the architectural whole is more impressive than its parts, despite the participation of Eero Saarinen and Philip Johnson.

Approach is customarily made from Columbus Ave., up long, low steps into the main plaza. Most impressive at night, when the center fountain and facades are lit, the **New York State Theater** is on the left, **Avery Fisher Hall** on the right, and the rounded arches of the **Metropolitan Opera House** directly ahead. To reach the **Vivian Beaumont Theater** and **Mitzi Newhouse Theater**, cut between the Opera House and Avery Fisher Hall. The larger structure to the N is the **Juilliard School**, a prestigious arts college. The Beaumont building incorporates the research **Library and Museum of the Performing Arts**, a branch of the public library system. To the s of the Opera House is **Damrosch Park** with its **Guggenheim Band shell**. In warmer months, the pedestrian spaces are enlivened by outdoor cafés, ice cream kiosks and wandering street musicians.

To greater or lesser degree, the buildings reveal Classical inspiration informed by Modernist sensibilities, from austere to romantic in interpretation according to the predilections of their designers. Each enjoys the presence of large-scale artworks by notable painters and sculptors. Avery Fisher Hall, with the New

York Philharmonic in residence, has Richard Lippold's *Orpheus and Apollo*; the Opera House, two Marc Chagall murals; the New York State Theater, a Lee Bontecou and a Jasper Johns, among others.

Restaurants are the **Allegro Café** (*noon-8pm*) and **Fountain Café** (*noon-midnight*) in Avery Fisher Hall, and the **Grand Tier** (*open to ticketholders 2hrs before performances*) in the Opera House. Guided tours of the Center last approximately 1hr (☎ *877-1800 ext. 516*). Backstage tours of the Opera House are also available (☎ *582-3512*). Box office telephones are listed by theater under *Nightlife*.

Lincoln Tunnel
Map 4O1 ▨ *only when crossing W-E.*
The three tubes of the tunnel were completed in 1937, 1945 and 1957. That in the middle is the longest, at more than 1½ miles. They connect the city of Weehawken in New Jersey with W 38th St. in Manhattan, providing an additional Hudson River crossing.

Little Italy
Map 3S5.
Sicilian and Neapolitan immigrants made this their urban hamlet during the same period (1880-1925) that European Jews were establishing their Lower East Side community on the other side of *The Bowery*. Bounded on the w by Lafayette St., and by Houston St. and Canal St. to the N and S, the neighborhood is shrinking, but still vibrant. The quarter was always small, for arriving Italians and their children dispersed quickly throughout the five boroughs. But this warren of narrow streets and stunted tenements became symbolic of the Old Country and retains that flavor. Gray-haired women, dressed in black, clutch string bags as they move from fish store to bakery while their menfolk play *bocce* or sip espresso in murky coffee houses. The *Festa di San Gennaro* in Sept booms with brass bands and sizzles with booth after booth of sausage and *calzone*. (See *Walk 3* on pages 45-47.)

Lower East Side
Map 3R5.
Although immigrants of every race and nationality have made this shabby tenement district E of *The Bowery* and N of Canal St. their first stopover, its identity for many decades was East European Jewish. Millions of indigent Slavs, Poles, Russians and Lithuanians poured into these mean streets, from 1870 until harsh new laws stemmed the flow in the 1920s. They lived in 5-story buildings without plumbing, two or three families to an apartment, a population density that surpassed that of Calcutta. The lucky ones were pushcart peddlers, the others labored in the sweatshops of the garment trade. Yiddish was the prevailing tongue, and at one time there were 500 synagogues. Blacks and Hispanics now dominate, but a taste of that former era — and some remarkable shopping bargains — can be had along **Orchard St.** On Sun, the three blocks between **Delancy St.** and **E Houston St.** are the liveliest on the Lower East Side, so jammed with shoppers, residents, and merchants that cars are banned. Discount stores are the reason, most of them selling clothing, but also luggage, fabrics, shoes, and accessories. Bargain-seekers pick their way through the blare of salsa and disco music, past signs in at least four languages, beneath clothes hung above like heraldic banners. Designer items can be found at prices 20-50 percent below retail, if you are willing to accept

the inconveniences of communal changing rooms, shabby fixtures, and harried and often brusque sales people. Do not go on Fri or Sat, when almost everything is closed and the absence of crowds leaves the streets less safe and less interesting.

Madison Square Garden
8th Ave. (33rd St.), NY 10001 ☎ *564-4400. Map 4P3* ✖✖ ▬
Opening times vary according to events scheduled.
The present complex is the fourth version on the third site. Only the first two were even in the vicinity of Madison Square, nor did any of them have plants or flowers in sufficient quantities to justify the "Garden" label. In all its manifestations, from 1871 to the present day, Madison Square Garden has been concerned with sports and popular entertainment. It has a circus, ice shows, hockey, basketball, horse and dog competitions, rodeo, prizefighting, and rock concerts.

For no good reason, the architecturally imposing Penn Station was razed to street level in 1968 to permit the construction of this current insipid building. Incredibly, plans are afoot to abandon this structure and erect a *fifth* version.

Marble Collegiate Church 🏛 †
272 5th Ave. (29th St.), NY 10001 ☎ *686-2770. Map 5P4.*
Open Mon-Sat 9am-6pm, Sun for services only.
An 1854 edifice by Samuel A. Warner, it was commissioned by a congregation of the Dutch Reformed faith, which had its roots in the earliest settlement. The official landmark designation is due as much to age as to architectural worth. Consistent with its time, both Gothic and Romanesque motifs were used in a satisfactory (if not especially striking) blend.

Metropolitan Museum of Art 🏛 ★
5th Ave. (82nd St.), NY 10028 ☎ *879-5500 (office)*
☎ *535-7710 (recorded information)* ☎ *570-3949 (concerts, lectures). Map 7L4* ✖✖ ✗ *on rented tapes* ▬ ▬ ✦ ▬
entrance on 5th Ave. (80th St.). Open Sun, Tues-Thurs 9.30am-5.15pm, Fri, Sat 9.30am-8.45pm. Closed Mon and some holidays (check ahead) ▣ *children under 12 accompanied by adult. Photography without flash permitted, except at special temporary exhibitions.*
Grand in concept and numbing in scope, this is the largest repository of art and antiquities in the Western Hemisphere. There are 18 departments and 248 galleries, with well over one million prints, paintings, sculptures, furnishings, costumes, ceramics, musical instruments, armor and reassembled sections of ancient temples and palaces. Barely 25 percent of the collection is on view at any one time. There are, in addition, three libraries, two auditoriums, an art and book store, a gift store, a cafeteria, a restaurant with table service, and a snack shop. Concerts, films and lectures are also staged.

It might all be intimidating, were it not for an imaginative administration determined to enhance accessibility. Huge, colorful banners billow from the 5th Ave. facade, touting the two or three special exhibitions that are always on offer. These nearly always tie in with popular enthusiasms of the moment — Chinese costumes, the treasures of Tutankhamen, Viking artifacts — the better to draw infrequent museum-goers who are unfamiliar with the permanent exhibits. Galleries are laid out in an orderly manner; attendants are gracious and often speak other languages; and there are special programs for children and ready

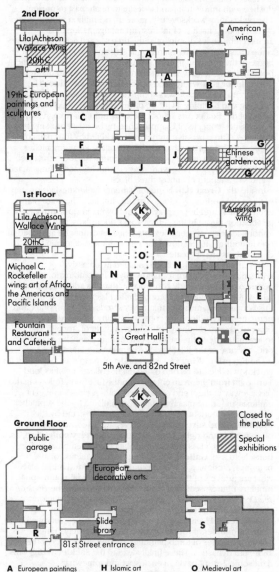

2nd Floor

Lila Acheson Wallace Wing
20th C art

19th C European paintings and sculptures

A

A'

B

B

C

D

F

H

I

J

J

G'

Chinese garden court

G

1st Floor

Lila Acheson Wallace Wing

20th C art

Michael C. Rockefeller wing: art of Africa, the Americas and Pacific Islands

Fountain Restaurant and Cafeteria

American wing

K

L

M

O

N

N

O

E

P

Great Hall

Q

Q

Q

5th Ave. and 82nd Street

Ground Floor

K

Public garage

European decorative arts.

Slide library

81st Street entrance

R

S

Closed to the public

Special exhibitions

A European paintings
B Musical instruments
C Drawings and prints
D Recent acquisitions
E Sackler wing
F Greek and Roman art
G Chinese paintings

H Islamic art
I Ancient Near Eastern art
J Asian art
K Lehman Pavilion
L French period rooms
M English period rooms
N European sculpture and decorative arts

O Medieval art
P Greek, Cypriot and Roman art
Q Egyptian Wing
R Uris Center for Education
S Costume Institute

access for older or disabled people. There is an air of authority flushed with innovation, and a desire to relate past to present. The philosophy works: yearly, more than 5 million people visit.

The building itself is of interest, an amalgamation of the architectural styles dominant at the time of each addition. Its core is the unassuming Ruskinian Gothic structure that was the first home of the museum in 1880. The only major edifice within the boundaries of Central Park, its front then faced W into the trees. This exterior is now enclosed by the **Lehman Pavilion**. The familiar 5th Ave. facade was completed in 1902, reorienting the building and dictating its future development. Best defined as being of the Beaux Arts school for its blending of Roman and Renaissance conceits, it is approached by broad steps rising from the street. Three massive arches are bracketed by four pairs of impressive columns with Corinthian capitals. Resulting niches were intended to house figures representing the four epochs of human history, but these were never commissioned. Wings reach N and S to a length of almost three blocks.

Inside, the **Great Hall** is the fulfillment of a Piranesi vision, but without the oppressive gloom that this implies. There are plants and benches, and huge sprays of cut flowers in stone urns. An information booth in the center stocks floor plans, and makes announcements of special events. The Met cannot be absorbed in one lightning tour. Sit down for a moment and determine which departments are of greatest appeal.

The curatorial staff has been engaged in a massive reorganization program for nearly 20yrs, in combination with a period of ambitious new construction that has added four major wings. Although this two-pronged effort is essentially complete, this is an organic museum that never stands still. Temporary and permanent exhibitions are constantly being mounted, and many other works are routinely shuffled in and out of storage. The following guide to the galleries can therefore only be a general one, because of the likelihood of frequent modification.

The **Egyptian Wing** (★) is as good a place to start as any, for it is acknowledged to be one of the major collections of its kind. Turn right from the main entrance on the first floor, following the passageway at the N end of the Great Hall. A child's innocent enthusiasm for the macabre may be stimulated by the sepulcher of Lord Chamberlain Per-nedbi that is seen first, and by the **mummies and sarcophagi** displayed in the corridors leading off to the left and right. There is a superb **jewelry collection**, as well as textiles, glass and ceramic objects of ceremonial and household use. **Gallery 31** is a long room of meticulous paintings, facsimiles of those found in temples and burial places. Next are artifacts of the Ptolemaic period, including numerous funerary figures, sculptures and reliefs. Papyri from the *Book of the Dead*, a compilation of medicinal formulas and religious rituals, date from around the 5thC BC.

Galleries 2-15 encompass the 1st-18th dynasties, followed by a similar number of rooms devoted to the delicately crafted reliefs, facsimiles of tomb paintings and funerary relics of the 18th-30th dynasties. These finally lead to the **Sackler Wing**. This handsome 2-story pavilion encloses (and somewhat overwhelms) the **Temple of Dendur**. A gift of the Egyptian government, it was painstakingly dismantled, pieces numbered and charted, and sent here for reassembly. Light, through a vast bank of glass in the N wall, bathes the temple and reflects on the water of the U-shaped pool that frames it. Reorganization continues in adjacent galleries.

To maintain historical sequence, return to the Great Hall and cross to **Gallery 11**, where a portion of the **Greek, Cypriot and Roman collection of statuary and ceramics** is on view. Many of these pieces were contributed by the first director of the museum, Luigi Palma di Cesnola, who was responsible for their discovery and excavation. Just beyond is the **Fountain Restaurant** (*open Sun, Tues-Thurs 11.30am-3.30pm, Fri-Sat 9.30am-8pm*) and **Cafeteria** (*open Sun, Tues-Thurs 9.30am-4.30pm, Fri-Sat 9.30am-8pm*).

Turn right, W, just before the restaurant and enter the **Michael C. Rockefeller Wing**. Opened in 1982, it houses, in 3,900sq.m (42,000sq.ft) of exhibition space, superb examples of the arts of Africa, Oceania and pre-European America. The wing, and much of the art within, were donated by Nelson A. Rockefeller and named after his son, who disappeared on an anthropological expedition in 1961. There are more than 1,500 objects on display, including Papuan masks of bark cloth and cane, Olmec jade and ceramic figurines, Mayan reliefs, wood carvings of Benin and the Ivory Coast, and Eskimo (Inuit) sculptures. These sprawling rooms adjoin the **Nathan Cummings Collection**, with a narrower but comprehensive focus on pre-Columbian art and artifacts of Mexico, Mesoamerica and South America. Stone sculptures, ornamental censers, ceremonial masks and North American Indian crafts are viewed in engrossing profusion.

Continuing W through the Rockefeller Wing, the new, 2-story (and mezzanine) **Lila Acheson Wallace Wing** is encountered. It houses part of the museum's growing collection of 20thC art, defined to include Europeans and Americans born in the 19thC, but who lived into this century. The range, therefore, includes sedate academic painters, Post-Impressionists, Cubists, and figurative painters, as well as Abstract Expressionists. There are works by Picasso, Max Beckmann, Thomas Hart Benton, Matisse, Georgia O'Keeffe and Pollock, which include such famous paintings as Picasso's portrait of *Gertrude Stein* and Ivan Albright's *Fleeting Time Has Left Me Cold*. An entire long room houses a single environmental work of the artist Robert Rauschenberg. It is titled ¼ *mile or 2 furlongs*, and since only approximately *one* furlong is on view, perhaps there is more to come. Another gallery devotes itself to modern design in architecture and furniture, and yet another to prints and drawing. There is a rooftop sculpture garden.

Return again to the Great Hall and go down the corridor to the right of the central staircase. This leads into the section devoted to **medieval art**. After a clockwise circuit of the tapestries and ecclesiastical objects, make your way to the **arms and armor gallery**, which is dominated by a mounted troop of knights, and augmented by heraldic banners, crossbows and other armaments.

A door in the N wall leads into the enclosed garden court of the **American Wing**. Trees, 19thC statues and a reflecting pool provide a quiet resting place beneath a glass roof. At the N end is the 1824 Greek Revival facade of a former Wall St. bank. Enter the door at the right to view portions of the most extraordinary collection of **American furniture and decorative arts** in existence. Three floors of 18 period rooms and 12 galleries proceed from Colonial times (1630) into the Federal period, ending c.1825.

Installations still in progress will carry the story forward to the early 20thC. Splendid Chippendale bureaux and paintings of the **Hudson River School** are joined with comprehensive assortments of silver, pewterware, antique glass, ceramics and textiles. For a chronological view, begin on the third floor of the wing and walk down.

Afterwards, leave the garden court by the doorway at the s corner. Pass through a large **gallery of European sculpture and decorative arts**, which covers essentially the same period as the American Wing. Bear right, then left, through the **English period rooms**. Just beyond is the entrance to the **Lehman Pavilion**, where Robert Lehman's collection of early Italian and 19th and 20thC French art is displayed in modern galleries and somber period rooms, the latter reconstructed from his house on W 54th St. Among the Italian works are drawings by Leonardo da Vinci and Botticelli. Of the later period, Ingres' *Portrait of the Princess of Broglie* is characteristic of his uncanny aptitude for naturalistic reproduction. The Fauvists, an Expressionist offshoot of Post-Impressionism, are represented by Vlaminck and Derain. A quick circuit of the wing is sufficient. Leave the door through which you entered, noting in passing the 1880 facade of the original museum building. Turn right into the **French period rooms**, which include a reconstructed 18thC Parisian shopfront, and boudoir furnishings commissioned by Marie-Antoinette. An adjoining room has additional **European sculpture and decorative arts**. Return to the Great Hall. This is a good interval at which to break off the visit, saving the rest for another day.

Picking up where we left off, mount the central staircase at the w of the Great Hall. Remarkable riches are confronted on the second floor, and the layout does not lend itself to a programed tour. Straight ahead are the enormously popular **galleries of European paintings**. They commence with large Baroque canvases of debatable content but undeniable drama. Continuing w, a maze of smaller galleries reveals the gems of the **Dutch collection**. Rembrandt's *Aristotle Contemplating a Bust of Homer* is the work of the artist's mature years, less theatrical than some of his earlier masterpieces. The concern with light remains, but it is a subtle mist, not a blinding shaft through clouds or portal. An oddity was Rembrandt's decision to clothe Aristotle in contemporary dress. The *1660 Self Portrait* (★) is an unsparing examination of his late middle age, the face pallid and corpulent, but with dignity intact. Vermeer was also intrigued by the properties of light, but in a narrow optical sense. The flesh of his *Young Woman with a Water Jug* (★) has the luminosity of an eggshell lit from within by a candle flame. Any emotional impact is vitiated by the serenity of his subject matter and compositions, but he inspires admiration for his flawless technique.

For powerful imagery, move on to the **Spanish section** and El Greco's *View of Toledo*. This was his only landscape and one of his greatest works — a big, somber canvas, which conveys an uneasy sense of foreboding through its lowering storm clouds. The portrait of *Juan de Pareja* (★) by Velázquez was acquired in 1970, the most costly single purchase the museum had made until that time. Velázquez was perhaps unequaled in his sensitive portrayal of character, and in this painting he focuses all his skill on bringing the humanity of a friend to eternal life.

The connecting **French galleries** include fine examples of Claude and Watteau, as well as Poussin's celebrated *Rape of the Sabine Women*.

Complete your tour of the European galleries with a wander through the **English rooms**, where portraits by Reynolds and Gainsborough hang alongside Turner's visionary cityscape, *The Grand Canal*.

To the N of these rooms is an enchanting accumulation of lutes, sitars, gongs, temple bells, nose flutes, sarindas and other exotic **musical instruments**. Return to the top of the central staircase and turn left into a corridor given to **recent acquisitions** and **drawings and prints**.

This empties into the **André Meyer galleries**, an important collection of 19thC European art. Turn left into a room of drawings by Degas, Renoir and Manet. In the center are Degas' bronzes of dancers — his favorite subject. Only one piece of Degas sculpture was exhibited in his lifetime, yet in this room alone are 12. In the second gallery is the charming miniature oil on wood, *The Dancing Class*, and a dozen more sculptures, all by Degas. The instinctive grace of his dancers is only made more profound by the odd angularity or awkward position, or the implied sheen of sweat brought on by endless repetition of exercises. Further confirmation of his mastery can be found in the third room, which is dominated by a large bronze figure (1922) with a tutu of real muslin.

Bearing right, you enter a large hall filled with heroic sculptures by Rodin and Maillol. Especially arresting is Rodin's tormented study of *Adam*. The rest of the Meyer galleries are devoted to paintings, a cornucopia of 19thC artistic fecundity. The transition away from both Classicism and Romanticism toward as yet unimagined frontiers is illustrated here in the manifold works of Corot and Courbet. The "Establishment" these artists competed with is also represented by the polished Neo-Classicism of Ingres. Despite Courbet's own strivings toward greater realism, he is said to have been dismayed by Manet's rejection of principles of perspective. In the 21 canvases by this younger artist, you can see striking concessions toward the two-dimensionality of the picture-plane. His flat, poster-ish portraits are almost devoid of shadow and simulated depth. Manet is often classified erroneously as an Impressionist, but his real kinship lies with such Post-Impressionists as Cézanne and Van Gogh, who are both equally well represented here. The scope and complexity of these works — most of them mounted in a large central room that does them full justice — is nothing less than breathtaking.

Eventually, these galleries lead into the **Islamic art collection**, the highlight of which is the **Syrian Nur Ad-Din House** (1707). The wall panels of the room produced here are modeled out of gesso, with ornate floral patterns and inscriptions in Arabic. Adjacent galleries show ceremonial vessels, chess pieces and silk carpets and hangings. Beyond the halls containing **Greek and Roman art** and **Ancient Near-Eastern art**, you reach the open balcony square above the Great Hall.

Continuing N past **Far-Eastern art**, go through the special exhibition areas until you arrive at the **Astor Court**. Yet another recent addition, it is a reconstruction of a Chinese garden of the Ming dynasty (1368-1644), based on an authentic example that still exists in Soochow. It is a pleasantly tranquil spot in which to pause for a while and reflect upon all that you have experienced so far within the walls of this vast treasure house.

Complete your tour by traveling two escalator flights down to the **Costume Institute**. Its biennial exhibitions have featured ancient Chinese garments, Parisian *haute couture*, and theatrical wardrobes.

Also down in the basement is the **Uris Center for Education**, created to introduce children and teenagers to the mysteries of art and history manifest in the floors above. There are frequent lectures and films intended to be shared with parents, as well as displays drawn from the larger collections.

Recorded cassette tours are available at moderate rentals, covering 21 subjects and galleries, some of them in languages other than English. There are also lectures, films and concerts ranging from discussions of painting techniques, to cinematic explorations of biblical and esthetic interrelationships, to recitals by the Juilliard Quartet. The museum takes on a festive, romantic air Fri and Sat evenings after 5pm, when the music of a string quartet fills the Great Hall, and cocktails are served on the candlelit balcony.

Midtown East
Map 5.
This concentration of corporate headquarters, foreign consulates, and publishing and advertising firms brings to it streams of business people and diplomats, and shoppers are inexorably drawn toward the fabled luxury emporia of 5th Ave. Coping with this influx are many of Manhattan's most exclusive hotels (**Palace**, **Waldorf-Astoria**, **Grand Hyatt**) and restaurants (**Four Seasons**, **Lutèce**, **Le Cygne**). It's also a residential area, but only for people who needn't concern themselves with the price of a second Mercedes. Penthouses with roof terraces, gardens and even swimming pools perch above the East River, their foliage visible from the streets. Principal sights are *St Patrick's Cathedral*, the *United Nations Headquarters*, *Grand Central Terminal*, and those exemplars of the International Style in architecture, *Lever House* and the *Seagram Building*.

Morris-Jumel Mansion 🏛
Jumel Terrace (near W 161st St.), NY 10032 ☎ 923-8008. Map 10E3 ▨ ✗ Open Tues-Sun 10am-4pm. Closed Mon. Subway 1 to 157th St.; B to 163rd St.-Amsterdam Ave.
Given its age (1768), Georgian core, and Federal overlay (1810), the mansion warrants attention for its architecture alone. But great historical figures lived and loved and dined here, and as is only fitting, ghosts are reported to have materialized. Roger Morris was the builder. Although a friend of George Washington, he was a loyal subject of the King and left the country at the outbreak of the Revolution. Both Washington and the British general Henry Clinton made the house their headquarters during the War. After a period of service as a tavern, it was bought by French wine merchant Stephen Jumel for his wife Eliza. They renovated the house in Federal style and filled it with Empire furniture, much of which is still here.

The Jumels held lavish parties and banquets, which encouraged New York Society to overlook the rumor that Eliza was the illegitimate child of a prostitute. She reportedly started an affair with Aaron Burr before Stephen died in 1832, surprising only in part because the former Vice President was then in his seventies. Scheming Eliza and the brilliantly devious Burr kept house for a while after Stephen's death, but it was not a happy match and he soon moved out. Burr's room is at the top of the stairs, and there is a portrait of Eliza in her 80th year. The ghosts? A Hessian soldier and Eliza herself. Perhaps they are aided by the secret passageways.

Murray Hill
Map 5P4.
A low-key residential quarter with indistinct boundaries, Murray Hill lacks the kind of attractions that capture the attention of developers and tourists. No doubt that suits the residents.

Following the usual progression from Colonial farmland to Federalist village to elegant suburb to bypassed backwater, Murray Hill managed to avoid the usually inevitable decay. Compressed by commercial development along the central N-S avenues, it is delineated, roughly, by Park Ave. and 3rd Ave. from 33rd St. to 42nd St. Strips of 19thC row houses and mews such as **Sniffen Court** (36th St., between Lexington and 3rd Aves.) have been transformed into quietly handsome private apartments and homes. Several good hotels trade the slightly out-of-the-way location for its relative tranquility, and a number of competent restaurants have opened in recent years.

Museo del Barrio
1230 5th Ave. (104th St.), NY 10029 ☎ *831-7272. Map 7J4* ▨ ✗ *Open Wed-Sun 11am-5pm. Closed Mon, Tues.*
The vitality of Hispanic culture is repeatedly validated by the changing exhibitions of photographs, paintings and crafts in this gallery of El Barrio (Spanish Harlem). Pre-Columbian figures and works by other modern Latin Americans broaden the appeal.

Museum of American Folk Art
2 Lincoln Square (Columbus Ave., between 65th and 66th Sts), NY 10023 ☎ *977-7298. Map 6M3* ▣ *Open 9am-9pm.*
Cast out of its crumbling former digs on W 54th St., the museum was without a home for three years. Now ensconced in a glass-enclosed plaza opposite Lincoln Center, it can once again display its charming collections of works by unschooled but talented American craftspeople from Colonial times to the present day. There is an enchanting assortment of weather vanes, carved and painted saints, whirligigs, toys, kitchen implements, quilts, store signs, bird decoys, and clean-lined furniture that predates the Danish Modern style by a century. Frequent temporary shows are mounted, and the popular gift shop sells examples of contemporary folk art — dolls, rugs, crafts — and has an excellent book selection. Permanent though it seems, this, too, is a way station. In 1992, the museum will move to still another facility, this one on W 53rd St., near the Museum of Modern Art. It is well worth following.

Museum of American Illustration
128 E 63rd St. (Lexington Ave.), NY 10021 ☎ *838-2560. Map 7M4* ▣ *Open Mon-Fri 10am-5pm, Tues 10am-8pm. Closed Sat, Sun, Aug.*
Rotating exhibitions of commercial art for books, magazines and print advertising are mounted, under the sponsorship of the Society of Illustrators. The permanent collection is augmented by theme shows and the eagerly-anticipated annual exhibition of award-winning works.

Museum of the American Indian   Presently part of
the *Audubon Terrace* complex, this has the largest collection of Native American artifacts in the United States.

Museum of Broadcasting
1 E 53rd St. (5th Ave.), NY 10022 ☎ *752-7684. Map 5N4* ▨ ✗ *by appointment* ✸ *Open Wed-Sat noon-5pm, Tues noon-8pm. Closed Sun, Mon. Mornings reserved for groups by appointment.*
More than 7,000 recorded radio and television programs from the 1920s to the present are available for transmission in 23

individual listening/viewing booths. Selected TV shows, changed daily, are presented on giant screens, usually illustrating a sociological, journalistic or dramaturgical point. Although the emphasis is on television, with particular attention to the years prior to the introduction of tape technology around 1960, there are recorded broadcasts by President Warren Harding and Lord Haw-Haw, as well as a lengthy catalog of commercials. While it might be wise to inquire about the availability of specific programs, no advance reservation is required.

Museum of the City of New York ★
5th Ave. (103rd St.), NY 10029 ☎ 534-1672. Map 7J4 🔳 *𝕏 ✳*
Open Tues-Sat 10am-5pm, Sun and holidays 1-5pm.
Closed Mon, major holidays.
A museum as lively as the city it celebrates, the five floors of this Neo-Georgian building are crammed with historical dioramas, antique playthings, model ships and decorative arts. Take the elevator to the top and work down.

On the fifth floor (which may still be closed for renovations) are two rooms from the first Rockefeller mansion, done up in High Victorian manner and featuring furnishings by English designer Charles Eastlake. On the third floor are the dollhouses and tiny trams, model farms and penny banks, miniature table settings and hobby horses. On the way out, linger over the Duncan Phyfe furniture, characterized by graceful curves, restrained inlays and stylized swags and lyres. Phyfe worked in Albany, NY and New York City from c.1783-1854, and borrowed from Hepplewhite, Sheraton and French Empire examples to formulate his own style.

The second floor has still more period rooms, ranging from the Colonial to the Theodore Roosevelt era. Model ships and displays trace maritime development from New Amsterdam onward, and spill over to the first floor. Space is left on the main floor for an engrossing multimedia presentation that spins through 400yrs of local history in barely 20mins, employing light, sound, and 24 synchronized projectors. Concerts and walking tours of the city are presented some Suns during warm weather.

After a visit, it may take a while to obtain a taxi, but the tawdry streets immediately E of the museum do not invite exploration.

Museum of Holography
11 Mercer St. (Canal St.), NY 10013 ☎ 925-0581. Map 2S4 🔳 *✳ Open Tues-Sun 11-6pm. Closed Mon.*
In its present state, holography may be only the first tentative flicker of a 21stC mass communication technique —film-in-the-round in your living room. Or it might be a technological trick that never develops beyond the level of a sideshow curiosity. At this unique museum, it is treated as an art form. Film is exposed to laser beams and mounted within a plastic cylinder. With illumination, the photographic image appears to be in three dimensions, changing as the observer walks around it. The effect is otherworldly and fascinating. Special exhibitions are mounted on a quarterly basis, with evening lectures.

Museum of Immigration   See *Statue of Liberty.*

Museum of Modern Art *(MOMA)* ★
11 W 53rd St. (6th Ave.), NY 10019 ☎ 708-9480 (current exhibitions) ☎ 708-9490 (films) ☎ 708-9500 (other info).
Map 5N4 🔳 *𝕏 ▣ Open Fri-Tues 11am-6pm, Thurs 11am-9pm. Closed Wed.*

Known with ironic affection by its acronym — MOMA — this daring and innovative museum first lobbied for the validity of modern art at a time when that belief was by no means conceded, then in later years assumed the role of arbiter. An artist represented in the collection is among the anointed, assured of at least a sliver of immortality.

It is alleged by some that the museum has retreated from the forward edge of the avant-garde, that it has grown conservative and protective of its stature. Evidence can be cited in support of that conclusion, but, given the uncertain directions of contemporary art over the last decade or two, caution is understandable. In any event, controversy is the life-blood of an institution such as MOMA.

Modern art is here defined as commencing with the Impressionists in the 1880s and, although the history of the many movements that have since evolved favors abstract and nonobjective modes, figurative options are also shown. Magic Realist Andrew Wyeth's *Christina's World*, for example, is one of the most popular canvases on view. The scope of the founders' intentions is demonstrated by the extensive film library and samples of superior design in such otherwise mundane objects as toasters and tableware.

An ambitious expansion program was recently completed, involving the construction of a new West Wing that nearly doubled gallery and storage space. About 30 percent of the permanent collection can now be placed on view.

The book and gift store is to the right of the main entry hall; the admission booths and information desk are straight ahead. Beyond these, an escalator takes you to two lower levels, housing the **René d'Harnoncourt Galleries**, which display temporary exhibitions, and the **Titus Theaters**. The glass wall bordering the hall gives access to the outdoor **sculpture garden**, a leafy retreat of pools and fountains dominated at the W end by Rodin's majestic *Balzac* and Gaston Lachaise's equally heroic *Standing Woman*. In counterpoint at the E end are monumental metal sculptures of more recent vintage, including works by Caro, Newman and Oldenburg.

To view the permanent exhibitions inside, return to the main hall. Take the escalator to the second floor and turn left into the first room of the painting and sculpture collection. Approximate chronological order of the development of modern art commences with the Post-Impressionists, represented here by *The Bather* and several smaller works of Cézanne. The next three galleries exhibit the work of Gauguin, Seurat, Redon, Toulouse-Lautrec (*La Goulue at the Moulin Rouge*) and Van Gogh (*The Starry Night*). A powerful study of three bathers by Derain dominates the smaller Matisses in the fourth room.

Next are the Cubists, primarily Georges Braque and Pablo Picasso. At the far wall, detour to the left to see Monet's vast angled triptych, and the only slightly smaller flat painting of his famous lily ponds. Retrace your steps and continue straight ahead, bearing right, past varied examples of Picasso's Cubist paintings and sculptures, large Léger canvases and a platform of sculptures by Brancusi. A large Chagall looks as fresh as if it were finished yesterday, however faint its Cubist elements. The Expressionists are highlighted by Wilhelm Lehmbruck's sculptures, *Kneeling Woman* and *Standing Youth*. Two rooms on, the eye must adjust to the linear geometrics and flat rectangles of 14 deceptively simple studies by Piet Mondrian. A large gallery, farther on, is devoted to Matisse; his vibrant tones

103

invest *The Red Studio* with delightful intimacy.

After two rooms of intriguing paintings by Klee, Kandinsky and Modigliani, another large space is devoted to Picasso. These astonishingly inventive sculptures and canvases show his advance beyond Cubism, as in the celebrated *Girl Before a Mirror* and *Head of a Woman*. His wrenching antiwar mural *Guernica*, installed here for more than 40yrs, has now been returned to Spain, in deference to the artist's wishes. But there is ample testimony to his genius in the works that remain.

Through the door to the right, a salon of Dadaists includes the once-shocking work of the French-born American Marcel Duchamp. Joan Miró is next, his light and witty work classified as Surrealist, but quite unlike the often dark visions of Dalí, Magritte and Pavel Tchelitchew that follow.

On the third floor, the American realists Andrew Wyeth and Edward Hopper are first on view, followed by abstractionist Stuart Davis. Bear left, then right, through two rooms of the early 1940s Abstract Expressionists, notably Newman, Gorky, Pousette-Dart, Rothko, De Kooning and Motherwell. Also displayed are works by the "Action Painter" Jackson Pollock, who galvanized the art world toward the end of that decade with his technique of applying paint in balletic swoops and traceries. A hiccup in the chronological layout, Room 6 contains Matisse's canvases jointly labeled *Swimming Pool*, but they are followed by more Abstract Expressionists.

The next large rooms are concerned with long-term rotating exhibitions of contemporary works that push the boundaries of even these mid-century pioneers. Expect to see assemblages by Robert Rauschenberg, plaster figures by George Segal, Jasper Johns' flag painting, Warhol's and Lichtenstein's Pop icons.

The architecture-and-design collection is displayed on the fourth floor, featuring industrial objects and handcrafted items of the last few decades; for example, bentwood chairs, Art Nouveau glass, office equipment, architect-designed furniture, television sets and even a 1946 Pinin Farina car. (A museum store annex at 37 W 53rd St., next to the American Craft Museum, sells objects deemed of similarly superior design.)

Museum of Natural History   See *American Museum of Natural History*.

New York Aquarium
Boardwalk (W 8th St.), Coney Island, Brooklyn, NY 11224
☎ *718-265-3474. Map 12F3* 🔳 💻 ♣ *Open 10am-5pm.*
From 1892 until 1941, the aquarium was in Castle Clinton (see *Castle Clinton National Monument*) in lower Manhattan. That monument was threatened by proposed highway construction, so the fish were transported to this new aquarium at *Coney Island*, on the southern rim of Brooklyn. It is a schizophrenic operation, part amusement center, part marine science laboratory. That does not diminish its appeal. Predictably, popular exhibits are the sharks, 2-ton Beluga whales, performing porpoises, and electric eels that light up bulbs. Some of them are flown to Florida for the winter, so the best time to go is between May and Oct.

New York Botanical Garden   Incorporating a river
and specialized gardens and ponds of astonishing diversity, these 250 acres constitute the northern half of the *Bronx Zoo and New York Botanical Garden* complex.

New York City Fire Museum

278 Spring St. (between Hudson St. and Varick St.), NY 10013 ☎ 691-1303. Map 2S3 ☑ ✱ Open Tues-Sat 10am-4pm. Closed Sun, Mon.

New York bristles with quirky and beguiling specialized museums tucked in out-of-the-way corners. They take little time to explore and often enchant in unexpected ways. This is one of them, and less difficult to locate than it used to be. The collection is the result of the recent merging of two smaller museums, in what was a former firehouse. A lovingly polished nickel-plated steam engine highlights the assembly of hand- and horse-drawn vehicles that date back to the 18thC, a time of great conflagrations in the city. Antique water pumpers, hose wagons, and examples of helmets and uniforms fill the rooms.

New-York Historical Society

170 Central Park W (77th St.), NY 10024 ☎ 873-3400. Map 6L3 ☒ Open Tues-Sun 10am-5pm. Closed Mon.

The name is misleading, for although the orientation is America as viewed from a New York perspective, the net is widely cast. Founded in 1804, the society moved to its present home in 1908. Although it lives in the shadow of the *American Museum of Natural History*, just across the street, the five floors of galleries are well worth perusal. Some galleries are open only on a rotating basis, and many objects that were once on view have been withdrawn, including the horsedrawn carriages formerly displayed in the basement. This is sadly due to a current need for financial retrenchment,

There are examples of folk art, period rooms, works in silver, Colonial maps and prints, early American toys and carvings, farm and household implements. The fourth floor is devoted primarily to portraits and landscapes by painters of the Hudson River School; the third floor has a collection of antique toys, far fewer in number than on display in the past, but entrancing nonetheless.

The highlight of the second floor is the **World of Tiffany** collection, with dozens of the valuable stained-glass lamps by the turn-of-the-century designer. On the walls of the entry hall are the drawings and watercolors of birds by the naturalist John James Audubon. On the ground floor, paintings, maps and drawings illustrate the city's growth from the days of Dutch rule.

New York Public Library

5th Ave. (42nd St.), NY 10018 ☎ 790-6161. Map 5O4 🗶 Open Mon-Wed 10am-9pm, Thurs-Sat 10am-6pm. Closed Sun, holidays.

The city-wide library system has more than 6 million volumes and three times as many related materials — much of it in this, the main branch. They are housed in what many regard as *the* paradigm of the Beaux Arts style that was in vogue at the beginning of the 20thC. Certainly its 5th Ave. facade is more subdued than that of the flamboyant *Metropolitan Museum of Art*. Beyond the famous pair of reclining lions (sometimes called Patience and Fortitude), long steps and a terrace lead up to the Roman portico.

The library is for reference, not for lending, but there are frequent exhibitions of books and prints. A copy of the Declaration of Independence written by Thomas Jefferson is on view, as is a desk once owned by Charles Dickens. *Bryant Park* is on the other side of the block.

New York University 🏛

Washington Sq., NY 10003 ☎ 598-3127. Map 2R4. Open Mon-Sat 8am-9pm. Closed Sun.

Founded in 1831, New York University is one of the largest private universities in the country. Its first permanent home was a Gothic Revival pile at the NE corner of **Washington Square** in Greenwich Village (see **Walk 4** on pages 47-49.). That was replaced by the present structure in 1894.

Over the last century, expansion has been unremitting, with a postgraduate School of Business Administration in the **Financial District**, a medical-dental complex on the **East Side**, a respected Institute of Fine Arts on 5th Ave., and a second campus in The Bronx. Fiscal difficulties in the 1970s forced the sale of the Bronx campus and other smaller units, but the university retains ownership of most of the buildings on the E and S sides of Washington Sq., as far over as Broadway and down to Houston St. In recent years, the university has enjoyed a markedly enhanced perception of its academic stature. The schools of law and medicine are ranked among the best in the nation. Distinguished teachers and graduates have included Samuel Morse, Thomas Wolfe, Jonas Salk, Joseph Heller, Albert Sabin, Lillian Hellman and Edward Koch.

Numismatic Society   See **American Numismatic Society.**

Oases

Walking the streets of Manhattan can come to feel like a mental and physical pummeling. Tranquil retreats abound when feet and legs are ready to give out, places to sit or plan or read awhile — and they are free. Churches and libraries (see **Useful addresses** on pages 17-18) are obvious choices. Here are some others.

AT&T Building
550 Madison Ave. (55th St.).
Tables and chairs are available all around the street-level arcade, protected from rain and snow, but not the cold.

Crystal Pavilion
805 3rd Ave. (50th St.).
A three-level atrium offers tables and chairs, artificial waterfalls, plants, and several stores and restaurants.

Ford Foundation
42nd St.(between 1st & 2nd Ave.).
One of the first enclosed atriums is a jungle of trees and plantings, with a pool. Open Mon-Fri 9am-5pm.

Hotel Parker Meridien
118 W 57th St. (near 6th Ave.).
To gain building code variances, the developers included a walk-through public atrium lined with tables and chairs. There are rest rooms down the stairs to the right.

IBM Garden Plaza
590 Madison Ave. (56th St.).
Tall bamboo trees, flowers, chairs, and — scarcest of commodities — clean public rest rooms.

New School for Social Research
66 W 12th St. (near 6th Ave.).
Pass through the lobby, with chairs and telephones, to the terrace and sculpture garden beyond.

Olympic Tower
645 5th Ave. (51st St.).
Another office building atrium, with a waterfall and cafés.

United States Courthouse
40 Center St. (Foley Square).
Rest rooms, seating, snacks — all in or off the main lobby — but you have to pass through a metal detector to gain entrance.

Whitney Museum at Equitable Tower
7th Ave. & 51st St.
Similar facilities to **Olympic Tower**, above.

Whitney Museum of American Art at Philip Morris
Park Ave. & 42nd St. (opposite Grand Central Terminal).
One of several neighborhood branches of the Whitney, this is a high-ceilinged gallery with sculptures by contemporary Americans. Several tables and chairs are placed about, there is a coffee bar, and it's air conditioned.

World Financial Center
Battery Park City.
The splendid **Winter Garden** is one of the city's great new urban spaces, with benches and restaurants beneath towering palm trees.

Old Merchant's House

29 E 4th St. (Broadway), NY 10543 ☎ 777-1089. Map 2R4 ▨ Open Sun 1-4pm, other times by appointment. Closed Aug.
No one seems to be certain, but the house is attributed to Minard Lafever, pre-eminent architect of the early 19thC. The design falls between Federal and Greek Revival, and was completed as a speculation in 1832. Merchant Seabury Tredwell bought it in 1835. His family lived here until 1933, and since then it has been restored and preserved by the Historic Landmark Society. The original furnishings and floor coverings are still in place, and there is an intriguing secret passage.

Paley Park

3 E 53rd St. (5th Ave.). Map 5N4. Open Mon-Sat 8am-6pm. Closed Sun, Jan.
A chunk of valuable midtown real estate was here employed, not as a multistory garage or apartment building, but as an enclosed "pocket" park. The combination of trees, tables, chairs and simulated waterfall was underwritten by the former chairman of the board of the Columbia Broadcasting System and was presented as a gift to the people of New York City. It is so popular there is often a line.

Pan Am Building 血

200 Park Ave. (45th St.), NY 10017. Map 5O4 ◩ ¥ Open 6am-2am.
Praise has not been the Pan Am's lot, even before its completion in 1963. By forming a visual octagonal wall across Park Ave., it does almost nothing right. The fact that Bauhaus doyen Walter Gropius had a hand in it is little compensation. A fatal accident in 1977 even ended its rooftop heliport function.

Pierpont Morgan Library 血

29 E 36th St. (5th Ave.), NY 10016 ☎ 685-0610. Map 5P4 ▨ Open Tues-Sat 10.30am-5pm, Sun 1-5pm. Closed Aug, Mon, and Sun in July.
One of the quiet pleasures of subdued *Murray Hill*, the library was constructed for financier J. Pierpont Morgan in 1902 by the omnipresent firm of McKim, Mead & White. The Neo-Classical design reflects Pierpont Morgan's passion for the Italian

Renaissance. An unobtrusive 1928 addition was finished 15yrs after his death, and a nearby 45-room mansion, purchased in 1988, will soon double the size of the facility.

Consistent with its name, the building is primarily a repository of rare books, illuminated manuscripts, and other documents of the Middle Ages and Renaissance, but there is also a great deal more that warrants attention: stained glass, sculpture, enamel- and metal-work, and a number of somber Italian and Flemish paintings. The **West Room**, with its carved, painted ceiling and red damask curtains, has been kept exactly as it was during Pierpont Morgan's lifetime.

Planetarium, Hayden   See *American Museum of Natural History*.

Police Academy Museum
235 E 20th St. (2nd Ave.), NY 10003 ☎ 477-9753. Map 5Q5
🖼 ✱ Open Mon-Fri 9am-3pm. Closed Sat, Sun, holidays.
Installed on the 2nd floor of the city's police academy, where fledgling cops trot briskly and earnestly down the halls between classes, the museum makes a forthright depiction of crime prevention and punishment in New York. Displays of the improvised weapons used by teenage street gangs are mixed with semihistorical lethal artifacts of the gangster era. Much of the material is unlabeled, and the collection is modest in scope, so don't make a special trip. It is an opportunity to eavesdrop on cop talk, however.

Prospect Park
W of Flatbush Ave., Brooklyn. Map 12E3. Subway D, M, QB to Prospect Park.
Frederick Law Olmsted and Calvert Vaux collaborated on this landscape design (1866-74), as they had on the larger *Central Park* in Manhattan. Many think this is the better of the two, with fewer roads and a more imaginative composition of wooded glades, water, and pathways. A small **zoo** established in 1935 along Flatbush Ave. contains elephants, zebras, monkeys and bears (☎ *965-6560, open 11am-4pm; call ahead, as restoration is underway*).

Nearby is the **Lefferts Homestead**, built in 1783 in the Dutch Colonial style, and fitted out with period furnishings (☎ *965-6560, open Wed-Sun 10am-4pm, Jan-Mar open weekends only; closed Mon, Tues*).

In gentler times, this bucolic setting adjacent to the *Brooklyn Museum* and *Brooklyn Botanic Garden* would constitute a rare urban retreat. Sad to say, it is the victim of frequent acts of vandalism and lack of funds. Go only during daylight.

Queensboro Bridge
Map 5N5 🖼
Once it was possible to drive halfway along this bridge over the East River and turn right into an elevator that lowered to **Roosevelt Island** (formerly Welfare Island). For safety and security reasons, that service was ended in the mid-1970s, when the island became home to an ambitious new residential community, called Southtown, which was an attempt to integrate all economic classes in new housing financed by both public and private funds. No cars are allowed, and travel to and from the island is now by cable car and a new subway line. The bridge, symbolic of *East Side* glamor, appears in dozens of old movies.

Queens-Midtown Tunnel
Map 5O5 🚇
This two-tube, four-lane East River tunnel is of note only because it is likely to be the one used by arrivals from LaGuardia and JFK airports. It emerges between 36th and 37th Sts. in Manhattan.

RCA Building
After a change in corporate ownership, this Rockefeller Center skyscraper is now known as the *GE Building.*

Richmondtown Restoration 🏛 ★
441 Clarke Ave., Staten Island, NY 10306 🕿 *718-351-1611. Map 12F2* 🚇 ✗ *by appointment* 🖭 ✱ *Open Wed-Fri 10am-5pm, Sat, Sun, and holidays falling on Mon 1-5pm. Closed Mon, Tues and other major holidays. Ferry from Battery Park. Take a taxi or 113 bus from the Staten Island Ferry terminal.*
Eventually this is to be a museum village of more than 30 buildings — restored, reconstructed, reassembled, re-created — ranging from the early Colonial period up to the 19thC. The Staten Island Historical Society has been working on this project for 40yrs, and while progress is painstakingly slow, the rewards are evident. Several buildings are fully furnished and open to the public, among them a colorful general store and a 1696 elementary school. Costumed artisans give demonstrations in pottery, leatherwork, weaving and printing. The grounds include a mill pond, and picnicking is encouraged.

Riverside Church 🏛 ✝
490 Riverside Dr. (122nd St.), NY 10027 🕿 *222-5900. Map 8I2* 🚇 *Open 8am-10pm.*
Despite the 74-bell carillon and 20-ton bell at its top (both the largest of their kind anywhere in the world), the 120m (392ft) tower of this interdenominational church looks vaguely like a Gothic 1930s office building — and is, in part. There is an **observation deck**, which affords a sweeping panorama of the Hudson River from Wall St. to the *George Washington Bridge* (*open Mon-Sat 11am-3pm, Sun 12.30-3pm* 🕿 *749-7000 for times of carillon performances*).

Riverside Park
Maps 8&10E-F1-2.
New Yorkers owe an eternal debt to Frederick Law Olmsted and Calvert Vaux, the 19thC landscape architects who created *Central Park, Prospect Park* in Brooklyn, and this sylvan strip of trees and hills bordering the Hudson River. It runs from W 72nd St. to W 125th St., banked to the E by a wall of handsome apartment houses and blemished only by the Hudson Parkway, which was built along its length in the 1930s. The **Soldiers and Sailors Monument** (*W 89th St.*) and *General Grant National Memorial* (*W 122nd St.*) are within its boundaries.

Rockefeller Center 🏛 ★
Map 5O4.
John D. Rockefeller Jr. put together the grand scheme for this 22-acre compound of office towers — a "city within the city." It has an ordered integrity that is in sharp contrast to such flashy later edifices as *Trump Tower*. The heart of the complex is between 5th and 6th Aves. and 49th and 50th Sts. Here are found the sights familiar from tourist literature, most of them completed

in the 1930s. Dominating is the *GE Building* (the former **RCA Building**), facing E. While it does not compare in scale or inventiveness with the contemporary *Chrysler Building*, it bears a mantle of restrained elegance. At the NW corner of its base is the Art Deco **Radio City Music Hall**, with a breathtaking vaulted interior in which rock concerts and elaborate revues are staged. To the E, directly in front of the entrance, is a sunken plaza, which is an ice-skating rink in winter and an outdoor café in summer. A gold statue of *Prometheus* floats above. At the approach of Christmas, a tree more than 21m (70ft) high is placed behind him. Still farther E, banks of plants and flowers take up the center of a pedestrian mall that ends at 5th Ave. (See *Walk 1* on page 42.)

St Bartholomew's Church 🏛 ✝

*109 E 50th St. (Park Ave.), NY 10022 ☎ 751-1616. Map **5O4** Open 8am-6pm. Closes 3pm during major holidays after Sun services.*

Providing a welcome antidote to the slab-sided canyon of midtown Park Ave., this pinkish pile of glorious Byzantine-Romanesque excess features Stanford White's **triple portals** (1903), salvaged from an earlier church by James Renwick, located downtown on 24th St. The present church opened in 1919, and the prominent dome was finished in 1930. See it quickly, for the Episcopalian church has financial problems, and developers are casting covetous eyes. Concerts take place some Sunday and Tuesday afternoons.

St Mark's-In-The-Bowery 🏛 ✝

*2nd Ave. (10th St.), NY 10003 ☎ 674-8112. Map **3R5**. Open 9am-5pm.*

One of the oldest houses of worship in Manhattan, this church was built on farmland in 1799. The basic structure of the building is Federal, with a Greek Revival steeple added in 1828. Dutch Director-General Peter Stuyvesant is buried here, in ground that he once owned. A fire in 1978 destroyed much of the roof and interior of the church, but costly restoration has returned it to its former condition. There is a long, and continuing, tradition here of music, poetry and dance.

St Patrick's Cathedral 🏛 ✝ ★

*5th Ave. (51st St.), NY 10022 ☎ 753-2261. Map **5N4** except by prior approval. Open 7am-8pm.*

When James Renwick submitted his drawings in 1850, the fashion for Gothic Revival was on the wane. By the time the cathedral was completed in 1888, it must have seemed dated. No matter, for the style returned to favor soon afterward, and by then St Patrick's was already in the ranks of the timeless. Echoing great cathedrals of Europe (for Renwick formulated his ideas after intense study of European examples), it is part lacy stonework, part soaring caprice, part massive pretense. Authenticity might have demanded flying buttresses, but the site would not accommodate them and they were not required structurally, for the roof was lighter than in the earlier Gothic prototypes.

The siting of the cathedral was to cause consternation in some quarters. At the time, Irish immigration had reached sufficient proportions to be threatening to the Protestant majority. The latter found it distasteful in the extreme to endure such a blatant monument to the Roman faith, especially in the midst of a neighborhood chosen by the wealthy as refuge from the masses downtown. In time, both groups came to uneasy union, in the face of succeeding waves of even less familiar creeds.

St Paul's Chapel ▥ †
Broadway (Fulton St.), NY 10002 ☎ 285-0874. Map 2U4.
Open 8am-3.45pm.
The only existing nonresidential building in New York that
predates the Revolution (1766), it holds its own against the
silvery glass curtain walls of the *World Trade Center*, at least
when viewed from street level. Made of Manhattan schist
quarried at the site, the exterior facing is brownstone. Apart from
the steeple, added in 1794, it is authentic Georgian, inside and
out, although the blue and pink paint was perhaps not always so
vivid. Architect Thomas McBean is believed to have been a pupil
of James Gibbs, who designed St Martin-in-the-Fields in London.

Chandeliers of Waterford crystal dominate the interior, and the
altar screen (1787) is by Pierre L'Enfant, the Frenchman who later
planned Washington, DC. George Washington put in frequent
appearances during his first presidential term. His pew is marked.
The graveyard is a shaded resting place for footsore souls still
living, and there are lunchtime concerts of classical music on
Mon, Tues and Thurs.

Seagram Building ▥
375 Park Ave. (52nd St.), NY 10022. Map 5N4.
First came *Lever House*, just across Park Ave., then the Seagram
(1958). After them, the glass-and-metal box International Style
went downhill, swallowed up in greed and misinterpretation of
its deceptive simplicity. (For confirmation of that conclusion,
simply look s to the *Pan Am Building*.) The Plaza in front of the
Seagram may appear banal but, considering the almost
unbelievable cost of midtown property, even this much walking
space seems generous. The narrow slab looming above is the
color of well-aged bourbon, consistent with the preoccupation of
the client, a prominent distiller. Ludwig Mies van der Rohe was
the architect, Philip Johnson his assistant.

Snug Harbor Cultural Center ▥
914 Richmond Terrace, Staten Island, NY 10301
☎ 718-448-2500. Map 12E2 ▣ to grounds and most
exhibitions ▣ some exhibitions and performances. Open
8am-dusk ✗ weekends. Ferry from Battery Park. Take a
taxi or S1 bus from the Staten Island Ferry terminal.
Sailor's Snug Harbor, a wealthy charitable foundation providing
shelter for retired merchant seamen, purchased these 80
waterfront acres in 1831. The organizers proceeded to build, in a
grand manner that might seem inconsistent with their mission.
Their dedication left a trove of more than 20 contiguous
buildings representative of the Greek Revival, Italianate, Victorian
and Beaux Arts modes. One of the architects was Minard Lafever,
as prominent in the early 19thC as Stanford White, 75yrs later.

Now renamed and designated a National Historic Landmark
District, Snug Harbor is still in the process of often-tentative
conversion to an arts center. Should all the acquired buildings be
utilized eventually for that purpose, it would be an
unprecedented complex. As it is, only a few galleries are
presently in use, and on a limited schedule. Fiscal concerns and
public indifference appear to be frustrating the great plans of the
trustees. In the meantime, the complex is a compressed lesson in
19thC architecture.

SoHo ★
Map 2S4.

Whoever coined the name no doubt had the famous London quarter in mind, but the two places have little in common. This "SoHo" is a contraction of "SOuth of HOuston St." (Incidentally, that street is pronounced "HOWston," not "HEWston.") Barely three decades ago, SoHo was a dreary industrial district with broken concrete sidewalks piled high with boxes of refuse and pot-holed streets of worn Belgian blocks. Trucks backed into loading bays, rows of sewing and die-cutting machines clattered and thumped behind grimy windows, crates of fabrics and plastics were trundled about by forklifts and bowed backs. At night, everyone left.

Apart from the condition of the streets and those buildings that have thus far escaped renovation, that description no longer applies. In the early 1960s, artists of the New York School, no longer content with easel painting in conventional studios, sought ever-larger work space. The problem was cost. They discovered the lofts of what was then called "The Valley" — 5- to 10-floor buildings with vast unpartitioned rooms designed for warehouses, shipping firms and labor-intensive light industries. Marginal businesses were closing up, and artists moved in. This was illegal, according to zoning laws. Yet they doubled their transgression by adding living spaces to their new studios, installing bathrooms and kitchens. Hanging plants and curtains were glimpsed from the streets. In due course, other artists with similar needs — film-makers, dancers, sculptors — followed the leaders.

By 1970, the trickle became a torrent. Since the municipal authorities could no longer ignore the fact that their ordinances were being violated, they simply changed them. Bona fide artists *could* now live in the converted lofts.

SoHo went from cultural work place to artistic community to general free-for-all in just a few years. Bars, restaurants, food and craft stores catering to artists were supplemented by branches of established uptown galleries. Stockbrokers and lawyers bought up the lofts and fitted them out with saunas, billiard tables, and luxury bathrooms. Rents skyrocketed and many artists left. Nevertheless SoHo remains a vital, passionate community, despite pretentious boutiques and eating places that charge breathtaking prices.

Saturday is the time to go, for the art-lover's ritual gallery tour and a drink at an engaging pub. (See *Guide to the galleries* on page 29.) Along the way, observe the **cast-iron facades** for which the district is also known. After a brief mid-19thC period during which SoHo was the fashionable center of town, hotels and stores were displaced by factory buildings. To dress them up, iron-cast motifs taken from European palaces were prefabricated in sections and assembled on the site, apparently an American innovation. Entire buildings were erected in four or five months by this method. Although they proved to be not fireproof and the technique was abandoned in the early 20thC, more than 200 examples survive. They are notable for their **gargoyles**, **Corinthian columns**, and **ornamentation** and **sculptural detail** taken from Venetian, Romanesque and French Second Empire examples. Most of them are within an official landmark district created by the city to ensure their preservation.

SoHo is bounded by Houston St., Canal St., Sullivan St. and Broadway. The main street is West Broadway, and the oldest house (1806) is at 107 Spring St.

South Street Seaport 🏛 ★
*Museum Visitor's Center: 12 Fulton St. (between South St.
and Front St.), NY 10038 ☎ 669-9424 for recorded
information. Map 3U5 🎫 ✗ 🍴 ♣ ☕ ⇌ 🕊 Museum
buildings open 10am-5pm. Closed Christmas and New
Year's Day.*

A living museum-in-progress, the Seaport contributes mightily to
the resurrection of lower Manhattan as a place to live and stroll
and cherish. Beginning with a group of volunteers interested in
preserving a segment of New York's maritime past, an alliance
was forged with commercial interests to underwrite restoration of
some of the last remaining blocks of early 19thC buildings and of
a growing collection of antique sailing vessels. The largely
salutary result is an expanding neighborhood of tasteful shops
and restaurants that has proven to be immensely popular with
both natives and visitors. Standing just s of the Brooklyn Bridge,
its appeal has at its heart seven ships of the early steam and
clipper days, all docked in the East River. Their masts and spidery
rigging stand in arresting contrast to the majestic backdrop of
Wall St. skyscrapers. Most of them are in a seemingly endless
process of renovation and ongoing maintenance, but they easily
convey a sense of the romantic epoch that made the city the
busiest port in the New World.

Most of the ships can be boarded by visitors. Prides of the fleet
are the four-masted, metal-hulled bark *Peking* and the classic
1885 square-rigger *Wavertree.* Among the others are the 1906
lightship *Ambrose* and an 1893 fishing schooner, the *Lettie G.
Howard.* Cruises of the harbor can be taken aboard replicas of
the paddlewheeler *Andrew Fletcher* or the steamboat *De Witt
Clinton* (*Apr-Nov* ☎ 406-3434) and on the schooner *Pioneer*
(*May-Sept* ☎ 669-9400). They vary in length from 90mins-3hrs,
including twilight cocktail cruises and evening music cruises.
Combination museum and cruise tickets are available. Jazz
concerts are among the special events held during the warmer
months.

Seafarers required land-based support services, and the
developers have taken them into account. Restoration is nearly
complete on the 11-block official national historic district
adjacent to the piers. More than $5 million has been spent on
quayside rows of Greek Revival, Georgian, Federal and Victorian
warehouses and ships' chandleries. Venerable **Schermerhorn
Row** and **Front St.** have undergone careful renovation, with
much of their interior space given over to retail enterprises. A
new 3-story structure was opened in 1983. Dubbed the **"Fulton
Market,"** it is crammed with specialty food stores and sidewalk
cafés. Nearby is what remains of the old Fulton Fish Market,
source of most of the fresh seafood served in Manhattan's better
restaurants.

The **Cannon's Walk** block of buildings opposite the Fulton
Market is partly old, partly new, and contains a variety of stores,
exhibition galleries, and a theater showing a slick multiscreen
film about the evolution of the district, entitled *The Seaport
Experience.* Another 3-story pavilion, **Pier 17**, was erected on an
overwater platform N of the ships. Opened in 1985, it contains
100 stores and restaurants. (See *Walk 2* on pages 42-45.)

Spanish Institute
*684 Park Ave. (68th St.), NY 10021 ☎ 628-0420. Map 7M4
🔲 Open Mon-Sat 11am-6pm. Closed Sun.*
The home of the Center for American-Spanish Affairs is an

architectural echo of the neighboring neo-Georgian structure, erected in 1926. Frequent lectures, recitals and art exhibits showcase Spanish writers, poets and artists. Classes are offered in Spanish and Catalan.

Staten Island Zoo
613 Broadway (Forrest Ave.), Staten Island, NY 10310
☎ *718-442-3100. Map 12E2* 🔁 🅭 *on Wed* ✱ *Open 10am-*
4.45pm. Ferry from Battery Park. Take a taxi or 107 bus
from the Staten Island Ferry terminal.
Specialization can make otherwise modest institutions rival grander establishments blessed with better resources. Although this zoo is of principal interest to residents of Staten Island, its reptile collection rivals any in the US. There are specimens of every known type of rattlesnake, an aquarium and a well-regarded collection of birds.

Statue of Liberty ★
Liberty Island, New York Harbor, NY 10004 ☎ *732-1236.*
Map 12D3 🔁 🅭 *Open 9am-6pm. Ferry from Battery*
Park every 30mins 10am-4pm. Tickets sold in Castle
Clinton National Monument.
A description of "Miss Liberty" is as enlightening as one of a telephone. Everyone knows what she looks like, although the first sight of her is undiminished by *déjà vu*. French sculptor Auguste Bartholdi created her out of thin, beaten copper panels, with the engineering counsel of Gustave Eiffel, a man of recognized expertise in such matters. At 46m (151ft), the statue dwarfs that wonder of the ancient world, the Colossus of Rhodes. Extensive renovation prepared her for the 1986 centennial.

While the cost of the statue itself was underwritten by French contributions, the American public was slow to come up with the requisite matching funds to build the pedestal. It took nearly 20yrs from its first conception to the unveiling, in 1885. The statue weighs 225 tons, each eye is 75cm (2ft 6in) wide, and the tip of the upraised torch is 120m (395ft) above sea level. Inside, an elevator carries visitors halfway up, and 168 steps lead to the perforated crown. This gives a remarkable view of the bay, from the *Verrazano Narrows Bridge* to the spires of Manhattan. The *American Museum of Immigration* is housed in the points of the star-shaped base. Its exhibits emphasize the contributions, rather than the travails, of the immigrants who created a nation. Their story is told by photographs, dioramas, slide shows, and other displays. Visitors on ferries leaving after 2pm for the Statue of Liberty may not be able to get up to the crown due to long lines. Waits can be as long as 2-3hrs.

Temple Emanu-El
5th Ave. (65th St.), NY 10021 ☎ *744-1400. Map 7M4. Open*
10am-5pm; services Fri 5.15pm, Sat 10.30am. For services,
enter by 5th Ave. door; at other times, by E 65th St. door.
The largest Reform Jewish synagogue in North America, it can accommodate 2,500 worshipers. Limestone is the primary material, buttressed by steel. Its size is the principal attraction for sightseers, given the ambiguity of its half-Turkish, half-Italianate make-up.

Theater District
Map 4O3.
Depending upon context, Broadway is either the city's longest

avenue or a synonym for the theatrical district through which it passes on its diagonal slash through midtown. And **Times Square** is essentially the intersection of that famous street and 7th Ave.

Within the area bounded by 40th St., 55th St., 6th Ave. and 8th Ave. are many large movie houses and most of the major legitimate theaters. The huge electrified signs and marquees that gave Times Square the sobriquet "Great White Way" are still there, although they now advertise Japanese cameras and electronic gadgets more than coming attractions. Crowds of gawkers, New Jersey teenagers, matinee ladies from the suburbs, French sailors, winos, hustlers, and tourists from everywhere, fill the streets. On New Year's Eve, they are wall-to-wall, more than 100,000 strong (but watch it on television).

Despite repeated efforts to clean it up, 42nd St. between 7th and 8th Aves. remains a sludge of pornographic movie houses, prostitutes, addicts and troublemakers. Avoid it, and the northerly stretch of 8th Ave. it joins, but don't be deterred from seeing a show on the streets nearby. Restaurants in the area cater to every taste and budget. Few are more than middling-good, most are noisy, but they specialize in pre- and post-show meals.

Theodore Roosevelt Birthplace
28 E 20th St. (5th Ave.), NY 10003 ☎ 260-1616. Map 5Q4 ✉ ✗ Open Wed-Sun 9am-5pm. Closed Mon, Tues.
The 26th President (1901-9) was born in this house in 1858 and lived here until 1873. The Roosevelts were a large and wealthy family even then, and this Greek Revival house, rebuilt to original specifications, reflects that prosperity. In the five period rooms open to the public, careful attention has been paid to authenticity. The parlor is agleam with crystal chandeliers and gilt-framed mirrors. Plump horsehair sofas and chairs are arranged in inviting groups, and fringed satin curtains frame the tall windows. The result is a faithful impression of elegant solidity consistent with the time and social class of its original occupants.

Trophies reflect Roosevelt's roles of rancher, big-game hunter, explorer and soldier. Tiger and bear skins cover the floor of one room, and there are branding irons, a stuffed lion, uniforms and cavalry bugles. Yet this complex man — a progressive Republican at home, an imperialist abroad — was above all a dedicated public servant. One glass case after another, filled with campaign buttons, public documents, family records and letters, and newspaper cartoons, attests to the energy he applied to that calling. (See also *Gramercy Park*.)

Tibetan Museum   See *Jacques Marchais Center of Tibetan Art*.

TriBeCa
Map 2T4.
When the artists who resurrected *SoHo* were forced out by landlords and speculators who saw the profits to be realized in sales to non-artists with regular incomes, many simply moved a few blocks s and w. They called their new homestead TriBeCa, for "TRIangle BElow CAnal St." Inevitably, the SoHo phenomenon is asserting itself, with galleries, bars, restaurants and funky nightclubs. Down here, where streets have names instead of numbers and the straightforward grid of uptown does not apply, the approximate boundaries are West St. to Church St. and Barclay St. to Canal St.

Trinity Church 🏛
Broadway (Wall St.), NY 10006 ☎ 285-0872. Map 2U4 ✗
Open 7am-6pm ⬚ Museum open 9-11.45am, 1-3.45pm,
Sat 10am-3.45pm, Sun 1-3.45pm.

The first Trinity Church was erected here in 1698, entirely of wood. That burned down in 1776, in the first of the two great fires that decimated old New York. The second version was razed in 1839, and the present Gothic Revival manifestation (by Richard Upjohn) went up in 1846. No one has seriously considered washing the outside since, and the red sandstone is now so black it nearly shines. Over the intervening years, additions have included a chapel (1913) and bronze entry doors (1894) modeled on those of the Baptistry in Florence. A small museum displays photographs and artifacts relating to the history of the church. Pause in the graveyard (now under renovation) for a glance at the memorials to statesman Alexander Hamilton and steamboat inventor Robert Fulton.

Trump Tower
725 5th Ave. (56th St.) ☎ 832-2000. Map 5N4 ⬚ ▯ ⇌
Open Mon-Sat 8am-10pm. Closed Sun.

Only one of many monuments built by, and dedicated to, New York's most visible multimillionaire, this office-residence-store tower characteristically falls on the glittery side of luxe. Donald Trump has never been accused of restraint nor reclusiveness, and his showmanship, revealed in this flossy structure, begins with exterior terraced stepbacks from the 3rd through to the 8th floors, each planted with trees and ivy. Inside, more real trees line the entrance hall, which leads to an atrium aglint with brass and polished marble and a 3-story waterfall cascading into a sunken courtyard. There is a bistro-style café down below, and a restaurant on the 5th floor. On the intervening floors there are representatives of such pricey shops as Cartier, Blantre, Charles Jourdan and Abercrombie & Fitch.

Ukrainian Museum
203 2nd Ave. (12th St.), NY 10003 ☎ 228-0110. Map 3R5 ⬚
Open Wed-Sat 1-5pm. Closed Mon, Tues.

Embroidery is the specialty — on garments, textiles and ritual panels — but the intricately decorated Easter eggs are equally entrancing. There are two galleries, also featuring folk carvings and metalwork.

Union Square
Map 5Q4.

In the 1930s, the 3.6-acre park was a vigorous if shabby version of Speakers' Corner in London's Hyde Park. Anarchists, trade unionists, radicals and simple eccentrics mounted soapboxes and endured hecklers. Its decline accelerated after World War II, and it eventually became the habitat of drug peddlers and prostitutes. An increased police presence and a major beautification project completed in 1985 encouraged families and office workers to return there, and new restaurants and stores have opened.

United Nations Headquarters
1st Ave. (45th St.), NY 10017 ☎ 754-1234. Map 5O5 ⬚ ✗
⇌ ▯ Open 9am-5.20pm.

John D. Rockefeller Jr. donated the East River site, and the first three buildings were ready for occupation in 1952. Despite the presence of a number of significant works of art by Marc Chagall and Barbara Hepworth, the overall visual effect of the complex is somewhat vapid, in the manner of quasi-governmental edifices.

Most offices and rooms are closed to the public, but are of little general interest. The library is open to scholars and journalists. 1hr tours with multilingual guides leave about every 10mins from the Main Lobby of the **General Assembly Building**. That is the low structure with the concave roofline to the N of the simple slab of the **Secretariat Building**. The latter is probably the more familiar from photographs.

Tickets to sessions of the General Assembly, the Security Council and certain other meetings can be obtained at the Information Desk shortly beforehand. (*Admission is free, but on a first-come basis; starting times are usually 10.30am and 3pm.*) The opening of the General Assembly, usually Mon of the third week in Sept, is the most intriguing time to go.

Outsiders can lunch at the Delegates' Dining Room on the top floor of the **Conference Building**, which sits astride the FDR Drive at the edge of the river. They are seated in order of arrival; no reservations are accepted (*lunch only, Mon-Fri*). A coffee shop in the public concourse is open daily (*9.30am-5pm*). Nearby stores sell souvenirs, books, UN postage stamps, and handicrafts of many nations.

Upper West Side
Map 6J2.

Of all the recently resurgent neighborhoods — *SoHo*, *TriBeCa*, *Chelsea*, **Park Slope** in Brooklyn — the Upper West Side most resists easy classification. It is too large, for one thing — from Central Park W to the Hudson River, and from 59th St. to as far N as 120th St., according to some definitions. Secondly, it lacks the handy ethnic, social or cultural identity of other districts. Well-to-do refugees from the more fashionable *East Side* have long lived here, in such still desirable apartment houses as the gabled *Dakota Apartments*. But they understandably chose the narrow strips along *Central Park* and Riverside Drive, and the blocks in the middle were allowed to fester.

Many people mark the renaissance of the Upper West Side from the completion of the *Lincoln Center* (1966), and this event was no doubt influential. Another factor was the escalating rents of Greenwich Village, which drove out writers and other professionals associated with publishing and communications. The newcomers spruced up their apartments, their buildings, even whole blocks. They opened gourmet and book stores and brought new life to those already there. Pubs of sufficient atmosphere attracted customers whose conversation was of royalty contracts and writer's block. Dim, woody bistros featuring allegedly Provençal cuisine proliferated at such a rate that natives used to refer to one stretch of Columbus Ave. as "Quiche Alley." Ratification of the area's new-found panache was the arrival of Eastsiders, who not long ago were insisting that only the imminent demise of a close relative would cause them to cross Central Park.

Diversity continues, with smart boutiques beside seedy but colorful *bodegas*, working-men's bars adjoining glittery singles' hangouts, upper-crust Bohemians jostling with welfare mothers in corner delis. Important sights and institutions include the *American Museum of Natural History*, the *New-York Historical Society*, the *Cathedral Church of St John The Divine*, *Columbia University*, *General Grant National Memorial* and the city's grandest boulevard, Riverside Drive.

Van Cortlandt Mansion and Museum 🏛

Van Cortlandt Park (242nd St. and Broadway), Bronx, NY 10471 ☎ 543-3344. Map 13B4 🔲 ✗ Open Tues-Sat 10am-4.45pm, Sun noon-4.45pm. Closed Mon. Hours may vary: see below. Subway 1 to 242nd St.-Van Cortlandt Park.

George Washington spent a lot of time in and around New York, usually with British troops hot on his heels. This country house (1748), with its deceptively modest stone exterior, served as one of his headquarters, as did the *Morris-Jumel Mansion* in Manhattan. It has elements of the Dutch Colonial style, but is essentially Georgian. Note the carved faces in the window keystones. Unlike most of the city's historic houses, it remains in a preserved rural setting, although the nearby meadows are now playing fields. Nine rooms are open to the public, including a cellar kitchen with a Dutch oven, and a parlor with a spinet and excellent Chippendale pieces. On display are Delftware and English china, crewelwork, cooking implements, a dollhouse and unusual cupboard bed. Recently renovated and under new administration, the opening hours may vary; call ahead.

Verrazano Narrows Bridge

Map 12E2-3 🔲 only when crossing W-E.

When opened in 1964, it became the longest suspension bridge in the world. England's Humber Bridge surpassed it in 1981. Two decks and 12 lanes link Staten Island and points w with the Belt Parkway in Brooklyn. Giovanni da Verrazano was an Italian explorer in French employment, who is believed to have been the first European to sail into the bay. The New York Marathon starts at the w end of the bridge in Nov.

Villard Houses (Palace Hotel) 🏛

451 Madison Ave. (51st St.), NY 10022. Map 5N4.

This U-shaped Italian Renaissance palace, commissioned by German-born financier Henry Villard, was a departure for the firm of McKim, Mead & White. As the most popular architects of the late 19thC, they had dabbled in most revivalist styles except this one. In effect, these are six connected brownstone houses unified by a Roman esthetic. After various changes of ownership, they were purchased by Harry Helmsley. He was prevailed upon to restore them and erect his **Palace Hotel** to the E. The houses were incorporated into the overall design and became part of the hotel. The cost was substantial, but the result is a triumph of enlightened development.

Washington Square 🏛

Map 2R4.

Now it is the heart of *Greenwich Village* — playground, meeting place, open-air venue for street musicians, de facto campus of *New York University*. Over the centuries, it has been put to many uses, including hunting preserve, potter's field, public execution place and military parade ground. Brick Greek Revival row houses of the 1830s survive along the N side. Stanford White's **Washington Arch** (1892) marks the s end of 5th Ave., while Philip Johnson's **Bobst Library** dominates the SE corner. (See *Walk 4* on pages 47-49.)

Wave Hill Center for Environmental Studies

675 W 249th St. (Independence Ave.), Bronx 10071 ☎ 549-3200 Map 13B4 🔲 Sat and Sun 🔯 weekdays. Open 10am-4.30pm; longer in summer, so check ahead.

A distinguished estate with sweeping views of the Hudson River and the craggy cliffs called the Palisades, Wave Hill has been home to a British UN ambassador as well as Mark Twain and Theodore Roosevelt. Its 28 acres were bequeathed to the city of New York for use as an environmental study center. Nature trails and gardens are open to the public, and an outdoor sculpture exhibition is mounted every summer. Concerts are scheduled occasionally, some live and some recorded programs by another former resident, Arturo Toscanini. Call ahead for events, as listings are difficult to find in local publications, and funding difficulties may affect future plans. A visit can be co-ordinated with one to nearby *Van Cortlandt Mansion*.

Whitney Museum of American Art 🏛 ★

*Madison Ave. (75th St.), NY 10021 ☎ 570-3676 (general information), ☎ 570-0637 (film information). Map **7M4*** 🔲 *Tues 6-8pm and at all times for senior citizens and students* 🔳 *at all other times* 🕑 *Open Tues 1pm-8pm, Wed-Sat 11am-5pm, Sun noon-6pm. Closed Mon, holidays.* The nation's foremost repository of solely American modern art is a subject of virtually unending internal and external controversy, lately revolving around its incumbent leadership and a planned addition to the landmark building. Depending upon whose interests are promoted — or ignored — the show called the Whitney Biennial is predictably cited as presumptuous, bland, stunning, inept and seminal. The ambitious survey of art by currently active painters and sculptors rarely fails to outrage or dismay the creative community, which may be fairly taken as evidence that the museum is doing something right. As befits the basic premise, the exhibition has ranged from such luminaries of the moment as James Rosenquist and Wayne Thiebaud to fresh unheralded talents, from the arrestingly experimental to polyresin sculpture so lifelike it all but breathes. There are, in addition, avant-garde films, slide and video presentations of "site works" by conceptual artists, and dance programs and events that endeavor to push conventions beyond their limits. The Biennial is normally held from late Jan to mid-Apr.

At other times, works of particular schools and trends are exhibited. They are supplemented by rotated selections from the permanent collection. Virtually every major American talent since 1900 is represented. Among the later artists are Willem de Kooning, Louise Nevelson, David Smith, Andy Warhol and Hans Hofmann; the earlier ones include Stuart Davis, Edward Hopper, George Bellows and Reginald Marsh. But the strength of the Whitney lies in its refusal to settle back and wait for artists to establish themselves. The trustees take chances, from acquiring kapok-and-vinyl "soft" sculptures, to rooms of randomly-tuned radios, to heaps of fabric and timber. In the process, they make curious choices, but their nerve is refreshing.

All this came about through the energy and commitment of Gertrude Vanderbilt Whitney, a sculptress who happened to be rich. She began by expanding her studio in *Greenwich Village* into exhibition space and purchasing the work of unacknowledged young artists. Periodic moves to larger premises led from 8th St. to 54th St. to the present location. As is often true of New York museums, the Whitney building (1966) is as provocative as the creations it houses. Marcel Breuer met the requirements of his clients with the sort of unconventional solution for which he was noted. The building is sheer on three sides, but the facade rises in three cantilevered tiers from the moated patio below street level, the top floor looming over the sidewalk and the suspended bridge connecting sidewalk with lobby. The granite sheathing is pierced by asymmetrically placed trapezoidal windows. Interior walls are, in part, raw concrete, bearing the impressions of the grains of the forming planks.

Some 50 Alexander Calder mobiles and stabiles are positioned around the courtyard and can be seen through the tall plate glass windows of the basement floor. A new wing is planned.

A small airy cafeteria edged with potted trees serves lunch, snacks and cocktails. The Whitney has three smaller branches (*33 Maiden Lane in the Wall St. district; opposite Grand Central Station at 125 Park Ave at 42nd St.; and in the Equitable Center at 787 7th Ave. and 51st St.*).

Woolworth Building 🏛

233 Broadway (Barclay St.), NY 10007. Map 2T4 🔲 Open Mon-Fri 9am-5pm. Closed Sat, Sun.

Although best known as the consulting architect for the *George Washington Bridge*, Cass Gilbert was a favorite of tycoons and Federal bureaucrats, largely on account of his unabashed enthusiasm for the Neo-Classicism in vogue during the 50yrs bracketing the turn of the century. His 1907 Beaux Arts **US Customs House** (next to *Bowling Green*) bows only to the *Metropolitan Museum of Art* in effusive grandeur. It is said that he drew inspiration for that design from the Paris Opera House, and there is little question that the British Houses of Parliament played a role in his Woolworth commission. Replete with Gothic traceries and terra-cotta gargoyles, a blend of modern technology and stylistic nostalgia that so often fails, this "Cathedral of Commerce" is one of the most successful of the first generation of skyscrapers.

From its completion in 1913 until the opening of the *Chrysler Building* in 1930, Woolworth's monument to himself and his empire of nickel-and-dime stores was the tallest in the world. The observation floor has long been closed to the public, but you can step into the lobby to admire the terra-cotta and marble walls, bronze ornamentation, and vaulted ceiling.

World Financial Center 🏛

Battery Park City (West St., between Vesey and Liberty Sts.), NY 10048 ☎ 945-0505. Map 2U4 🔲 ⇌ 🖳 Open 7am-1am.

An ambitious cluster of buildings that contributes mightily to the resurgence of lower Manhattan as a place to live and play as well as work, this new complex is the centerpiece of the multi-use Battery Park landfill development. It stands opposite the *World Trade Center*, at the cusp of the Hudson. Included in its beguilements are a marina for those who can afford such extravagances, an unobstructed vista of the Statue of Liberty and Ellis Island, 40 shops, and, at last count, seven restaurants, including the already celebrated **Hudson River Club** (☎ 786-1500).

All these cluster around the fabulous **Winter Garden**, a stunning urban space rivaling *Grand Central Terminal* and *Rockefeller Center*. Under its vaulted glass-and-steel roof is a grove of palm trees, each at least 60ft high, yet dwarfed by the soaring atrium. Cafés are gathered around them, for a cappuccino or a full meal, and a gleaming marble staircase rises at the E end. Music, art exhibits, and other entertainments are frequently staged. The Garden is especially dramatic at sunset, as it is oriented w, looking toward the New Jersey shore and the Lady in the Harbor.

World Trade Center 🏛

Church St. (Liberty St.), NY 10007 ☎ *466-7377. Map 2U4* 🚇
◄€ ☰☰ 💻 ✳ *Observation decks open 9.30am-11.30pm.*
Long before their completion in 1974, the twin towers of the World Trade Center encountered censure, on both esthetic and environmental grounds. They were visually banal, displaced a thriving market district of little charm but much vitality, threw the lower Manhattan skyline out of balance, and placed unnecessary strain on public transportation and services.

Those complaints are now irrelevant. Rentable space was leased, stores and restaurants were installed, and there is not a more stunning vista in the urban world. At 411m (1,350ft) they are eight stories taller than the *Empire State Building*, but were surmounted within months by the Sears Building in Chicago.

The **observation decks** are in 2 World Trade Center, and nearly 2 million visitors a year take the quarter-mile trip to the summit. There is an **enclosed deck** on the 107th floor, and an open rooftop promenade on the 110th. The latter is not for the vertiginous, nor is it open in blustery or otherwise inclement weather. On a clear day, you can see 75-100 miles. Most of the 40 stores and 22 restaurants are at ground level or below, but the **Windows on the World** restaurant in 1 World Trade Center takes advantage of the views from the 107th floor.

The **Vista International Hotel** between the towers opened in early 1981, the first important downtown hotel in more than 100yrs.

Yeshiva University

187th St. (Amsterdam Ave.), NY 10033 ☎ *960-5400. Map 10C3. Subway 1 to 181 or 191 Sts.*
This is both the largest and the oldest Jewish university in the Western Hemisphere, and it first began in 1886 as a seminary called Yeshiva Eitz Chaim. Now a fully-fledged university with more than 7,000 students engaged in both undergraduate and postgraduate studies, it still maintains reverence for its origins while drawing wide respect for its courses in medicine and the mathematical sciences. The main building is a Moorish-Byzantine extravaganza of tiles, cupolas, minarets, domes and arches, completed in 1928.

Yeshiva University Museum
Yeshiva University Library, 2520 Amsterdam Ave., NY 10033 ☎ *960-5390* 🚇 *Open Tues-Thurs 11am-5pm, Sun noon-6pm. Closed Mon, Fri, Sat.*
A rich collection focuses on the Jewish experience, through photography, religious objects, paintings, and scale models of ten famous synagogues of the ancient world.

Yorkville

Map 7L5.
Germans were among the earliest substantial 19thC immigrant groups, and many settled in this Upper East Side district centering on 86th St. They were speedily assimilated, and had largely dispersed by the 1930s. Traces of their occupation remain, with a *bierstube* or two, several bakery-coffee houses, and some dark-paneled restaurants specializing in *wienerschnitzel* and *sauerbraten*. Prodigals return for the **Steuben Day** parade in mid-Sept.

Where to stay

An unprecedented surge in hotel construction signaled the emergence of the city from the miasma of the 1970s. It hasn't abated. At least 20 major new hotels are set for completion by 1992, many in areas, such as **SoHo** and the **Financial District**, where few or none presently exist. The **Times Square** area alone has attracted five, in addition to the monster **Marriott Marquis** and the several others already in place. Most will be large, but a parallel trend is to smaller, luxury hotels operated in the European manner: examples are **The Mark** and **Parc Fifty One**.

Most of these thousands of new rooms are of the super-deluxe (||||||) category, however, and there's the rub. New York already has the highest room rates in the nation, but with occupancy levels steady at more than 75 percent, there is little incentive to lower prices. Those budget accommodations that do exist are almost invariably mean and soulless, and there are few enough even of those. Little is available that might be compared in cost and homeyness to family-run Italian *pensioni*. There are efforts to rectify this situation. For one possibility, see *Bed & Breakfast* at the end of this section.

Otherwise, the best that can be expected in the inexpensive and lower mid-priced price categories is a reasonably clean room with minimal amenities: no more than a private shower, air conditioning, and a TV set; and none of those is certain. Some of the better hotels in this category (in price bands |■□ and |■□) are listed under *Further recommendations* on page 135.

At the other end of the scale, full baths, ankle-deep carpets, and meticulous housekeeping are the rule, and such additional touches as refrigerators, fresh-cut flowers, closed-circuit movies, and mints at the bedside are common. While 24hr room service is widely available at this level, canny travelers tend to avoid using it. Breakfast, for example, can easily cost four times what it does at a coffee shop around the corner. The same *caveat* applies to snacks or bottles of liquor or wine purchased in the hotel rather than from an independent store.

Whatever their classification, a majority of the worthiest choices are found in midtown **Manhattan**, in an area bounded by 3rd Ave. and 7th Ave. from 38th St. to 60th St. There is a scattering through the **Upper East Side**, a handful w of **Times Sq.** and a half-dozen motels near the **airports**. Rates are moderated somewhat by location, season, and duration of stay. To make up for the absence of businessmen, for example, hotels devise weekend package plans to attract suburbanites and tourists with such extras as theater tickets or brunches, and up to 40 percent off standard room rates. Availability of discounts fluctuates with occupancy levels, obviously, and finding a room at any price can be a chore between Apr and Oct, especially on short notice. On those occasions, it is wise to inquire at hotels outside the immediate midtown area, particularly those in the **Gramercy Park** and **Murray Hill** districts. Ideally, reservations should be made at least a month in advance.

Children under 16 often may stay in their parents' room at little or no extra charge. Ask when reserving. Several hotels have swimming pools and other recreational facilities to keep teenagers occupied, and lists of baby-sitters are customarily available. Dogs and other pets are usually prohibited or discouraged. Garage parking is rarely free, and most levy an in-and-out charge when cars are used.

Sales and occupancy taxes add 18.25 percent plus $2 to room bills. Tipping is expected, need it be said, but is not especially complicated. Tip the bellman about $1 per bag, and something extra if they are heavy. A doorman expects something for merely opening a car door, and about $1 if he devotes some time to hailing a taxi. Add 15 percent to the bill for room service waiters unless a service charge is added. Chambermaids are accustomed to receiving about $1 per night for routine cleaning. Unless stated otherwise, all the hotels listed below have elevators, air conditioning (▤), private baths, room TV (▢) and telephone (▣), and accept American Express (AE), Diners Club (◑) and other major credit cards. A 1989 state law allowed hotels to install minibars in their guestrooms, and many of them now offer that amenity. Nearly all these hotels have facilities for disabled persons (&), at least in terms of access. Many have rooms with wider doors and modified bathrooms. Inquire when reserving. Similarly, all but the smallest hotels have conference rooms for at least small groups, and most can supply audiovisual and related equipment.

Hotels classified by area

Lower Manhattan (below 14th St.)
Vista International ////
Gramercy Park/Murray Hill (E 14th St.-E 42nd St.)
Doral Court //// ✿
Doral Park Avenue ////
Doral Tuscany ////
Gramercy Park ///▢
Morgan's ////
Sheraton Park Avenue ////
Lower West Side (W 14th St.-W 42nd St.)
New York Penta ////
Midtown East (E 42nd St.-E 59th St.)
Berkshire Place ////
Beverly /▢ ✿
Grand Hyatt //// 🕮
Halloran House ///▢
Inter-Continental ////
Leow's Summit //▢
Lexington ///▢
Middletowne ///▢ ✿
New York Helmsley ////
Palace //// 🕮 🏛
Peninsula //// 🕮
Plaza //// 🕮
Roger Smith Winthrop ///▢ to ////
St Regis-Sheraton //// 🕮
Swissôtel Drake ////
United Nations Plaza //// 🕮
Waldorf Astoria ▤/// to //// 🕮
Midtown West (W 42nd St.-W 59th St.)
Algonquin ///▢
Dorset ////

Essex House ////
Helmsley Park Lane ////
🕮
Holiday Inn Crowne Plaza ////
Howard Johnson's //▢ ✿
Milford Plaza /▢
New York Hilton ////
Novotel ///▢
Omni Park Central ////
Parc Fifty One //// 🕮
Parker Meridien //// to ////
Ramada Inn /▢
Ritz-Carlton ////
St Moritz ////
Salisbury /▢ ✿
Sheraton Centre ////
Sheraton City Squire ////
Warwick ///▢ to ///▢
Wyndham /▢ to //▢ ✿
Upper East Side (E 60th St.-E 95th St.)
Barbizon //▢
Carlyle //// 🕮
Lowell ////
Mark, The //// to //// 🕮
Mayfair Regent //// 🕮
Pierre ////
Plaza Athénée //// 🕮
Regency //// 🕮
Stanhope //// 🕮
Wales /▢ ✿
Westbury //// 🕮
Upper West Side (W 60th St.-W 96th St.)
Mayflower ///▢ ✿

Algonquin
59 W 44th St. (near 5th Ave.), NY 10036 ☎ 840-6800 or 800-448-8355 ✆66582 🖷944-1419. Map 504 ///▢ 200 rms ▤ ▢ ⇌

Location: Near Grand Central Terminal. Dorothy Parker, George Kaufman, Robert Benchley and others traded japes and aphorisms around the famous Round Table

Hotels

here. That is history. But this turn-of-the-century hotel is still the clubby choice of many literary and theater folk. The lobby, crowded with sofas, wing chairs and ill-matched tables, has the feel of a well-used country inn. Afternoon tea and cocktails can be taken there. A bell on each table summons the waiter. While many of the baths retain their ancient fixtures, extensive redecoration and renovation by the new owners is perking up the once-shabby rooms. While an evening in the **Oak Room** cabaret is a treat, dining at the hotel is not, unless one has a taste for bangers and bubble and squeak.
🍷 🍴 ♪

Barbizon
140 E 63rd St. (Lexington Ave.), NY 10021 ☎ *838-5700 or 800-344-1212* ◉ *220060* ⊛ *753-0360. Map 7M4* ▥ *342 rms* ▣ ⇌
Location: At center of the Upper East Side. The Gothic and Romanesque architectural details of the exterior, speak of a past era when the Barbizon was a sanctuary for young ladies of gentle breeding. Men were allowed only in the lobby, to which residents were summoned when their escorts arrived. That was a time between chaperones and the sexual revolution, which proved fatal to such enterprises. Now, after protracted renovations in the mid-1980s, the Barbizon is a first-class hotel open to all. Standard rooms are small, but with their creamy color schemes and uncluttered furnishings, they manage not to feel cramped. Even in their costlier configurations, they represent a substantial savings over the better-known luxury hostelries in the vicinity. That may change, for new owners have announced plans to transform the hotel into a European-style spa. In the meantime, some suites have terraces and kitchenettes,and a number of rooms have good views.
« 🍷 ♪

Berkshire Place
21 E 52nd St. (Madison Ave.), NY 10022 ☎ *753-5800 or 800-843-6664* ◉ *710-581-5256* ⊛ *308-9473. Map 5N4* ▥ *420 rms* ▣ ⇌
Location: Near Rockefeller Center, St Patrick's Cathedral. Formerly a no-nonsense executive stopover, but now aggressively promoted with advertising and generous weekend packages. Suburban couples escaping the kids find themselves
124

treated to breakfast in bed, chocolates at bedside and bowls of fresh flowers, all at almost half the price of the same rooms Mon-Thurs. Harmonious tints of green, peach and beige accompany tasteful seating arrangements and decorative accessories. The handsome lobby soothes with print fabrics, potted palms and ivy, amidst which you can take an above-par afternoon tea. Added to these allurements are the best 5th Ave. stores, just outside the door.
🏊 🍷

Carlyle 🏨
35 E 76th St. (Madison Ave.), NY 10021 ☎ *744-1600 or 800-227-5737. Map 7L4* ▥ *500 rms* ▣ ⇌
Location: Upper East Side, one block from the Whitney Museum. Many hotels pretend to offer continental standards of hospitality, but here the grand traditions of Europe really are emulated. Over-sized rooms pamper with bathroom phones and custom toiletries. Most have serving pantries and well-stocked refrigerators. There is 24hr room service, and the cashier exchanges foreign currency until midnight. Pets are permitted at an extra charge, and dog walkers are on hand. Afternoon tea is an event, as is an hour spent with stylish singer-pianist Bobby Short or the jazz musicians and vocalists who often appear in his stead in the **Café Carlyle**. **Bemelmans' Bar** is the clubby home of murals by the famous author and illustrator of the Madeline books. It is scotch-and-soda country, with piano music from 5.30pm. Limousines stand ready to shuttle guests to midtown stores and theaters. A new health club is being built — about the only thing the Carlyle doesn't have to undergird its near-flawless reputation.
⌂ 🍷 ♪

Doral Court ♧
130 E 39th St. (Lexington Ave.), NY 10016 ☎ *685-1100 or 800-624-0607* ⊛ *889-0287. Map 504* ▥ *248 rms* ⇌ ▣
Location: Near Grand Central Terminal and the United Nations. One of a trio of ingratiating Doral hotels in upper Murray Hill, a complete overhaul qualifies it as a new entry. To the bare-bones amenities of others in its class are added remote-control TV and VCRs, bathrobes, refrigerators, and, on request, in-room exercycles. (Guests have access to a fully equipped fitness center nearby.) King-sized

beds, commodious dimensions, and a soothing Sister Parish-style decor are the norm. Downstairs, the **Courtyard Café** is favored by neighborhood executives, who use it for every animated meal of the day. Rates are at the low end of the expensive range, and are cut by 40 percent on weekends, when free parking is included.

🏠 🍸

Doral Park Avenue

70 Park Ave. (38th St.), NY 10016 ☎ *687-7050 or 800-847-4135* ☎ *968872* ☎ *808-9029. Map 5O4* |||| *220 rms* ⊟
Location: Near Grand Central Terminal. Murray Hill doesn't have the gloss and hum of the midtown core, but that is its virtue. This serene stopping-place, small by Big Apple standards, makes the most of its setting. Reasonable needs are skillfully met, without fuss or show, although the restaurant and room service close down early. Bedrooms have refrigerators and computer ports; some have serving pantries. There are two restaurants and a sidewalk café in summer, and most central office buildings and tourist sights are within walking distance. Guests can use a nearby health club.

🏠 🍸

Doral Tuscany

120 E 39th St. (near Park Ave.), NY 10016 ☎ *686-1600 or 800-847-4078* ☎ *640243* ☎ *779-7833. Map 5P4* |||| *143 rms* 🏠 ⊟
Location: Near Grand Central Terminal and United Nations. One of the best dollar-for-dollar values in its class, it charms in many small details — at the entrance, a large thermometer-barometer; on the desk, an arrangement of flowers; in the bedroom, a serving pantry with a refrigerator stocked with soft drinks; in the bathroom, a telephone and 3-nozzle massaging showerhead; outside the window, another thermometer. Even exercycles are available. It is quieter by many decibels than its larger cousins deeper in the midtown district, yet is only a few blocks farther from the action. **Time and Again** is as good a restaurant as can be found in the immediate neighborhood. The capable staff treats guests with an avuncularity that is at once amusing and reassuring. Conventioneers and tour groups are never in evidence, and the hotel is less likely to be booked up on short notice.

🏠

Dorset

30 W 54th St. (near 6th Ave.), NY 10019 ☎ *247-7300 or 800-227-2348* ☎ *581-0153. Map 4N3* |||| *400 rms* 🏠 *nearby* ⊟
Location: Near Rockefeller Center and Museum of Modern Art. The fact that more than half its rooms are under permanent lease is testimony to the desirability of this underpublicized hostelry. The paneled lobby is a welcoming retreat from the midtown bustle, the front desk staff uncommonly amiable. Personalities from the nearby television network headquarters lunch at the streetside bar-café. Some rooms have pantries and balconies. There is no charge for children under 14 sharing their parents' rooms.

🏠 🍸

Essex House

160 Central Park S (near 6th Ave.), NY 10019 ☎ *247-0300 or 800-645-5687* ☎ *125205* ☎ *315-1839. Map 5N4* |||| *810 rms* 🏠 ⊟
Location: On Central Park, near Lincoln Center and shopping areas. Although it aspires to rank with the cream of Manhattan hotels, the Essex House falls short. Participants in large conferences and formal dinners mill about the paneled and chandeliered lobby at all hours, and **Devereux's** restaurant is satisfactory, but no more. That said, however, the hotel qualifies as a runner-up to the best. Its location is excellent, the staff speaks 18 languages, the bedrooms are spacious. (Ask for one with a view of the park.) There are scales in the bathrooms for weight-watchers; and when the maid turns down the bed at night she leaves a chocolate mint. Bills can be paid in foreign currency. One-night family rates offer a good deal.

🍸

Grand Hyatt 🏨

42nd St. and Park Ave., NY 10017 ☎ *883-1234 or 800-228-9000* ☎ *645616* ☎ *697-3772. Map 5O4* |||| *1,407 rms* 🏠
Location: Next to Grand Central Terminal. A leader in the 1980s hotel boom, this addition to the Hyatt holdings also takes a giant share of the credit for the continuing rehabilitation of E 42nd St. The effect of the place is sleek, showy, and quintessentially New York, even though, by the standards of others in the chain, this Hyatt is downright sedate. There is drama in

125

abundance in its exuberant architecture. The effect of the 4-story atrium is horizontal rather than vertical, one side knuckling out over the street. There is a tiered waterfall beneath a vast spidery wire sculpture, rows of greenery, great columns cloaked in brass and steel. All rooms have color and cable TV, there is a health club with sauna, squash and tennis, and **Trumpet's** is one of the city's better hotel restaurants. The costlier "executive floors" are called the **Regency Club**.
☜ ♈

Halloran House
525 Lexington Ave. (near 48th St.), NY 10017 ☎ *755-4000 or 800-223-0939* ⊕*668844* ⊛*751-3440. Map* **5O4** ///□ *650 rms* 🖼 ⊟

Location: Midtown East, near Grand Central Terminal and United Nations. Livelier than most of the rather anonymous commercial hotels that stretch Lexington Ave., Halloran House offers concierge service for theater tickets and limousines, two restaurants and a bar named after the owner — **Biff's Place** — that swings to jazz or pop from 5pm until whenever. The bedrooms satisfy basic needs, with the welcome addition of small personal safes in the closets.
🐾 ☜ ♈

Helmsley Park Lane 🏨
36 Central Park S (near 5th Ave.), NY 10019 ☎ *371-4000 or 800-221-4982* ⊕*668613* ⊛*319-9065. Map* **5N4** //// *640 rms* 🖼 ⊟

Location: Across from Central Park, near stores and Lincoln Center. Much used to be made of the fact that Harry and Leona Helmsley, owners of half a dozen New York hotels, chose to live in this one. The in-house management sets high standards, for although this modern high-rise cannot achieve the grace of the older luxury hotels, it certainly tries. Lavish applications of brocade and suede dress the corridors and public rooms. There is a concierge to secure theater tickets and limousines. Try afternoon tea in the **Park Room** and you won't be disappointed. The higher the room on the park side of the hotel, the better the views.
⊄ ♈ 🐾

Holiday Inn Crowne Plaza
1605 Broadway (49th St.), NY 10019 ☎ *977-4000 or*

800-465-4329 ⊛*333-7393. Map* **4O3** //// *770 rms* 🖼 ⊟
Location: Times Square theater district. Place this gaudy newcomer in the jukebox subspecies of Post-Modernist architecture. The designer giddily admits he wanted the pink-and-burgundy exterior to look like a Wurlitzer, complete with huge bands of multicolored lights racing around the sides. Certainly no one can claim it is an intrusion on its Times Square neighborhood. Opened in Dec 1989, it was expected to appeal to businesspeople and a substantial proportion of foreign tourists, for whom it no doubt confirms everything they ever believed about the United States. Among its attractions are the largest indoor pool of any Manhattan hotel, 24hr room service, and three restaurants, one of which quickly drew good reviews. The executive floors have a private concierge.
☜ ♈ ♈

Inter-Continental
111 E 48th St. (Lexington Ave.), NY 10017 ☎ *755-5900 or 800-332-4246* ⊕*968677* ⊛*644-0079. Map* **5O4** //// *777 rms* 🖼 ⊟
Location: Near Grand Central Terminal and United Nations. A courtly European flavor persists here, announced by the lobby trademark, a large aviary with live birds. The spacious public areas and halls suggest bedrooms of larger dimensions than they usually prove to be, but thick walls and double windows keep them quiet. TV, AM-FM radio, free in-room movies, and 24hr room service remove the need to brave the streets for food and diversion. A fully appointed health club was inaugurated in 1990, with treadmills, weight-lifting and stair-climbing machines. They've even installed TV sets at eye-level in front of the Lifecycles. Sauna, steam, and massage are available. In the same healthy spirit, floors have been set aside for nonsmokers. The Theater District is only a few blocks w, and several celebrated restaurants are even closer. Within the building is the oldest pharmacy in New York, **Caswell Massey**, featuring soaps and hairbrushes that have their origins in Colonial times. There are several enticing weekend packages.
⊡ ♈ 🐾

Leow's Summit
569 Lexington Ave. (51st St.), NY 10022 ☎ *752-7000 or 800-223-*

0888 ⊕ 147181 ⊛ 758-6311. Map 5N4 ⅢⅢ 770 rms ▭ ⊑
Location: Near midtown shopping and United Nations. All the usual comforts are to be found in this large, international-breed hotel, right down to the concierge. Once inside, you might be in any of its counterparts in Lisbon, London or Rio. There are few surprises, good or bad, but then, prices are comparatively low for this part of town. Refrigerators, bathroom telephones, in-room movies and radios are standard. The well-equipped fitness center is welcome. For additional indulgences, ask for a room on the ESP (Extra Special Patron) plan, but expect a surcharge. One weekend package includes theater tickets, dinner, free parking and unlimited use of the health club; another, of the "no-frills" variety, squeezes costs down to the budget level.
♈ ⬥ ⅄

The Lowell
28 E 63rd St. (near Madison Ave.), NY 10021 ☎ 838-1400 ⊕ 275750 ⊛ 319-4230. Map 7M4 ⅢⅢ 60 rms ⊑
Location: Residential street near Central Park Zoo. The first thing you notice about The Lowell is its rose-and-cream-tiled Art Deco exterior, a mild visual shock on this sedate block. Erected as a residential hotel in the late 1920s, it had gone through several ownerships and marked decline until its recent facelift. There is much to distinguish it now from its midtown rivals. In a city of sealed glass and steam heat, all of the casement windows open, and 34 of the units have woodburning fireplaces. There are real books on the shelves, and live plants, cut flowers, twice-daily maid service and two bathrobes in every bathroom. None of the rooms is exactly alike, although a crisp contemporary look sets the tone. The charming **Pembrooke Room** is hidden away on the second floor, serving breakfast, lunch and afternoon tea. Management promotes highly personal attention and is discreet almost to a fault about its more celebrated clients — the reason they keep coming back.
▭ ⅄

The Mark ▣
Madison Ave. and E 77th St., NY 10021 ☎ 744-4300 or 800-843-6275 ⊛ 744-2749 Map 7L4 ⅢⅢ to ⅢⅢ 86 rms ⊑

Location: Upper East Side, among art galleries, near Metropolitan Museum of Art. Madonna slept here. Since it can be assumed that she can stay where she wants, the new Mark obviously has something going for it. After all, the **Carlyle**, dowager empress of Manhattan hostelries, is just across the street. Two-thirds of these units are suites, and those on the top three floors — 14 to 16 — garner the raves. Up there, the details include meticulously crafted moldings, custom-designed fabrics, marble bathrooms, and plush Italianate furnishings. King-sized beds and coffee-makers are the norm. Many of the suites have wet bars or terraces, most have serving pantries, and all have VCRs. (Video cassettes are available for rent.) The lower floors are scheduled for similar treatment, so ask for a renovated unit. Many good restaurants are within a few blocks, but the one downstairs is more than satisfactory.
▭ ⅄

Mayfair Regent ▣
610 Park Ave. (65th St.), NY 10021 ☎ 288-0800 or 800-223-0542 ⊕ 236257 ⊛ 737-0538. Map 5M4 ⅢⅢ 199 rms ▭ ⊑
Location: Upper East Side, in art and antiques country. The Mayfair Regent has earned a respect bordering on the reverential. In part, this reflects the personal attention that is only possible when the number of guests is carefully limited. More important is the flair of a management that learned its trade at such establishments as London's Connaught and Venice's Gritti Palace. Its success in replicating the atmosphere of such exalted caravanseries can be seen in the number of privileged Europeans, many of them in the Italian fashion field, who make this their home in New York. They gather for high tea and cocktails in the vaulted lobby lounge, a fantasy of arabesque flourishes that might have been the creation of a markedly secular caliph. The presence on the premises of the redoubtable **Le Cirque** restaurant lends even more stature, although it is independently operated. A majority of the accommodations are suites, sumptuously appointed. Ceilings are high, feet sink in plush carpets, wood and metal surfaces glow, colors soothe in dove gray and peach and beige. Some suites even have working fireplaces, a warming thought on a blustery

Hotels

January night. Bathrooms are supplied with oversized terrycloth robes that actually fit adults taller than jockeys and towels that wrap twice around the body. Guests confronted with a rainy day will find an umbrella hanging in the closet. When price is not a factor, this beauty has few equals.

Mayflower ♥
Central Park W (61st St.), NY 10023 ☎ 265-0060 or 800-223-4164 ❹ 4972657 ⓇP 265-5098. *Map 4N3* ▥▥ 400 rms ▱ ☷
Location: Near Lincoln Center. The otherwise resurgent Upper West Side is woefully short of decent hotels. The Mayflower hasn't had any serious competition there in living memory. It still hasn't. Although it is not in the same league as the East Side leaders, it remains a reliable choice. The parkside **Conservatory Café** has live entertainment and an above-par Sunday brunch. Suites with pantries cost no more than a standard double at many crosstown competitors. That makes for a loyal client roster of musicians, film-makers, and executives who don't want to sacrifice convenience or comfort to the dictates of their budget-keepers. They get spacious rooms with traditional furnishings, many with park views, and most with serving pantries with refrigerators. Weekday morning coffee is served gratis in the lobby.

Middletowne ♥
148 E 48th St. (near Lexington Ave.), NY 10017 ☎ 755-3000 or 800-321-2323 ❹ 640543. *Map 5O4* ▥▥ 192 rms ▱
Location: Midtown East, near Grand Central Terminal. Visitors settling in for a week or more sometimes wish it were possible to trim the overhead of full hotel services in exchange for more homelike quarters. They can do that here, trading room service waiters and elaborate lobbies for comfortable rooms equipped with full kitchens, including stoves, refrigerators and, if desired, silverware and crockery. Some suites have fireplaces and/or terraces. Rates might be negotiable for longer stays. There is neither bar nor restaurant, but both are abundant in this neighborhood.
▱ ▱

Morgan's
237 Madison Ave. (near 37th St.), NY 10016 ☎ 686-0300 or 800-334-3408 ❹ 288908 *Map 5P4* ▥▥ 154 rms ▱ ☷
Location: Busy avenue near Morgan Library and the Empire State Building. Call it a "boutique hotel." The owners do, and they know whereof they speak. Two of the principals were responsible for the original Studio 54 and the **Palladium** mega-disco (see *Nightlife*). It is zippy, youthful, and trendy enough to draw Mick Jagger, Billy Joel and executives of the fashion and design industries. To highlight this in-the-know status, there is no identifying sign outside and never will be. Guests are whisked into rooms of almost Oriental simplicity decked in chic black, white and gray tones. Built-in storage walls are of gray-stained bird's-eye maple, the low beds covered with pinstriped duvets. There are refrigerators, and this is one of the few hotels in the city with stereo cassette decks as well as VCRs in its rooms. (The front desk can provide videocassettes from its library.) A fresh-faced staff provides twice-daily housekeeping and 24hr room service. The duplex penthouse suite has a dramatic view of the Empire State Building.
Ⓨ

New York Helmsley
212 E 42nd St. (3rd Ave.), NY 10017 ☎ 888-1624 or 800-221-4982 ❹ 127724 ⓇP 986-4792. *Map 5O5* ▥▥ 793 rms ▱ ☷
Location: Near Grand Central Terminal and United Nations. One of the chain assembled or built by Harry Helmsley, this one is geared to the expense account crowd, and on the assumption that traveling executives have little time for ceremony, it is forthright rather than frisky, although all comforts are provided. Multilingual stenographers are available. Breakfast trays arrive with the *Wall Street Journal.* Rooms are crisply conservative. When business people go home for the weekend, sharply discounted rates draw the suburbanites for museum-hopping and Broadway shows.
▱

New York Hilton
1335 6th Ave. (53rd St.), NY 10019 ☎ 586-7000 or 800-445-8967 ❹ 238492 ⓇP 757-7423. *Map 5N4* ▥▥ 2,131 rms ▱ ☷
Location: Midtown, at Rockefeller Center. Big, brassy and bustling, this vertical town within the city makes it unnecessary to brave the weather.

Everything is here, from stores to secretarial services to a week's worth of bars and restaurants and live entertainment. Of the many types of room, only the claustrophobic singles are to be avoided. Comforting features include closed-circuit movies and heated bathroom floors. Half-day rates are available for lie-downs and wash-ups between shopping excursions and theater matinees. The separate **Towers** floors are less trampled by the humanity that engulfs the rest of the building. ♈ ♈ ♋

New York Penta
7th Ave. (33rd St.), NY 10001
☎ *736-5000 or 800-223-8585*
⊕ *220318* ⊛ *502-8712. Map 4P3*
||||| *1,700 rms* ⊸ ⊒
Location: Across the street from Penn Station. Large, anonymous, unremarkable, this giant looks in all significant ways like an aging version of dated modernity. Look upon it as an alternative to more luxurious stops, perhaps when they are full or when business or pleasure requires ready access to Penn Station, *Madison Square Garden* or the *Garment Center.* Tariffs are moderate, by local standards, and the rooms are comfortable enough.
♈

Novotel
226 W 52nd St. (Broadway), NY 10019 ☎ *221-4542 or 800-221-3158* ⊕ *220352* ⊛ *765-5369. Map 4N3* |||⌃ *470 rms* ▣ ⊒
Location: Midtown theater district. Proof positive that American hotel designers do not own exclusive rights to bad taste, this European-owned tower first assaults the eye by its orange-and-green exterior. It is, in addition, built above an existing 4-story commercial building of grim aspect. The lobby is on the 7th floor, and so riotously gaudy that words fail to describe it. None of this is meant to suggest that the Novotel is not comfortable, for the usual services and facilities of its class are at hand, and it is quieter than might be expected. All rooms have color cable TV and either one king-sized or two double beds. Nonsmoking rooms are available. Visitors intent upon a week of theater are within a few blocks of all the major houses.

Omni Park Central
870 7th Ave. (56th St.), NY 10019
☎ *247-8000 or 800-843-6664*

⊛ *541-8506. Map 4N3* ||||| *1,295 rms* ⊸ ⊒
Location: Midtown, near Carnegie Hall, Theater District. This former Sheraton hotel has been revamped with an eye-catching lobby, a brasserie-style dining room, and new furnishings and fresh paint from top to bottom. Standard bedchambers are nothing special. The preferred rooms and suites are on the "Omni Classic" upper floors, which enjoy such perquisites as free copies of the *New York Times* and arrays of complimentary toiletries. *Carnegie Hall* is across the street and the theater district only a few blocks away.
♋ ♈

Palace 🏨 🏛
455 Madison Ave. (50th St.), NY 10022 ☎ *888-7000 or 800-221-4982* ⊕ *640543* ⊛ *355-0820. Map 5N4* ||||| *773 rms* ▣ ⊒
Location: Midtown, near shopping. Preservation of worthwhile buildings has a checkered history in New York. More often than not, commerce has triumphed over heritage. Not so the Palace. Bent upon erecting a princely flagship for his real estate empire, Harry Helmsley was persuaded not only to spare the proud Villard Houses from demolition, but to restore them to their 1886 opulence. The Franco-Italianate interiors were lovingly scrubbed and mended, revealing marble inlays, Tiffany glass, frescoes, rich paneling, gold-leaf ceilings, and intricately carved wood friezes. His efforts were rewarded by a fat dossier of enthusiastic press notices. In the adjoining modern tower, guest rooms are unusually spacious and continue the theme with huge Baroque headboards, soft velvets, and tasteful Louis XV reproductions. Despite the recent hotly publicized legal and financial problems of Helmsley and his wife Leona, standards haven't noticeably faltered. The concierge, for example, can arrange for translators in nearly 40 languages. There aren't ten other hotels in town that can match this experience.
🍴 ♈

Parc Fifty One 🏨
152 W 51st St. (7th Ave.), NY 10019 ☎ *765-1900 or 800-338-1338* ⊕ *147156* ⊛ *541-6604. Map 4N3* ||||| *178 rms* ⊒
Location: Opposite Equitable Center, walking distance from theaters. Briefly known as the Grand Bay

Hotel, the Parc Fifty One has yet to imprint itself on the New York consciousness. It will, it will. For one thing, it is the only true luxury hotel in its central midtown neighborhood. For another, it is intimate and discreet, no doubt reasons it has been discovered by people who seek those qualities — Carol Burnett, John Cleese, Jane Fonda, and Julio Iglesias, among them. Personalized, anticipatory service prevails, from the front desk to 24hr room waiters to the off-lobby lounge, yet never crosses the line into undue chumminess. The gadgets and goodies that have endeared themselves to travelers who can afford this level of cosseting are, naturally, in place. Press a button on the wall of your suite, and a television set descends from its hiding place in a mirrored cube. All rooms have two multiline telephones with fax hookups, and in their bathrooms are hairdryers, robes, and another TV to catch the morning news. Courtesy limos leave each morning for Wall Street. And when the Sun *New York Times* is delivered, it comes with white gloves so the ink won't smear on the guest's hands. Now we couldn't have that, could we?
♈

Parker Meridien
118 W 57th St. (6th Ave.), NY 10019 ☎ 245-5000 or 800-543-4300 ⓕ 307-1776. Map 4N3 ⏸ to ⏸ 600 rms ▣
Location: Near Central Park, Rockefeller Center and Carnegie Hall. Air France is the parent company, and the Gallic touch is evident, if not as pervasive as its advertisements insist. Aubusson tapestries adorn the walls, a multilingual concierge attends to arrangements for reservation theater tickets and limousines, and the bars and restaurants smack of the Champs-Élysées. The jogging track, the squash and racquetball courts, and the whirlpool and sauna cater to the fitness mania of the contemporary international businessperson, who can then cool down in one of the 100 lavishly appointed "executive apartments." Breakfast in bed includes croissants and is usually accompanied by a copy of the *International Herald Tribune*. All rooms have stocked mini-bars and closed-circuit movies. The hotel dining room, the **Maurice**, is about to present itself in a new light after a period of closure. Weekend package plans include buffet breakfasts and welcome champagne. Corporate discounts are available.
≈ ♈ ♈

Peninsula 🏨
700 5th Ave. (55th St.), NY 10022 ☎ 247-2200 or 800-223-5652 ⓕ 4976154 ⓕ 903-3949. Map 5N4 ⏸ 251 rms ▣ ≈
Location: In heart of 5th Ave. shopping, near Museum of Modern Art. The jinx on this property has been lifted, or so it would seem. It was built in 1905 as a twin to the St. Regis-Sheraton, one of the luxury addresses of that day. By the 1960s, it had deteriorated badly. Then it was bought by a Swiss entrepreneur with more money than taste, and after eight tenant-less years he and his Nova Park had neither. It was resurrected as Maxim's de Paris 2yrs later, but the paint was barely dry before it was sold to the Hong Kong Peninsula group. They now have what might be the most-photographed lobby in the city, a grand staircase sweeping down in the glow of a spectacular chandelier. There are antiques everywhere, including the guestrooms, along with Art Nouveau flourishes, marble, and plush carpeting. The rooftop fitness facility takes up three levels, including weight and aerobic rooms and an indoor swimming pool. Cocktails and high tea are served in the splendid lounge, and while the restaurant, **Adrianne's**, has yet to fire great enthusiasm, the setting can't be faulted.
≈ ♈ ♈

Pierre 🏨
5th Ave. and 61st St., NY 10021 ☎ 838-8000 or 800-332-3442 ⓕ 127426 ⓕ 758-1615. Map 5N4 ⏸ 700 rms ▣ ≈
Location: Across from Central Park, near museums and stores. Monarchs and presidents select the Pierre, the New York outpost of the Canadian Four Seasons chain. Stretch limousines line the curb outside and studiously inconspicuous men often stand about whispering into micro-transmitters. There isn't a safer address in town. Marble baths and floral-painted basins are happy touches, as are magnifying shaving mirrors and electrically operated window drapes. The staff members make notes of preferences in flowers and other idiosyncracies and try to remember names. Barely half the rooms are available to temporary visitors, but they are

given no hint of second-class status. Reserve as far ahead as possible.

🏨 🛥 《

Plaza 🏨

5th Ave. and 59th St., NY 10019
☎ *759-3000 or 800-228-3000*
☏ *236938* ☏ *759-3167. Map* **5N4**
||||| *900 rms* ▣ ≕
Location: Corner of 5th Ave. and Central Park. Klieg lights and cameras are a frequent presence around the famous exterior, for the Plaza continues to serve as Hollywood shorthand for Manhattan glamor. Although a hair too populist to stand among the most elite hostelries, the Plaza remains a living symbol of between-the-wars opulence. Indeed, it has been declared a National Historic Landmark. In honor of that, new owner Donald Trump continues to scour away flaws, and he has for once resisted putting his name on it, which is his usual practice. Walls are thick, ceilings high, and floors carpeted, making for unusually quiet bedrooms and suites. In the public areas, brass window- and door-frames gleam, and statuary and capitals sparkle. Afternoon tea in the central Palm Court evoke the Gatsby-Fitzgerald era, complete with Viennese strings, and the atmospheric **Oak Bar** is so popular that it requires a *maître d'* to control the crowds. The several restaurants serve only fair food, and an effort is being made to upgrade the cuisine of the handsome **Edwardian Room**. There is 24hr room service, and many rooms overlook Central Park. The best of 5th Ave. shopping is directly outside.

《 ♟ ♪

Plaza Athénée 🏨

37 E 64th St. (near Madison Ave.), NY 10021 ☎ *734-9100 or 800-225-5843* ☏ *6972900* ☏ *772-0958. Map* **5M4** ||||| *160 rms* ▬ ▣ ≕
Location: Upper East Side, near bistros, shopping and Central Park. Literally no expense was spared to transform what was the lackluster Hotel Alrae into a paragon of the Continental standard of superb innkeeping. The aged, tiered structure was stripped to the shell and rebuilt, from plumbing and wiring to the lavish use of Brazilian mahogany in the public rooms, and padded silk wallcoverings in the spacious suites. The overhaul cost $50 million, and operating expenses are as dazzling a testament to intent — the monthly florist bill is said to

total $100,000. Now it matches up favorably with such paragons as the **Carlyle** and **Mayfair Regent**. Only the sourest curmudgeon can find serious fault, apart from the smallish rooms. Consider this roster of amenities, by no means complete: cable TV with remote control; newspaper delivered each morning; every message delivered by phone, at the desk *and* to the guest's room; room safes; bathroom scales; bathrobes; blissful tranquility; superb dining in the glamorous *fin de siècle* setting of **Le Regence**.

🏨 ♟

Regency 🏨

Park Ave. and 61st St., NY 10021
☎ *759-4100 or 800-223-0888*
☏ *147180* ☏ *826-5674. Map* **5N4**
||||| *400 rms* ▣ ≕
Location: Upper East Side, amidst exclusive stores and galleries. Cherished by New York's power elite and their compatriots from across both oceans, the Regency is the ideal place for those compulsive capitalists who roll out of bed and hit the floor running. The downstairs **540 Park** restaurant is *the* place to conduct pre-office morning meetings. Waiters make photocopies betwixt serving eggs and pouring coffee. Out-of-towners lacking local health club membership can keep in fighting trim in the lower lobby fitness center, which is equipped with stationary bicycles, rowing and skiing machines, jogging treadmill, Nautilus machines, whirlpool and sauna. Even on-the-go entrepreneurs expect their comforts — and they certainly get them. A small person could almost take up residence in one of the 400 bathrooms. Apart from the customary fixtures, each bathroom has a powerful hairdryer, a refrigerator, a telephone, a set of scales, bathrobes, and a TV set. The spacious bedrooms have large-screen TV with remote controls, and are furnished in what might be called Corporate Louis XVI. Afternoon tea is served in the bar-lounge, and a limousine office arranges suitable transportation. Reserve rooms or suites well ahead.

🏨 ♟ 🛥 ♪

Ritz-Carlton

112 Central Park S (near 6th Ave.), NY 10019 ☎ *757-1900 or 800-223-7990* ☏ *757-9620. Map* **5N4** ||||| *300 rms* ▣ ≕
Location: On Central Park, near Lincoln Center. A drumbeat of

gushing press notices attended the transformation of the old Navarro into the new Ritz-Carlton, but the expectations proved to be too grand. It was compared to London's Connaught, a serious strain on credulity. True, the location is excellent, and such celebrities as Warren Beatty no doubt appreciate the quiet of a hotel free of conventioneers and package groups. In the suites he presumably inhabits, there are hunting and horticultural prints, chintz, leather wing chairs, antique pine and carved mahogany. Any visiting Briton will feel at home. Reserve one of the rooms overlooking Central Park, disregard the expense, and anyone will be content. Try to economize, and the room is apt to be cramped and the housekeeping offhand. Service is solicitous and proper, however, and the first-floor **Jockey Club** restaurant is soothing for the power lunches of its international clientele. Right now, expect a first-class hotel at over-reaching tariffs.

🏨 🥂 ◁€

Roger Smith Winthrop
501 Lexington Ave. (47th St.), NY 10017 ☎ *755-1400 or 800-445-0277* ✆*238032* ✆*319-9130. Map 5O4.* ▥ *to* ▥▥ *183 rms* 🍽
Location: Slightly N of Grand Central Terminal and the United Nations. Once the temporary resting place of Willie Lomans and the employees of parsimonious airlines, ongoing rehabilitation has made the hotel a worthy option for vacationers, too. Still old-fashioned in some ways, none of them important, it has been upgraded in most regards. Rooms are large, pleasant, unsurprising. Each has a coffee maker, a nice touch, along with a refrigerator and the morning newspaper outside the door. Prices include continental breakfast, an unusual practice in New York that effectively lowers the room rate. The new restaurant, opened in 1990, has yet to establish a reputation. Weekend discounts are attractive.

St Moritz
50 Central Park S (6th Ave.), NY 10019 ☎ *755-5800 or 800-221-4774* ✆*668840* ✆*751-2952. Map 5N4* ▥▥ *772 rms* 🏨 🍽
Location: Overlooking Central park, near theaters and shopping. Decades of advertisements in *The New Yorker* magazine proclaimed it the "Biggest Little Hotel" in town,

but most citizens know it for its sidewalk café. Rooms are compact, but those high in front seem larger by virtue of the expansive views of the park. The entry to the street-level **Rumplemayers** restaurant is, improbably, lined with stuffed animals; ice cream concoctions are the big item. Since an Australian entrepreneur has spent a reported $180 million to purchase it, perhaps there will soon be noticeable improvements in service and housekeeping.

🏨 🥂 ◁€ 🍷

St Regis-Sheraton 🏨
2 E 55th St. (5th Ave.), NY 10022 ☎ *753-4500. Map 5N4* ▥▥ *520 rms* 🏨 🍽
Location: Midtown, near Rockefeller Center. Unlike most of its contemporaries of the turn of the century — decayed, demolished or converted to other uses — the 1904 St Regis prevailed. Even back then, it cost financier John Jacob Astor nearly $6 million to build and furnish what was to be the tallest hotel in the city. In opulent detail, it rivaled the **Waldorf-Astoria**, its principal competitor for the carriage trade. Astor went down with the *Titanic*, and now his grand-luxe hotel has undergone a year-long bow-to-stern renovation. Presumably they will retain the famous buffed brass doorman's booth, the commodious bedchambers, intricately carved moldings, and the Maxfield Parrish mural in the **King Cole Room**.

🏨 🍷

Sheraton Centre
811 7th Ave. (52nd St.), NY 10019 ☎ *581-1000 or 800-325-3535* ✆*421130* ✆*262-4410. Map 4N3* ▥▥ *1,842 rms* 🏨 🍽
Location: Near Rockefeller Center and Theater District. When it opened as the Americana, the jibe was that is was "a little far from the beach," implying its style was more appropriate to Miami than New York. This was not unfair, but things have improved somewhat under the Sheraton aegis. Tranquility cannot be claimed an asset in a place this large, and service is highly variable. Yet the rooms are comfortable, if uninspired, and every midtown tourist attraction is within walking distance. Major upgrading was reserved for the luxury section known as the **Sheraton Towers**, which has a separate reception area on the 46th floor with its own express elevator and lobby bar-

restaurant. The rooms are not usually larger than those below, but come with extra touches — electric blankets and shoe-polishers, nightly turndown service, bathrobes, and complimentary continental breakfasts. Rates are about 20 percent higher.
✔

Sheraton City Squire

790 7th Ave. (near 51st St.), NY 10019 ☎ *581-3300 or 800-325-3535* ⬛ *640458* ⊗ *541-9219. Map 4N3* ⫿⫿⫿⫿ *720 rms* 🖼 ⇌
Location: N edge of Times Sq. Theater District. Another vertical motel, and hardly one designed to add luster to the Sheraton name. Maintenance is lacking and rooms are small. Still, there is a swimming pool and its situation is central. Only for those who expect nothing of a hotel but a clean bed.
🏊 ⇌

Sheraton Park Avenue

45 Park Ave. (37th St.), NY 10016 ☎ *685-7676 or 800-325-3535* ⬛ *421308* ⊗ *889-3193. Map 5P4* ⫿⫿⫿⫿ *175 rms* 🖼 ⇌
Location: Murray Hill, s of Grand Central Terminal. A substantial remove from its uptown Sheraton cousins, in both quality and situation, this reminds many travelers of their favorite London hideaway. The oak-lined lobby and its library set the cultivated tone. Fireplaces in some rooms and the prevailing calm of corridors and public spaces buttress that impression. Previously this winning ambience came at a price somewhat lower than those hotels closer to midtown. Recent renovations have changed all that, but it remains a very pleasant stop. Extras include a concierge, free shoeshines, TV speakers in bathrooms, and floors reserved for clients who don't smoke. The jazz club downstairs has loyal patrons. Just don't expect a bargain.
🖼 🏊 ♀ 🎵 ⇌

Stanhope 🏨

995 5th Ave. (81st St.), NY 10028 ☎ *288-5800 or 800-828-1123* ⊗ *517-0088. Map 7L4* ⫿⫿⫿⫿ *132 rms* 🖼 ⇌
Location: Opposite Metropolitan Museum of Art. What was once a comfortably unremarkable stopping place has been transformed, with little regard for cost, into a hostelry of unabashed luxury. Scores of rooms were sacrificed, their walls torn down to shape far more

spacious bedrooms and suites. Baccarat crystal chandeliers, 18thC lobby furniture and hand-loomed carpeting are merely partial evidence. Amenities baskets are a common feature in hotel bathrooms of this class — but these are by Chanel. Room furnishings are several notches above even this rarefied norm: European fabrics and designs are executed with *élan*, and real plants of all sizes are set around to provide warmth. No lamps bolted to tables here, nor the blizzards of promotional announcements that usually clutter hotel desks and TV sets. Tariffs, of course, are among the highest in Manhattan, a fact rather smugly acclaimed in institutional publicity. But clients in a position to pay are accorded such niceties as complimentary transportation to midtown, in Mercedes Benz limousines. The restaurant operation has yet to rouse the approbation of local food critics, but tea in the salon, and people-watching from the summer sidewalk café, compensate.
🏨 ♨ ▢ ▢

Swissôtel Drake

440 Park Ave. (56th St.), NY 10022 ☎ *421-0900* ⊗ *147178. Map 5N4* ⫿⫿⫿⫿ *640 rms* 🖼 ⇌
Location: Midtown East. It can confidently be observed that the Swiss know how to run hotels. Their takeover here has brought renewed luxury and crispness of operation to a once-faltering establishment. The **Restaurant Lafayette**, for example, is one of the city's best, in or outside of hotels. Fine wines are served by the glass in the plush bar, to the tunes of the nightly pianist. Upstairs, the spacious rooms leading off the twisting halls reveal such touches as hideaway refrigerators, AM-FM radios, and first-run movies. A same-day laundry service is available. The prime East Side venue is a bonus, and things can only improve with the $52 million renovation now underway. A new Park Ave. entrance is contemplated, as are five new high-speed elevators, very much needed.
✔ 🎵

United Nations Plaza 🏨

1 United Nations Plaza (44th St.), NY 10017 ☎ *355-3400* ⊗ *128603* ⊗ *702-5051 Map 5O5* ⫿⫿⫿⫿ *427 rms* ⇌
Location: Near United Nations Headquarters. The hotel's "International Style" of architecture is appropriate to its ownership by

the eponymous world organization. The first-floor restaurant has settled into steady competence after years of uncertainty. Its Sun brunch is excellent. Guest rooms begin on the 27th floor. The views are arresting, and they can also be enjoyed from the huge indoor swimming pool. On the 39th floor is a tennis court, exercise room and sauna. Felicitous touches include made-to-order breakfast doughnuts, baskets of fruit on arrival, jogging maps, and limousine service to Wall St. and the theater and garment districts.

⟨ℰ ≈ ↝ ⚘ ♪

Vista International

3 World Trade Center, NY 10048 ☎ *938-9100 or 800-258-0505* Ⓦ *661130* Ⓕ *321-2237. Map 2U3* ⫿⫿⫿⫿ *825 rms* ▢ ⇔

Location: At base of World Trade Center. Apart from filling a glaring need (since 1836 no one had built a major hotel in lower Manhattan), the Vista has enhanced a neighborhood. Its dining-rooms are cuts above those of most of its competitors, and add such weekend features as a sumptuous seafood buffet and a Country and Western Fair with live music. Rooms are conventionally comfortable, with such amenities as alarm clocks, AM-FM radios and closed-circuit movies. "Vista Club" rooms on the 20th and 21st floors enjoy complimentary breakfasts with morning newspapers, a private lounge with free drinks and *hors d'oeuvres*, and a special concierge. All guests have access to the jogging track, racquetball courts, sauna and swimming pool on the top floor. Upper floors still have good views of the harbor, despite the construction of Battery Park City between the hotel and the river. Weekend packages include champagne reception, buffet lunch, and free use of the fitness center.

≈ ⚘ ♈ ♪

Waldorf-Astoria 🏨

301 Park Ave. (49th St.), NY 10022 ☎ *355-3000 or 800-445-8667* Ⓦ *666747* Ⓕ *872-6380. Map 5O4* ⫿⫿⫿⫿ *to* ⫿⫿⫿⫿ *1,600 rms* ▢ ⇔

Location: Midtown East, near Grand Central Terminal. The original Waldorf, a name long synonymous with luxury, gave way to the Empire State Building. This replacement threw open its doors in 1931, its public rooms a paean to the Art Deco fashion of that period. A very costly facelift has restored the classic lobby and anterooms to their former glory. All the amenities that

might be expected are here, and the rooms and suites of the **Towers** section are superior or equal to anything of their like in the city. In effect a hotel within the hotel, the Towers, with its own reception desk and concierge (*entrance on 50th St.*), is completing its own $30 million renovation. That includes refinished hardwood floors, original oil paintings, and period European furnishings. The lower floors of the main building are crowded with a remarkable variety of stores, bars and restaurants, among them the famous **Peacock Alley**, a kind of indoor sidewalk-café. There are several top restaurants within walking distance of the hotel, although every meal for a week could be taken within the hotel itself.

⫏⫎ ♈

Warwick

65 W 54th St. (6th Ave.), NY 10019 ☎ *247-2700 or 800-223-4099* Ⓦ *147179* Ⓕ *957-8915. Map 5N4* ⫿⫿ *to* ⫿⫿⫿⫿ *419 rms* ▢ ⇔

Location: Midtown, near TV network headquarters and Museum of Modern Art. Overshadowed by the mammoth **Hilton** across the street, this medium-sized hotel offers the same proximity to the major television headquarters and Broadway theaters but at lower tariffs. Not long ago, it was characterized by slapdash housekeeping and a clumsy decorative scheme. New management and a substantial infusion of funds have changed that. Maintenance has markedly improved, as has service. The middle-level executives who constitute much of the custom are kept in mind, with two-line telephones and "voice mail" (in effect, an answering machine for each room.) Many bedrooms are larger than the New York norm, and some have refrigerators. In the third phase of renovation, the vintage bathrooms are to be transformed with marble. Seniors receive 25 percent discounts off standard rates, and weekend discounts are deep. The Warwick now ranks with any midtown stopover in its price category, and is superior to most.

⫏⫎

Westbury 🏨

15 E 69th St. (Madison Ave.), NY 10021 ☎ *535-2000 or 800-225-5843* Ⓦ *125388* Ⓕ *772-0958. Map 7M4* ⫿⫿⫿⫿ *325 rms* ▦ ▢ ⇔ AE ◉

Location: Upper East Side, amidst smart boutiques and art galleries.

The huge Trust House Forte chain does not always impress in Europe, but its exceptional Forte Exclusive subdivision harbors only hostelries of the very highest order — Paris' Plaza Athénée and Madrid's Ritz among them. The Westbury handily adheres to such exalted standards. Converted from a 1920s apartment house, this fashionable and luxurious retreat endeavors to retain a residential quality — that is, if one normally lives with crystal chandeliers, 17thC tapestries, and lavish displays of dewy-fresh flowers. Lobbies often give an inaccurate foretaste of the rooms upstairs. Not here. This one features marble and Oriental carpets, and the bedrooms carry through on that promise. They, too, have glowing semi-antique rugs and do not stint in space or detail, although some baths are on the dainty side. Even the smallest single rooms are cozy, not cramped, and are equipped with remote-control TV, clock radios, two-line phones, and useful work desks. Most have connections for computer modems and fax machines, and cellular telephones can be rented at the front desk. A health club with sauna, whirlpool, and weight machines has just been installed. The revamped **Polo** restaurant is excellent, and the lounge has a piano player during cocktail hour. In a city of superb hotels, the Westbury has few peers. ⌂ ▼ ◤

Wyndham ❀
42 W 58th St. (near 5th Ave.), NY 10019 ☎ *753-3500. Map 5N4* ❙❒ *to* ❙❙❒ *202 rms* ▣ ≡▭
Location: Near corner of Central Park and 5th Ave. To one of the most desirable locations in town is added the buffed patina of a Cotswolds inn. The owner-managers live on the premises. Many of their guests are theater folk settling in for long runs on Broadway. These rooms weren't designed by computer imaging. Fitted with one-of-a-kind pieces and near-antiques, they have the look of the loving care of a genteel remittance man with nothing else to distract him. (If only some of the old-shoe charm had rubbed off on the gruff gents at the front desk.) There is a reasonable bar and the restaurant is good enough; no room service, though. At these remarkably low prices, reservations must be made 4-6wks ahead.
⌂ ▼

Further recommendations
Beverly ❀ (*125 E 50th St. (Lexington Ave.), NY 10022* ☎ *753-2700 or 800-223-0945*❙❒ ▣ ≡▭). Located in Midtown East, near Grand Central Terminal. Reasonable prices and fair-sized rooms. **Gramercy Park** (*2 Lexington Ave. (21st St.), NY 10010* ☎ *475-4320 or 800-221-4083* ✆ *505-0535*❙❙❒ ≡▭ ⌂). Near Gramercy Park, away from main traffic arteries. A relatively quiet situation, plus access to an attractive private park nearby. **Howard Johnson's** ❀ (*851 8th Ave. (near 52st St.), NY 10019* ☎ *581-4100 or 800-223-0888* ✆ *974-7502*❙❙❒ ▣ ≡▭). Shares the virtues and the liabilities of other midtown motels. Ready access by car, yet within walking distance from the major theaters. Moderate tariffs. **Lexington** (*48th St. and Lexington Ave., NY 10017* ☎ *755-4400 or 800-223-0888* ✆ *751-4091*❙❙❒ ▣ ≡▭). Near Grand Central Terminal and United Nations. One of the more pleasing stops along this noisy commercial strip. Most of the bedrooms are not large. Good weekend discounts. **Milford Plaza** (*270 W 45th St. (8th Ave.), NY 10036* ☎ *869-3600 or 800-221-2690* ✆ *944-8357* ❙❒ ➤ ≡▭). In the heart of the Theater District. Reasonable rates, and a generous 1-5 night discount package. **Ramada Inn** (*790 8th Ave. (near 49th St.), NY 10019* ☎ *581-7000 or 800-223-0888* ✆ *974-0291*❙❒ ▣ ≡▭ ⇄). In the Midtown Theater District. Relatively modest family rates — and a swimming pool (a rare facility). Good value, crisp decor and exemplary maintenance. **Salisbury** ❀ (*123 W 57th St. (between 6th and 7th Aves.), NY 10019* ☎ *246-1300 or 800-223-0680*❙❒ ▣ ≡▭ ⌂ ◤). Across from Carnegie Hall. Many refurbished rooms with big new beds, some with serving pantries. **Wales** ❀ (*1295 Madison Ave. (92nd St.), NY 10028* ☎ *876-6000 or 800-223-088* ✆ *860-7000*❙❒). In Upper East Side, near Guggenheim Museum. Many rooms and suites have an airy Edwardian flair. Well positioned for Madison Ave. stores.

Manhattan East suite hotels
Business people and families willing to forgo some conventional services receive in return one- to three-bedroom suites at the price of standard

doubles in the glossier hotels. Quoted prices are per suite, not per person, so children can be accommodated on convertible sofas without extra cost. Since all suites have kitchenettes, further economies can be made on meals and snacks. From outside New York State, you can make reservations for any of the following Manhattan East hotels (☎ *1-800-637-8483, ext. 139*). Individual local numbers are given below. All the following are moderately priced, and American Express (▨) and Diners Club (◖◗) are accepted:
Southgate Tower (*31st St. & 7th Ave.* ☎ *563-1800*), health club and restaurant; **Dumont Plaza** (*34th St. & Lexington Ave.* ☎ *481-7600*); **Shelburne Murray Hill** (*37th St. & Lexington Ave.*); **Eastgate Tower** (*222 E 39th St. (near 2nd Ave.)* ☎ *687-8000*), bar, garage, café; **Beekman Tower** (*49th St. & 1st Ave.* ☎ *355-7300*), rooftop bar, restaurant, garage; **Plaza Fifty** (*50th St. & 3rd Ave.* ☎ *751-5710*); **Lyden House** (*320 E 53rd St. (near 2nd Ave.)* ☎ *888-6070*), garage; **Lyden Gardens** (*215 E 64th St. (near 3rd Ave.)* ☎ *355-1230*); **Surrey** (*76th St. & Madison Ave.* ☎ *288-3700*).

Bed & Breakfast

The impersonality and often breathtaking expense of a stay in New York have inspired efforts to get round those twin liabilities. One answer is the bed-and-breakfast movement. Although it isn't comparable to those of the British model (or the usual American version, for that matter), the attempt is laudable. The agencies named below are essentially referral services, matching up clients with hosts. The variety of lodgings is considerable, from SoHo lofts to East Side townhouses to high-rise apartments. In some, the owners are present, to provide welcome, advice, and breakfast. In others, they are not, but leave stocked refrigerators and numbers where they can be reached. With that diversity, and the frequent modifications of rosters, quality is unpredictable. But prices are as much as 60 percent less than standard hotel rates, and the opportunity to live as New Yorkers is appealing to those who don't require conventional hotel services.

An advance deposit must be paid, usually equal to the first night's fee. Some, not all, agencies accept credit cards. A minimum stay is required, usually at least two nights. Several day's notice of cancellation are required for refund of deposits. Be clear about requirements when making reservations. Hosts often do not allow smoking, or young children. This is a volatile field, and no guarantees can be made about accommodations, or even the continued existence of the referral services listed below:
Abode Bed and Breakfast (*P.O.Box 20022, NY 10028* ☎ *472-2000*); **Bed and Breakfast Network of New York** (*134 W 32nd St., Suite 602, NY 10001* ☎ *645-8134*); **New World Bed & Breakfast** (*150 5th Ave., Suite 711, NY 10011* ☎ *675-5600 or* ☎ *800-443-3800*); **Urban Ventures** (*306 W 38th St., NY 10018* ☎ *594-5650*).

Where to eat

In New York, eating is a basic need elevated to an event, a debating issue, an investment opportunity, conversation topic, even reason for existence. There are 28,000 eating places in the five boroughs, more than half of them in Manhattan alone.

Ask Americans who have spent time away from home what they most missed and it will likely be that mythic two-inch-thick slab of steak seared a charred mahogany outside, rosy-pink within, captured juices flowing at the stroke of the knife. Seafood is nearly as popular, and the ultimate fantasy dish might well be lobster and beef, unfortunately described on the menus of indifferent eateries as "surf and turf." If anything can be accurately labeled as American food, this is it: beef and seafood, simply prepared, in hefty portions. These twin yearnings are easily satisfied in New York, at tariffs ranging from the almost reasonable to the heartstopping.

But this type of cooking is essentially straightforward, and wonderment must be sought elsewhere. In this city of immigrants, that has never been a problem. Exponents of every major cuisine fostered on the inhabited continents compete for attention. The classic modes are purveyed in abundance: French, inevitably, with admirable representations of the *nouvelle* and *haute* cuisines, but also Russian, Czech, Polish, Swiss, German and Hungarian; Chinese, of course, in most of its variations, but also Korean, Indian, Japanese, Thai, Filipino, Indonesian and Pakistani; Italian, in all its manifestations, but also Greek, Portuguese, Spanish and Armenian; Mexican, but also Brazilian, Cuban and West Indian. In all, more than 30 national gastronomies are represented, supplemented by such hybrids and subspecies as Kosher Chinese, Soul, Puerto Rican, Polynesian, Jewish and Cuban Cantonese. And there is the catch-all "continental" category, harboring all manner of predilections, but usually with a Gallic rallying point.

Over the last decade, the unflagging quest to sample the latest undiscovered variation on the act of eating escalated to fevered proportions. "New American" cooking, borrowing the techniques and affectations of the *nouvelle* vanguardists, has been applied to all manner of formerly distinctive regional styles, especially Creole-Cajun and Tex-Mex (the latter rechristened "New Southwestern"). Celebrity chefs from California, who made their reputations by applying Asian and French procedures to devoutly domestic ingredients (a result sometimes described as "Chinois"), brought their acts to the Big Apple. Suddenly, every neighborhood that aspired to chic had restaurants grilling exotic fish over hot coals of mesquite (wood from an otherwise worthless tree that Texans were happy to sell by the carload to gullible Yankees). Baby vegetables, Louisiana blackened redfish, and designer pizzas topped with such oddments as asparagus and avocado became stupefying clichés. The price to pull a chair up to one of these experimental tables was, in most cases, staggering.

An inevitable reaction has set in. Bistros are back, with lower tariffs and food in portions fit for humans, not Lilliputians. Flavor sells, not effete presentations too precious to disturb. Cuisines that were poorly represented now enjoy adept portrayals. Splashy neon grazing places, with the size and noise level of railroad terminals, have nearly disappeared. Revolution has slowed to evolution, and the dining scene is the better for it. New York can boast the widest selection of good to superior restaurants in its history.

Happily for the gourmand, ethnic groups cling more tenaciously to their food preferences than to their creeds and ikons, although they have had to adapt local ingredients to the recipes of their former homelands. Availability and quality of produce, along with dietetic need, have always influenced culinary invention, and it is best to approach the restaurants of New York with an understanding of the many styles of cooking. Chunks of Maine lobster and Long Island littleneck clams may be

137

substituted for the cuttlefish and sheep innards in the *paella* of Valencia, but it will be no less tasty for that. American caviar does not yet match the vaunted Caspian standard, but it is half the price, and vastly superior to the inky lumpfish roe masquerading in the supermarkets. A few transplanted chef-proprietors still air-freight Dover sole and Brittany turbot, out of chauvinistic myopia or simple snobbery, but their bay scallops and bass were harvested within 100 miles. And while Americans don't share the French interest in larks and pigeons, the local quail, duckling, and duck *foie gras* are unsurpassed.

These efforts to duplicate the fare once set before them by parents and mentors inevitably attract audiences from the larger community. Although restaurants of French, Italian, and Chinese cuisine dominate every listing of the city's top-drawer establishments, no matter how immutably classic they pretend to be, they too continue to change and diversify. Sauces are lighter, vegetables are lifted from the pot while their flavor remains, ingredients retain their separate identities. Even the once stodgy Cantonese, Neapolitan, and Provençal kitchens have aired out moldering recipe books and applied new techniques.

None of this is to assert that every meal is sublime. As everywhere, mediocrity and ineptitude prevail. Bringing together the elements that comprise an agreeable dining experience proves elusive. Several of the prettiest restaurants feature grumpy personnel and indifferent, if rarely appalling, food. On the other hand, above-average viands are often set before customers in garish or dreary quarters so cramped it is difficult to raise a fork.

The selection that follows is but a wisp of a hint of the available choices. As far as possible, it reflects a consensus of the best restaurants in the city — numerous others of all prices and styles can be found throughout New York, and for a guide to the most likely locations see *Area planners* on pages 37-41. Although the price range is necessarily skewed toward the higher end, every attention has been given to selecting restaurants offering reasonable value for money. In that spirit, this edition has dropped a number of good but prohibitively expensive restaurants in favor of cheaper eateries. That is small sacrifice, for chefs are doing wondrous things with humbler ingredients. The listings include a number of newer restaurants that appear to have sufficient strength to beat the odds against survival in a very tough business. The usual caveats still apply: even the hardiest performers stumble, through changes in management, departures of key personnel, or simple off days. Loyalists will continue to exchange blows over the relative virtues of **Christ Cella** and **The Palm**, **Le Bernardin** and **Le Cirque**, all recommended here. No amount of arbitration will resolve the disputes, and anyway, they're fun.

What to expect

In the luxury category — achieved or pretended — four discernible strata of staff are usually present, although this is breaking down, too. The *maître* (or *maîtresse*) *d'hôtel* greets customers in calibrated degrees of warmth or *hauteur* at the entrance to the dining area. He (or she) checks reservations, assigns seating, and often escorts guests to their tables. The captain then takes over. Assigned responsibility for a specific section of the room, he brings menus, advises on unlisted specials, points out specialties of the house. He might never return, concentrating on directing his minions. Or he might take orders for cocktails and meals, supervise or perform tableside preparations, even pour water and fill wine glasses. Waiters are the work-horses, identified by less formal attire. Depending upon the organizational structure, they may absorb some or all of the captain's duties, as well as bringing food, drinks, and wine. The busboy, younger and in still another costume, clears dishes, replenishes bread baskets and empties ashtrays. One other post has virtually disappeared — that of the *sommelier* or wine steward.

New York waiters — and New Yorkers in general — have an undeserved reputation for churlishness. Service can be lackadaisical, and individuals are sometimes sullen or arrogant, but in roughly the same proportion as in any large city. More frequently, complaints are of benign ineptitude, for there is a shortage of formally trained employees. The slack is taken up by recent arrivals to the city, by immigrants, students, and the legions of young actors, dancers and artists drawn here every year. As often as not, their spriteliness compensates for their lack of experience, especially in those places in which food is less than the main event.

Foolish or irritating practices persist, but appear to be fading. Waiters used to be instructed to say, "Hi! I'm Lance [or whoever] and I'll be your server tonight." They were then called upon to recite long rosters of unlisted starters and main courses, complete with descriptions of their preparations (a taxing exercise in memory retention for both sides of the transaction). Now, their superiors have shortened their lists of daily specials or have hit upon the obvious device of typewritten addenda to the regular menu. "Auctioning" is less widespread. That's when "Lance" arrives at the table with four plates and asks, "Who gets the chicken?" (his memory bank apparently full to bursting with his prior recitation). One other irritating practice is less common than it was. That was when Lance swooped by and inquired, at the precise moment a patron had forked a piece of meat into his mouth, "Is everything all right?" Helpless nodding was the only possible response.

Advance reservations are essential for restaurants of the upper tiers. Some ask for a telephone number so that reservations can be confirmed on the day of the anticipated meal. Despite such precautions, so many customers make reservations they do not honor that restaurants are forced to overbook. Often this results in knots of people waiting at the door or in the bar, their appointed times ticking away. The imperious manner of some hosts is clearly a defense against the angry remonstrances of clients left waiting for their tables. Another annoyance is the effort of restaurateurs to impose two complete sittings of customers in a lunch hour that comfortably accommodates only one. The attempt to serve as many "covers" (meals) as possible is understandable, given the overheads of a business in the city, but this can ultimately be a disadvantage to the restaurant. Indeed, many restaurants thought to be impervious to customer disgruntlement have been struggling.

There are other lapses. Year-round availability of usually seasonal commodities can delight, as with oysters in non-"R" months, and fresh fruit in Feb. But this convenience is expensive. Winter tomatoes can be as hard as croquet balls, and April apples too often taste like potatoes. In traditional restaurants not bitten by the *nouvelle* bug, prodigious portions of food can dismay, as with prime rib hanging over the rim of the plate, leaving little room for the heap of cottage fries. Travelers accustomed to spicy-hot seasonings may be disappointed by the mildness of

Indian and Mexican dishes. Insistence on authentically fiery food usually produces results.

Cocktails, wines and other drinks

Although liquor consumption by Americans is at a three-decade low, the custom of a pre-dinner cocktail or two persists. If trying one for the first time, be forewarned that they are large and potent. The best-known is the Martini, which is two to three ounces of gin or vodka with a splash of dry vermouth, usually served with a twist of lemon peel or a couple of olives, and with or without ice. Some people still order a Manhattan, a sweetish mix of rye whiskey with red vermouth, swirled with bitters and topped with a cherry. Combinations and variations are endless. Even at a conservative count, there are no fewer than 1,000 recognized cocktails and related concoctions. Some are favored for particular meals or foods — the Bloody Mary for brunch, and the Margarita before Mexican or Latin meals. A glass of white wine, perhaps with a dash of cassis (kir) or soda water (spritzer), or mineral water with lime is often preferred to the harder liquors, especially at lunchtime, and bourbon and Scotch have suffered steep declines in sales. The practices of smoking cigarettes and drinking cocktails throughout a meal are still seen, but are regarded as gauche, at least in more sophisticated places. A city ordinance even requires larger restaurants to provide sections for nonsmokers. Although still wines are appropriate for most cuisines, beer is thought satisfactory for Middle-European, Chinese, Mexican and Indian meals.

New Yorkers were long reluctant to embrace the wines of California. This attitude was part pretension and part pragmatism. Seaports tend to face across the water rather than inland, and European bottlings were substantially cheaper than the Cabernets and Zinfandels of the West. Currency fluctuations changed that, and now more than 70 percent of all wines drunk in the US are from California. This is not deprivation. Blind tastings in Paris and elsewhere have proved that the wines of the Gironde and Napa valleys bear separate but equal virtues. Labels to look for are Robert Mondavi, Sterling, Heitz Cellars, David Bruce, Stag's Leap, Charles Krug, Beaulieu, Burgess, Caymus and Mayacammas, among many others. Popular-priced wines are blends of several varieties of grapes and typically carry names suggestive of type — "Chablis," "Burgundy," "Chianti" — or such fanciful appellations as "Emerald Dry" or "Rhine Garten." The better pressings are comprised primarily (at least 51 percent or more) of a single varietal grape, and bear that name, without adornment. Some are familiar to European wine buffs, others are native strains or hybrids. Among the prominent reds are Cabernet Sauvignon, Petite Sirah, Pinot Noir and Zinfandel; favored whites are Chardonnay, Chenin Blanc, Johannisberg Riesling and Sauvignon Blanc. Weather is a factor in California wines, but its influence is less pronounced than in Europe. Recent estimable red vintages are those of 1978, 1980, 1984, and 1985. Least successful years were 1979, 1983, and 1988. Whites have stayed on a fairly even keel, but are best drunk within 3yrs of bottling.

New York State is a distant second in production, accounting for only 10 percent of domestic consumption. Its Finger Lakes and Hudson Valley vineyards are best known for sparkling wines, but a number of vintners create worthy blends of offbeat varietals, and wineries recently established on eastern Long Island are doing well. Look for Bridgehampton, Clinton, Benmarl, and Bully Hill.

Beers are served at glacial temperatures, and imported brands are sold everywhere, in greatest profusion at pub-style restaurants. Brewed decaffeinated coffee is widely available. Tap water is excellent.

Budget strategies

As dinner for two at a top restaurant can easily match the tariff for a night in a good hotel, funds set aside for a New York vacation or business trip can evaporate at an alarming rate. However, there are ways to economize. Consider taking the "splurge" meal at lunch, rather than at dinner, when prices are as much as 40 percent lower. Same room, same waiters, same food. Luncheon menus are merely a little shorter. Take advantage of the increasing availability of wine by the glass, as they are often from respectable bottles, and there is less waste.

In the eternal effort to make maximum use of their staff and facilities, many restaurants offer pre- or post-theater menus. They usually require that patrons order before 7pm or after 10.30pm, and choices are obviously somewhat limited — but discounts can be as large as at lunchtime. Weekend brunch is another way to sample the wares of a restaurant that otherwise seems out of reach. Seek out those places with fixed-price (*prix fixe*) meals, now becoming the rule at high-class eateries. Although the price per person does not include drinks, tips, taxes, or (sometimes) dessert, the check is less likely to be a shock. Scrutinize that check carefully. Deliberate overcharging is rare, but lapses in addition aren't, and some owners now add a service charge, in the European manner. Don't tip twice.

Families and large groups can eat very well in ethnic restaurants, at a fraction of the cost of a meal at one of the temples of cuisine. Chinatown, Little Italy, Chelsea, and Greenwich Village are filled with inexpensive Italian *trattorias,* Spanish *restaurantes,* Japanese noodle stores, Kosher delicatessens, and pizza parlors. Low-priced Chinese restaurants are everywhere, and many old-style taverns have counters laden with simple but abundant meats, sausages and vegetables. And, if you must, there are branches of all the major franchised fast-food stores.

Restaurants classified by area

**Lower Manhattan
(below Canal St.)**
Bridge Café, The ▯ to ▯▯ 🛳 ✿
Golden Unicorn ▯▯ to ▯▯ ✿
Hee Seung Fung ▯▯ ✿
Montrachet ▯▯ to ▯▯▯
Odeon ▯▯▯
Phoenix Garden ▭ 🛳 ✿
Thailand ▯▯ ✿
Windows On The World ▯▯ ▯▯▯
  and ▯▯▯
**SoHo/Greenwich Village
(Canal St.-14th St.)**
Amici Miei ▯▯▯
Benny's Burritos ▭ 🛳 ✿
Chanterelle ▯▯▯
L'Ecole ▯▯▯
Gotham Bar and Grill ▯▯▯ to ▯▯▯
Greene Street Café ▯▯▯
Jane Street Seafood Café ▯▯▯
K-Paul's ▯▯▯
One Fifth ▯▯▯

Mulino, Il ▯▯▯
Sabor ▯▯ ✿
Vanessa ▯▯▯ to ▯▯▯
**Chelsea
(W 14th St.-W 23rd St.)**
Ballroom, The ▯▯▯
Cadillac Bar ▯▯▯
**Gramercy Park/Murray Hill
(E 14th St.-E 42nd St.)**
Park Bistro ▯▯▯ to ▯▯▯
Salta in Bocca ▯▯▯
Union Square Café ▯▯▯ to ▯▯▯ ✿
**Midtown East
(E 42nd St.-E 59th St.)**
Aurora ▯▯▯ △
Bukahara ▯▯▯ ✿
Christ Cella ▯▯▯
Cygne, Le ▯▯▯ △
Dawat ▯▯ to ▯▯ ✿
Four Seasons ▯▯▯ △
Hatsuhana ▯▯▯
Lutèce ▯▯▯ △

141

Restaurants

Oyster Bar and Restaurant
Palm, The
Quilted Giraffe, The
Rosa Mexicano
Sichuan Pavilion
Sparks
Take-Zushi

Midtown West
(W 42nd St.-W 59th St.)

Aquavit
Bernardin, Le
Cabana Carioca
Carnegie Delicatessen
Carolina
China Grill
Cité, La
Palio
Petrossian
Raga
Réserve, La
Russian Tea Room, The
Sam's
Sea Grill, The
21 Club
Un Deux Trois
Wylie's

Upper East Side
(E 60th St.-E 96th St.)

Arcadia
Arizona 206 and Café
Aureole
Cirque, Le
Contrapunto
Côte Basque, La
Elaine's
Mortimer's
Pamir
Parioli Romanissimo
Relais, Le
Veau d'Or, Le

Upper West Side
(W 60th St.-W 96th St.)

Alcala
Amsterdam's
Café des Artistes
Café Luxembourg
Ginger Man, The
Kasbah, La
Shun Lee
Tavern On The Green

Brooklyn

Gage and Tollner
River Café

Restaurants classified by type of cuisine

Afghan
Pamir

American
Amsterdam's
Arcadia
Arizona 206 and Café
Aureole
Bridge Café, The
Cadillac Bar
Carnegie Delicatessen
Carolina
Christ Cella
Gage and Tollner
Ginger Man, The
Gotham Bar and Grill
Jane Street Seafood Café
K-Paul's
Oyster Bar and Restaurant
Palm, The
Sam's
Sea Grill, The
Sparks
Union Square Café
Vanessa

Chinese
China Grill
Golden Unicorn
Hee Seung Fung
Phoenix Garden
Shun Lee
Sichuan Pavilion
Wylie's

Continental/International
Café des Artistes
Café Luxembourg
Elaine's
Four Seasons
Greene Street Café

Mortimer's
One Fifth
River Café
Tavern On The Green
21 Club
Windows On The World

Cuban
Sabor

French
Aurora
Bernardin, Le
Chanterelle
Cirque, Le
Cité, La
Côte Basque, La
Cygne, Le
L'Ecole
Lutèce
Montrachet
Odeon
Park Bistro
Petrossian
Quilted Giraffe, The
Relais, Le
Réserve, La
Un Deux Trois
Veau d'Or, Le

Indian
Bukahara
Dawat
Raga

Italian
Amici Miei
Contrapunto
Mulino, Il
Palio
Parioli Romanissimo
Salta in Bocca

Japanese
Hatsuhana *III*☐
Take-Sushi *III*☐
Latin American
Benny's Burritos ☐ 🍴 ♣
Cabana Carioca *I*☐ ♣
Rosa Mexicano *III*☐
Middle Eastern
Kasbah, La *I*☐ to *III*☐ ♣

Russian
Russian Tea Room, The *IIII*
Scandinavian
Aquavit *III*☐ to *IIII*
Spanish
Alcala *III*☐
Ballroom, The *IIII*
Thai
Thailand *I*☐ ♣

Alcala
349 Amsterdam Ave. (near 76th St.), NY 10023 ☎ 769-9600. Map 6L3 III☐ ☐ ■ AE ◉ VISA Open for dinner daily.
The brief fad for Spanish *tapas* was barely a tremor this side of the Atlantic, submerged beneath the Pan-Global gastronomic earthquakes of the last decade. Americans who never got around to eating these tasty bar snacks don't know what they're missing. They can find out here. It looks like Madrid, the long bar lined with platters of fresh anchovies, delicately fried squid, mussels, marinated olives, seafood salad, and whatever else the kitchen has chosen to prepare that day. The room is cleaner and airier than the *tascas* of the country of origin, not filled with smoke and refuse. Authentic tiles line both floors and walls.

The bar and the proper dining room don't start getting full until after 9pm, true to Spanish practice. It's easy enough to fill up on *tapas*: there are 20 or 25 on view or available to order — just keep pointing and eating until sated. If a full dinner is desired, the roast sucking pig is one of the best choices, the paella less impressive.

Amici Miei
475 West Broadway (Houston St.), NY 10012 ☎ 533-1933. Map 2T4 III☐ ☐ AE ◉ VISA Open daily.
SoHo starts at this congenial bar-trattoria, and it works hard to meet the social and dining needs of its knowing patrons. Apart from its full lunches and dinners, it offers, in lieu of the usual peanuts and pretzels, a filling happy hour snack of roast peppers and sun-dried tomatoes with chunks of bread. A grazer's delight of antipasti is also made available, selections of which can constitute a meal. Champagne brunch and special weekday lunches are appetizing in both price and flavor, and can be served either in the multileveled brick-walled interior or on the small summer patio.

Amsterdam's ♣
428 Amsterdam Ave. (near 81st St.), NY 10024 ☎ 874-1377. Map 6L2-3 I☐ ☐ ■ ☐ ■ AE ◉ ◉ VISA Open daily.
Its reputation as a singles bar overshadows its desirability as a rendezvous for Westsiders who know a dining bargain when they eat one. The reason for the primary identity is evident any evening after 6pm, when the bar at front is elbow-to-elbow with good-looking people waiting for a table and, with luck, a stranger of the opposite gender with whom to share it. Star attractions, however, are the racks of chicken and duck on rotating spits in the open kitchen. They send off maddeningly appetizing aromas and come to the table with three-green salads and side orders of super French fries. Simple and tasty, they are, and at prices that make Manhattan seem downright affordable. There is another, similar branch downtown (*454 Broadway ☎ 925-6166*).

Aquavit
13 W 54th St. (between 5th and 6th Ave.), NY 10019 ☎ 307-7311. Map 5N4 III☐ to IIII ☐ ■ ♀ AE ◉ VISA Closed Sat lunch, Sun.
This bright and saucy place has filled a vacancy as the only authentic Scandinavian in Manhattan. Behind the Museum of Modern Art and below an imposing Beaux Arts building that now houses a private bank, its entry floor is blond wood, and a long bar faces tables at a leather banquette. At the rear is a glass panel with a view of treetops. They prove to be the potted greenery of the formal dining room one level below. A domed glass vat at one end of the bar is filled with colored versions of aquavit, the Scandinavian firewater, served ice-cold in stemmed glasses. The usual chaser is beer, and both Danish and New York brews are on draft. At lunchtime only, those intricate open-faced sandwiches (*smørrebrød*) are available, evoking fond memories of Copenhagen's

143

Tivoli. Snacks and light meals include gravlax with mustard sauce and dill, and a *smörgåsbord* plate of herring, bleak roe, liver pâté and *vasterbotten* cheese, and salmon terrine. All are delectable. Downstairs, complete dinners might include monkfish with saffron, snow grouse or loin of venison. The menu is changed frequently. Fixed price lunches are a relative bargain for this level of quality. This welcome newcomer has beaten the frightening odds faced by all New York restaurateurs.

Arcadia

21 E 62nd St. (between Madison Ave. and 5th Ave.), NY 10021 ☎ *223-2900. Map 5N4* ▥ ▭ ▦
▣ ▣ ▦ *Closed Sun.*

Anne Rosensweig ascended rapidly into the pantheon of celebrity chefs at this, her compact and innovative Upper East Side showcase. Much in demand as a consultant, she isn't always on the premises, but her kitchen staff performs well in her absence. The menu is avowedly New American, with the customary borrowings from other continents — such delectables as crab cakes lying on a fricassée of corn, tomatoes, and *favas*, and pasta with mint-cured salmon, dill, and Jerusalem artichokes. At lunch, her trademark lobster club sandwich is a witty send-up of country-club banality, and immensely satisfying, to boot. In warm weather, the front opens, to allow two sidewalk tables. The relatively larger room in back is ringed with paintings in the manner of Thomas Hart Benton, the quintessential middle American muralist. A semicircular booth in the corner frequently encloses famous faces. Everyone else pretends they don't notice. Service is crisp, but without much warmth, and it can be forgetful. Those customers who have grown accustomed to nonsmoking sections in restaurants should know that this one is too small to have one. The food is so good that such minor carps hardly matter.

Arizona 206 and Café

206 E 60th St. (near 3rd Ave.), NY 10022 ☎ *838-0440 Map 5N5* ▭ *to* ▥ ▦ ▣ ▣ ▦ *Open daily.*

When it arrived on the scene, the then-exotic Arizona 206 single-handedly created the lust for New Southwestern victuals. That fad has dissipated, and the inevitable copycats never did manage to

duplicate the panache of this, the champ. The handsome main rooms are straight out of picture-book Santa Fe. They are also hard-surfaced stucco, which explains the often high noise level. That's small sacrifice for its lessons in this great regional cuisine, one that fires the palate without (necessarily) scorching the gullet. Essential ingredients of this cooking — cactus pears, poblano chilies, and such — are foreign to the shores of the Hudson, which partly explains the high prices in the main rooms. So, in a trend gaining favor throughout the city, a no-frills annex has been attached, offering fewer, less complex dishes at sharply lower tariffs. Not a jot of taste is lost. For proof, try the black bean soup — not nearly as humble as it sounds. Both sections are open daily for lunch and dinner. Bloomingdale's is just a traffic light away.

Aureole △

34 E 61st St. (near Madison Ave.), NY 10021 ☎ *319-1660. Map 5N4* ▥ ▦ ▣ ▣ ▦ *Closed Fri and Sat lunch, Sun.*

No restaurant opening was more eagerly anticipated than this. Charles Palmer made his bones at the **River Café** in Brooklyn, and when he set out on his own across the East River, his route was eagerly charted by food groupies. He didn't disappoint them. There is the space — two stories of a townhouse on the toney East Side. The downstairs looks out on a garden; upstairs is an airy, more private loft. Conservative and understated, the dining rooms are outfitted with banquettes, mostly in muted tones, and there are wall reliefs of assorted animals — deer, swans, geese. Huge baskets of flowers provide the color. Service is amiable, and not the least pompous.

And, there is the food — self-described as "progressive American," and hitting all the right notes. Appearing one night were yellowfin tuna *carpaccio* on a medley of mushrooms, partridge dumplings, sole wrapped in crisp-cooked potato and garnished with baby clams and fresh-snipped thyme twigs. Desserts, in the word of the astonished lady at the next table, are "killers." Young pastry wizard Rich Leach, and his staff of three, fashion remarkable concoctions. The daunting chocolate plate, for one, has a dollop of chocolate mousse, a glob of chocolate Bavarian, rolled wands of striated white and dark chocolate, and a chocolate basket with a chocolate lid. No chocolate freak can resist it. Palmer has leapt into the front rank of New York chefs and didn't even get his feet wet.

Aurora ⌂
60 E 49th St. (between Madison Ave. and Park Ave.), NY 10022 ☎ 692-9292. Map 5N4 ▥ ▯ ▤ � AE ▣ ▥ ▨ Open daily.

As a newcomer to the *haute* sweepstakes, Aurora did nearly everything right, and was rewarded by a band of sophisticated loyalists. That hot blush of success has faded, after chef changes and rumors of instability, but it remains a most agreeable choice. Far too often, establishments in this stratum treat their patrons as supplicants eager to endure *hauteur*, pretension, favoritism and bare inches of eating space. Aurora righted those wrongs. The welcome is uncommonly warm, the captains (who do most of the work) are helpful without being patronizing, friendly without being familiar. The lighting is flattering, the tables set well apart, the seating as comfortable as can be found. And the food, of the *nouvelle* Franco-American tradition, avoids the taint of preciousness. Diners looking for something to complain about might choose the decorative scheme, which features 2- and 3-dimensional representations of bubbles: in the carpet, the plates, the uniforms, and almost everywhere else. Highly polished wainscotting tempers the effect, as does the muted hum of satisfied conversation.

The Ballroom
253 W 28th St. (off 8th Ave.), NY 10001 ☎ 244-3005. Map 4P3 ▥ ▯ ▦ ▤ ⏃ ♪ ♥ *(sometimes).* Closed Sun dinner, Mon.

Spanish cuisine has received short shrift in the city. It deserved better than the pallid *paellas* and limp *gazpachos* that New Yorkers came to accept as representative, and it got it when chef Felipe Rojas-Lombardi emerged as a force on the local culinary scene. He started with a fresh look at *tapas* — the tasty snacks Spaniards take before, after, or in lieu of meals. They are laid out along the handsome bar: platters of marinated sliced sow ears, chunks of rabbit, fist-sized quail, scallop *seviche*, fried squid rings. The display changes by night and season. Venturesome young customers snaffle up these goodies as they absorb the live flamenco guitar. Two or three *tapas* constitute

a light meal, but the full dinner is not to be shunned. The management also lays on a cabaret in a separate room, so once settled in, there's hardly a reason to leave, unless it be the highish prices.

Benny's Burritos ▦ ♣
113 Greenwich Ave. (Jane St.), NY 10014 ☎ 633-9210. Map 2R3 ▯ No credit cards. Open daily.

Neon and plastic laminates are to be expected at a place with a name such as this, and that's what you get at Greenwich Village's *numero uno* tortilla joint. But burritos this good aren't found in abundance this far N and E of the Rio Grande, so pay the surroundings no attention. These Tex-Mex gifts to the world are about the length and thickness of an average forearm, the huge tortilla encasing such maddeningly tasty innards as black beans, cheese, guacamole, sour cream, rice, and shredded chicken or beef. Enchiladas and quesadillas are other possibilities. There's another branch (*93 Ave. A, near 6th St.*) on the shabbier Lower East Side.

Le Bernardin ⌂
155 W 51st St. (near 7th Ave.), NY 10001 ☎ 489-1515. Map 4N3 ▥ ▰ ▤ ▣ ▥ Closed Sun.

The grandfather of the chef-proprietor was a fisherman, and his father was a fisherman who also ran a bistro. So it is in the natural order of things that Gilbert Le Coze chose to open a seafood restaurant. His first gained two stars from Michelin. This one, in the new Equitable Building, was an instant success, and so demanding that he closed the one in France. In the eyes of many New Yorkers, including the author, his creation is at the very apex of the local gastronomical pyramid. A meal at Le Bernardin is honeyed mellifluence, from entrance to satisfied departure. That assessment assumes, to be sure, that the patron is not a fish-hater. Mr Le Coze allows only a single meat entrée to sully the purity of his oceanic fare. He has had to make a few concessions to the relative naiveté of Americans as regards the exotic creatures that form part of his repertoire. The "sea squab" turns out to be blowfish, hardly a staple table item this side of the briny. But such subterfuge is infrequent, and he introduced sea urchin, skate and tuna *carpaccio* to his eager (and monied) acolytes, along with supernal preparations of grouper, scallops, halibut, and red snapper, among many. The room is large and warmly furnished, its soaring ceilings sheathed in glowing wood, and the walls hung with innocuous paintings of fishermen, and still lifes. The staff is friendly (when encouraged to be) and helpful. "*Scrape* the flesh of the skate from the shell," advises the captain when asked, "don't slice it like steak." Their pride in working here is evident, and many graduated from such estimable places as **Lutèce** and **Le Cirque**. Their chef, one says, "can tell at a glance whether a cod has been out of the water six hours or 24," and "fish stores save their best for him." A thoughtfulness gratefully acknowledged is a menu that is printed in large, readable type, without hyperbole, and in English.

It will come as no surprise that such munificence comes at a price. Save a little by ordering wine by the glass — there are two reds and two whites available daily, evenly divided between French and California vintages. And avoid those few dishes with supplementary charges over and above the *prix fixe*. But if at all possible, do not miss what may be one of the most memorable dining experiences of a lifetime.

The Bridge Café ☕ ✿
279 Water St. (Dover St.), NY 10038 ☎ 227-3344. Map 3T5 ▯▯ to ▯▯▯ ☐ ☖ Closed Sat lunch. No reservations. No cards.
Wavy floors, a stamped tin ceiling, and a well-used bar-counter attest to the age of this venerable seamen's watering hole. It is believed that the core structure went up in 1801, although there have inevitably been remodelings.

Since the recapture of the café from disintegration a number of years ago, an imaginative menu at fair tariffs has drawn a loyal clientele of politicians from the nearby Civic Center, and aware New Yorkers from the burgeoning lower Manhattan and Brooklyn communities. Everything is at its freshest — fish, vegetables, fowl. The blackboard of the day's fare changes daily, according to market availability. Among the seasonal staples, chili, calamari, tortellini and omelets are dependable. Wines are priced at only slightly above retail, and there are several imported beers on tap. Irish coffee with real whipped cream is sufficient reason to stop by after a chilly day at the nearby South Street Seaport.

Bukahara ✿
148 E 48th St. (between Lexington Ave. and 3rd Ave.), NY 10017 ☎ 838-1811. Map 5O4 ▯▯▯ ☐ ☖ Ⓨ 🆎 ☖ ⊙ 💳 Open daily.
Diners are encouraged to use their fingers, not silverware, to eat this splendid Indian food. That's why the hot towels precede, not follow, the meal, and the napkin is an oversized bib. Digging a hand into a salad with a vinaigrette dressing is some people's notion of sensuality. If it isn't yours, order a knife and fork and plunge into sublimely tender and aromatic tandoori chicken and lamb. The lights in their perforated copper shades are low, the wooden tables and chairs are massive, and they rest on Oriental rugs. (The eponymous Bokharas hang on the walls.) This is easily one of the two or three most accomplished Indian restaurants in Manhattan. That in mind, lunch and weekend brunch are remarkably inexpensive. The only regret is not being able to finish everything, so substantial are the portions.

Cabana Carioca ✿
123 W 45th St. (near 6th Ave.), NY 10036 ☎ 581-8088. Map 5O4 ▯▯ ☐ ☖ Ⓨ ☖ ⊙ 💳 Open daily.
When the tariffs of the city's best-known restaurants seem dizzying, consider the ethnic restaurants. This one is on a midtown block handy to the Broadway theaters. Brazilian food has not caught the attention of the larger populace, so a full dinner for two here is still very reasonable. Inside, the place looks as if it were once a hut on the banks of the Amazon River, blaring with bright colors and gaudy folk paintings. The tropical drinks (try an inhibition-loosening *caipirinha*) are a fitting way to contemplate the joyously raucous scene. No one need remain an outsider for long. The luncheon buffets are an uncommon bargain, but if the national dish, *feijoada*, is on hand, don't hesitate. A boggling portion of the black stew of beef, pork, and sausage is easily enough to share between 2-3 people. Or, take the safer route of shrimp *paulista*. The best soup is *caldo verde*. Desserts are the bland Latin norm.

An annex called **Cabana Carioca II** has opened down the street (*#133*). It strives for a glossier tone, which takes away some of the fun, but serves essentially the same dishes.

Cadillac Bar
15 W 21st St. (near 5th Ave.), NY 10010 ☎ *645-7220. Map 5Q4* ⫴ 🞐 📖 ⏣ 🅰🄴 ⊕ 📷 🆅🆂🅰 *Closed Sat lunch.*

And now for something completely different. On the frontier of Chelsea sits a transplanted Texas bar — big, of course, and brassy, naturally. The floor is bare and the ceiling is high. Up there, the ducts, pipes and cables are all orange. Reaching about 3m up the walls are layer upon layer of graffiti. The management encourages this defacement by its young patrons, assuming they demonstrate a modicum of taste. Order a Tequila Shooter from the comely cowgirl waitress, her chest crisscrossed with bandoliers (filled with shot-glasses instead of bullets). In her holsters she carries a bottle of tequila and a bottle of 7-Up, and pours some of each in a glass, covers it with a piece of paper and pounds it on the table while making a mirror-cracking unearthly screech. Toss it down and give her back the glass. Toward the end of the week, people stack up six deep around the rectangular bar (with its canopy of empty beer bottles). Authentic Mexicans shine shoes and take photos of customers in embroidered sombreros. And the food? It's Tex-Mex, and not too bad. Try the *fajitas, carnitas*, or *cabrito* (baby goat). No reservations are accepted in the evening, except for larger parties, but with that "Shooter Girl" around, time passes quickly. Open late every night.

Café des Artistes
1 W 67th St. (Central Park W), NY 10023 ☎ *877-3500. Map 4M3* ⫴ *to* ⫴⫴ 🞐 📖 🅰🄴 ⊕ 🆅🆂🅰 *Open daily.*

George Lang transformed this long dreary dining room into one of the liveliest bistros on the West Side. Praise for the rejuvenation lies more with the menu than the decor, if only because the decor needed less effort — with touch-ups, a nostalgic 1920s glow was wrested from the former dowdiness. Murals by Howard Chandler Christy, featuring chastely voluptuous nudes, are set off by banks of plants and ornate mirrors. Vaguely familiar faces lean over hurricane lamps and snowy napery. The already ambitious card is supplemented by several daily specials in all categories. Among recent memorable offerings are a grilled swordfish paillard with mustard sauce, roast duck with brandied pear *compôte, pot au feu*, and *cassoulet*. The very popular weekend brunch has featured curried seafood stew, and a meal-in-itself *pâté* and *charcuterie* platter. The setting and the excellent value for money deservedly keep this satisfying retreat among those consistently favored by New Yorkers, year after year. One could wish for a trace more warmth from the service staff, but there is little else to fault. Men must wear jackets after 5pm. Reservations are essential.

Café Luxembourg
200 W 70th St. (near Amsterdam Ave.), NY 10023 ☎ *873-7411. Map 6M2* ⫴⫴ 🞐 📖 🅰🄴 ⊕ 📷 🆅🆂🅰 *Closed Mon-Sat lunch.*

This, the younger sibling of TriBeCa's **Odeon**, replicates the jovial blend of funk and professionalism that made that estimable *boîte* such a solid success. It might be the ultimate Upper West Side restaurant, serving as it does a community with a happily confused identity of high-minded art, New Wave frivolity, traditional Bohemianism and simple urban striving. The Deco-Moderne setting of marble and mirrors, jazzy window treatments and colorful tiles is filled from late afternoon to early morning with an ecumenical spectrum of social types: elderly neighborhood couples, flamboyant singles, young executives and conceptual artists. They come for food that observes fashion and stimulates all the appropriate senses, but doesn't demand the sham reverence of those places that imagine a *sole meunière* to be the equivalent of a Bach sonata. Daily appetizer, entrée and wine specials supplement the set menu. The nightly *prix fixe* dinner, served between 5.30-6.30pm, is about half the price of a regular meal.

Carnegie Delicatessen 🍴 ✿
854 7th Ave. (55th St.), NY 10019 ☎ *757-2245. Map 4N3* 🞐

The co-owner of this prototypical Jewish "deli" was a minor media star, abetted by Woody Allen, who chose the Carnegie as a set for one of his films. That fact is duly noted on the menu. The waiters are, by turns, rude, chatty and amusingly cynical. Eating (it can't be called dining) at the Carnegie means sitting elbow to elbow at tables crammed together in rows, with requisite bowls of free pickles placed at intervals among them. Matzo ball soup and cheesecake are winners.

Be forewarned: when they describe their sandwiches as "gargantuan," it is not hyperbole. A construction of turkey and beef brisket is 6 inches high, with nearly a pound of each meat inside. It could satisfy a family of four. There is often a line out onto the sidewalk, but it moves quickly. They only close between 4am and 6.30am.

Carolina
355 W 46th St. (8th Ave.), NY 10036 ☎ 245-0058. Map 4O3 ▥▥
▭ ▤▤ ⬚ ▣ *ⱽⁱˢᵃ*

Mislabeling is a not-infrequent by-product of New York's enthusiasm for domestic regional cuisines. The states of North and South Carolina may be in the Southeast, but this "Carolina" features the cooking of the Southwest. No matter. Most of what comes out of the open kitchen tastes just fine, be it grilled salmon or swordfish steak or racks of barbecued ribs slow-cooked over mesquite coals. This is simple, tangy fare that sets the nostrils flaring even before it arrives at the table. To start, there is corn chowder or hot smoked sweet sausage with roasted peppers. To follow, bourbon baked ham with black cherry sauce or meltingly tender beef brisket. The snug back room, beyond the kitchen, is visually opened with wrap-around mirrors and a pyramidal skylight, but the tables out front are less crowded. It remains one of the better choices along the theater district's "Restaurant Row."

Chanterelle
2 Harrison St. (Hudson), NY 10013 ☎ 966-6960. Map 2T4 ▥▥▥
▭ ▣▣ ⬚ ▣ *ⱽⁱˢᵃ Closed lunch, Sun, Mon.*

Anti-establishmentarians develop their own rituals, uniforms and convictions. It once seemed that every bar and restaurant in the new Bohemia of lower Manhattan was to be a garage or loft, stripped to bare brick walls, hung with green industrial lamps and filled with potted ferns. Chanterelle has only its lofty space in common with its neighbors. Now in a new, larger, TriBeCa location, it retains the spare serenity of its earlier incarnation, with only a huge vase of flowers to soften its conspicuously hard-edged minimalism. The obsessive chef-owner pursues his trade with not a trace of frivolity, which may be counted among his few failings. His productions demonstrate respect for

148

basic tenets of *nouvelle cuisine*, but few of the extremes to which some of his colleagues have gone. Furthermore, measured growth is evident. If the meal taken there last year was good, the one tonight almost surely will be better. The menu changes constantly. Reserve ahead.

China Grill
60 W 53rd St. (near 6th Ave.), NY 10019 ☎ 333-7788. Map 5N4 ▥▥▥▥
▭ ▤▤ ⬚ ▣ *ⱽⁱˢᵃ Closed Sat and Sun lunch.*

Much of the first floor of CBS headquarters — tagged "Black Rock" for its dark granite facing — is set aside for a restaurant. The first four attempts failed, but this one succeeded. The cavernous block-to-block space has no carpets or drapes to absorb sound, and the buzz of 400 diners soon builds to a roar, helped by a stereo system thumping out rock music. The type of Californian cuisine often called "Chinois" is served in this arena of manufactured chic, the marriage of Eastern and Western ingredients and techniques symbolized by the open kitchen in the corridor between the two dining rooms. On one side, Asians cook with huge woks, on the other, Occidentals use skillets. What they produce can be stunning. No one believes the "crispy spinach," the leaves of the humble vegetable flash-fried in peanut and sesame oil to the texture of ancient paper about to crumble. Nubbins of warmed raw tuna arrive in lightest tempura batter, a feat comparable to sautéing ice cream. "Confucius Chicken Salad" comes in a much larger helping, a fitting prelude to the tasty "Grilled Dry Aged Szechuan Beef," tossed in scented oil and cilantro. Since all dishes are served Chinese-style (to share), two people can ease the bite of the check by ordering only one appetizer, one main course and one dessert. Advance reservations are nearly always necessary, especially for dinner, when the thin and rich nightbirds flock to this aviary.

Christ Cella
160 E 46th St. (7th Ave.), NY 10017 ☎ 697-2479. Map 4O3 ▥▥▥▥
▭ ▣▣ ⬚ ▣ *ⱽⁱˢᵃ Closed Sat lunch, Sun.*

Call it "Krisella" or "Kreechella." Either way, it is a place for people who like their food simple — and are willing to pay for it. The two floors of this 1926 landmark steakhouse are assertively plain, with bare floors, indifferent seascapes on the walls, uncushioned chairs and waiters in aprons. Patrons unknown to the management can be shunted to the bleaker upstairs rooms. There isn't a written menu, but the recited selections do not tax the memory. Basic appetizers are shrimp or crabmeat cocktails, spinach or Caesar salad; entrées are roast beef, sirloin steak, huge lobsters, veal or lamb chops, broiled fish, scallops; desserts are cheesecake, ice cream. Obviously, people who prefer drama or elegance or intricacy of preparation should go elsewhere. Those who have business to conduct, without distraction, find Christ Cella suits their purposes exactly. Men are expected to wear jacket and tie.

Le Cirque ⌂

58 E 65th St. (near Madison Ave.), NY 10021 ☎ 794-9292. Map 5M4 ▥▥▥ ▭ ▬ ▆ *AE* ◉ *Closed Sun.*

Some of the ladies who lunch here are principally concerned with staying below their normal weight and with which $5,000 designer dress to wear for the next benefit for the homeless. Others are key players in the mightiest circles of finance, politics and Hollywood. Presumably, a few even go for the food, which is excellent. It does not, however, distract from the mutual ogling and exchanges of insider gossip that charge the atmosphere. After all, their companions often include such folk as Nancy and Ronald Reagan, Sylvester Stallone, assorted Vanderbilts, and, of course, Woody Allen. Their arena is a lovely, flower-bedecked room ringed by banquettes, the tables scant inches apart (the better to eavesdrop). Mere mortals are allowed to attend, providing they dress well and have made reservations 2wks ahead and confirmed them the day before. They cannot expect the best tables, reserved for the regulars, but they will not be placed too far from the action, and they are not subjected to the *hauteur* of other places of similar pretense but less achievement. Rarely are restaurants of this exalted order so unintimidating. Sirio Maccioni orchestrates. He is one of those personages known by his first name, a transplanted Italian who rules his domain with unquestioned, if velvety, authority. The chef is French, and the menu reflects both influences. Sirio insists that he invented *pasta primavera*, a dish so good it has become a cliché. In a show of currently fashionable menu rustication, the otherwise plebeian *pot au feu* is here brought to new heights of perfection. Desserts are splendid. For all this, the final reckoning is no more staggering than at the few other restaurants with which Le Cirque can be fairly compared.

La Cité

120 W 51st St. (near 7th Ave.), NY 10019 ☎ 956-7100. Map 4N3 ▥▥▥ *to* ▥▥▥ ▭ ▬ ▆ *AE* ◉ *VISA Main room closed Sat and Sun lunch; grill open daily.*

This midtown extravaganza was a hit from the day it opened its doors. Inevitably, time was needed to bring all components into smooth synchronization, especially the serving staff, which floundered quite a bit at the outset. There's a good idea lurking here — a Manhattan version of a Parisian brasserie, coupled with a plainer, more casual grill room offering similar food at somewhat lower prices. The deviation from their Gallic models is that neither facility can be regarded as an inexpensive or even moderately-priced destination. That aside, there is much to compel a visit, not least their proximity to the theater district and the possibility of a snack or a meal any time from 11am-2am. The main room is a dual-level Art Deco phantasmagoria with giant chandeliers and crimson velvet banquettes; the adjoining grill is quieter and less conspicuously decorated. Chicken, fish, and steak in their less complicated guises are safest. To get out the door with bank account nearly intact, consider the big rich crock of onion soup in the grill, which is accompanied by a basket of five honorable chewy breads. It brings back memories of Les Halles. Just the thing for after *The Phantom of the Opera*.

Contrapunto ♣

1009 3rd Ave. (corner of 60th St.), NY 10022 ☎ 751-8616. Map 5N5 ▥▥▥ ▭ *AE* ◉ ◉ *VISA Open daily.*

The minimalist quasi-Milanese setting is on the second floor overlooking lively Third Avenue, above another bar-restaurant called **Yellowfingers** and next door to **Arizona 206**. Very bright track lighting, wooden chairs, a perky espresso machine, and glass tops

149

over white tablecloths are the extent of the decor. Concentrate on the food. It is fetchingly fresh pasta, dressed rather than sauced. Mushrooms of the season are grilled, peppered, sprinkled with minced garlic and parsley, drizzled with oil — a delicious starter. *Bresaola parmigiano* (dried beef with oil and cheese) is good, too. All manner of pasta forms are tossed with sweet pepper slivers, or with tomato and Pecorino cheese, or with exotic fungi, or with Ricotta, grated nutmeg and chopped chives. Italian-style *gelati* are made right here, in such surprising flavors as praline, grapefruit and white chocolate. Chocolate fudge cake is a boggler. They don't take reservations, so expect a wait, probably in the downstairs bar.

La Côte Basque ⌂
5 E 55th St. (near 5th Ave.), NY 10022 ☎ *688-6525. Map 5N4* ▥▥
▢ ▦ ➡ AE ◉ ◑ ▨ *Closed Sun.*

Henry Soulé introduced serious *haute cuisine* to New York, and his disciples soon began opening places of their own on every midtown block. La Côte Basque was one of the maestro's creations, and he died while working here in 1966. Not long after, it looked as if the restaurant might expire as well, but it was resuscitated by chef-proprietor Jean-Jacques Rachou in the early 1980s. Soulé would be proud of his successor, for Rachou is not afraid to create such familiar fare as *cassoulet* and tarragon chicken, in generous portions that would make the avatars of *nouvelle cuisine* blanch. The disingenuously homey room even retains its red banquettes and the original Lamotte murals of the Basque coast, flying in the face of the current design school that dictates hard polished surfaces and seating that looks better than it feels. Its resultant popularity with the privileged over-40s set causes traffic jams in the vestibule, especially at lunchtime. Unless known to the management, persons with 1.30pm reservations can expect to wait 15mins or more. The flavors of some dishes can prove somewhat wan, as in one special appetizer with saffron in its name but none visible in its taste or color. Another irritation is that the menu is only in French, an affectation that deserves prohibition by law. However, the staff is gracious and anticipatory, the customers genteel and/or celebrated, and the prices, although

high, are not unreasonable. Good-to-excellent wines are served by the glass. The lunch menu is up to 40 percent cheaper than dinner.

Le Cygne ⌂
55 E 54th St. (Madison Ave.), NY 10022 ☎ *759-5941. Map 5N4* ▥▥
▢ ▦ ➡ AE ◉ ◑ ▨ *Closed Sat, Sun.*

You may very well have your best meal in New York at "The Swan." The host treats with equal favor patrons old and new, celebrities and unknowns, and his captains harbor no lofty notions of their station: he makes menu suggestions, clears dishes, and fills glasses, with grace and warmth. This second home (next door to the original) is in cool grays and slate blue, severely Modernist outside and faintly nautical (as in *QEII*) within. The upstairs room is as soothing as the main floor, if a touch more frenetic at peak hours. Bouquets of flowers are everywhere. Fixed-price lunches and dinners are not inexpensive, and with supplementary charges and injudicious wine selection, dinner for two can rocket into the stratosphere.... and higher.

Dawat ♣
210 E 58th St. (between 2nd Ave. and 3rd Ave.), NY 10022 ☎ *355-7555 Map 5N5* ▯ *to* ▥▯
▢ ▦ ➡ AE ◉ ◑ ▨ *Closed Sun lunch.*

In a city with a burgeoning number of restaurants of Indian and allied subcontinental persuasions, Dawat not only ranks at the top, it surpasses the genre. Count it among the best of any kind, and go for lunch to get a bargain in the process. The three special noon meals cost less than a couple of hamburger platters at far less distinguished eateries. The "light" fish lunch, for one, arrives in bowls and little copper pans — one with curried tilefish, another with gingered cauliflower, a third with rice and vegetables, plus a salad, mango chutney, yogurt, and a superb rendition of the puffy bread *nan*. At dinner, a comparable spread, with drinks, wine, and dessert can race toward the ▥▥▥ price band. Service is, if anything, overly attentive. The decor is restrained, with groupings of carved heads spotlighted on salmon-pink walls.

L'Ecole ▨
462 Broadway (Grand St.), NY 10013 ☎ *219-3000 Map 2S4* ▥▥▯
▦ ➡ AE ◉ ◑ ▨ *Closed Sun.*

On the seedy SE edge of SoHo, an airy light-filled ground-floor space stops passers-by in their tracks. It is a vision of understated elegance, with French country chairs, spinning overhead fans, and a small wine bar. Despite appearances, it is a classroom for students in the respected French Culinary Institute. The ambitious menu changes monthly. There are glitches in service and presentation, as charitable patrons will understand, but the overall performance is admirable. Besides, the fixed-price lunches and dinners are considerably cheaper than can be expected elsewhere for food of equally high intent. The wine card features several bottles a day, at retail prices, not the usual 100 or 200 percent markup. Go give the kids a chance to show what they've learned. In a few years, you'll have to pay a lot more for their services.

Elaine's
1703 2nd Ave. (near E 88th St.), NY 10028 ☎ *534-8114. Map 7K5* ⬚⬚⬚ ⬚ ⬚ *Closed Sat and Sun lunch.*
Luminaries of the literary world and, by mutual attraction, from show business and politics, make this saloon-restaurant their own. The proprietress takes care of them, saving their favorite tables and shooing away *paparazzi* and gawpers. There is no reason to believe they come for the mainly Italian food, for it is only adequate, and may account for the fact that no one shows up before 10pm.

Four Seasons △ ⬚⬚⬚
99 E 52nd St. (Park Ave.), NY 10022 ☎ *754-9494. Map 5N4* ⬚⬚⬚ ⬚ ⬚ ⬚ ⬚ ⬚ ⬚ *Open Mon-Sat noon-3pm, 5-11.30pm.*
Lunch is the main event here, and the so-called **Grill Room** is the arena. Publishers soothe brand-name authors and their agents in a daily ritual in which every change of table or occupant is duly charted. Unknowns are hustled up and out of sight into the Grill Room Siberia, a small room with a portrait of James Beard to compensate for being away from the action. The dinner locus shifts to the **Pool Room**, with its floral bounty and marble-bound pool. It is a vaulted space 3 stories high, at the base of the Seagram Building. Some find it rather arctic, but the tables are comfortably spaced, and much of the artwork is rotated four times a year. Officially designated a

landmark space, it is the first restaurant in New York to be so honored. The food, usually of the highest quality, is almost worth the prices. The scope is broad enough to qualify for the catch-all "continental" label, with chocolate cake the preferred topper. The superior cellar highlights American vintages. Fixed-price pre-theater dinners are a way to sample at lower cost.

Gage and Tollner ⬚⬚⬚
372 Fulton St. (near Borough Hall), Brooklyn, NY 11201 ☎ *(718) 875-5181. Map 3V7* ⬚⬚⬚ ⬚ ⬚ ⬚ ⬚ *Closed Sat lunch, Sun.*
This is an officially designated landmark, handy to Brooklyn Heights. The gaslit Gay Nineties atmosphere is authentic, because it opened in 1879. It hasn't changed much since, and some of the staff look as if they might have been around as long. They wear emblems attesting to their years of employment. Seafood has always been its *raison d'être*, and the bisques and soles and snappers are all good, in some cases surpassingly so. Of late, the food has taken a turn toward the American South, with she-crab soup and chicken baked in parchment both well worth a try.

The Ginger Man ♣
51 W 64th St. (near Broadway), NY 10023 ☎ *399-2358. Map 6M3* ⬚⬚⬚ ⬚ ⬚ ⬚ ⬚ *Open daily.*
Sustenance, not wonderment, is the function of the hamburgers and full dinners in this cozy, crowded tavern-restaurant directly across Broadway from the Lincoln Center. The patrons, after all, are either anticipating or savoring the ballet or opera or concert they will attend or have just left. In that frame of mind, a profound culinary experience would be wasted, even if it were available. Serviceability is therefore the keynote, and simplicity the greater virtue. Choose from the menu accordingly. From 6-8pm and 10pm until closing it is jammed, from the glass-enclosed sidewalk room all the way to the back. Keep in mind the possibility of a quiet breakfast in the grill-room snuggery, especially when it's cold enough outside for a fire within.

Golden Unicorn ♣
18 E Broadway (Catherine St.), NY 10038 ☎ *941-0911. Map 3T5* ⬚⬚ *to* ⬚⬚⬚ ⬚ ⬚ ⬚ ⬚ *Open daily.*

Two gaudy floors in a building just E of Chatham Square herald the presence of a much-noted new Hong Kong restaurant. *Dim sum* and Cantonese cooking spark the joyful din, as trolleys rattle by laden with goodies, and patrons exclaim over the inventive seafood specialties. To make the most of it all, go with a gang of four or more dedicated eaters.

Gotham Bar and Grill
12 E 12th St. (5th Ave. and University Place), NY 10003
☎ *620-4020. Map 2R4* ▥▥ *to* ▥▥
▭ ▭ AE ◉ ◎ ▦ *Closed Sat and Sun lunch.*
Despite the folksy name, there is little that is self-effacing about this high-rise monument to contemporary American cooking. It is large, bustling, and, abetted by New Age music on the stereo, inevitably loud at peak dining hours. The food is testimony to the puissance of relentless culinary invention, each dish one step ahead of cliché: warm skate salad, duck *terrine*, goat cheese ravioli, veal *carpaccio*, and, of course, pasta with almost anything. In less capable hands, it could be dismissed as all flash and fad, but Alfred Portale is a master, not a follower. Allowing for the occasional breakdown behind the swinging doors, a meal here is almost certain to be memorable. The head chef's trademark towering presentations — pyramids of food in imminent danger of collapse — help to imprint a visual, as well as gustatory, impression. (Freud might have something to say about Portale's edible edifice complex.) If anything is lacking at Gotham, it is that sense of playfulness that reminds us that a meal is not a benediction, but something we have to do again in a few hours.

Greene Street Café
101 Greene St. (near Prince St.), NY 10012 ☎ *925-2415. Map 2S4*
▥▥▭ ▾ ♪ AE ◉ ◎ ▦ *Open daily.*
An all-inclusive drinking-dining-entertainment center, its interior expands beyond the SoHo norm, with walls of brick and groves of greenery within a towering cube of space modified by balconies and staircases. The young and uniformly attractive servers are capable of reeling off numbingly long lists of daily specials. A playful global cuisine is the inclination of the busy kitchen, with a New American

orientation. Most preparations are well above par, and prices are surprisingly fair. It is easy to start with early evening cocktails in the active front bar, and stay past midnight. Piano or chamber music usually accompanies dinner (allowing for the latest enthusiasm of the hyperactive owner, Tony Goldman) and there is jazz most nights at 11pm (for which there is a cover charge and a two-drink minimum for non-diners). It is essential to make a reservation. Next door is an allied enterprise, the **SoHo Kitchen** (*#103* ☎ *925-1866*), its featured attraction a huge Cruvinet that can serve glasses of wine from up to 100 bottles. The simpler fare of burgers and pizzas doesn't compete for attention.

Hatsuhana
17 E 48th St. (between 5th Ave. and Madison Ave.), NY 10017
☎ *335-3345. Map 5O4* ▥▥ ▭ AE
◉ ◎ ▦ *Closed Sat lunch, Sun.*
The idea of ingesting raw fish was once daunting to Americans. Now, *sushi* and *sashimi* are just two more food categories among ever-expanding dining options. Hatsuhana helped in this acceptance, and remains a heavy favorite of enthusiasts. It is authentic, the close quarters make it easy to strike up a conversation, dieters can save calories, the cost isn't high, and a full meal is light enough to precede 2hrs in a theater seat. Young Japanese adroitly slice quivering fresh tuna and shrimp, wrap them in sheets of kelp, top with salmon eggs, arrange them artistically on lacquered trays of vinegared rice, all within inches of the diners at the two long narrow pine counters. Most customers eat at the *sushi-sashimi* bars, where they can see their food prepared. But there are tables, too. Stop off also at their other branch (*237 Park Ave.*
☎ *661-3400*).

Hee Seung Fung ♣
46 Bowery (near Elizabeth St.), NY 10013 ☎ *374-1319. Map 3S5*
▥ ▭ ▦ *No cards. Open daily.*
There is an uptown branch of "HSF," but this is the original. Although full meals are served after 5pm, the source of its success is Hong Kong-style *dim sum*, available from 7.30am on. These are tasty morsels in appetizer portions, of apparently limitless variety. The division of labor is clear: waiters bring drinks (for which you pay immediately) and the check. In

between, waitresses trundle endlessly by with trolleys loaded with dumplings, sliced fowl, shrimp rolls and assorted exotica. You choose what appeals. Be selective, for something better is just behind. When the place is crowded, strangers may be seated at your table. They don't remain strangers long, and if they are Chinese-Americans, they can be of help in identifying the contents of dishes. Dinners are inexpensive, but better can be had a block or two in any direction.

Jane Street Seafood Café
31 8th Ave. (Jane St.), NY 10014
☎ 243-9237. Map 2R3 ▥ ◻ ☿
ᴀᴇ ◉ ᴠɪsᴀ Open daily, dinner only.
This is a hint of spare and salty New England in the NW corner of Greenwich Village. The ceiling is low and of molded tin, the walls exposed brick, tables are bare wood, and there is even a fireplace — with a fire, when weather dictates. Wear your most comfortable clothes, arrive in a patient mood, since there will be a wait, and eventually settle in to a meal composed of produce fresh from the market. Everyone raves about the bread, the coleslaw, the chowder, but those are merely starters. Little that follows will disappoint. Steamed lobster, for one, is done as well as it can be. No advance reservations are accepted, but the bar in front is convivial.

La Kasbah ♣
70 W 71st St. (Columbus), NY 10023 ☎ 769-1690. Map 6M3 ▥ to ▥ ◻ ▬ ᴀᴇ ◉ ᴠɪsᴀ Closed Sat-Thurs lunch, Fri.
No one need know a thing about the kitchen's *glatt* kosher cooking rules to appreciate these five tasty versions of *couscous*, mounded with chicken, lamb, or vegetables. Given the size of the portions, appetizers, although available, aren't really necessary. The setting isn't the Middle Eastern seraglio that might be imagined. Tables are snugly spaced, in peach-colored rooms with aqua trim. Lamb is the most expensive item, of course, but even it will not spoil the pleasant surprise of the reckoning. Early-bird specials are available Mon-Thurs until 6pm, at even lower prices.

K-Paul's
622 Broadway (between Bleecker St. and Houston St.), NY 10012 ☎ 460-9633. Map 2R4

▥ ◻ ▬ ᴀᴇ ◉ ᴠɪsᴀ Dinner only. Closed Sat, Sun.
With his famous New Orleans restaurant and a heavily-touted and influential cookbook, Paul Prudhomme was almost singlehandedly responsible for thrusting Cajun cooking into the national consciousness. For a time, his signature recipe for blackened redfish threatened to put that over-exploited creature on the endangered species list. Eventually, inevitably, he brought his formidable reputation and exceedingly robust self to New York, presumably on the theory that you haven't really "made it" unless you have prevailed in the Big Apple. It was intended to be a road trip, a tryout to see if America's most distinctive regional cuisine could travel well. The lines immediately formed along lower Broadway, and still do, so K-Paul's is now a permanent presence. Here is the place to see what Cajun popcorn (batter-fried crayfish) and gumbo are all about. Fortunately, Mr. Prudhomme has relented on his "no reservations" policy. Unfortunately, he commutes between his two enterprises, and there is a perception that the kitchen doesn't perform as well in his absence.

Lutèce ⌂
249 E 50th St. (near 2nd Ave.), NY 10022 ☎ 752-2225. Map 5O5 ▥ ◻ ▬ ᴀᴇ ◉ ᴠɪsᴀ Closed Sat and Mon lunch, Sun.
Lutèce was long the standard against which any American restaurant that presumed to purvey French cuisine was measured. Hardly half a dozen establishments in New York approach its mark, and probably not that many in the rest of the country. While to dine here is very nearly an honor — reservations must be secured at least 3wks in advance — no one is made to feel less than an eagerly anticipated guest. Rank, class, prominence and frequency of visits have no discernible bearing on treatment at the hands of the staff. That is the way it should always be, of course — especially at these prices — but too rarely is. The captains contrive to be attentive but not unctuous, friendly but not familiar, helpful but never patronizing. This exquisite balance, which carries from reception to appetizer to entrée to coffee, is orchestrated by chef-proprietor André Soltner and his wife, who functions as *maîtresse d'*. They have been here more than

25yrs, and he is one of the few men in America that the great chefs of France acknowledge as their equal. He emerges from the cramped narrow kitchen periodically, in unsoiled whites, circulating among his patrons to make suggestions and answer questions. Human endeavor can only aspire to perfection, however, and there are quibbles. The famous **Garden Room** is a trifle too unassuming for such a grand reputation, and some of the waiters are entirely too avuncular and offhanded, especially with customers for whom this is a once-in-a-blue-moon event. Those grumbles aside, simply stab at the card, or attend to the captain's recitation of unprinted specials. The cellar is a library of great vintages of Bordeaux and Burgundy, usually at breathtaking prices. A secondary list of serviceable wines offers rational substitutes, and white wine is served by the glass.

Montrachet
239 West Broadway (between Walker St. and White St.), NY 10013 ☎ *219-2777. Map 2T4* ▥▯ *to* ▥▯ ▭ ▰ *AE Closed Mon-Thurs and Sat lunch, Sun.*
The walls are painted in neutral tones, with no pictures or other embellishments. There are no flowers on the tables. The staff is dressed in black from chin to toe. That sort of self-conscious minimalism certainly focuses attention on your companions and the plates set before you. This is no privation, for what appears there is excellent. Unlike many chefs, who burn themselves out on appetizer fireworks and then slide quickly into banality, Debra Ponzek lengthens her patrons' attention span with main courses and desserts every bit as arresting as her starters. The daily game and seafood specials demand consideration, and the soufflés and praline ice cream with bananas are conversation-stoppers. Food this good rarely comes at prices so reasonable, at least for the lower two of the three fixed-price meals always available. When entering a cab uptown for the journey to TriBeCa, by the way, make sure to specify *West* Broadway, where there is a cluster of restaurants, and not just Broadway, where there are none. Reservations are necessary — jacket and tie are not.

Mortimer's
1057 Lexington Ave. (75th St.), NY 10021 ☎ *517-6400. Map 7L4*
154

▥▯ ▭ ☿ *AE* ▰ ▭ *VISA Open daily, dinner only.*
The ingredients of success cannot be isolated, otherwise everyone would do it. What wizardry transforms a restaurant with indifferent food at middling-high prices in unremarkable surroundings into a *de facto* semi-private club for powerhitters, trendsetters, and their eager followers? Probably even the owners of Mortimer's don't know, and utter small prayers that they don't unwittingly jar the composition out of balance. Apparently they haven't, for their success no longer has to do with the fashion of the moment. Mortimer's has crossed over into institutional status. To witness the phenomenon at flood stage, drop in after 11pm. A parade of lovelies and their attendants, some of them celebrated, fill the big bar and modest dining room. If they choose to eat, it is from a conventional continental menu featuring such items as gravlax and *paillard* of chicken. Considering the floor show, prices are reasonable.

Il Mulino
86 W 3rd St. (Bleecker St.), NY 10012 ☎ *673-3783. Map 2R4* ▥▯ ▭ ☿ *AE Closed Sat lunch, Sun.*
Italian restaurants in the Village used to mean checkered tablecloths, melted candles in old Chianti bottles and watery sauces on overdone spaghetti. Il Mulino is a good deal more ambitious, and its efforts have paid off. Limousines and expensive foreign sedans line drab W 3rd St. on weekend nights, and often reservations for Sat evening must be made 3wks ahead. Except for those nights, the welcome is gracious and service is deft and knowledgeable. A dish of nibbles arrives with cocktails and the menu. Have the *prosciutto* with ripe figs, and the soft-shell crabs when they're available. Otherwise, you won't go wrong with any of the various pasta offerings, the fish or shellfish. The value received is greater than at most of the posh Italian eateries of the Upper East Side, and at no sacrifice in ambience. Go for lunch to avoid the crowds. Men should wear jackets.

Odeon
145 West Broadway (Thomas St.), NY 10013 ☎ *233-0507. Map 2T4* ▥▯ ▭ *AE* ▰ ▭ *VISA Open Sun-Fri noon-3pm, 7pm-2.30am, Sat 7pm-2.30am.*

This is an "Art Moderne" cafeteria of World War II vintage, left pretty much as it was, with a speckled marble floor and chrome tubular chairs with leatherette upholstery. Some customers show up in green cropped hair, others wear Wall Street pinstripes. Most, however, are simply jeans-and-tweeds sorts of the TriBeCa-SoHo art community. They come for semi-*nouvelle cuisine* concoctions of *mahi-mahi*, gingered roast duck, chilled black bean soup, or whatever the chef has devised. Steak au poivre and roast chicken with mashed potatoes are comforting counterparts to the jazzier entries. Full dinners are served until 12.30am, light suppers until 2.30am, and the clientele grows more entertainingly bizarre as the night wears on.

One Fifth
1 5th Ave. (8th St.), NY 10003 ☎ 260-3434. *Map 2R4* ▯▯▯ 🔲 🔳 ⚡ *Closed Mon-Fri lunch.*

As the name suggests, One Fifth is at the base of 5th Ave., a half-block from Washington Square Park. Salvaged artifacts from a ship called the *Caronia* set the nautical tone. For the moment, it is deemed a steakhouse, and, given its moderate prices, a welcome alternative to its far costlier but better-known uptown competitors. Weekend brunch is enjoyable, to be remembered, perhaps, before a tour of the twice-annual outdoor art show.

Oyster Bar and Restaurant
Grand Central Terminal (42nd St. and Vanderbilt Ave.), NY 10017 ☎ 490-6650. *Map 5O4* ▯▯▯ 🔲 🔳 ⚡ 🔳 🔳 *Closed Sat, Sun.*

Reclaimed from oblivion in the late 1970s, this venerable 1913 fishhouse is better than ever. The cavernous vaulted space is sheathed in beige tiles, its high arches echoed by pinlight traceries. When seasons and shipments overlap, the menu is crammed with more than 120 items, changed daily according to availability. The day's catch can include such rarities as *loup de mer*, shark, sea urchin, sand dab and ray. Up to 10 types of oyster are usually on hand, along with chowders, pan roasts, stews, lobsters and crabs. Lake sturgeon, salmon and trout are smoked on the premises. Nearly everything is super-fresh, not too surprising in a place with this high volume. The simplest preparations are best. Service is speedy, without

flourishes. There is an excellent list of California white wines. Since they do not close between lunch and dinner, unhurried pre-theater meals are possible. To avoid the lunchtime cacophony of the main room, ask for a table in the adjoining "Saloon." Otherwise, the greatest deficiency is the churlish attitude of the gentleman at the entry podium.

Palio ⌂
151 W 51st St. (near 7th Ave.), NY 10010 ☎ 245-4850. *Map 4N3* ▯▯▯ *to* ▯▯▯ 🔲 🔳 ⚡ 🔳 🔳 *Closed Sun.*

Vivid expressionist murals by Sandro Chia surround the striking horseshoe marble bar inside the entrance. Snacks called *sfiziosi* are available here all the time, just right as an appetite-assuager before the curtain rises. To the right is an elevator that carries the sleekly turned-out crowd to the restaurant proper, one floor up. That large but not oppressive room melds almost *shibui* wall-and-window treatments with crisply upholstered black chairs and white tablecloths. Each table has a silver bowl of rosebuds. Wide aisles permit easy passage for diners and waiters, an amenity to be cherished, given the cost of unoccupied floor space in Manhattan. Despite that room to maneuver, service can get a trifle confused at times, perhaps because most of the staff is more comfortable with Italian than English. Food is of the *nuova cocina* variety, often a little *too* light for those accustomed to heartier fare from the land of origin. Infelicities are being scoured away, however, and this continues to be an excellent choice for business meals by day and dressy couples at night. Get to the bar before 6pm, and always reserve ahead for meals. Men are expected to wear jacket and tie.

The Palm
837 2nd Ave. (near E 45th St.), NY 10017 ☎ 687-2953. *Map 5O5* ▯▯▯ 🔲 🔳 🔳 *Closed Sat lunch, Sun.*

Steak is the reason for The Palm, and for its annex across the street, **Palm Too** (☎ 697-5198). Admirers of precisely seared slabs of unadorned prime cow flesh are a manly lot, it would appear, and impatient with the fancy rituals of those swishy French places. Beef is what they want, and they get it, along with loaves of hashed brown potatoes, preceded by shrimp and followed by cheesecake, all in stupefying portions. Sawdust is on the floor, faded cartoons line the walls and ceiling, and women are mostly decorative, preferably silent. The bored waiter recites the menu, for none is written, and there isn't all that much to remember. Those inclined to stoking up in such places insist that this is one of the three best steakhouses in New York, and are willing to pay for the privilege. Reservations for lunch, none for dinner.

Pamir ✿
1437 2nd Ave. (near 75th St.), NY 10021 ☎ 734-3791. Map 7M5 💶 *to* 💶💶 ⬜ ▬ ▦ ◉ 💳 *Open daily, dinner only.*
Another way to shave expenses with ethnic food? Try Afghan, and try it here, for it is packed with satisfied wallet-watchers every night. It conjures up a central Asian club of the sort Indiana Jones lays waste, with the red ceiling, guttering candles, and Oriental rugs on walls and floor. Staff members are eager to please, explaining every dish. They are especially attentive to children, but all ages are represented, partly because nothing too weird arrives on the plate. *Kabobs* are favorites, and the heady scents of *cilantro* and cardamom drift lightly on the air.

Parioli Romanissimo ⌂
1466 1st Ave. (near 76th St.), NY 10021 ☎ 288-2391. Map 7L5 💶💶 ⬜ ▦ ◉ *Dinner only, closed Sun, Mon.*
No satisfactory explanation is advanced for the practice — primarily of Chinese and Italian restaurants — of not listing on the menu dishes that are nonetheless nearly always available. They do that here, but the food, hidden or not, is so good and the ambience so amiable that grousing is small-minded. Be sure to reserve ahead, for they cannot serve more than 50-60 at a time. Among your fellow diners are certain to be an actor or two, a fashion designer, a recognizable power broker. They come here to eat, not to ogle their peers, which makes a refreshing change from other celebrity hangouts.

Although the starters and main courses are estimable, you can do worse than to hand the menu unread back to the captain and inquire about delights they might be concealing in the kitchen tonight. He will not be evasive, and if he mentions game, have it.

Park Bistro
414 Parke Ave. S (near 29th St.), NY 10016 ☎ 689-1360. Map 5P4 💶💶 ⬜ to 💶💶💶 ⬜ ▬ ▦ ◉ 💳
One of the latest districts to undergo gentrification is lower Park Ave., and this white-hot bistro is making the most of it. It is hysterically popular just now, standing-room-only at both lunch and dinner. It only hints at its humble inspiration, however, with cheeky compilations that don't ignore culinary inventions of recent years. There's sautéed skate wing in vinegar sauce with cabbage, *terrine* of rabbit, roasted monkfish with fennel and tomato *coulis*. As usual, lunch is the time to keep costs within reason. Always reserve; men usually wear jackets.

Petrossian
182 W 58th St. (7th Ave.), NY 10019 ☎ 245-2214. Map 6N3 💶💶💶 ⬜ ▬ ▦ ◉ 💳 *Open daily.*
The famed Parisian firm of Petrossian provides sustenance for those who can't get through the week without periodic infusions of *foie gras* and fish eggs. To showcase their products in the New World, they opened this decidedly upscale bistro-takeout-boutique in a Beaux Arts building that has hints of Right Bank origins. Immediately inside the entrance are glass cases filled with such essential edibles as duck and goose terrines, truffles, smoked silver eel and Scottish trout, *mousselines* and Russian caviar (including Beluga, Osetra and Sevruga). For those who intend to make a habit of such delectables, sterling silver *presentoir* sets are for sale. A right turn leads into the restaurant, a snug Art Deco setting with marble floors and nudes etched on the mirrors behind the angled bar. The tables are already set with Champagne flutes, should any patrons miss the thrust of the enterprise. Deft young Europeans bring copies of the aforesaid *presentoirs*, heaped with caviar, or impeccably arranged plates of the several "Petrossian Teasers," such as roulades of smoked sturgeon with wild mushrooms or bouquets of shrimp with smoked cod roe. Main courses are half *nouvelle*, half classical French, and nearly always excellent. The vodka is Russian, of course, and the house champagnes are available by the glass. For all the *de luxe* ingredients, the fixed price meals are almost reasonable, and they include pre- and after-theater dinners as well as Sun brunch. This outpost of the good life deserves

better than the tepid ratings accorded it by local critics.

Phoenix Garden 🍴 ♦
46 Bowery (near Elizabeth St.), NY 10013 ☎ *962-8934. Map 3S5*
▢ ▢ *No cards. Open daily.*
Fans of Chinese food have been infatuated for years with the fiery Hunan and Szechuan cuisines, with a parallel contempt for that of Canton. This is understandable, if only for all the preceding decades of insipid *won ton* and *chow mein.* Yet, properly done, Cantonese cooking is subtle, varied and most decidedly worthy of attention. In this regard the Phoenix Garden might just be the leader in all New York. The owners haven't made it easy. The room couldn't be plainer nor the exterior less beguiling — a dingy, littered alley drilled through a commercial block. But the adventure is abundantly rewarded. Unlike in many Chinatown eateries, staff recommendations can be trusted. These might be "pepper and salty shrimp," "boneless duck's feet" or "shark fin soup," all far tastier than they sound. Leave selections in the waiter's hands. You won't regret it.

The Quilted Giraffe 🛆
15 E 55th St. (near Madison Ave.), NY 10022 ☎ *593-1221. Map 5N4* ||||| ▦ ▭ AE ▣ ▣ VISA
Closed Sat lunch, Sun, Mon.
The owners, a husband-and-wife team by the predestined name of Wine, are a peripatetic pair. Testing themselves at a restaurant in upstate New York, they brought their act to the big town on the crest of the early enthusiasm for *nouvelle cuisine.* Many thought they were too hot not to cool down. In a way, they were right. The Wines have matured and achieved a steadier hand at the controls. Excessively innovative dishes, some of which bordered on the simply silly, were removed from the menu; the original decor of ceramic and stuffed giraffes departed the premises. Soon enough, the establishment was deemed to have joined **Lutèce** and **Le Cirque** at the tip of the pyramid. Then, ever restless, they moved to the AT&T Building, in a room of brushed steel, marble, and gray leather banquettes, the chilly post-industrial effect of which is moderated by sprays of flowers. While innovation is still important to Mr. Wine, it does not supersede all other considerations. His passion is tempered by an apparent entrancement with the culinary arts of Japan, filtered through an obviously boundless imagination. It is evident in the ingredients, all top of the bin and many of them shipped daily from their upstate farm. The most delicate of touches show themselves in the fabrications that appear on the plate, drawing every last wisp of natural flavor from fish and vegetable. Wine himself delivers dishes to the table when anyone orders the highest-priced *Kaiseki* dinner. (He's the one in kitchen whites who looks a little like Dan Quayle.) His staff is as precisely trained in all nuances of service as any to be found. There is no point in mentioning specific dishes, for they don't remain long on the menu. Suffice that disappointments are few. Very few. Save this for a landmark birthday, a silver anniversary, or the conclusion of a major business deal. Whether even those events are worth the cost of monthly sustenance for a family of four is an issue to be resolved in the heart of each patron.

Raga ♦
57 W 48th St. (near 5th Ave.), NY 10036 ☎ *757-3450. Map 5O4* ||||▢
▢ ▦ AE ▣ ▣ VISA *Closed Sat and Sun lunch.*
The Indian restaurant that deviates from the grease-stained stereotype is no longer a novelty. But Raga achieves a blend of exotic formality while preserving an unpatronizing authenticity in its dishes. There is tandoori, if you must, although the popularity of simple broiled chicken is a puzzlement in the presence of eggplant *bhurta, nargisi kofta* and *jingha chat.* The 8-course lunch buffet is cheap, and almost makes dinner irrelevant. Some of the staff might profit from a stint in charm school. Many nights, there is live flute or sitar music.

Le Relais
712 Madison Ave. (64th St.), NY 10021 ☎ *751-5108. Map 7M4* |||||
▢ ▦ 🚗 AE
A beneficiary of the present bistro craze, Le Relais is thriving well beyond the lifespan that might have been predicted for it more than 10yrs ago. The food, which is no better than adequate, is not central. The crowd is. They gather on velvet banquettes, beneath walls crowded with framed mirrors and etchings, gaggles of East Siders seated haunch to denimed haunch, and aproned waiters who remain calm and

cogent despite the clamor. The short menu is adjusted to seasonal availabilities, but might include sorrel soup, bass cloaked in seaweed, tender soft-shelled crabs and rosy-centered lamb. Save it for a warm day, when tables are set out on the sidewalk and the interior is less claustrophobic.

La Réserve ⌂
4 W 49th St. (near 5th Ave.), NY 10020 ☎ 247-2993. Map 5O4 ▥▥▥
▱ ▤ ■ AE ⊙ ⊙ VISA *Closed Sat lunch, Sun.*

There are people who have no need to agonize over which Manhattan restaurant to select for the big splash — they simply rotate. **Lutèce** on Tues, **Le Bernardin** on Wed, **La Côte Basque** on Thurs and La Réserve on Fri. At least they *look* like the same crowd, with their immaculately coiffed hair, winter tans, and flares of gold at wrist and throat. Two large rooms are illuminated by chandeliers of Venetian glass and decorated with large murals of game preserves. The china is Limoges and the balloon-shaped goblets allow the proper savoring of a Château Laffitte. The food is *haute*, with an up-to-date concern for presentation. Mediocrity is not permitted, nor is novelty for novelty's sake. Tables are closely placed, but not oppressively so, and service is efficient, if not warm. The pre-theater dinner, which must be ordered between 5.30-6.45pm, is a less expensive way to sample the kitchen's wares. Although it can take weeks to reserve a table at others of this class, 2-3 days' notice is usually sufficient here.

River Café ⌂
1 Water St., Brooklyn, NY 10001 ☎ 522-5200. Map 3T6 ▥▥▥ to ▥▥▥
▱ ◁⟨⟨ ▤ 🚗 ⌂ AE ⊙

The breathtaking views of the Manhattan skyline from this remodeled barge beneath the Brooklyn Bridge more than compensate for the frequent changes of the guard behind the stoves. Deficiencies are infrequent, the result of daring rather than indifference. Depending upon who is cooking at the moment, the culinary mix is usually part Gallic conceit, part chauvinistically native produce. Ingredients are Key West shrimp, Smithfield ham, California snails, New Jersey pheasants — resolutely American — but the twin sauces, aspics and *terrines* cry out their Old World origins. Furnishings are agreeable — bamboo,

bentwood and the requisite portholes — but the decor is the vista, which reaches from the Statue of Liberty to the Empire State Building. The best time to be there is at dusk, when interior illumination is kept low. A piano is played, and tables are set out on the terrace in summer. Sunday brunch is popular, and reservations are always essential.

Rosa Mexicano
1063 1st Ave. (58th St.), NY 10022 ☎ 753-7407. Map 5N5 ▥▱▱
▱ ▤ AE ⊙ ⊙ VISA

The fever for Mexican food came later to New York than to other parts of the country, so its converted enthusiasts are often unschooled in that great cuisine. Hybrid Tex-Mex and New Southwestern variations confused the issue further, and the management feels compelled to make it known on their menu that "you may not find some of the Americanized dishes associated with Mexican food." Authenticity aside, these dishes are singularly satisfying. In a city of rubbery, store-bought tortillas, the chefs at Rosa Mexicano make their own. In contrast to the usually vapid yuppie Margaritas, these are concocted with fresh lime juice and premium tequila, and are deceptively benign. Given the difficulties of obtaining proper ingredients (there are scores of different chilies used in Mexican cooking, from mild to incendiary) this kitchen so carefully replicates south-of-the-border recipes that patrons are transported to Veracruz and Cuernavaca. Duck comes in a creamy green pumpkinseed sauce with a hint of serrano; raw bay scallops are marinated in lemon juice, chili, and coriander. Off-menu specials often feature recipes from one or more of Mexico's regional cuisines, such as Yucatán's shredded peppery pork, slow-baked in banana leaves. Even the mango ice cream is made on the premises. The wine list is adequate, but this food cries for real Mexican beer —*Corona* or *Dos Equis*. Reservations are essential.

The Russian Tea Room
150 W 57th St. (near 7th Ave.), NY 10019 ☎ 265-0947. Map 4N3 ▥▥▥ ▱ ▤ AE ⊙ ⊙ VISA

Restaurants where celebrities gather are notorious for indifferent food, but a number of eccentricities endear the Tea Room to Woody Allen, Jackie O, Rudolf Nureyev, Liza Minnelli, Joseph Heller and

Max von Sydow (to drop the names of some regulars). There is the fact that it really does serve Russian food, rare in these parts. Christmas decorations wreathe the light fixtures — all year. No two of the many clocks have the same time. And perhaps most of all, as violinist Isaac Stern said, it is "a private-professional club where the public is allowed." Noncelebrated folk with the wherewithal to afford attendance are not, however, permitted to approach the stars, which helps assure their frequent return. While gazing upon each other, they dip into borscht, dine on salmon *kulebiaka* or *shashlik*, and rhapsodize over the finest grades of caviar, especially in concert with *blinis*. Surely the Tea Room will sail majestically into the next century, its slogan intact— "Slightly to the left of Carnegie Hall." But by all possible means, avoid consignment to the upstairs "Siberia."

Sabor ✿
20 Cornelia St. (near Bleecker St.), NY 10014 ☎ 243-9579. Map 2R3 ⫽ ▯ ▭ AE ◆ ◑ VISA

Cuban food is direct and unassuming, a blending of dishes from the Iberian homeland with the ingredients and tang of the Caribbean. There isn't a better place in the city to make its acquaintance than Sabor. The setting is a narrow former storefront on a tatty side street in the Village, the principal decorative element of which is a 19thC stamped tin ceiling. Start with a birdbath-sized Margarita, made with fresh lime. Move on to plump, tender mussels dressed in a saffron-tomato sauce, or to *escabèche* (a cool, firm piece of fish hidden beneath a blanket of crisp pickled vegetables). *Pollo con comino* is boneless baked chicken breast marinated in lime juice, cumin and garlic, accompanied by strips of onion and sweet pepper. Don't be put off by the implications of *ropa vieja* — "old clothes" — for this Cuban classic is in fact shredded beef tossed in a piquant sauce of tomato, cloves and cinnamon. There isn't an ounce of pretension or a misstep in taste from entrance to departure.

Salta in Bocca
179 Madison Ave. (near 33rd St.), NY 10016 ☎ 684-1757. Map 5P4 ⫽ ▯ ▭ AE ◆ ◑ VISA Closed Sun.

It is an inexplicable truism that the most sublime of dishes in northern Italian restaurants are often not listed on the menu. Patrons must ask, or hope, that the captain will volunteer the information. At Salta in Bocca, the fried cornmeal known as *polenta* falls into this secretive category, perhaps because it requires so much muscle to prepare. It arrives with a variety of garnishes, all tasty. Pasta dishes can be shared as an appetizer, as can mussels or clams. This reasonableness is carried through to the prices. Although this unassuming trattoria rivals the best in town, the final accounting is within the grasp of almost any budget. Simply ignore the dreadful paintings, and arrive for dinner, not lunch.

Sam's
152 W 52nd St. (near 7th Ave.), NY 10019 ☎ 582-8700. Map 4N3 ⫽ to ⫽⫽ ▭ AE ◆ ◑ VISA Closed Sun.

Actress Mariel Hemingway is "Sam," and this is her second restaurant. The powers at the Equitable Building wisely invited her to open here as an informal and far less expensive alternative to **Le Bernardin** and **Palio**, both securely ensconced just a few yards away. The huge interior is reasonably attractive, with a lower noise level than might be expected. Hamburgers with chewy shoestring potatoes equal any to be had, and the juicy pork chop with blue cheese sauce is an understandable favorite. At night, the kitchen is somewhat more ambitious. Sea scallops with wild rice and sautéed black bass with herbed *polenta* are two worthies. In anticipation of the theater, for which Sam's is ideally situated, consider one of the imaginative pastas, such as penne with duck liver and artichokes. Only those who choose to have two or three courses, dessert, and the top wine in the cellar will receive a check that edges into the expensive range.

The Sea Grill
19 W 49th St. (near 5th Ave.), NY 10020 ☎ 246-9201. Map 504 ⫽⫽⫽⫽ ▯ ▭ AE ◆ ◑ VISA

When the skating rink at the foot of the GE Building in the Rockefeller Center was overhauled, it was the management's intent to upgrade the eating places that bordered the popular arena. They didn't have to reach too high, given the feeble performances of a succession of previous occupants. The fact that the Sea Grill turned out to be far

159

better than required was a surprise to many. The decor is neither flashy nor dowdy, with comfortable leather chairs allowing views of skaters (in winter) twirling outside, and cooks flashing knives and spatulas over the fashionable open grill. It is an atmosphere in which both businesspeople and adult tourists feel at ease. The menu leans toward regional American dishes, an elastic rubric that incorporates grilled fish, chowders, oysters Rockefeller, charred *pompano* and chicken, and the San Francisco invention, *cioppino* (seafood stew). Entrance to the restaurant is from the glass bubble on 49th St. Reservations are recommended, particularly at lunchtime. There is outdoor dining in good weather. The companion restaurant across the rink is the **American Festival Café** (*20 W 50th St.* ☎ *246-6699*). With its broader menu and lower prices, it may be a better choice for families, although the food doesn't rank with that of the Sea Grill.

Shun Lee

43 W 65th St. (near Broadway), NY 10023 ☎ *595-8895. Map 6M3* IIII *to* IIII ▭ ☲ AE ⊙ ⊙ VISA

One of an erstwhile chain that introduced high style in Chinese restaurants, this is a happy diversion from, and improvement upon, the quiche-and-burger emporia that dominate the Lincoln Center neighborhood. One might even go there simply to eat, rather than to fuel up for a session of Puccini or Bach. The black-and-white decor is enlivened at the entrance and in the lounge, with *papier mâché* dragons and monkeys with glowing red eyes. Spicy Szechuan and Hunan cuisines were introduced to New Yorkers by the owners, and the chili oil is shaken with a generous hand, if requested. When a full meal might rest too heavily on the stomach during a night at the opera, the *dim sum* served at the adjoining **Shun Lee Café** (*43 W 65th St.* ☎ *769-3888*) is just the ticket.

Sichuan Pavilion

310 E 44th St. (near 2nd Ave.), NY 10017 ☎ *972-7377. Map 5O5* IIII ▭ ☲ AE ⊙ ⊙ VISA

Authenticity is overrated, as can be attested by anyone who has braved some of the cherished peasant stews of the Mediterranean. Yet the early infatuation with Sichuan (née Szechuan) preparations doubtless produced travesties, and who could complain of the importation of ten

chefs from the People's Republic to bring enlightenment? That was what management did when this Midtown East eatery first opened, and there were revelations. The spritz of freshness and novelty has flattened now, but this remains one of the few noteworthy Chinese restaurants in the neighborhood. Many of the recipes presented are unique to this restaurant, and the dishes listed on the menu under the heading "First Time Served In America" deserve particular attention.

Sparks

210 E 46th St. (near 3rd Ave.), NY 10017 ☎ *687-4855. Map 5O5* IIII ▭ ☲ AE ⊙ ⊙ VISA *Closed Sat lunch, Sun.*

As testament to human perversity, business boomed after a Mafia chieftain was gunned down outside after a meal here. They didn't really need the boost. As Manhattan steak houses go, this is one of the best, its huge chops and lobsters as succulent and overpriced as any in town. What makes it notable is that few restaurants of any category can match its inventory of fine wines. European wine buffs can here test the virtues and vintages of California, from Mondavi to Mirassou and dozens of other vintners. There are French, Spanish and Italian bottles, too. Between sips, stick to the simplest of beef preparations.

Take-Zushi

71 Vanderbilt Ave. (near 46th St.), NY 10017 ☎ *867-5120. Map 5O4* IIII ▭ ▦ ▦ ☥ AE ⊙ ⊙ VISA *Closed Sat lunch, Sun.*

Sushi and *sashimi* — raw fish with and without rice — are sufficiently commonplace now to draw distinctions between their purveyors. Many *sushi* chefs pursue their craft with a *ninja*'s fierce solemnity. That can be offputting, especially for a neophyte diner who would like a little advice along with the showy knifemanship. Friendliness is a hallmark of this branch of a growing family-owned chain, from the barman in the bamboo-and-slate vestibule to the kimonoed waitresses and the chefs themselves. While their command of the English language runs from not bad to unintelligible, they go out of their way to instruct gently on the niceties of this specialized sort of eating. They might urge that you begin with the unadorned buttery-soft "fatty tuna," or that you stir a little horseradish in your dish of soy sauce, or that the yellowtail rolled with rice in seaweed sheets is best eaten with the fingers, not chopsticks. It results in a far more gratifying evening of culinary theater than at those places where the eating of uncooked fish is regarded as a mystic ritual. Don't accept a table upstairs.

Tavern On The Green
Central Park W (67th St.), NY 10023 ☎ 873-3200. Map 6M3 ||||
□ ■ 🚗 🚠 ⏰ AE 💳 💳 ☷

Tavern On The Green is one of those places that must be mentioned simply because it is there and everybody knows about it. Once a barn for the sheep that wandered in the adjacent meadow, it has been a restaurant for much of this century. Successive managements have consistently fallen short in matching the dining experience to the promise of the building and the park surroundings. The latest to try is a Mr Leroy, an apostle of the "eat-with-the-eyes" theory of restaurateurship. His version is visually provocative, crammed with carved plaster, etched mirrors, and a profusion of brass, crystal and copper ornamentation. Some describe the experience as "festive"; others call it noisy, disorganized, and pretentiously cute. The food can be good, but it is impossible to predict which dishes at what hours. Service is erratic. Despite all this, out-of-towners and many New Yorkers love it. Maybe you'll agree. To find out, try the unusually inexpensive pre-theater dinner.

Thailand ✿
106 Bayard St. (Mulberry St.), NY 10013 ☎ 349-3132. Map 2T4 ||⊃ □ ■ *Closed Mon.*

It might seem sacrilegious to venture into Thai food while in Chinatown, for a year of uninterrupted consumption would not exhaust the Szechuan, Mandarin, Cantonese and Hunan cuisines to be sampled in its perhaps 200 restaurants. But this admittedly seedy little place across from Columbus Park deserves consideration, and its prices are as low as any in the neighborhood. The menu is bewilderingly comprehensive, with nearly 100 listed items. A party of four can take advantage of the variety.

21 (Twenty-one) Club
21 W 52nd St. (near 5th Ave.), NY 10019 ☎ 582-7200. Map 5N4
|||| □ AE 💳 💳 ☷ *Closed Sat (in summer), and Sun.*

Once a Prohibition-era speakeasy, "21" went on to become a sanctuary for the power elite. Celebrities are on view, but the carefully tonsured and garbed regulars that frequent the place are more often senior partners in important law firms, executives of multinational corporations, or the men who decide who will be permitted to run for political office. It is not a club in the sense of excluding the general public, but strangers are granted no more than distant courtesy. Under new management, the food has improved.

Un Deux Trois ✿
123 W 44th St. (near Times Sq.), NY 10020 ☎ 354-4148. Map 4O3 ||⊃ □ ■ AE 💳 💳 *Closed Sat and Sun lunch.*

Its allegiance to the brasserie archetype is not slavish, but with its vast ramshackle room, paper tablecloths and hearty rather than delicate victuals, the point is made. At lunch, its clients run to executive sorts, but at nightfall, a disco-theater crowd prone to spiky hair and violet cheekbones mingles with specimens of the Concorde Set. Most of the servers are exactly what they appear to be — actors, singers, dancers. Your host may be the tenor who has "aged from Vivaldi to Mozart" during his tour of duty. Selections from the regular menu — roast chicken, steak au poivre — are preferable to the daily specials.

Union Square Café ✿
21 E 16th St. (near 5th Ave.), NY 10003 ☎ 243-4020. Map 5Q4 ||⊃ to |||| □ ■ AE 💳 💳 *Closed Sun.*

Were this writer informed he could eat in only one Manhattan restaurant for the rest of his days, he would choose the Union Square Café. That assumes, of course, that they don't change a thing. Certainly not the welcome by a host who appears so delighted to see you that you hardly notice he is steering you to the worst table in the house. Not the bubbly, knowing waiters (hunky) and waitresses (dishy), who manage to convey the impression, however untrue, that they wouldn't mind if they never made it to the Broadway stage as long as they could keep working here. Not the food, the very model of pan-oceanic eclecticism, with myriad flavors that explode in the mouth at every bite. And definitely not the prices, about half what uptown emporia charge for eats of comparable quality. It couldn't start to take itself too seriously, either. Keep such whimsical notes as the yellowfin tuna "burger," served on a seeded roll. And don't touch the big expressionist murals of floating nudes, or alter the composition of the crowd, which seems, for a change, less interested in "making the scene" than in enjoying itself. Even solo diners are not set adrift, especially if a platter of iced oysters and a flinty Chardonnay at the mahogany bar satisfies their notion of lunch. Put this beguiling place on the must-list, right up there with the Metropolitan Museum of Art and the Empire State Building.

Vanessa

289 Bleecker St. (7th Ave.), NY 11014 ☎ *243-4225. Map 2R4* IIIII *to* IIIII ⬜ ▦ ⵑ 𝔸𝔼 ⊡ ⬤ 𝕍𝕀𝕊𝔸 *Open daily, dinner only.*
Elegance is not to be expected in artily iconoclastic Greenwich Village. But here is an exception. The handsome space is painted a creamy plum, with glints of brass, and floors and fixtures of bare oak. The staff appears to comprise young careerists rather than the usual theatrical hopefuls. They bring staples of the New American tradition — free-range poultry, Gulf shrimp, duck *foie gras*. Appetizers and desserts are best. Comforting touches abound, with harp music or jazz at certain hours, and flowers and cloth towels in the rest rooms. While not cheap, prices are lower than at similar uptown enterprises. Business suits dominate.

Le Veau d'Or

129 E 60th St. (near Park Ave.), NY 10022 ☎ *838-8133. Map 5N4* IIIII ⬜ 𝔸𝔼 *Closed Sun.*
If there has ever been a moment when this place was not packed with ravenous humanity, it has escaped the memory of its habitués. Staff and patrons are a congenial lot, though, patient with each other in the presentation and consumption of consistently good mid-level food. Something more than a bistro but less than a *temple de cuisine*, it manifests none of the hyper-trendiness of the former nor the solemnity of the latter. Walls are chock-a-block with travel posters, inconsequential paintings, and objects of Gallic origin. Seating is fairly comfortable — but guard against dipping your elbow in your neighbor's *vichyssoise*.

Windows On The World

1 World Trade Center, NY 10048 ☎ *938-1111. Map 2U4. Three restaurants, all* ⬜ ▦ ▬ 𝔸𝔼 ⊡ ⬤ *The Cellar in the Sky* IIIII *dinner only, closed Sun. The Hors d'Oeuvrerie* III ⋘ ↻ *The Restaurant* IIIII ⋘ *closed Sun dinner.*
There are three distinct eating places under the **Windows On The World** umbrella, all of them in the N tower on the 107th floor. Enduring the wait at the reception desk of **The Restaurant** can be a chore, but persevere, for it justifies the temporary aggravation. Surely there is no more stunning urban vista anywhere — sparkling spires, bands of winking sapphires, silvered waters and webs of bridges. All is made available to view from tiered tables in a muted spaceship environment. As is usual in rooftop restaurants, competence on the plate proves elusive, but the fixed-price dinner at least eases the fiscal bite. The premise of **The Hors d'Oeuvrerie** is to make entire meals of appetizers, a gimmick that was overdue. The starter dishes of different countries — Chinese *dim sum*, Spanish *tapas* — are featured on a rotating monthly basis. Jazz performers are on duty from 4.30pm until closing. Reservations are unnecessary. **The Cellar in the Sky** has no views, but attempts to compensate with ambitious 7-course meals enhanced by five different wines. They have only a single sitting each evening (dinner only) for a maximum of 36 diners.

Reservations are essential for **The Cellar** and **The Restaurant**, often at least 2wks in advance. Avoid the hectic Sunday buffet and brunch. Wines available at the complex are often superb, and are reasonably priced.

Wylie's ✿

59 W 56th St. (6th Ave.), NY 10019 ☎ *757-7910. Map 5N4* II ⬜ 𝔸𝔼 ⊡ ⬤ 𝕍𝕀𝕊𝔸
There is no pretense here, just a barbecue joint featuring chili, baby back ribs, fried chicken, corn-on-the-cob, and brick-sized loaves of fried onion rings. It is very popular, so a wait for a bare formica table is likely. Avoid the cacophony of the 2nd floor, dominated by large parties competing for audibility. A good selection for those on a budget, those wanting an informal lunch, or parents with children in tow, either here or at the other branch (*891 1st Ave., at 50th*).

Good fast food

It isn't necessary to resort to the ubiquitous representatives of the franchised food chains for a quick snack or a light meal. Here are some alternatives.

Broome Street Bar   363 West Broadway (Broome St.) ☎ 925-2086. Salads, sandwiches and "pub grub" in SoHo.

Fine and Shapiro   138 W 72nd St. (near Broadway) ☎ 877-2874. One of the better Jewish delis.

1st Wok   1374 3rd Ave. (78th St.) ☎ 861-2600. One of a growing Szechuan chain.

Great Jones   54 Great Jones St. (near the Bowery) ☎ 674-9304. Low-cost Cajun.

Hamburger Harry's   157 Chambers St. (near West Broadway) ☎ 267-4446. Imaginative variations on America's favorite sandwich.

John's Pizzeria   278 Bleecker St. (near 7th Ave. S) ☎ 243-1680. Long lines for consensus top pizza. There's another branch at 408 E 64th St.

Moondance Diner   55 Broadway (Wall St.) ☎ 226-1191. Untricky diner chow, just as it says. Always open.

Tien Fu   180 3rd Ave. (near 16th St.) ☎ 505-2000. Situated in Gramercy Park district. Chinese lunch is a particular bargain.

Tony Roma's   400 E 57th St. (near 1st Ave.) ☎ 308-0200. Northern outpost of Florida barbecue chain. Onion ring loaf is super-sized.

Tortilla Flats   767 Washington St. (W 12th St.) ☎ 243-1053. Tex-Mex temptations in the West Village.

Veselka Coffee Shop   144 2nd Ave. (9th St.) ☎ 228-9682. Honest renditions of Polish and Ukrainian dishes.

Open late

When dinner has been deferred to avoid nodding off in the theater or concert hall, it can be distressing to learn that the nearby restaurant takes no orders after 10.30pm. The following places stay open well past midnight. Some of them are described in greater detail in the above section.

Brasserie   100 E 53rd St. (near Park Ave.) ☎ 751-4840. Sort-of French, best-known for being open 24hrs.

Cadillac Bar   15 W 21st St. (near 5th Ave.) ☎ 645-7220. Fun Tex-Mex. Open until 2am Mon-Thurs, 4am Fri-Sat.

Carnegie Deli   854 7th Ave. (near 55th St.) ☎ 757-2245. Open until 4am.

Columbus   201 Columbus Ave. (69th St.) ☎ 799-8090. Ignore the food and ogle the celebs. One of the owners is Mikhail Baryshnikov. Open until 2am.

Corner Bistro   331 W 4th St. (Jane St.) ☎ 242-9502. Greenwich Village chili-burger-and-brew café.

Empire Diner   210 10th Ave. (22nd St.) ☎ 243-2736. Retro-glitz, often bizarrely costumed disco-goers. Open 24hrs.

Hard Rock Café   221 W 57th St. (near Broadway) ☎ 489-6565. Inspired by London's original. Raucous, jammed, loud — definitely for younger revelers. Open until 4am.

Odeon   145 West Broadway (Thomas St.) ☎ 233-0507. "New American" in TriBeCa. Open until 2.30am.

P.J. Clarke's   915 3rd Ave. (55th St.) ☎ 759-1650. Tavern food, lively mixed crowd. Open until 4am.

Stage Deli   834 7th Ave. (near 54th St.) ☎ 245-7850. The Carnegie Deli's closest competition in location and quality. Open until 2am.

Wilson's   201 W 79th St. (Amsterdam Ave.) ☎769-0100.
Comfortable pub-eatery, ideal after visiting Lincoln Center.
Open until 4am.
Wollensky's Grill   205 E 49th St. (between 2nd Ave. and
3rd Ave.) ☎753-0444. Cheaper sidecar to Smith & Wollensky's
steakhouse. Open until 2am.

Sunday brunch

More lunch than breakfast, brunch is now an established
event in New York. Usually offered in a fixed-price menu, it
can be buffet or table service. Informality is the rule, and it is
a way to sample the wares of restaurants that can be
prohibitively expensive during the week. These are just a few
of many. Normal hours are 11am or noon-3 or 4pm. Reserve
ahead.

Café des Artistes   1 W 67th St. (near Central Park W)
☎877-3500. Very popular, soothing setting.
Darbár   44 W 56th St. (near 6th Ave.) ☎432-7227. Bargain
northern Indian buffet.
La Métairie   189 W 10th St. (W 4th St.) ☎989-0343. Small,
somewhat pricey Village French. Try other branch too (*1442
3rd Ave, near 82nd St.*).
Pig Heaven   1540 2nd Ave. (near 80th St.) ☎744-4887.
Gimmicky Chinese, featuring pork and an overdone barnyard
theme. Enjoyable, nonetheless.
Le Régence   37 E 64th St. (near Madison Ave.) ☎606-4647.
The lovely dining room of the Hotel Plaza Athénée; very
French.
El Rio Grande   160 E 38th St. (3rd Ave.) ☎867-0922. Large,
yuppie-single Tex-Mex in Murray Hill.
The Russian Tea Room   150 W 57th St. (near 7th Ave.)
☎265-0947. Celebrity roost; blinis are the perfect brunch.
Avoid upstairs room.
Sarabeth's Kitchen   423 Amsterdam Ave. (near 80th St.)
☎496-6280. Delectable omelets, waffles, pancakes. Another
branch too (*1295 Madison Ave., near 93rd St.*).
20 Mott Street   20 Mott St. (near Pell St.) ☎964-0380.
Superb, inexpensive *dim sum*. Packed on weekends.

Nightlife & the performing arts

On the evidence of what is available, it might be inferred that half
the population of New York never sees the light of day. Following
cocktails and dinner, there can be opera, ballet, a symphony
concert, a Broadway musical. After that, they can choose the late
show at a cabaret or supper club, or drop in at a dance club or
jazz loft. Many places stay open until 4am, and most revelers find
that's enough. But the hardy and knowledgeable move on to
transient after-hours bars, essentially illegal and with the lifespan
of a fruit fly, but thriving. Finally, perhaps, they decompress with
croissants or bagels at a 24hr Art Deco diner.
    The rest of us, however, must make choices. Before we do,
some considerations. Apart from on opening nights, theaters
impose no dress codes. Many restaurants and nightclubs do,
however, if only to prohibit denim clothing. That being the case,
it is advisable to plan an evening with an eye on compatible
districts and events. For instance, don your dressiest outfit and
combine a deluxe restaurant with the trendiest of clubs or
cabarets, all on the East Side. For an evening in SoHo-Greenwich

Village, jeans and a sweater will do for a pub crawl, dinner, and a jazz or rock club. Something in between is suitable for opera or ballet at the Lincoln Center, a post-theater supper and intimate conversation at a piano bar, all on the West Side.

Liquor laws are liberal. Establishments serving alcoholic beverages are required to close between 4am-8am (Sun 4am-noon), although most do not open before 11am, and lock up whenever business is slow. Anyone 21 and over can purchase liquor, although some bars and clubs set a higher age limit and require two items of positive identification.

Bars and clubs offering live entertainment often fix a "cover" charge that is, in effect, an admission fee; and the range can be considerable, depending on the standard or elaborateness of the show. In dance clubs it tends to rise with the chicness of the place. It might be collected at the door or simply added to the check. Typically, in such places, there is also a "minimum" charge for consumption of beverages and/or food, per person.

Fine food and music are rarely found in combination. Getting something to eat — a hamburger, a bowl of chili — is nearly always possible, but in general expect no more than alleviation of hunger pangs. Exceptions are such establishments as **The Ballroom** in Chelsea, which serves excellent food and lays on cabaret and dancing, and the **Greene Street Café**, where the owner is determined to create an all-inclusive dining-and-entertainment complex (for these two see *Restaurants*).

To learn who is appearing where, consult the entertainment listings of the Fri and Sun editions of *The New York Times*, the weekly magazines *New York* and *The New Yorker*, and, for more offbeat diversions, the weekly newspaper *The Village Voice*. Even then, call ahead for reservations and to inquire about last-minute changes in hours and performers.

There has been no attempt here to locate sexually-oriented clubs, theaters, massage parlors or movie theaters. They soon make themselves apparent, and in any case are too ephemeral for print. It is sufficient to note that all predilections are accommodated. For guidance, check *The Village Voice* and that tasteful journal, *Screw*. Prostitution is illegal, although that does not dissuade its practitioners. While streetwalkers are flamboyantly visible around Times Sq., their sisters who work hotel bars are cautious and less readily identifiable.

Ballet
Surely no other city enjoys ballet in such abundance and variety. In addition to a dozen or more locally-based companies, the troupes of other cities and nations are regular visitors. There are four principal venues.

Brooklyn Academy of Music
30 Lafayette Ave. (downtown Brooklyn), NY 11217 ☎ *718-636-4100. Map 12D2.*
Known for experimental works and frequent appearances by the Martha Graham and José Limon troupes and the Pennsylvania Dance Company.

City Center
131 W 55th St., NY 10019 ☎ *246-8989. Map 4N3.*
The Joffrey Ballet, the Alvin Ailey Dance Theater, and the Paul Taylor Dance Company.

Metropolitan Opera House
Lincoln Center, NY 10023 ☎ *580-9830. Map 6M3.*
Host for the American Ballet Theater, which long had Mikhail Baryshnikov

Nightlife and the performing arts

as its artistic director and has seen performances by most of the other famous Russian emigrés.

New York State Theater
Lincoln Center, NY 10023 ☎ 870-5570. Map 6M3.
Home of the New York City Ballet.

Bars

Passing the night in a bar (or several) is a common diversion and, except when it becomes an addiction, not as decadent as it sounds. Certainly there are hundreds of bars devoted to nothing more elevating than the diligent consumption of alcohol. But the owners know that success lies in distractions. These may be no more than the preservation of antique trappings — stamped tin ceiling, potbellied stove, stained-glass window — but can escalate into exciting meals, collections of imported beers and wines, live music and entertainments of every description, or dancing. Or it may be simply a matter of creating the kind of environment that attracts crowds of like-minded seekers-after-companionship. The roster that follows merely indicates the possibilities. Unless otherwise noted, all bars are open seven days a week, usually from 11am or noon until at least 2am, and serve food.

Fake Tiffany lamps and dark-stained plywood too often substitute for atmosphere in American bars, along with inept imitations of the British or Irish pub. Exceptions exist, however. **Fanelli's** (*94 Prince St. in SoHo ☎ 226-9412, closed Sat, Sun*) predates the Civil War, and looks it. Neighborhood workingmen share it with the recent artistic immigrants. **McSorley's Old Ale House** (*15 E 7th St. ☎ 473-9148*) is even older, and did not miss a working day during the 13yr experiment called Prohibition. Only two decades ago did they grudgingly allow women inside the door. There still isn't a sign to mark **Chumley's** (*86 Bedford St. in Greenwich Village ☎ 675-4449*), and it retains the Bohemian aura of Edna St Vincent Millay and Eugene O'Neill. Yellowing book jackets of former clients line the walls, and there is a working fireplace in winter. Good 'burgers, too. O. Henry was a regular patron of **Pete's Tavern** (*129 E 18th St. ☎ 473-7676*), which opened in 1864. They have sidewalk tables for warm weather dining, with mostly Italian food. **Joe Allen** (*326 W. 46th St. ☎ 581-6464*) looks older than it is, perhaps because of the photos of Leslie Howard, W.C. Fields, and Billie Holliday. The battered bar frequently supports the tailored elbows of stars of the New York-based soap operas. Food was recently upgraded. The venerable **P.J. Clarke's** (*915 3rd Ave. at 55th St. ☎ 355-8857*) remains dark and cobwebby in the corners, with sawdust beneath the feet; an archetypal Irish saloon, but the clientele wears three-piece suits now, and chatters of media campaigns and TV audience shares. Serious beerdrinkers have a home at the boutique brewery/bar/restaurant, **The Manhattan Brewing Company** (*40 Thompson St. ☎ 219-9250*). The **White Horse Tavern** (*W Hudson St. and 11th St. ☎ 243-9260*) was established in Greenwich Village in 1880. Dylan Thomas, Norman Mailer, poet Delmore Schwartz and Brendan Behan gathered there. British pub grub — shepherd's pie, steak and mushroom pie — is on the menu of the 1868 **Landmark Tavern** (*626 11th Ave. at 46th St. ☎ 757-8595*). Drop in after the theater, but before midnight, or for Sunday brunch.

Bars with shorter histories but as much atmosphere include:
Blue Mill Tavern (*50 Commerce St., in Greenwich Village* ☎ 243-7114), a former Prohibition speakeasy; **Broome Street Bar** (*363 West Broadway, in SoHo* ☎ 925-2086); **Harvey's Chelsea** (*108 W 18th St.* ☎ 243-5644); tavern restaurant **The Lion's Head** (*59 Christopher St., in Greenwich Village* ☎ 929-0670) — literary lions, that is; and **Prince Street Bar** (*125 Prince St., in SoHo* ☎ 228-8130).

Wine bars, where the titular tipple is the only one available, never quite caught on. Some conventional bars have installed Cruvinets, and have more and better selections than the usual jug wines. Among these are **I Tre Merli** (*463 Broadway* ☎ 254-8699), **SoHo Kitchen and Bar** (*103 Greene St.* ☎ 925-1866), and **Lavin's** (*23 W 39th St.* ☎ 921-1288).

Desperate loneliness pervades hotel bars, and the occupants seem to exude their disinclination to venture more than 100ft from their bedrooms. Among the dozen exceptions, so engaging that even New Yorkers stop in, are **Bemelman's Bar** in the plush **Carlyle** (*Madison Ave. and 76th St.* ☎ 744-1600). Jazz piano is the backdrop, and the justification for the cover charge. The bar of the **Algonquin Hotel** (*59 W 44th St. near 5th Ave.* ☎ 840-6800) is still a charmer, burbling with talk of book packages and theatrical contretemps. Bankers' pinstripes dominate at the handsome **Oak Bar** of the **Plaza** (*5th Ave. and 59th St.* ☎ 759-3000), where the principal diversion is eavesdropping on the collision of egos.

The hope of human contact, of conversation, however brief, is a primary motive for bar-hopping. When it became clear that increasing numbers of unmarried people were choosing to retain that status, the "singles bar" became an explicit entity. Few unencumbered folk admit to visiting such places, which leaves open the question of why they flourish nevertheless. And, of course, they fall into categories, subject to unpredictable change and fashion. A note of cautious sobriety has pushed its way into the once super-heated sexuality of such places, owing to the spread of herpes, then AIDS. However, that hasn't slowed the quest for commitment nor the inclination to engage in an evening's flirtation. Allegiances shift, but try:

Amsterdam's   428 Amsterdam Ave. (81st St.) ☎ 874-1377
Café Iguana   235 Park Ave. S (19th St.) ☎ 529-4770
Caramba   684 Broadway (3rd St.) ☎ 420-9817
Cheyenne Social Club   417 Lafayette St. (E 4th St.) ☎ 979-7550
Jim McMullen's   1341 3rd Ave. (77th St.) ☎ 861-4700
Lucy's Retired Surfers   503 Columbus Ave. (84th St.) ☎ 787-3009
Tortilla Flats   366 W 12th St. (Hudson St.) ☎ 627-1250

These are located all over town, but other places of similar intent will be encountered in the same areas.

Cabarets and supper clubs
Gorgeous chorines (as chorus girls were known), over-plumed and under-dressed, once descended sweeping staircases to the strains of Cole Porter, attended by top-hatted tap-dancing young men. Those days are gone, except in Las Vegas, but leaner versions persist, with contemporary variations. Expect cover charges and indifferent food at unjustified prices. Our suggestions:

Amazonas

492 Broome St. (near West Broadway), NY 10013 ☎ *966-3371. Map 2S4* ═ 𝝥 ⅋ AE ⊙ *Open daily.*

Here is a supper club with an ingredient usually missing at such establishments: decent food. It is Brazilian, with a seafood stew called *mariscada* heading the list. Peruse the menu over a *caipirinha*, the potent national cocktail that blends sugar-cane brandy and lime juice. Mostly-continuous live renditions of the infectious salsa beat keep diners moving in their seats.

Blue Angel

323 W 44th St. (between 8th and 9th Aves.), NY 10036 ☎ *262-3333. Map 4O3* ═ 𝝥 ⅋ AE ⊙ ⊙ *Open nightly.*

This is about as close as New York comes to the traditional revues of such fabled Parisian nightclubs as the Lido and Moulin Rouge. The energetic cast of 20 singers and comely showgirls zips through its paces so deftly that the viewer hardly notices that the entire endeavor seems a trifle wan and dated in our jaded age. There is no cover charge if you eat dinner, and there is live music for dancing before and between shows, which are at 9 and 11.30pm. Jackets required for men. Next door is **The Nile** (*327 W 44th St.* ☎ *262-1111*), which features belly dancers and Middle Eastern food.

Café Society

Broadway at 21st St., NY 10003 ☎ *529-8282. Map 5P4* ═ 𝝥 ⅋ AE ⊙ WA *Closed Sun.*

The name is a reference to the fabled style-setters of the 1930s and 1940s, and the stunning Art Deco interior certainly recalls that era immortalized by scores of Hollywood musicals. Three or more orchestras perform for dancing 6 nights a week, from swing to lambada, and there are occasional revues, as well. Next door is, of all things, **Society Billiards** (*10 E 21st St.* ☎ *529-8600*), a ritzy pool hall for the upper crust, or at least upwardly mobile.

Chippendales

1110 1st Ave. (61st St.), NY 10021 ☎ *935-6060. Map 5N5* AE *Closed Sun-Tues.*

It's only fair: at this "Ladies Only" show, women get to ogle muscular young waiters without shirts, and equally blessed colleagues who take off nearly all their clothes to a disco beat. The male strippers have their set routines — cowboy, motorcycle cop, Zorro, whatever — just like their female counterparts. The more daring members of the squealing audience stuff dollar notes into the G-strings of the dancers in expectation of a kiss and an overt squeeze of glistening flesh. Alien males are permitted to enter after 10.30pm.

Club Paradise

15 Waverly Place (near Washington Sq.), NY 10003 ☎ *533-3048. Map 2R4. Open nightly.*

The "hottest tropical bar on the island" — their description — puts on hip-swiveling reggae and Latin rhythms nightly. Three shows on Fri and Sat, with a free after-midnight buffet of Caribbean edibles. They keep their regulars coming back with such gimmicks as that, sometimes waiving the cover charge and offering half-price drinks for brief periods during the evening.

Delta 88

332 8th Ave. (26th St.), NY 10001 ☎ *924-3499. Map 4P3* ═ 𝝥 ⊙ WA *Open nightly.*

Gustatory sustenance is middling soul food and icy beer, served until midnight or later, and at an all-you-can-eat Sun evening buffet. Nourishment for the spirit are groups — changing every night — who give their all to gospel, rhythm 'n' blues standards, and occasional butt-kickin' country.

Duplex

55 Grove St. (near 7th Ave. S), NY 10014 ☎ *255-5438. Map 2R3* ♫ 𝝥 ⅋ *Open nightly.*

Upstairs is a cabaret in which revues and individual music and comedy acts are staged. More than 20yrs ago, it was the testing ground for performers who went on to high-profile careers, including Woody Allen and Rodney Dangerfield. It continues that function, despite the unpredictability of such enterprises. Downstairs, young couples and singles, alert to the possibilities of new friendships, crowd around the piano. Many of them step up to the open microphone and burst into songs by Jerome Kern or Stevie Wonder. In such a traditional neighborhood of aspiring actors and singers, this means that many of the volunteers are, in truth, reasonably talented. It makes for a convivial group, and conversations are easily struck up.

Michael's Pub
211 E 55th St. (near 3rd Ave.),
NY 10022 ☎ *758-2272. Map 5N5*
🍸 🎵 AE ◨ ◨ 🎬 *Closed Sun.*
In a dim, woody chain of rooms that
suggests some fleeting exposure to
the British pub, the varied offerings
include such name comedians as
Joan Rivers and Sid Caesar, jazz
singers such as Anita O'Day, and
jazz combos that often favor the
swing era. On Mon, the program
shifts to Dixie, and Woody Allen is
known to sit in at clarinet when he's
in the mood. Music starts at 9.30pm.

The Oak Room
Algonquin Hotel, 59 W 44th St.
(near 6th Ave.), NY 10036
☎ *840-6800. Map 5O4* AE ◨ ◨
🎬 *Open Sun, Mon.*
In a renewed tradition, this room in
the venerable hotel favored by
British actors and Manhattan literati
now features cabaret vocalists,
usually accompanied only by a
piano. Such singers as the ageless
Julie Wilson and Margaret Whiting
construct eclectic programs of tunes
by Sondheim, Kern and other
Broadway composers. Nightly
shows are usually at 9.15pm and
11.15pm, but scheduling may be
adjusted to accommodate
performers and the season. Dinners
are offhandedly served and
indifferently prepared. Focus on the
music, which is customarily very
engrossing for fans of the genre.

Rainbow!
30 Rockefeller Plaza (GE
Building), NY 10017 ☎ *632-5100.*
Map 5O4 ▭ 🎵 🎵 ◨ ◨
Rainbow Room closed Sun, Mon.
The glamor has returned with a
vengeance to what was once the
premier supper club in Manhattan.
Two years and millions of dollars in
renovations were worth it. The
famous Art Deco extravaganza **The
Rainbow**, at the top of the GE,
once again conjures images of Fred
Astaire and Ginger Rogers whirling
across the revolving dance floor,
beneath hundreds of pinlights
pulsating to the music. From 7.30pm

onward, there is continuous music
from the 12-piece dance band that
shares the stand with a similar group
that swings to a Latin beat. Even the
food is good, although expensive
(the cover charge is higher on Fri
and Sat). Another new feature is the
transformation of the once ordinary
bar-lounge. Called the **Rainbow
Promenade**, its floor was raised
40cm (16ins) and the walls opened
in banks of glass to take maximum
advantage of the most stunning vista
in New York. As a bonus, they serve
delectable "little meals" that are the
ideal pre-theater snack: grilled
shrimp, Cajun sausage and three
types of caviar are some of the
dishes likely to be encountered.
Even by itself, the Promenade is on
a par with the Metropolitan Museum
of Art as a "must see" destination in
New York.
  In another part of the complex is a
small supper club with slightly
lower tariffs — **Rainbow & Stars**
— offering intimate cabaret
entertainment. Tony Bennett was
the opening act, but not all
performers are of that impressive
magnitude. Nostalgia is an apparent
factor in their selection, with the
likes of the McGuire Sisters and Jack
Jones. Men must wear jacket and tie
in all areas of the club. Reservations
are essential in both the main room
and the cabaret.

Sounds of Brazil
204 Varick St. (near Houston
St.), NY 10014 ☎ *243-4940. Map*
2S3 ▤ 🎵 🍸 AE 🎬 *Closed Mon,*
Tues.
Familiarly known as "S.O.B.," this
colorful and persistently lively club
is known more for its Latin
American and African dance music
than for the merely serviceable
Brazilian food. It is frequented by a
buoyant cosmopolitan crowd that is
not even distracted by the
offhanded decor, largely made up of
masks and hanging gourds. Dinner
is served from 7pm, and the
admission charge is lower if you eat
there. Friday and Saturday are the
big nights.

Cinema
Films are of profound concern to many New Yorkers, often to
the point of reverence. In strong-mindedly rejecting the
foolishness of the notorious Cannes event, for example, the
New York Film Festival (*Alice Tully Hall, Lincoln Center,
mid-Sept to early Oct*) overcompensates on the side of
solemnity. No prizes are awarded, no starlets drop their bras,
and few outsiders notice that anything happened. Worthwhile

films are introduced, nonetheless, some of which go on to limited release. "Art" films — usually foreign-made and of slim domestic appeal — are showcased by managers who no doubt pray for the occasional hit. A few of these do happen. Many are subtitled.

Theaters specializing in such films include:

Angelika Film Center   Houston and Mercer Sts.
☎995-2000

Art Greenwich Twin   Greenwich Ave. and 12th St.
☎929-3350

Carnegie Hall Cinema   7th Ave. and 56th St. ☎265-2520

Carnegie Screening Room   887 7th Ave. (57th St.)
☎757-2131

Cinema 3   59th St. (near 5th Ave.) ☎752-5959

Lincoln Plaza   Broadway (near 63rd St.) ☎757-2280

Paris   4 W 58th St. (near 5th Ave.) ☎688-2013

The Public Theater   425 Lafayette St. (near E 4th St.)
☎598-7150

Seaport Cinema   210 Front St. (South Street Seaport)
☎608-7889

In addition, several movie theaters specialize in revivals, often in "festival" or retrospective form. They can be high-minded or high camp, composed of movies foreign or domestic, anything from 1-50yrs old.

Such theaters include:

Anthology Film Archives   32-34 2nd Ave.(2nd St.)
☎477-2714

Biograph Cinema   225 W 57th St. (Broadway) ☎582-4582

Bleecker St. Cinemas   144 Bleecker St. (LaGuardia Pl.)
☎674-2560

Cinema Village   33 E 12th St. (near University Pl.)
☎924-3363

Thalia SoHo   15 Vandam St. ☎675-0498

Theater 80   80 St. Mark's Pl. (near 1st Ave.) ☎254-7400

Waverly Twin   323 Ave. of the Americas (W. 3rd St.)
☎929-8037

Several museums have regular film programs. The most comprehensive is at the **Museum of Modern Art** (*11 W 53rd St. (6th Ave.) ☎ 956-7070*). Also try the **Museum of the Moving Image** (*35th Ave. and 36th St. ☎ 718-784-4520*).

For general movie showtime information ☎777-3456.

Classical music

Avery Fisher Hall (*Lincoln Center ☎ 874-2424*) is home for the New York Philharmonic and its East German conductor, Kurt Masur. Chamber orchestras, string quartets and instrumentalists are heard at **Alice Tully Hall** (*Lincoln Center ☎ 362-1911*). The National Orchestra of New York uses **Carnegie Hall** (*57th St. and 7th Ave. ☎ 247-7800*), while groups and individual artists use the attached **Weill Recital Hall**.

A service similar to "TKTS" (see page 178) offers half-price day-of-performance tickets for music and dance events. Look for the booth in Bryant Park on 42nd St., near 6th Ave. (*☎ 382-2323 (after 12.30pm), open Tues, Thurs, Fri noon-7pm, Wed, Sat 11am-7pm, Sun noon-6pm. Closed Tues-Sat 2-3pm*).

Other venues are:

Brooklyn Academy of Music   30 Lafayette Ave., Brooklyn
☎718-636-4100

Kaufman Concert Hall   1395 Lexington Ave. ☎ 427-4410
Merkin Concert Hall   129 W 67th St. ☎ 362-8719
Town Hall   123 W 43rd St. ☎ 840-2824

Comedy

As an alternative to cabaret or a show, try stand-up comedy. Its most typical manifestation is in the form of showcase clubs, in which parades of would-be comics are given opportunities to test their material before live audiences. Should you attend, don't sit near the stage unless you are prepared to be the object of the performers' jibes. Non-Americans and even non-New Yorkers are apt to find many references obscure.

Caroline's
332 8th Ave. (26th St.), NY 10001 ☎ *924-3499. Map 4P3* 🏛 ⬛ ▣ *Closed Mon.*
Selectivity is the rule here, for most of the performers in the spotlight have garnered at least a measure of journalistic or television attention. They are given time to develop their material, with less pressure from lines of novice comedians standing anxiously about for their turns. The surroundings are not as barren either, with mirrors and neon sculptures brightening the walls. Expect high prices. Success with this formula led to the opening of another branch by the same name at the South Street Seaport (*89 South St., Pier 17* ☎ *233-4900*). It attracts the bigger names, as well as an affluent young Wall St. crowd.

Catch a Rising Star
1487 1st Ave. (78th St.), NY 10028 ☎ *794-1906. Map 7L5* 🎵 🏛 ⬛ *Open nightly.*
Continuous streams of singers and comedians, all unpaid, but so anxious to perform that they line up every week for auditions. Two masters of ceremonies keep the pace brisk. Much of the humor is ethnic, very local in origin, and often mystifying to outlanders.

Comedy Cellar
117 MacDougal St. (near Bleecker St.), NY 10012 ☎ *254-3630. Map 2R4* 🎵 🏛 ⬛ ▣ *Open nightly.*
This is one of several showcase clubs where young comedians can try out their material on a live audience and pray that a producer will be sitting there and be impressed. A few of them make it. Arrive early, as performances start around 9pm. It's underneath the Olive Tree Café.

Comic Strip
1568 2nd Ave. (near 81st St.), NY 10028 ☎ *861-9386. Map 7L5* 🎵 🏛 ⬛ ▣ ▣ *Open nightly.*
One of the younger comedy showcases, with most of the qualities of the others. The emphasis is on fledgling comics, but with some singers. More misses than hits, but that's the nature of the game. Shows begin about 9pm, with a second at 11.30pm Fri, Sat.

Dangerfield's
1118 1st Ave. (near 61st St.), NY 10021 ☎ *593-1650. Map 5N5* 🎵 🏛 ⬛ ▣ *Open nightly.*
Stand-up comic Rodney Dangerfield grew weary of life on the nightclub circuit and so opened his own place, where he now holds forth two or three times a night, if he's in town. When he is away on television or movie assignments, able comedians fill in. On Sun at 9.30pm, the stage is given to aspiring talents, some of them funny.

Improvisation
358 W 44th St. (near 9th Ave.), NY 10036 ☎ *765-8268. Map 4O3* 🎵 🎵 🏛 *Open nightly.*
The first of the showcase clubs, and therefore able to boast the longest list of alumni who went on to successful careers as comics and singers. The by-play between performers and hecklers can get vicious at times, and it is painful to watch obvious failure. But people crowd in to hear the ones who have true promise.

Rags to Riches
226 E 54th St. (3rd Ave.), NY 10022 ☎ *688-5577. Map 5N5* 🎵 🏛 ⬛ ▣ *Open nightly.*
Manhattan's youngest comedy club avoided several clichés of the breed. It's spacious, with 300 seats. A mural of the famous skyline replaces the customary bare brick wall as a backdrop. And comics work the crowd during the 5-8pm happy hour as well as from 9pm-1am.

171

Stand Up New York
*236 W 78th St. (near Broadway),
NY 10024* ☎ *595-0850. Map 6L2*
🎵 AE CB VISA *Closed Sun.*
This is a bare-bones operation, with
packed tables, straight-backed
chairs, exposed pipes and wiring,
and a painted brick wall as
backdrop for the performers.
However, it is the only comedy club
on the West Side, and a few of the
comics who have appeared here
went on to achieve a modicum of
success in more prominent arenas of
showbiz. The usual schedule has
three comedians performing a night,
not counting the master of
ceremonies, who does parts of his
own routine between acts. Often,
they return as a group to engage in
improvisations based upon code
words solicited from the audience.
Shows begin Sun-Thurs 9pm, Fri
8.30pm and 11pm, Sat 7.30pm,
10pm and 12.30am. There is a cover
charge and a two-drink minimum
per person, but it's not expensive, as
these things go.

Country and western

New Yorkers, who prefer to think of themselves as worldly,
were the last to adopt this otherwise beloved American genre.
Responding some years back to a fad fueled by such movies
as *Urban Cowboy*, they took to wearing snakeskin boots and
pearl-button shirts, and supporting radio stations and clubs
that specialized in the heartfelt plaints of Waylon Jennings
and Willie Nelson. That burning fixation has faded to a
flicker, but a few places carry on for the diehards.

Foot-stompin' and hootin' by transplanted Texans from
Houston and Brooklyn sets the walls atremble from 10pm on
at the **Rodeo Bar** (*375 3rd Ave.* ☎ *683-6500*). It's open
every night, and there's no cover charge. **Cottonwood Café**
(*415 Bleecker St.* ☎ *924-6271*) is a little ol' chunk of Texas
plunked down in Greenwich Village, but is so friendly and
relaxed that even native New Yorkers fit right in. Distinctions
blur at **Eagle Tavern** (*355 W 14th St* ☎ *924-0275*), for they
mix bluegrass, country and Irish folk music on different
nights.

When the Lone Star Café was down in Greenwich Village, it
billed itself as "the biggest and best honky-tonk north of
Abilene." Now, the **Lone Star Roadhouse** (*240 W 52nd
St.* ☎ *245-2950*), and moved to larger quarters in the theater
district, it has broader tastes in music. Different bands are on
every night, playing just about anything that will get toes
tapping — blues, gospel, 1950s rock 'n' roll, and, of course,
country. Many of the accouterments of the old Lone Star have
been salvaged, along with the better-than-average Texas
vittles and brews for which it was known. Loyalties of country
purists have now been transferred to **O'Lunney's** (*915 2nd
Ave.* ☎ *751-5470*), still a fair approximation of a Waco beer
hall. See also *Pop/folk/rock*.

Dance clubs

Discotheques nearly disappeared after their 1960s heyday,
revived and faded in each of the next two decades, and now
seem once again as healthy as ever. Obviously, predictions on
their fate are difficult to make. Of those that persist, some are
cavernous spaces ablaze with multimillion-dollar special
effects that would do credit to *Star Wars*; others are simply
cafés that shove aside a few tables after the dishes are cleared
away. Most are expensive, with cover and minimum charges,
and stiff prices for drinks.

References to "disco music" are met with sneers by habitués.
"Disco is dead," they insist. No matter that it sounds pretty
much the same to the unattuned ear. It is now called "house

music," or in the case of its more strident, metallic versions, "acid house." To fogeys over 40 this may be a nuance without a difference. Otherwise, old rules apply. It's still difficult to get into the clubs-of-the-moment, with entrance denied or tendered by hard-eyed centurions at the door. Being appropriately bizarre in dress, or rich, or famous, or in the company of a particularly comely young woman, may help. Or not. Approach with a firm grip on your ego.

Limelight

47 W 20th St. (5th Ave.), NY 10011 ☎ 807-7850. Map 5Q4 ●
AE Open nightly.
Years ago, this was the hottest club in town for the usual 6mths. Those days are long past, but the club seems to have survived bankruptcy. Call ahead to make sure, then go to see what enthralled the night people for so long. It's a converted church, stained-glass windows intact, and seating in side chapels and on upholstered pews. Candles and lasers provide illumination. The androgynous models and celebrities have disappeared, but at least mere mortals can get inside the doors.

Mars

28-30 10th Ave. (13th St.), NY 10014 ☎ 691-6262. Map 2Q2 ●
◆ AE ◑ ◻◻ Closed Mon-Wed.
This 5-story warehouse and meat-packing plant at the edge of the Hudson was transmogrified into a club by the creator of **Tunnel**. Its decor, if such it might be called, is comprised primarily of urban refuse — walls of outdated computer chips, vintage TV sets, lava lamps, African masks, and equipment left over from the building's former function. Dressing right is the key to getting in, apparently interpreted by the rope attendants as lots of leather and/or lots of skin. Each floor has different sounds — house music at painful levels, slightly less loud New Wave, Germanic industrial-synth, and, when the rooftop terrace is open in summer, reggae.

Palladium

123 E 14th St. (between 3rd and 4th Ave.), NY 10003 ☎ 473-7171. Map 5Q4 ● ◆ AE ◑ ◻◻ ◻◻ Closed Mon, Tues.
The creators of **Studio 54** roared back after a brief court-induced absence, to set the night ablaze with still another monument to frivolity. Their 7-story phantasmagoria attracted the positive attention of no less a presence than the architecture critic of *The New York Times*. Elements of the rococo theater this once was are now augmented with

towering sculptural dividers, vast Post-Modern murals and clusters of TV monitors bouncing with the impressionistic imaginings of experimental video artists. Naturally, every member of — or aspirant to — the international glitterati made the scene. It's far less exclusive now, since the management has to fill more than 10,000 sq.ft of space.

Régine's

502 Park Ave. (49th St.), NY 10022 ☎ 826-0990. Map 5O4 ▤ ● ◆ AE ◑ ◻◻ ◻◻ Closed Sun.
The local branch of the flamboyant Parisienne's international chain. No longer chic, but the people and surroundings are pretty, the prices less so. Dinner is served until midnight, but don't go to eat, and nurse your drinks.

Red Zone

440 W 54th St. (between 9th and 10th Ave.), NY 10019 ☎ 582-2222. Map 4N3 ▤ ● ◆ AE Closed Sun-Wed.
Bucking the trend to smaller, more intimate clubs, Red Zone occupies much of a city block, with a claimed 14,000 sq.ft. on two floors. Every disco-technology of the last 20yrs is employed and updated on the ground floor — lasers, smoke machines, big screen projections, strobes — and **42** loudspeakers. Upstairs is calmer, quieter (as these things go), with a restaurant serving trendy eats. Flamboyant gays, S&M studded leather fans, drag queens, and celebs recognized by their first names, constitute much of the crowd, but suits and stockbroker ties are as much in evidence. Have dinner and they waive the cover charge.

Roseland

239 W 52nd St. (near Broadway), NY 10019 ☎ 247-0200. Map 4N3 ● ◗ ◻◻ AE ◻◻ Closed Mon-Wed.
More than 60yrs old and resisting repeated threats to its existence, this grand old ballroom carries on with two orchestras playing 1930s swing and 1940s Latin American rhythms until 11pm each night. Then it

Nightlife and the performing arts

switches to disco. All ages waltz or samba with each other or with professional dance teachers. Huge buffet-style restaurant.

setting that could have been conceived by George Lucas. Suppers are served. You will pay dearly.

Stringfellow's
35 E 21st St. (near Park Ave. S), NY 10010 ☎ 254-2444. Map 5Q4 ⊟ ♈ AE ⊙ ⊙ VISA Open nightly.
A New World outpost of an established London enterprise, this super-tech disco opened to a flurry of overheated criticism and then proceeded to impose such an exclusive entry policy that very few New Yorkers were able to get in. Try early in the week. If you are very fit, chic and gorgeous, and arrive in a stretch limousine (your own, not rented), then perhaps you will get past the social arbiters at the door. If this is no problem, join your equals in a boggling, state-of-the-art

Tunnel
220 12th Ave. (27th St.), NY 10001 ☎ 244-6444. Map 4P2 ● AE ⊙ VISA Open nightly.
This, too, was once *the* status club. The Concorde set, the severely strange and the breathlessly trendy have fled to warmer climes but it still pulls in enough players to fill a space as long as two end-to-end football fields. The decor is vaguely Moorish seraglio, with many alcoves and crannies in which to escape the crowds. High entrance fees tend to suppress the numbers of the very young, but the need to fill the place makes it less exclusive than many other clubs.

Jazz
America's most exportable art form may have been born in New Orleans and journeyed up the Mississippi to Kansas City and Chicago, but the ultimate destination was New York. Jazz musicians were not — *are* not — certain of recognition until they appeared and were accepted here. One of their number was credited with the invention of that celebrated nickname for the metropolis: "I made it, brother, I'm going to the Big Apple."

Jazz flourished and grew in New York from World War I into the 1950s. It hung on in the face of the onslaught of Elvis, The Beatles and their progeny. Now it is back, more vital than ever, and in all its permutations — Dixieland, swing, fusion, mainstream, bop, progressive, and wildly experimental. It is performed in old-line clubs on the scene for 50yrs and in fifth-floor "lofts" no more settled than Bedouins. Concerts are also mounted in the halls of colleges and churches all over town. Call the **Jazzline** — ☎ 718-465-7500 — for a daily recorded announcement. Here are 12 of the 50 possibilities:

Angry Squire
216 7th Ave. (23rd St.), NY 10011 ☎ 242-9066. Map 4Q3 ♪ AE ⊙ Open daily.
Another pub-tavern contributing to the Chelsea renaissance, with fittingly British cookery that is at least as authentic as American hamburgers in London. The music is mainstream and hard bop.

from the midtown original and infrequently signs up stars of that luminosity. Buffs still think it is worth the trek. Lesser-known practitioners such as the Jimmy Heath and Paul Ostermayer quartets are the capable rule, with occasional appearances by such legends as Milt Jackson.

Birdland
2745 Broadway (105th St.), NY 10025 ☎ 749-2228. Map 6J2 ⊟ ♪ AE ⊙ ⊙ VISA Open nightly.
The fabled Birdland of the 1940s and 1950s hosted jazz greats Charlie Parker and Dave Brubeck, and others of their prominence. This upper West Side club is far removed

Blue Note
131 W 3rd St. (Ave. of the Americas), NY 10012 ☎ 475-8592. Map 2R4 ⊟ ♪ AE Open nightly.
Arguably New York's premier jazz showcase, their roster of performers has included just about every notable performer, past and present, from Sarah Vaughan and Dizzy

174

Gillespie to Illinois Jacquet and Chick Corea. Naturally enough, with that caliber of musician, it is packed with fans nearly every night. Headliners have two shows during the week, three on Fri and Sat, and afterwards, a house trio jams on until 4am. Weekends, there are matinees with late brunch.

Bradley's
70 University Pl. (11th St.), NY 10003 ☎ 228-6440. Map 2R4 ☿ ♫ AE ◉ ◉ VISA Open daily.

Dim, smoky, bubbling with conversation. The 'burgers are good and the progressive mainstream duos and trios at the end of the long bar even better. They tune up twice nightly, somewhere around 10pm and midnight.

Carlos I
432 6th Ave. (near 10th St.), NY 10011 ☎ 982-3260. Map 2R4 ☿ ♫ AE ◉ ◉ VISA Open nightly.

With a friendly crowd in the bar and bands with as many as 12 musicians, this is decidedly *not* one of those hushed halls in which jazz is often heard. Given the club's name and the Caribbean food it serves, it isn't surprising that the music veers toward Afro-Latin rhythms, although the range is wide. Arthur Prysock, Thuli Dumarkude, the World Saxophone Quartet and the Henry Threadgill Sextet have all performed here. Sun afternoon jazz brunch sessions start at 1.30pm. Try the seafood.

Fat Tuesday's
190 3rd Ave. (17th St.), NY 10003 ☎ 533-7902. Map 5Q4 ☿ ♫ AE ◉ ◉ VISA Closed Sun.

Once upon a time, this was Joe King's Rathskeller, a magnet for generations of collegians. The main floor hasn't changed, in spirit. Singles mingle, 'burgers are munched, pitchers of beer are quaffed. Downstairs is a separate place. Jazz prevails, largely of the progressive mainstream variety. There is a hefty cover charge, and the minimum is best consumed in liquid form. Sets are usually at 8pm, 10pm and, on weekends, midnight.

Fortune Garden Pavilion
209 E 49th St. (3rd Ave.), NY 10017 ☎ 753-0101. Map 5O5 ═ ♫ AE ◉ ◉ VISA Open daily.

Here's a twist: Jazz *and* good Hong Kong-style food, a peculiarly New York blend. Music in the main-floor restaurant is by duos and trios on the order of Clark Terry, and in the

downstairs lounge, by singer-pianists, sometimes accompanied by bassists. Three sets nightly.

Knitting Factory
47 E Houston St. (near Lafayette St.), NY 10012 ☎ 219-3055. Map 2S4 ☿ Open nightly.

Quartets and quintets squeeze onto a tiny stage to deliver narratives on improvisation in the modernist mode. Elbow-to-elbow patrons tend to be an attentive, appreciative lot who treat the music as centerpiece, not backdrop. There are usually two sets a night, the first between 8 and 9pm. An admission fee is charged.

Sweet Basil
88 7th Ave. (Bleecker St.), NY 10014 ☎ 242-1785. Map 2R3 ═ ♫ AE ◉ VISA Open daily.

Mainstream jazz in an attractive brick-and-wood setting, with such artists as Nat Adderley and Chris Conner. Music starts at 10pm; or show up for Sat and Sun afternoon sessions and avoid the cover charge.

Village Gate
160 Bleecker St. (Thompson St.), NY 10012 ☎ 475-5120. Map 2R4 ☿ ♫ ⬚ AE ◉ VISA Open daily.

Stability is not a characteristic of jazz emporia, but the "Gate" grooves on, now approaching its fourth decade. Performers range from good to unsurpassed, their preferences from be-bop to fusion to salsa. They're housed in a large, comfortable, noisy room. Music starts from 10pm. The multilevel complex also puts on comedy acts, revues, theater, chamber music, to name but a few.

Village Vanguard
178 7th Ave. S (near 11th St.), NY 10011 ☎ 255-4037. Map 2R3 ☿ ♫ Open nightly.

Landmark cellar club approaching its 50th anniversary. Mainstream jazz, mostly, often by large bands and the likes of Milt Jackson and Mel Lewis. Shows start at 10pm.

Zinno's
126 West 13th St. (near 7th Ave.), NY 10011 ☎ 924-5182. Map 4Q3 ═ ☿ ♫ AE ◉ VISA Open Mon-Sat noon-2.30pm, 5.30-10.30pm; bar until 1am.

First-rate duos and trios (there isn't room for more) split themselves between the bar and dining room nightly to tender immaculate versions of blues and mainstream jazz. It's a cozy layout, not unlike a party at a friend's house. The bonus is good food — exceedingly rare at

175

Manhattan jazz showcases. Here, it's northern Italian, and the pastas are especially tasty. They make the minimum consumption charge easy to meet, although patrons aren't compelled to eat. An entertainment charge is levied, too. Sets usually start at 8 or 9pm. Be warned that reservations are essential if you intend to eat.

Opera

Full-scale productions are mounted during extended seasons of the Metropolitan Opera Company and the New York City Opera at the **Metropolitan Opera House** (*Lincoln Center* ☎ 580-9830) and the **New York State Theater** (*Lincoln Center* ☎ 870-5570). **City Center** (*131 W 55th St.* ☎ 581-7907) is an important site for smaller touring and regional companies.

Gilbert and Sullivan and Victor Herbert fans support a year-long season at the **Light Opera of Manhattan** (*316 E 91st St.* ☎ 831-2000).

Singing principals of these and other companies perform in concerts in other venues around the city, including:

Brooklyn Academy of Music   30 Lafayette Ave. (downtown Brooklyn) ☎718-636-4100
Carnegie Hall   57th St. and 7th Ave. ☎247-7800
Kaufman Concert Hall   1395 Lexington Ave. ☎427-4410
Town Hall   123 W 43rd St. ☎840-2824

Amateurs and young professionals form the companies of the **Amato Opera Theater** (*319 Bowery* ☎ 228-8200) and the **Bel Canto Opera** (*220 E 76th St.* ☎ 535-5231).

Pop/folk/rock

Some of these clubs have survived decades of changing fashions, but many opened yesterday and will close tomorrow. Always call ahead to learn of scheduled acts, prices, dress code, and present policies.

See also *Country and western* and *Cabarets and supper clubs*.

The Back Fence
155 Bleecker St. (Thompson St.), NY 10012 ☎ *475-9221. Map 2R4* 🍸 🎵 *Open daily.*

A Greenwich Village haunt of more than 40yrs standing, it's just the place to recapture whichever segment of that period constituted one's youth. The milling, happy, noisy participants in that quest are suburbanites sliding into their middle years, ageing hippies or their latter-day reincarnations, and graduate students and faculty from nearby New York University. Performers are part of the same spectrum, re-creating golden rock-and-roll oldies and folkie laments from the halcyon days of social protest and flower power. A few are known to suggest that songs have been written since 1970, but not often. Dress is very casual. There is a two-drink minimum, but they are inexpensive.

The Bitter End
149 Bleecker St. (near La Guardia Pl.), NY 10012 ☎ *673-7030. Map 2R4* 🎵 🎵 *Open daily.*

Since the 1960s, when it showcased Bob Dylan and Joni Mitchell, this has been one of the most influential rooms in New York. It is still snug and plain, but with an unusually good sound system and acoustics. Genres represented run from folk to jazz to rock and their subspecies. Shows are usually at 9pm and midnight, but call ahead.

Bottom Line
15 W 4th St. (near Washington Sq.), NY 10003 ☎ *228-7880. Map 2R4* 🎵 🎵 *Open nightly. No cards.*

Lines form days in advance for tickets to the celebrated acts, more likely to appear here than anywhere else in the city. One-night stands are

the rule for a catholic schedule of
top performers, leavened with
groups judged to be on the way up.
Any musical persuasion might show
up — bluegrass, New Wave, folk,
blues, jazz, pop.

Café Carlyle
*Madison Ave. and 76th St., NY
10021* ☎ *744-1600. Map 7L4* ⬛
🛇 🜔 *Closed Sun, Mon.*
Bobby Short is at the piano and in
full silky voice about half the weeks
of the year. An eternal favorite with
the older strata of local society and
the Establishment, his métier is the
show tunes of Cole Porter, Rodgers
and Hart, and George Gershwin. His
renditions of songs obscure and
celebrated are as smooth as hot
butter on glass. You will pay dearly
to hear them.

CBGB
*315 Bowery (Bleecker St.), NY
10012* ☎ *982-4052. Map 2R4* 🍷
🛇 *Open nightly.*
Once the home of imported British
punk, this grungy but
unintimidating ex-garage now
promotes less nihilistic New Wave
rockers. For those over 30, a visit
now qualifies as a nostalgia trip.

The Ritz
*254 W 54th St. (Broadway), NY
10010* ☎ *541-8900. Map 2R4* ◼
🛇 ☙ *Open nightly. No cards.*
The management cares how their
big rock palace looks as well as
sounds — it's a restored rococo
opera house — but it's uncertain

whether the young crowd notices.
Some are skinheads, some sport
chains and leather, and many are
teenagers from suburban fringes
trying hard to look *bad*. Serious
slam-dancing sometimes erupts on
the huge dance floor, to New Wave,
white rap, and classic and
underground rock. International
bands are as well-known as Kid
Creole and the Coconuts and Ricky
Skaggs or as obscure as The Cramps
and The Radiators. Anyone whose
complexion has cleared up will feel
like an antique. Kids who can pass
for 16 will love it. Seats can be
reserved in the balcony, general
admission downstairs. No food, no
credit cards, and steep prices for
watery drinks.

Sweetwater's
*170 Amsterdam Ave. (68th St.),
NY 10023* ☎ *873-4100. Map 6M2*
⬛ 🛇 🄰🄴 🜔 🄲🄳 💳 *Closed Mon.*
This can be just the right place for
winding down after a cultural stint
at the Lincoln Center. The usual
format is a singer backed by a small
instrumental group. The thrust is
toward a glossy mix of pop, rock
and soul. Two shows nightly.

Tramps
*125 E 15th St. (near Irving Pl.),
NY 10003* ☎ *777-5077. Map 5Q4*
⬛ 🎵 🛇 🄰🄴 🜔 💳 *Open
nightly.*
Blues in all its variations is the
staple, although experimental jazz
features from time to time.
Comfortable tavern atmosphere.

Theater
Broadway, the avenue, long ago gave its name to Broadway,
the theater district. Few of the 36 theaters actually front on
that thoroughfare, however. Rather, they cluster around
Times Sq., the intersection of Broadway and 7th Ave. Here
are the lavish musicals, popular intimate comedies and,
against heavy odds, occasional serious dramas.

Economics mitigated against experimentation, so that role
was traditionally assumed by what came to be known as
"Off-Broadway" — smaller houses with lower overheads and
greater daring. Many of these are found in and near
Greenwich Village, but they are also located throughout
Manhattan. In recent years they have grown somewhat more
wary, in effect serving as a pre-Broadway tryout circuit,
although few productions manage the long step into the big
time. Alternative theater, often raw and wildly avant-garde, is
known as "Off-Off-Broadway." These productions —
happenings — are mounted in garages, churches, lofts,
backrooms of restaurants, galleries, anywhere.

Good seats at a hit musical are extremely expensive; seats
are not cheap even at the back of the auditorium. There are

ways to reduce the bite, however. Productions nearing the end of their runs issue "twofer" passes to stores and hotels: take these to the box office of the appropriate theater and you'll receive two tickets for the price of one. Or, visit the **TKTS** booth at the N end of Times Sq. after 3pm on the day you wish to attend. Last-minute cancellations and unsold seats are made available at substantial discounts, although not for all plays, of course. There is another TKTS booth at 2 World Trade Center.

Many theaters accept telephone orders for tickets to their current productions. Their numbers are listed in the daily "Theater Directory" of the *New York Times*. Have a credit card ready when calling. If there is time, tickets can be mailed; otherwise they are picked up at the box office, usually on the day of performance. There are independent tickets-by-telephone agencies, as well, representing large numbers of theaters and the several sports arenas. Those with considerable coverage include **Telecharge** (☎ *239-6200*) and **Teletron** (☎ *246-0102*). They take orders 24hrs a day, 7 days a week. **Ticketmaster** (☎ *307-7171*) and **Hit Tix** (☎ *564-8038*) concentrate on Off-Broadway venues. A surcharge is added to credit card purchases. There are also **Ticketron** outlets throughout the city and suburbs at which tickets can be purchased for most Broadway and Off-Broadway productions (and concerts and sports events, too). Ticket brokers and hotel concierges can handle requests, but be sure that their handling fee will not exceed the going rate.

Shopping

All the world's goods pour into Manhattan. There is no material need, and few of the psychic kind, that is not supplied by its shops and stores. Many objects and services are offered at heart-stopping prices, but more often at costs equal to or below those of the countries of origin. Peruvian folk art to Japanese video recorders, Belgian lace to Colombian emeralds, Florentine leather to Chinese porcelain — if it isn't here, somewhere, it probably isn't worth having. Those who shop as a form of recreation cannot exhaust the possibilities for diversion. Those who regard it as a chore can, with prior research, march into a single store and emerge minutes later with the precise product required.

At this center of the nation's garment industry, clothing is available in bewildering profusion. Milanese and Parisian couture are represented, of course, often in salons devoted exclusively to the work of a single house. Native designers challenge them on every front, especially in sportswear and ready-to-wear. Part of the success of Calvin Klein, Bill Blass, Geoffrey Beene, Ralph Lauren and Anne Klein is attributable to their willingness to design for broader markets. While custom tailoring is still available, careful sizing in both men's and women's ready-to-wear garments largely eliminates the need. The better shirts, for example, are calibrated in both neck and sleeve size, and dresses are proportioned to body type — petite, junior, misses, women's — as well as size.

Photographic and home electronic equipment is consistently sold below list price. High volume permits this, and heavy competition also requires it. Many camera dealers bypass the US distributors, for example, to purchase directly from Japanese manufacturers, thereby eliminating intermediate price rises. With more than 90 percent of the nation's publishers quartered here, discounting of new books is widespread, all languages are represented, and rare and out-of-print volumes are quickly located. Specialization reigns, and stores can concentrate exclusively on Marxism, homosexuality, feminism, travel or detective novels. Jewelry and unset gems, musical instruments, kitchenware and fashion accessories are of the highest quality and at accessible prices.

The picture is not entirely blue sky and clear sailing, of course. Objects of substantial age, such as antiques or Oriental carpets, are available in quantity, but are invariably over-priced. Be wary, too, of stores that proclaim in foot-high letters that they are going out of business: some of them have had those signs up for years. Check labels and identifications carefully, especially on watches and electronic equipment. Unknown brands aren't worth the risk, and some are made to look like products of reputable companies, right down to names with only one letter changed. Street vendors peddle scarves, umbrellas, belts, almost anything portable. Their prices are low, but remember that they move about and might not be at the same site tomorrow.

Weekday mornings are the best times to shop, lunch hours and Sat the worst. The only days on which virtually everything is closed are Thanksgiving (*last Thurs in Nov*), Christmas and New Year's Day. Other holidays are used as an excuse for sales. Although Sun is still usually a day off, many large stores now open on Sun afternoon. As a rule, midtown stores are open from 9.30am or 10am until 6pm, Mon-Sat, with late closing 8pm or 9pm on Thurs eve. Elsewhere, the hours reflect the religious convictions or life-styles of the communities. In Bohemian Greenwich Village and SoHo, doors may not open until noon, but close as late as midnight. Jewish-owned businesses of the Lower East Side and elsewhere are closed Fri afternoons and Sat, but open Sun. In the nine-to-five world of the Wall St. area, many stores close Sat as well as Sun.

Sales personnel, being New Yorkers, can be brusque or helpful, irritable or patient. For no obvious reason, assistants in camera stores and luxury clothing emporia are testy and/or indifferent in undue proportions. Generally, however, encounters will be pleasant and informative. While department stores are logical first stops in the quest for two or more unrelated items, they are frequently under-staffed, and the wait can be long at the payment and wrapping counter. Items of a more specific or unusual nature are more easily found in smaller stores. Their owners, fearing crime, often keep their doors locked, buzzing them open only after making snap judgments of potential clients. On that subject, incidentally, take care never to leave a handbag or wallet on a counter while signing a sales slip or examining goods. They can be snatched in a twinkling.

Credit cards are widely accepted, even in the smallest stores, although a minimum purchase price might be stipulated. Travelers checks are *not* regarded as simply another form of money. Supplementary identification is often required, and checks drawn in another currency are invariably refused. Personal checks from out-of-town banks are not welcomed, but individual managers can sometimes be persuaded to take them, with two or more types of identification, if the customer appears trustworthy.

While diversity prevails, certain streets and neighborhoods have taken on distinct commercial identities, with regard to either cost or similarity of merchandise. Even casual window-shoppers gravitate to the stretch of 5th Ave. from about 47th St. to 57th St., a half-mile of world-famous clothiers, jewelers, booksellers and purveyors of superior luggage and shoes. The same distinction applies along 57th St., especially between 1st Ave. and 5th Ave. Antique hunters and art lovers will want to explore Madison Ave., from 57th St. to 80th. Tucked between the galleries are scores of boutiques trafficking in leather goods, pet supplies, lingerie, materials for needlework, and clothing geared to expectant mothers, debutantes, urban cowboys and country squires.

Before settling on **Tiffany's** or **Cartier**, stroll both sides of 47th St. between 5th Ave. and 6th Ave. for a boggling pageant of jewelry and precious stones of every description and price. For art galleries, see *Guide to the galleries* on page 29. For discount designer and mass clothing, make the popular pilgrimage to Orchard St. on the Lower East Side, but go there *only* on Sun. For photographic equipment, head for 34th St. near Herald Sq. or for Lexington Ave. between 42nd St. and 52nd St. Crafts and offbeat articles of clothing are apparent on a gallery tour of SoHo and along the blocks of W 4th St. and Greenwich Ave., just w of 7th Ave. in Greenwich Village. The compilation that follows in the next few pages does no more than sketch the highlights.

Stores are open normal hours (*9.30 or 10am-5 or 6pm*) unless otherwise stated.

Antiques

If rarity and distinction are your criteria and cost is not, there are dozens of exclusive dealers along 57th St., Madison Ave. and the adjoining blocks. For antique porcelain, look at:

Chinese Porcelain Company   822 Madison Ave. (69th St.) ☎628-4101

Gem Antiques   1088 Madison Ave. (85th St.) ☎535-7399

James Robinson   12 E 57th St. (near 5th Ave.) ☎752-6166

Fine European furniture of the same period can be viewed at:

French & Co.   17 E 65th St. (near 5th Ave.) ☎535-3330

Old Versailles   315 E 62nd St. (near Lexington Ave.) ☎421-3663

Gene Tyson   19 E 69th St. (near 5th Ave.) ☎744-5785

Michael B. Weisbrod   906 Madison Ave. (73rd St.) ☎734-6350

Overseas visitors may be more interested in early American furnishings, quilts, and folk arts. Among stores focusing on these:

American Hurrah   766 Madison Ave. (67th St.) ☎535-1930

Geoffrey Goodman Antiques   825 Broadway (13th St.) ☎674-2673

Poor Richard's Antiques   37 W 20th St. (near 5th Ave.) ☎675-6477

Somethin' Else   182 9th Ave. (in Chelsea) ☎924-0006

Speakeasy Antiques   799 Broadway (11th St.) ☎533-2440

Spirit of America   269 W 4th St. (in Greenwich Village) ☎255-3255

The multifloored antique galleries of London and Paris have their counterparts here, too. There can be good buys, somewhat below the stratospheric price ranges of the stores already mentioned. Dealers in silver, enamel, crystal, music boxes, vintage clothing, china, paperweights, brassware and every category of bric-a-brac lease space at:

Manhattan Art and Antiques Center   1050 2nd Ave. (56th St.) ☎355-4400. 85 stalls.

New York Antique and Flea Market   145 E 23rd St. (near Lexington Ave.) ☎777-9609. 20 stores.

Auction houses

Auctions are a source of enlightenment and entertainment even for those who have no intention of bidding (*for a recorded announcement of the week's sales at these and other auction houses* ☎ *977-2579*).

Christie's
502 Park Ave. (near 59th St.), NY 10022 ☎ *546-1000. Map 5N4.*
Closest in stature to **Sotheby Parke Bernet**, Christie's is also a British house and nearly as comprehensive in its offerings. It has another branch, **Christie's East** at 219 E 67th St. (☎ *606-0400*).

Sotheby Parke Bernet
1334 York Ave. (72nd St.), NY 10021 ☎ *606-7000. Map 7M5.*
This result of a merger of British and American firms continues to hold center stage. They deal in snuff boxes, folk arts, antiquities, Oriental carpets, Impressionist paintings, toys, Judaica, Art Nouveau — everything.

Beauty parlors and hairdressers

Once the exclusive province of women, both skin-care centers and hairstylists now cater to men as well. The former retain their markedly feminine decor and emphasis, despite the fact that as much as 40 percent of their clientele is male. Hairdressers are increasingly unisexual (one might say multisexual) in character.

Facial treatments typically take an hour to an hour and a half. Inevitably, there are soft-sell efforts by attendants to sign you up for repeat sessions and costly creams and lotions. Advance reservation is essential. Many salons serve both men and women.

Borja and Paul   805 Madison Ave. (67th St.) ☎ 734-0477
Kenneth   19 E 54th St. (5th Ave.) ☎ 752-1800
Georgette Klinger   501 Madison Ave. (52nd St.) ☎ 838-3200
Lia Schorr   686 Lexington Ave. ☎ 486-9670 (half the clients are men)
Christine Valmy   767 5th Ave. (58th St.) ☎ 752-0303

At the following hairstylists, appointments are not always required, but call ahead for hours and rates.

Michael Kazan   16 E 55th St. (near 5th Ave.) ☎ 688-1400
Larry Mathews   536 Madison Ave. (54th St.) ☎ 246-6100
Nardi   143 E 57th St. (3rd Ave.) ☎ 421-4810
Vidal Sassoon   767 5th Ave. (near 58th St.) ☎ 535-9200

In a category all its own is **Astor Place Hairstylists** (*2 Astor Place, near Broadway* ☎ *475-9854*). It's a haircutting assembly line, with *100* barbers on three floors. They'll do anything for anyone's hair, male or female, including, but not restricted to, shaving a Batman or Mercedes-Benz logo on the back of heads. Tom Cruise might be in the next chair, and prices are moderate.

Books and records

Barnes and Noble
105 5th Ave. (18th St.), NY 10003 ☎ *807-0099. Map 4Q4* Ⓐ Ⓔ Ⓒ Ⓓ Ⓥ Ⓘ
Open daily.
One of a chain of 11 stores that concentrates on recent books at a discount. At most outlets, the selection is limited, but the 5th Ave. and 18th St. location has been called by Guinness the "world's largest bookstore." There are many bargains, with 10 percent off for paperbacks and up to 30 percent off for bestsellers. The principal uptown branch is at 5th Ave. and 48th St.

Bleecker Bob's Golden Oldies
118 W 3rd St. (near 6th Ave.), NY 10012 ☎ *475-9677. Map 2S4* Ⓒ Ⓓ Ⓥ Ⓘ
Open daily.
A Village institution, it has enough endearing quirks to amuse any

audiophile. It doesn't open until noon, but doesn't close until 1am (*3am Sat, Sun*). The huge inventory concentrates on rock in its many forms, but has disks of other musical persuasions, too. Head down if you must have that one hit record by the doo-wop group that disappeared forever in 1956.

B. Dalton Bookseller
666 5th Ave. (52nd St.), NY 10019 ☎ *247-1740. Map 5N4* AE CB VISA
The substantial stocks include thousands of titles on every imaginable subject at this flagship store of a chain of 800 outlets nationwide. More than 300,000 titles in stock.

Doubleday
724 5th Ave. (57th St.), NY 10019 ☎ *397-0550. Map 5N4* AE CB CB VISA *Open until midnight.*
Large three-level store. Every category is covered, with a marked emphasis on the performing arts. The store sells records, too.

Sam Goody
666 3rd Ave. (E 43rd St.), NY 10017 ☎ *986-8480. Map 5O4* AE CB CB VISA *Open also Sun noon-5pm. Another branch at 235 W 49th St.*
Records and tapes in all categories, and at a discount. Audio equipment, musical instruments and sheet music are also on sale.

Gotham Book Mart
41 W 47th St. (near 6th Ave.), NY 10036 ☎ *719-4448. Map 5O4* AE CB VISA
The founder of this revered bookstore was working in the store on her 100th birthday, 68yrs after she first opened these doors. Frances Steloff lives upstairs, and still makes periodic visits to see that things are running smoothly. Her clients list has included W.H. Auden, Warren Beatty, Gore Vidal, Henry Miller, Gertrude Stein and Dame Edith Sitwell, and the store is of particular appeal to creative artists. The stock is comprehensive and iconoclastic, with particular strength in poetry, and classic and experimental fiction.

Murder Ink
271 W 87th St. (near West End Ave.), NY 10024 ☎ *362-8905. Map 6K2* CB VISA
Bookstore dealing exclusively in crime mysteries.

New York Bound Bookshop
50 Rockefeller Plaza (near 5th Ave.), NY 10019 ☎ *245-8503. Map 5N4.*
Specializing in rare and out-of-print books as well as recent titles about New York, it also attracts clients for its old prints and for axonometric maps of midtown Manhattan, on which buildings are reproduced right down to the stairs and construction cranes.

Pan Am Newstand
200 Park Ave. (45th St.), NY 10017. Map 5O4. Open daily.
If this store on the main floor of the Pan Am Building doesn't have the latest copy of every magazine and periodical published in the civilized world, it's not for want of trying. There are more than 2,000 titles, attesting to the incredibly diverse interests of the tens of thousands of readers who pass here daily. To find it, take the escalators up from the main hall of Grand Central Terminal and bear right, past the new **Tropica** restaurant.

Rand McNally
150 E 52nd St. (near Lexington Ave.), NY 10022 ☎ *758-7488. Map 5N4* AE CB VISA
Maps and atlases, of course, and language books, travel guides and videos, and children's games.

Rizzoli
31 W 57th St. (near 5th Ave.), NY 10019 ☎ *759-2424. Map 5N4* AE CB CB VISA *Another branch at 454 West Broadway, in SoHo.*
The New York outlet of the prestigious Italian publisher, with books in several European languages, and classical background music in keeping with its studied elegance.

Strand
828 Broadway (12th St.), NY 10003 ☎ 473-1452 Map 2R4. Open also Sun 11am-5pm AE □ VISA
Shelf after shelf of mostly used books, in a gratifying clutter that ensnares book lovers for hours. Reviewers sell off their advance copies here at discounts.

Tower Records
4th St. and Broadway, NY 10012 ☎ 505-1505. Map 2R4. Open daily AE □ VISA
California-style merchandizing techniques are applied to the sale of records, tapes and videos in a manner that was a revelation to Easterners. Tower is *the* place to search for obscure titles, imported and domestic, as well as the latest pop hits. Both branches are huge, claiming as many as 50,000 different recordings in all formats. The downtown store has a classical music annex at 4th St. and Lafayette St. The discounted prices are good-to-excellent. They are open every day of the year.

Cameras and photographic equipment
Sales and discounts are the rule in this enormously competitive field. Check the full-page ads in the Sunday *New York Times* before setting out. Profit margins are slashed to the bone, which makes some floor managers irritable when you inquire if they will match the lower price for the same lens or projector at a store down the street. Ask anyway. When making a purchase, be certain it is handed over in a sealed factory carton.

Most stores listed below are open 7 days a week, and take major credit cards.

Camera World
104 W 32nd St. (near 6th Ave.), NY 10001 ☎ 563-8770. Map 5P4.
Nearly as well-stocked as **Willoughby's**, and holding frequent sales. It makes a point of carrying electrical products in foreign voltages.

47th Street Photo
67 W 47th St. (near 6th Ave.), NY 10036 ☎ 260-4410. Map 5O4
Arrive knowing exactly what make and model you want, since you'll get little advice, just low prices on cameras, computers, and electronic gear. The Orthodox Jewish owners close from 2pm Fri until 10am Sun. There's a larger branch at 115 W 45th St.

Grand Central Cameras
420 Lexington Ave. (near 44th St.), NY 10017 ☎ 986-2270. Map 5O4.
The personnel have proved consistently helpful, and the prices are good.

Hirsch Photo
699 3rd Ave. at 44th St., NY 10017 ☎ 557-1150. Map 5O4.
Prides itself on its attentiveness to individual needs.

Willoughby's
Main branch at 110 W 32ndSt. (near 7th Ave.), NY 10001 ☎ 564-1600. Map 4P3.
The largest of the photographic stores. Willoughby's accepts trade-ins, and members of staff speak several languages.

Clothing and shoes for men

Bancroft
363 Madison Ave. (45th St.), NY 10017 ☎ 687-8650. Map 5O4 AE □ VISA
While it sells a complete line of haberdashery, Bancroft may be best known for its wide selections in dress shirts in cottons and blends, and in unusual sizes not usually stocked by other stores. Moderate prices and frequent sales prevail.

Shopping

Barney's
7th Ave. and 17th St., NY 10011 ☎ 929-9000. Map 4Q3 💼 AE 🔲
Within the memory of most of its customers, Barney's was an out-of-the-way discount house that drew them to inconvenient Chelsea with promises of bargains. Those low-priced days are gone, but now men and women of every shape, height and girth come for the unrivaled range of garments in all sizes and fashions. They have installed a coffee shop in which to consider whether the Wall St., Rue de Rivoli or Via Condotti look is for you.

Brooks Brothers
346 Madison Ave. (44th St.), NY 10017 ☎ 682-8800. Map 5O4 AE
In an aberrant world, there is Brooks. Tradition cleaves to its stately spaces. This is the 170yr-old home of the natural-shoulder suit preferred by American business leaders and those who aspire to succeed them. Their conservative detailing has been altered somewhat in recent years, in deference to current taste and the fashion for physical fitness. But the trenchcoat purchased in 1970 is remarkably similar to the one bought yesterday.

Custom Shop
555 Lexington Ave. (50th St.), NY 10022 ☎ 759-7480. Map 5O4 AE 🔲 🔲 VISA
Men of proportions that don't quite fit off-the-shelf shirts — thick neck, short arms; thin neck, long arms — can stop here for made-to-measure cottons and cotton blends that cost not much more than average, depending on fabric and collar style. There is a minimum order of four, but first-time customers get a substantial discount. Custom suits are also available. There are several branches.

Dunhill Tailors
65 E 57th St. (near Park Ave.), NY 10022 ☎ 355-0050. Map 5N4 AE 🔲 VISA
They also sell ready-made suits, but their reputation is for custom tailoring in English cuts and fabrics. That Cary Grant was a steady client should be sufficient recommendation. Expect to pay handsomely for a suit that will last decades.

The Gap
145 E 42nd St. (near 3rd Ave.), NY 10017 ☎ 286-9490. Map 5O4 🔲 VISA *Open also Sun noon-6pm.*
This and seven other branches throughout Manhattan purvey jeans in every style, color and size — but from reputable manufacturers, not overpriced and shoddy, bootleg products. Also some tops and related sportswear.

Paul Stuart
Madison Ave. and 45th St., NY 10017 ☎ 682-0320. Map 5O4 AE 🔲 🔲 VISA
For the British-American or mid-Atlantic look, Paul Stuart has suits and sports jackets in a subdued palette of checks, herringbones, flannels and twills. The arm-holes are higher than those of the equally traditional **Brooks Brothers**, the shoulders are squared, the waists ever-so-slightly more suppressed. Most are of natural fibers, but there are some blends. Shirts come in an unusually broad range of sizes. There is a small women's department. The prices are middling-high.

A. Sulka
711 5th Ave. (55th St.), NY 10022 ☎ 980-5200. Map 5N4 AE 🔲 🔲 VISA
Made-to-measure silk shirts are the ultimate luxury in this exclusive store, but there are also suits, coats and accessories of comparably high standard. Monogrammed handkerchiefs make an affordable gift; custom cashmere bathrobes do not.

Sym's
45 Park Pl. (near Church St.), NY 10007 ☎ 791-1199. Map 2T4.
One of the more prominent discount men's stores by virtue of its insistent TV advertising, Sym's takes a center path in fashion and delivers good value. The labels are left in the garments so the customer can have an idea of their origins, and the original list price is followed on the tag with the Sym's price. Those willing to examine carefully three floors of racks and

counters can emerge with twice as much clothing as the same expenditure would obtain midtown, and that is the temptation.

Victory Shirt Company
345 Madison Ave. (near 45th St.), NY 10017 ☎ *687-6375. Map 5O4*
AE CB DC VISA

A boon to the odd-sized man or woman who doesn't care to pay for custom tailoring. Victory makes 100-percent cotton shirts of made-to-measure quality at ready-made prices. Some sweaters and ties are available, all in natural fibers. Monograms and alterations are available extras.

Clothing and shoes for women

Fiorucci
125 E 59th St. (near Park Ave.), NY 10022 ☎ *751-5638. Map 5N4* AE
CB DC VISA

Have an espresso while contemplating startling, imaginative and often popularly priced clothes that bear no allegiance to any fashion schools. Everyone calls it "fun"; and certainly no one who walks out in one of these zingy tops or slacks will lack attention.

Gucci
685 5th Ave. (54th St.), NY 10022 ☎ *826-2600. Map 5N4* AE CB DC VISA

Despite the not-unwarranted reputation of the sales staff for sullenness, flocks of moneyed patrons storm these four floors daily (*not Sun*). They are men and women who admire fine Italian craftsmanship in leather goods — shoes, belts, handbags and luggage — and don't mind wearing someone else's initials: the famed double G.

Charles Jourdan
725 5th Ave. (56th St.), NY 10022 ☎ *644-3830. Map 5N4* AE CB DC VISA

Imported French shoes of frolicsome panache — wispy sandals, and shoes in frothy hues, lighter than air but remarkably long-lived. There are men's shoes, too, but they are much more traditional. All are expensive, of course.

OMO Kamali
11 W 56th St. (5th Ave.), NY 10022 ☎ *957-9797. Map 5N4* AE CB DC VISA

One of the country's hottest designers has herself a 6-story showcase in a grandly refurbished old building just off 5th Ave. She covers the female form from beach to disco, office to dinner party, and throws in equally inventive clothing for children.

Polo/Ralph Lauren
867 Madison Ave. (72nd St.), NY 10021 ☎ *606-2100. Map 7M4* AE

Make an excuse to visit this stunning four-floor specialty shop even if the price tags make most shoppers blanch. America's most admired designer of the loose, classic look has outfitted the 1895 mansion to reflect every element of his wide-ranging interests. Antique furnishings and accessories are arranged in rooms authentic to the last detail, settings for the maestro's clothing for men and women. But be wary, for even the least expensive items cost hundreds of dollars.

Yves St-Laurent Rive Gauche
855 Madison Ave. (near 70th St.), NY 10021 ☎ *988-3821. Map 7M4*
AE CB DC VISA

From the striking front to the metal-and-leather interior, this boutique sizzles with the products of the restless mind of the celebrated French designer. Shirts, pants, shoes, dresses, suits, belts are at the leading edge of fashion. One pays dearly to participate.

Unique Clothing Warehouse
718 Broadway (Washington Pl.), NY 10003 ☎ *674-1767. Map 2R4* AE
DC VISA *Open also Sun noon-5.45pm.*

As an antidote to the jasmine-and-musk air of the 5th Ave. boutiques, or simply because it's Sunday, drop down to Greenwich Village. This repository of rugged working-man's apparel and military uniforms was the first, it is said, to recognize the inherent chic of such things. A few years later, the Parisian and Milanese couturiers were turning out their own versions for the Côte d'Azur. The prices are good, but the quality is variable, so choose very carefully.

Valentino

823 Madison Ave.(69th St.), NY 10022 ☎ 744-0200. Map 7N4 AE CD VISA

The legendary Valentino permits us to gaze on his trend-anticipating lines of dresses, sweaters and separates, and to marvel at fabrics and sartorial details that can be had only at very high prices.

Department stores

Abraham & Strauss

420 Fulton St. (Hoyt St.), Brooklyn 10001 ☎ 718-875-7200. Map 3V7.
Familiarly known as "A&S," this is Brooklyn's largest and best-stocked department store. Although somewhat low profile outside its home borough, it is comparable to **Macy's** in the breadth and price range of its offerings. That competition has grown sharper with the new branch near Herald Sq., on the site of the departed Gimbel's.

Henri Bendel

10 W 57th St. (near 5th Ave.), NY 10019 ☎ 247-1100. Map 5N4 AE CD VISA

While it avoids the flashy, Bendel's is at the forefront of fashion trends, at least among department stores. A step inside the door and a peek at size labels reveals that the cautious and/or amply proportioned shopper would best spend time elsewhere. Clothes boutiques take up the first floor, but there are five more floors above in which to consider stationery, table linens, shoes, cosmetics, household ware.

Bergdorf Goodman

754 5th Ave. (57th St.), NY 10022 ☎ 752-3000. Map 5N4 AE
On what is perhaps the most glamorous corner in New York, Bergdorf's follows through with unrivaled service and products. Furs, lingerie, fragrances, linens are of the highest order. To a degree, the store is shelter to the glossy boutiques of Givenchy, Halston, St-Laurent and their like. Men who can afford the tariffs are drawn to the new annex recently opened just for them across the street.

Bloomingdale's

1000 3rd Ave. (59th St.), NY 10022 ☎ 355-5900. Map 5N5 AE
Multitudes of New Yorkers and suburbanites slavishly follow the dictates of the great guru Bloomingdale, denying all the while that their living rooms are replicas of those in the store, that they dress like the models in the Sat newspaper ads, that the food they eat imitates the delights of the gourmet stores on the first floor. They need not be defensive, for they could hardly find a better model to follow. In the evening and on Sat they are as likely to drop in just to meet people similarly afflicted as to buy anything.

Lord & Taylor

424 5th Ave. (39th St.), NY 10016 ☎ 391-3344. Map 5O4 AE
Whether you want a cashmere sweater or a chair, curtain fabric or a crystal bowl, buy it here and it will remain a classic until its natural demise. That might be later than your own, for Lord & Taylor has been around well over a century, and it has no intention of alienating coming generations. Known mainly for sportswear, it also employs interior decorators to advise on renovations both modest and ambitious. Decisions can be made in comfort over soup and salad in one of the store's three cafés.

Macy's

Broadway and 34th St., NY 10001 ☎ 971-6000. Map 5P4 AE *Open also Sun.*
In recent years, Macy's has moved to occupy the area between the bland middle ground and the snappy upper-middle ground represented by **Bloomingdale's**. Most welcome innovations are the repository of kitchenware and gourmet foods called **The Cellar**, and an uncanny

reproduction of the trendy Irish saloon, **P.J. Clarke's**. The largest store in
the world (so they claim) has something for everyone, from antiques to
puppet shows.

Saks Fifth Avenue
611 5th Ave. (50th St.), NY 10022 ☎ *753-4000. Map 5O4* AE O
Scrupulously choreographed and relentlessly edited, Saks contrives to
retain its conservative image without descending into dowdiness. Clothes
are its strength, from sports to formal wear, as delineated by Bill Blass,
Oscar de la Renta and their colleagues.

Food and kitchenware
New Yorkers have always been interested in food and cooking, if
only to reproduce the cuisines of their homelands. The recent
enthusiasm for gourmet cookery has intensified that concern,
and these stores are booming. Try to avoid Sat.

Balducci's
422 6th Ave. (9th St.), NY 10011 ☎ *673-2600. Map 2R4* AE *Open
daily until 8.30pm.*
Enter Balducci's immediately after a large meal, or your eyes will grow
round as billiard balls and you will be seized with a compulsion to sweep
up heaps of everything in sight. You will be in competition with milling
throngs anxious to get their hands on the very same cheeses, pastries,
choice vegetables, thick slabs of prime meats, ringlets of homemade
sausages, smoked fishes, or lobsters. Absolute freshness of produce and
ingredients in cooked or baked products is the norm. It is always busy.

Bridge Kitchenware
214 E 52nd St. (near 2nd Ave.), NY 10022 ☎ *688-4220. Map 5N5* O
VISA *Closed Sun.*
The shelves are packed with quality utensils for the serious cook. Pick
through stainless carbon knives by several manufacturers, food processors,
graters, coffee grinders, bowls of steel and ceramic, copper molds, crystal.
The prices are neither exorbitant nor low: they are simply fair.

Caviarteria
29 E 60th St. (near Madison Ave.), NY 10022 ☎ *759-7410. Map 5N4*
AE O VISA
Unprepossessing inside and out, this small store is easy to dismiss. But the
distractedly helpful proprietor deals in the essentials of a calculated
seduction or a dinner designed to impress. His caviar is Iranian, Russian and
American. The last is a Californian experiment that appears to be
succeeding, and at half the price of the imports. He also stocks smoked
salmon, cheeses and related delicacies, and enjoys a substantial mail order
trade.

Dean & DeLuca
560 Broadway (Prince St.), NY 10012 ☎ *431-1691. Map 2S4. Open
also Sun 10am-6pm.*
Expensive, yes, but not unconscionably so, and the mark-up is justified
merely by the aroma encountered at the front door: coffee, freshly baked
bread, cheeses, fresh produce all contribute. This is a new location for the
popular SoHo food and houseware store. (The former address at 121 Prince
St. is to become an outlet for professional kitchenware.) White walls and
marble floors are the minimalist setting for 10,000 sq.ft. of exotic
mushrooms, pâtés, terrines, produce, cheeses, smoked fish, pastas, an
extraordinary selection of herbs, honeys and jams, and racks of kitchen
utensils, including whisks, cast-iron pans and oven-usable stoneware. Drink
it all in with a cappuccino at the handsome coffee bar near the front door,
perhaps with a fresh muffin or pastry. It's an obligatory stop for the city's
legion of foodies.

E.A.T.
1064 Madison Ave. (81st St.), NY 10028 ☎ *772-1586. Map 7M4* AE
Open also Sun 9am-5pm.
Prepared dishes and baked goods are made on the premises, from

sourdough and raisin bread to pâtés to complete meals. Teas, jams, salmon and cheeses are imported. Prices are as eye-popping as the food.

Zabar's

2245 Broadway (near 80th St.), NY 10024 ☎ 787-2000. Map **6L2** ⒜Ⓔ
⒞ ⒸⒹ ⒱⒤ⓈⒶ Open daily, Sat until midnight.

Balducci's and **Zabar's** are perennial contenders for the throne of gourmet stores, but Zabar's may have pulled ahead by virtue of its recent second-floor expansion for kitchenware. Absolute kitchen essentials — fish poachers and duck presses —take their place among food mills and copper pots. On the first floor, cheese, coffee, caviar, smoked fish, prepared terrines and entrees, pumpernickel bread, ice cream, coffee cake, chopped liver, herring, and other intoxicating sights and aromas battle for attention.

Jewelry

From the waiting limousines to the understated window displays and the hushed, almost ecclesiastical interiors, **Cartier**, **Harry Winston**, **Tiffany & Co.** and **Van Cleef & Arpels**, the Titans of the retail trade in gold, gems, silver and watches, breathe an ever-tasteful opulence. Dress for the occasion. All of them have a well-crafted trinket or two at modest cost for recipients back home who are impressed by the name on the gift box.

Department store marketing techniques are used by **Fortunoff**, and its stock is supplemented with fine jewelry and watches, antique silver and flatware. There are four floors, and prices are reasonable, as these things go.

While all these stores are within a few steps of each other, true comparison shopping is best undertaken along 47th St., between 5th Ave. and 6th Ave. Every imaginable sort of jewelry is on hand in shoulder-to-shoulder (and floor-upon-floor) stores that sell nothing else. Start at the **International Jewelers Exchange**, with its dealers installed in 84 cubicles, then work w along 47th St., crossing to the opposite side and returning e. Prices are often negotiable, so it's best to delay purchase until several trays of the desired object have been examined.

Cartier 5th Ave. and 52nd St. ☎753-0111
Fortunoff 681 5th Ave. (near 54th St.) ☎758-6660
International Jewelers Exchange 5th Ave. and 47th St.
☎869-8600
Tiffany & Co. 5th Ave. and 57th St. ☎755-8000
Van Cleef & Arpels 5th Ave. and 57th St. ☎644-9500
Harry Winston 718 5th Ave. (near 56th St.) ☎245-2000

Museum shops

Cultural curiosity and the acquisitive impulse are handily combined in the gift and bookstores of all the major museums and most of the smaller ones. While selections naturally reflect the concerns of the museums in which they are located — seafaring motifs at the *South Street Seaport*, folk art at the *Brooklyn Museum* — they interpret their missions with broad strokes. Given their auspices, trashy merchandise rarely slips onto the shelves. For the same reason, expect fair prices but no bargains. See individual entries in *Sights and places of interest* for addresses and telephone numbers.

Predictably, the store of the *Metropolitan Museum of Art* is largest, with excellent reproductions of many items in the collections, as well as art books and illustrated catalogs. The *Museum of the American Indian* has handcrafted "squash-blossom" necklaces, silver belt buckles, "concha" belts, and Navajo rugs. Reproductions of Egyptian jewelry and authentic Latin American ceramics and dolls are the specialty of the

Brooklyn Museum. Books and posters once dominated at the *Museum of Modern Art*, but its new design shop, on the opposite side of the street from the museum, has a greatly expanded inventory of exquisite glassware, pottery, flatware, cigarette lighters, garden shears and clocks. At the *Jewish Museum*, even Gentiles are drawn to the brass candlesticks and *menorahs*, *mezuzah* boxes, and the jewelry. Finally, there are quilts and crafts, antique and contemporary, at the *Museum of American Folk Art*.

Pharmacies
Despite their fanciful European imitations, not all American drugstores resemble supermarkets. Most concentrate on the sale of cosmetics, perfumes, toiletries, assorted sickroom and surgical devices and, of course, prescription and nonprescription medicines. Be sure to bring along your doctor's prescription. Foreign visitors should also bear in mind that certain drugs that can be bought without prescription at home require one here. Two of the oldest pharmacies in New York are **Caswell-Massey** (established 1752) and **Bigelow Pharmacy** (established 1838). The **Duane Reade** chain, with locations all over town, is noted for its discounts.

Bigelow Pharmacy   414 6th Ave. (near 8th St.), NY 10011 ☎533-2700. Map **2**R4. Still in its original quarters, and open every day.
Caswell-Massey   518 Lexington Ave. (near 48th St.), NY 10017 ☎755-2254. Map **5**O4. Closed Sun. Caswell-Massey blended soaps and colognes for George Washington and Sarah Bernhardt, and its products make good souvenirs.
Kaufman Pharmacy   Lexington Ave. and 50th St., NY 10022 ☎755-2266. Map **5**O4. Open 24hrs a day, 7 days a week.

Sports and camping equipment
Athlete's Foot   16 W 57th St. (near 5th Ave.), NY 10022 ☎586-1936. Map **5**N4. Runners stop here, or at one of its six branches, for its full line of footwear and warm-up suits.
Herman's   Midtown branches at 135 W 42nd St. (near Times Sq.), NY 10036 ☎730-7400. Map **4**O3. Also 845 3rd Ave. (near E 51st St.), NY 10022 ☎688-4603. Map **5**N5. One of the largest general sporting goods stores.
Hudson's   3rd Ave. and 13th St., NY 10003 ☎473-7321. Map **2**R4. Open also Sun. For camping and outdoor equipment.
Paragon   867 Broadway (near E 18th St.), NY 10003 ☎255-8036. Map **5**Q4. Open also Sun. Huge stock of general sporting goods.
Spiegels   Nassau St. and Ann St., NY 10005 ☎227-8400. Map **2**U4. Closed Sat in summer. For all sports goods in lower Manhattan, at discounted prices.

Toys
It is tempting to begin and end with **F.A.O. Schwarz**, but there are other stores too. All of them will wrap and ship.
F.A.O. Schwarz   767 5th Ave. (58th St.), NY 10022 ☎644-9400. Map **5**N4. Open also Sun. A wonderland of fantasies even for the most cynical adult, it qualifies as a not-to-be-missed sight. Imagine 10ft-high stuffed giraffes, storybook villages complete with dogs and street lamps, child-sized cars that really work, marionettes, electric trains and, of course, a vast selection of dolls, books and games... three floors of them.
Childcraft Center   150 E 58th St. (Lexington Ave.), NY 10022

☎753-3196. Map **5**N4. Focuses on sturdy educational toys.
Penny Whistle   1281 Madison Ave. (near 91st St.), NY 10028
☎369-3868. Map **7**K4. Young patrons are actually encouraged to
play with the dolls and games. Other branches in SoHo (*132
Spring St.*) and on the West Side (*448 Columbus Ave.*).
Toy Park   112 E 86th St. (near Amsterdam Ave.), NY 10024
☎427-6611. Map **6**L3 and 626 Columbus Ave. (near 90th St.), NY
10024 ☎769-3880. Map **6**K3. Extra-large toy emporiums, with a
play area for children so grownups can shop.

Wines and liquor

Equidistant from the vineyards of France and California, New
York samples the vintages of Old World and New. Special sales
are frequent, sometimes of wine from unexpected countries —
Lebanon, Chile, Yugoslavia. Their advantage is price, of course.
Choices can be bewildering, but the sales people at the following
stores are helpful, and their wares are exemplary for price and/or
variety.

   All are closed Sun; most accept credit cards and make deliveries.
Astor Wines & Spirits   12 Astor Pl. (near Lafayette St.)
☎674-7500. Map **2**T4.
Embassy Liquors   796 Lexington Ave. (near 61st St.)
☎838-6551. Map **5**N4.
Morrell & Co.   307 E 3rd St. (near 2nd Ave.) ☎688-9370. Map
3R5.
Sherry-Lehmann   679 Madison Ave. (E 61st St.) ☎838-7500.
Map **5**N4.
67 Wines & Spirits   179 Columbus Ave. (W 68th St.)
☎724-6767. Map **6**M3.
SoHo Wines & Spirits   461 West Broadway (Prince St.)
☎777-4332. Map **2**S4.

Sports and activities

The following guide to sports and leisure in and around New
York offers ideas for spectators and participants.

Spectator sports
Arenas and stadiums
Baker Field (*W 218th St. and Broadway* ☎ *567-7423*).
American football as played (usually poorly) by Columbia
University, one of the members of the "Ivy League" of prestigious
colleges; Sept-Nov.
Byrne Arena (*Meadowlands Sports Complex, E Rutherford, NJ*).
Opened in 1981; the venue for the professional basketball **Nets**
(☎ *201-935-3900*) and the **Devils** hockey squad (☎ *201-935-
6050*), as well as rock concerts, circuses, college basketball, and
other events. Get there by bus from the Port Authority Bus
Terminal on 8th Ave.
Giants Stadium (*Meadowlands Sports Complex, E Rutherford,
NJ*) Crowds fill the superb arena on Sun afternoons from late
Aug-early Dec to watch professional football with the **Jets**
(☎ *212-421-6600*) and the **Giants** (☎ *201-935-8222*); tickets
for regular-season games are nearly impossible to obtain.
Repeated experiments with professional soccer have failed, but
the 1994 World Cup competition in the US should renew interest,
and some of those games surely will be played in this stadium.

Madison Square Garden (*8th Ave. and 33rd St.* ☎ *563-8300*). Among its many guises, it is the home of **New York Rangers** ice hockey (*Oct-Apr*), **Knicks** basketball (*Oct-Apr*), and college basketball (*Nov-Apr*). Also boxing and wrestling matches and such special events as the circus, the Ice Capades, dog and horse shows, and rock concerts.

Nassau Coliseum (*Uniondale, Long Island* ☎ *516-794-4100*). Special musical and entertainment events are presented, as are the ice hockey games of the often successful **Islanders**.

National Tennis Center (*Flushing Meadows-Corona Park, Queens* ☎ *718-271-5100*) is the site of the annual US Open Championships (*early Sept*).

Shea Stadium (*126th St. and Roosevelt Ave., Queens*). The professional baseball **Mets** (☎ *718-507-8499*) play here (*Apr-Sept*).

Yankee Stadium (*River Ave. and W 161st St., The Bronx* ☎ *718-293-6000*). Home base (*Apr-Sept*) of the **Yankees**, who are frequent champions and one of the oldest teams in professional baseball.

Racetracks

Aqueduct (*108th St. and Rockaway Blvd., Queens* ☎ *718-641-4700*). The "Big A" features thoroughbred flat racing (*Jan-May and Oct-Dec; for routes and fares* ☎ *718-330-1234*). It can be reached by subway.

Belmont Park (*Belmont, Long Island* ☎ *718-641-4700*). Thoroughbred racing (*May-July, Sept-Oct*). The Long Island Railroad, departing from Penn Station, has special trains and fare-admission packages (☎ *739-4200 for information*).

Meadowlands (*Meadowlands Sports Complex, E Rutherford, NJ* ☎ *201-935-8500*). Most of the grandstands are enclosed at this new track, permitting comfortable viewing of thoroughbreds (*Sept-Dec*) and of trotters (*Jan-Aug*). Evening races can be watched from the **Pegasus** dining-room.

Roosevelt Raceway (*Westbury, Long Island* ☎ *516-222-2000*). Evening trotters go through their paces (*Jan-Mar, June-Aug, Oct-Dec*). Package fares on the Long Island Railroad from Penn Station include bus transfers and track admission.

Yonkers Raceway (*Yonkers, NY* ☎ *914-968-4200*). Easily accessible off the Gov. Thomas E. Dewey Thruway, N of The Bronx. The track is devoted to trotting races (*Mar-Apr, June-July, Sept-Oct and Dec*). Special buses leave from Port Authority Bus Terminal on 8th Ave.

Participant sports
Baseball
The national game can be played on fields all over New York. "Pick-up" teams come together for a few innings whenever a sufficient number of enthusiasts gather. Contact the **Heckscher Ballfields** (*Central Park, E of Central Park W at about 64th St.* ☎ *408-0213*).

Basketball
There are courts within a few blocks of nearly every address in Manhattan. These are usually occupied by local youngsters, or aging executives who take the game very seriously (☎ *360-8111 for the closest court*). Branches of the **YMCA** have gymnasiums (*215 W 23rd St.* ☎ *741-9220; 224 E 47th St.* ☎ *755-2410; and 5 W 63rd St.* ☎ *787-4400*), but there is a stiff fee for one-time use by nonmembers. Visitors who can present a membership card from a hometown "Y" can usually gain entrance for a limited number of times.

Sports and activities

Bicycling
Shops in most neighborhoods rent bicycles by the hour, day, or week — consult the Yellow Pages under *Bicycles*. City streets can be intimidating, so consider *Central Park*, as some of its roads are closed to cars midday and eves during the week and throughout the weekends. The **Loeb Boathouse in Central Park** (☎ *861-4137*) has bicycles for rent.

Boating and sailing
Rowboats are available at the **Loeb Boathouse in Central Park** (☎ *517-2233*). Rentals by the hour to anyone over 16. Children may go, if accompanied by an adult.

Sailing instruction is offered by the **New York Sailing School** (*City Island, The Bronx* ☎ *864-4472*).

Bowling
All the boroughs have bowling emporia, but the only one still in business in Manhattan is the 44-lane **Bowlmor** (*110 University Place* ☎ *255-8188*) in Greenwich Village. It's open until at least 1am every night.

Cricket
Immigrants from the British West Indies keep the imperial heritage alive, on pitches in **Flushing Meadows-Corona Park** in Queens (☎ *718-520-5900*), and in **Van Cortlandt Park** (*W 250th St. and Broadway* ☎ *430-1825*).

Diving
Instruction in SCUBA is given by the **Aqua-Lung School of New York** (*1089 2nd Ave.* ☎ *582-2800*), **Atlantis II** (*498 6th Ave.* ☎ *924-7556*), and **Scuba Plus** (*201 E 34th St.* ☎ *689-0035*), all in Manhattan. They also arrange diving trips for qualified divers. There are a number of intriguing wrecks in offshore waters.

Fishing
Anglers over 16 must obtain a license to use the freshwater lakes and rivers of New York City and State. These are readily available for a small fee at many sporting goods stores. Anyone can fish in salt water without a permit. Lakes within **Central Park, Prospect Park** (*Brooklyn*), and **Van Cortlandt Park** (*The Bronx*) contain such gullible species as catfish, bluegills and carp. Charters and party boats (each passenger pays a fare) are available at **City Island** (*The Bronx*) and **Sheepshead Bay** (*Brooklyn*).

Golf
There are no golf courses in Manhattan, although there are 13 in outlying boroughs. (*For information: The Bronx* ☎ *822- 4711; Brooklyn* ☎ *718-965-6511; Queens* ☎ *718-520-5311; Staten Island* ☎ *718-422-7640.*) Expect to wait for a tee-off.

Handball
New York City has more than 2,000 handball courts (☎ *397-3100 for the location of the nearest city-owned court in Manhattan*).

Horseback riding
Instruction and rent-by-the-hour are available at: **Claremont Riding Academy** (*175 W 89th St.* ☎ *724-5100*), classes for children, too; **Clove Lake Stables** (*1025 Clove Rd. Staten Island* ☎ *718-448-1414*); **Van Cortlandt Park Stables** (*Broadway and W 254th St., The Bronx* ☎ *549-6200*).

The trails for the **Claremont** wind through Central Park, and it has an indoor ring as well.

Ice-skating
The rink at the base of the **GE Building** in the Rockefeller Center has a constant crowd of spectators and so is used primarily by skilled and/or exhibition skaters. Central Park has two outdoor

rinks: **Lasker** (*near 110th St.*) and **Wollman** (*near the Zoo*). All are open Nov-Apr. The **Sky Rink** (*450 W 33rd St.* ☎ 695-6555) is large, indoors and on the 16th floor. Open all year, it has disco skating on Fri and Sat nights.

Skating is also permitted on natural lakes and ponds when there is safe ice cover, but it is wise to stick to the artificial rinks.

Racquetball and squash

So popular it threatens to eclipse tennis, racquetball is normally available only at membership clubs. Hotels often have arrangements with nearby clubs; check with the concierge. A few clubs are open to the public on a courts-available basis. Daily rates aren't *too* steep.

Among these are: **Grand Central Racquetball Club** (*25 Vanderbilt Ave.* ☎ 883-0994); **Manhattan Plaza Racquet Club** (*45 W 45th St.* ☎ 594-0554); **Manhattan Squash & Racquetball Club** (*41 W 42nd St.* ☎ 869-8969); **Park Avenue Squash & Racquet Club** (*3 Park Ave.* ☎ 686-1085); **Park Place Squash Club** (*25 Park Place* ☎ 964-2677). All are usually open 7 days a week, 7am-midnight. They sell or rent equipment, and credit cards are accepted. Reserve well ahead.

Hotels that have courts include the **Parker Meridien** and the **Vista International**.

Running

New York runners are a hardy breed, seen on every street, at all hours, in any weather. A morning jog or a serious 10-mile effort can follow any route, but certain areas and pathways are favored because of their even road surfaces, lack of vehicles and crowds, and relative freedom from air pollution.

Central Park has 30-plus miles of roads, providing substantial variety in distances and difficulty. Suggested routes:

• The fenced reservoir slightly N of the mid-point of the park has two cinder tracks. Enter the park at **Engineer's Gate**, at 5th Ave. and E 90th St. The inner track is 1.57 miles long.
• Slightly S of the reservoir is **The Great Lawn Oval**, with a measured circumference of half a mile and markers at 200m (220yd) intervals.
• A 6-mile loop follows the main drive around the perimeter of the park. Cut E or W for runs of 1, 2 or 4 miles. Enter at **Engineer's Gate**, or at W 66th St. beyond the Tavern On The Green restaurant, or just beyond the Zoo.

Less crowded parks are **Fort Tryon**, **Prospect** (*Brooklyn*), **Riverside**, and **Van Cortlandt** (*The Bronx*). The *New York Botanical Garden* (*also in The Bronx*) is ideal for runners, and is a worthy destination by itself.

For river vistas, try **Riverside Park** (*between 72nd and 96th Sts.*) and the promenades along the East River, with easy access S from **Carl Schurz Park**.

Road races of varying lengths are held every month in the city. For dates, times and registration details, contact the **New York Road Runners Club** (*9 E 89th St.* ☎ 860-4455). There are indoor tracks at: **McBurney YMCA** (*215 W 23rd St.* ☎ 741-9224); **92nd St. YMHA** (*1395 Lexington Ave.* ☎ 427-6000); **West Side YMCA** (*5 W 63rd St.* ☎ 787-4400).

Skiing

Cross-country skiing, with rolling terrain and gentle slopes, is available in **Prospect Park** (*Brooklyn* ☎ 965-6511) and at **Van Cortlandt Park** (*The Bronx* ☎ 543-4595). Equipment rental, instruction, tours to upstate and New England ski centers: all from **Scandinavian Ski Shop** (*40 W 57th St.* ☎ 757-8524) and **Sportiva Sporthaus** (*145 E 47th St.* ☎ 421-7466).

Swimming

Municipally-owned pools in the five boroughs are open from late May-early Sept. They tend to be shabby, crowded, and sometimes rowdy. Visitors are likely to prefer the pools at the following hotels, some of which are open to outsiders as well as guests: **Best Western Skyline** (indoor), **Halloran House**, **Harley**, **Holiday Inn Crowne Plaza** (indoor), **Parker Meridien**, **Sheraton City Squire** (indoor), **United Nations Plaza** (indoor), and **Vista International** (see *Hotels*).

Jones Beach State Park (*on the s side of Long Island*) has the finest public beach and related facilities in the region, and is less than an hour by car (*via Southern State Parkway, exiting s on Wantagh State Parkway*) or special bus from the Port Authority Bus Terminal. Municipal beaches are nearly always crowded, and the color of the water is often suspect, even when certified safe for swimming, but most are within reach by public transportation. *Coney Island* beach (*S Brooklyn*) is best known, but **Rockaway Beach**, to the E, is three times as long, with a tenth of the humanity. **Orchard Beach** (*near City Island in The Bronx*), and **Great Kills Park** (*Staten Island*) are also popular.

Tennis

Commercial tennis clubs usually have equipment shops, lounges, instructors, and lockers available. Many also offer saunas, air conditioning, swimming pools, weekend brunches and evening parties. There are indoor courts at: **Crosstown Tennis** (*14 W 31st St.* ☎ 947-5780); **Columbus Racquet Club** (*795 Columbus Ave.* ☎ 663-6900); **HRC Tennis** (*East River piers at end of Wall St.* ☎ 422-9300); **Manhattan Plaza Racquet Club** (*450 W 43rd St.* ☎ 594-0554); **Sutton East Tennis Club** (*488 E 60th St.* ☎ 751-3452); **Tower Tennis Courts** (*1725 York Ave.* ☎ 860-2464); **Turtle Bay Tennis & Swim Club** (*1 United Nations Plaza* ☎ 355-3400); **USTA National Tennis Center** (*Flushing, Queens* ☎ 718-271-5100); **Village Courts** (*110 University Place* ☎ 989-2300).

These are normally open 7 days a week from 7am-midnight; always call ahead to reserve a court and, if alone, to arrange a game. All boroughs have municipal courts, with more than 100 in Manhattan alone, but permits are required, and red tape slows the process. Fanatics should note the **Stadium Tennis Center** (*11 E 162nd St. in The Bronx* ☎ 293-2386, open Oct-May 24hrs a day*).

New York for children

From boat trips to children's zoos, New York is a city packed with interest for children. The following are some of the most enticing and popular possibilities.

Boat trips

Circle Line (*Pier 83, W 43rd St.* ☎ 563-3200). 3-hour trips around Manhattan Island may be a trifle long for the very young, but there are few dull moments for everyone else. Cruises depart at least 10 times daily (*Apr-Nov from 9.45am-5.30pm*), weather and demand permitting. Half-price for under 12s.

Ellis Island Ferry (*Battery Park, Lower Manhattan* ☎ 269-5755). Ferries cross to the famous old immigrant processing center (*daily May-Nov at 9.30am, 11.45am, 2pm and 4.15pm*). The fare includes a 1hr guided tour of the poignant national monument.

Staten Island Ferry (*Battery Park, Lower Manhattan*
☎ *248-8097*). The double-decker ferry leaves Whitehall St. pier
every 20-30mins. It passes the Statue of Liberty and provides
unparalleled views of bridges, harbor traffic and an imposing
skyline. Note that the terminals and ferries are shelter for often
substantial numbers of homeless people, a perhaps unsettling,
but rarely threatening circumstance.
Statue of Liberty Ferry (*Battery Park, Lower Manhattan*
☎ *269-5755*). Spectacular views from the crown of the famous
lady, and the ride from the city are included in the fare.
Sometimes, though, there's a long wait.

Children's theater

Courtyard Playhouse (*39 Grove St., near 7th Ave. S* ☎ *765-
9540, usually 2 performances daily on Sat and Sun*). Excellent
fare offered by the **Little People's Theater Company**.
Admission is inexpensive; reservations are essential. **First All
Children's Theater** (*37 W 65th St., near Central Park W* ☎ *873-
6400*). Musical productions with casts of children usually
Oct-May on Sat and Sun only; more frequent performances
during school vacations. **Hartly House Theater** (*413 W 46th St.,
near 9th Ave.* ☎ *666-1716*). The **On Stage** company mounts
several plays a year, including such classics as *Charlotte's Web*.
Ordinarily, there are two shows Sat, one Sun. Moderately
expensive admission; reservations necessary. **Jan Hus
Playhouse** (*351 E 74th St., near 2nd Ave.* ☎ *772-9180*). Plays
and musicals are presented on an irregular schedule, sometimes
two in an afternoon. Inexpensive. **Mostly Magic** (*55 Carmine St.
at Bleecker St.* ☎ *924-1472*) Magicians leaven their illusions with
laughs and puns, often assisted by recruits from the audience.
Best for under 10s. Shows are Sat afternoons; reserve. **New
Media Repertory Company** (*512 E 80th St, near 1st Ave.*
☎ *734-5195*). Unpredictable entertainments performed by child
actors on Sat during the school year. Aimed at 3-7s; inexpensive.
Open Eye: New Stagings for Youth (*270 W 89th St at West
End Ave.* ☎ *769-4143*). Excellent stagings of original and classic
productions, usually with music and dancing and aimed at
various age groups. Ignore the rather stuffy name. Prices are low
to moderate; reserve ahead. **Promenade Theater** (*2162
Broadway at 76th St.* ☎ *240-8202 or 677-5959*). The
Theaterworks/USA troupe puts on plays and musicals based on
the lives of historical and mythical figures, as well as grander
themes, all short enough to fit a child's attention span. Afternoon
shows Sept-June on Sat and Sun. **13th Street Repertory
Company** (*50 W 13th St., near 5th Ave.* ☎ *675-6677*). New
plays with music, based upon children's stories. Usually, two
shows Sat and Sun, all year. Inexpensive, but reservations are
essential.

Christmas decorations

The luxury shops and large department stores are ablaze with
holiday lights and window-dressing from late Nov-late Dec, and
midtown 5th Ave. is a glorious spectacle. The centerpiece is the
70ft tree with myriad winking lights looming above the skating
rink at the foot of the *GE Building*; the **Channel Gardens** that
lead into *Rockefeller Center* from 5th Ave. are transformed;
store windows and interior displays of invariable delight are
those of **Lord & Taylor** (*38th St.*), **Saks Fifth Avenue** (*50th St.*),
and **F.A.O. Schwarz** (*58th St.*).
 Elsewhere in Manhattan, a Christmas tree is framed within

Washington Arch in **Greenwich Village**, wreaths encircle the
necks of the lions outside the **42nd St. Library**, an elaborate
tableau of castles and elves fills the lobby of the *Museum of the
City of New York*, and a tree in the Medieval Hall of the
Metropolitan Museum of Art emphasizes the spiritual origins
of the holiday, supplemented by a panorama of 200 18thC figures
gathered about the birthplace of the Christ child. Down at **South
St. Seaport**, carolers arrange themselves into a living Christmas
tree while they sing.

Comedy and revue

Several nightclubs have afternoon or early evening sessions, in
some cases specifically for children. But inevitably clubs change
policy and others close, so always telephone for schedules and
prices. Remember that profanity is not uncommon in many comic
acts not directed at youngsters, and children under 16 usually
must be accompanied by parents.

The **Comic Strip** (*1568 2nd Ave., near 81st St.* ☎ *861-9386,
Sat 5pm, Sun 5.30pm*) has spotlighted professional stage
youngsters appearing in current TV and stage shows. **Caroline's**
(*Pier 17 in South St. Seaport* ☎ *233-4900*) has its comedy and
music club just for kids aged 7-13, complete with hot dogs and
soft drinks; not expensive. Periodic early shows have been
presented by **Chicago City Limits** (*351 E 74th St.* ☎ *772-8707*),
where no alcohol is served; by **Improvisation** (*358 W 44th St.,
near 9th Ave.* ☎ *765-8268*), one of the oldest comedy clubs in
town; and by **Stand-up New York** (*236 W 78th St.* ☎ *595-
0850*). Sat at 1pm is the time for children's cabaret at **Steve
McGraw's** (*158 W 72nd St.* ☎ *595-7400*). A similar event,
performed by children, is held each Sat noon at **The Duplex** (*61
Christopher St.* ☎ *255-5438*).

Concerts for young people

The **American Symphony Orchestra** and the **New York
Philharmonic** give irregularly scheduled concerts of classical
music directed at ages 6-16. Most are performed in the fall and
winter at **Carnegie Hall** (☎ *247-7459*) or **Avery Fisher Hall**
(☎ *874-2424*). Check newspapers for full details.

Events and entertainments

Big Apple Circus: New York's very own one-ring circus in a
tent, modeled after the intimate European troupes that have no
other equivalent in the US. Clowns cavort, aerialists execute the
fabled triple somersault, elephants dance, and jugglers and
acrobats twirl and tumble. Prices are low at this not-for-profit
enterprise; operation is most likely in summer and the Christmas
season. A frequent site is Damrosch Park in the *Lincoln Center*,
but it moves through all the boroughs.
Citicorp Center (*Lexington Ave. and 53rd St.* ☎ *559-4259*): the
atrium has free entertainment most days, but Sat afternoon is for
children, with music, magic, jugglers and puppets.
July 4th (Independence Day) festivities: an awesome
fireworks display is put on by Macy's Department Store, set off
over the East River. Among the better vantages are the **South St.
Seaport** and the **Brooklyn Heights Promenade**. Be there by
9pm. The **"Old New York"** celebrations take place at *Battery
Park* in lower Manhattan, with street performers and suitable
ceremonies from noon-dusk.
Storytelling in Central Park: at the **Hans Christian
Andersen Memorial** (*near 5th Ave. and 72nd St.*), stories are

read (*May-Sept, Sat at 11am*) to children, some of whom sit in the bronze lap of the master.

Hotels

Various discounts and incentives help keep costs within reason when children are in tow. Some hotels permit children under 12 (or 14, or even 17) to stay with their parents for free. Most will bring in an extra bed or cot at a small additional charge, making a substantial saving over the cost of separate rooms.

Alternatively, a suite sleeping 3-4 is often cheaper than two rooms. Reception desks or concierges normally have available lists of **baby-sitters**.

Swimming pools are an important feature for children, and the following Manhattan hotels and motels have them: **Best Western Skyline** (indoor), **Halloran House**, **Harley**, **Holiday Inn Crowne Plaza**, **Parker Meridien**, **Ramada Inn-Midtown**, **Sheraton City Squire** (indoor), **United Nations Plaza** (indoor), and **Vista International**. Most of these are listed under *Hotels*.

Museums and exhibitions

Belvedere Castle (*in Central Park, near 79th St. and s of the Great Lawn* ☎ 772-0210. *Hours vary* 🔲). Kids are delighted by the miniature castle itself, commanding a small hill beside a pond. Despite the ponderous name of the series of programs held inside (the forbiddingly titled "Central Park Learning Center"), more play than work goes on, and a wide variety of experiences is provided. At Christmas, children might make their own tree ornaments; in summer, there are nature walks and outdoor games related to the park. Call for details, and to reserve places.

Brooklyn Children's Museum (*145 Brooklyn Ave., between Eastern Parkway and Atlantic Ave.* ☎ 718-735-4400, *open Mon, Wed-Fri 2-5pm, Sat, Sun 10am-5pm* 🔲). The oldest (1899) children's museum in the US is in a new building. Exhibits cover basic technologies, social and natural history, and handling and participation are encouraged. Several levels support a steam engine, water-wheels, ladders, a windmill, hydraulic devices, plants and animals. There are thousands of objects and displays.

Junior Museum of the Metropolitan Museum of Art (*5th Ave. and 82nd St.* ☎ 879-5500, *ext. 351, open Tues 10am-8.45pm, Wed-Sat 10am-4.45pm, Sun and hols 11am-4.45pm*). Somehow it manages to be intellectually accessible to children under 12 without patronizing them. Exhibits, from the permanent collections and outside sources, introduce the arts and inspire a thirst for further exploration in the galleries upstairs. There is also a lively program of workshop demonstrations, films, and gallery tours.

Children's Museum of Manhattan (*212 W 83rd St., near Amsterdam Ave.* ☎ 721-1234, *open Tues-Fri 11am-5pm, Sat noon-5pm* 🔲). This modest museum emphasizes hands-on participation in games, displays and workshops concerned with natural history, conservation, culture and society. Puppetry and mask-making also take place.

In addition to the three museums mentioned above, many of the city's other museums also have presentations that are of interest for children. For addresses and opening times, and fuller details, see individual entries throughout *Sights and places of interest*.

American Museum of Natural History: the reassembled dinosaur skeletons, and dioramas of mounted animals and birds in simulated habitats are long-time favorites; but more vivid are the detailed depictions of the peoples and cultures of Asia, Central America and Africa; several rooms are set aside for schoolchildren, to increase their awareness of the museum through participatory exhibitions, games, performers, films, story hours and guided tours. The **Hayden Planetarium** is part of the facility, and on Sat during the school year (Oct-June) mounts a "Young People's Sky Show," which includes realistic overhead projections of galaxies and constellations, accompanied by music and narration. **Aunt Len's Doll and Toy Museum**: hundreds of antique toys, dolls and miniature houses crowd every inch of space in this refreshingly informal museum; visits by appointment only. **Brooklyn Museum**: programs on Sat and Sun introduce youngsters aged 6-12 to various parts of the collections through talks and demonstrations that do not abuse attention spans; art workshops are another feature. **Guinness World Records Exhibit Hall**: excess fascinates, and this set of tableaux of the longest, highest, shortest, fattest, oldest, youngest and most bizarre creations of man and nature never fails to grab attention. **Metropolitan Museum of Art**: apart from the **Junior Museum** on the basement level, the most alluring items for youngsters in the many collections seem to be the Egyptian tombs and mummies and the medieval arms and armor; older children are drawn to the special shows of the **Costume Institute**, and the recorded cassette tours are attractive. **Museum of Broadcasting**: children can enjoy tapes and kinescopes of radio and TV shows of the "olden times"; adults are usually just as intrigued, but some might wish to wait in Paley Park, next door. **Museum of the City of New York**: puppet shows (*Nov-Apr, Sat*) are the incentive to join in various "please touch" demonstrations of objects related to the history of the area; on Sun, there are concerts to which children over 10 are invited; and the gallery of toys and dolls on the 3rd floor is fascinating. **Museum of Holography**: ghostly three-dimensional images produced by laser technology provide a glimpse of the 21stC; free lectures (*Sept-May, Thurs eve*). **New-York Historical Society**: a scale-model of a Noah's Ark, populated by 300 animals, dominates the collection of vintage toys and dolls on the 2nd floor; storytelling, too. **Richmondtown Restoration** (Staten Island): costumed guides and craftsmen bring history to life in this re-created village, with demonstrations of weaving, wool-spinning, basketmaking, leatherwork, and cooperage. **South Street Seaport Museum**: the authentic tall ships of this open-air museum are diverting for all ages, and there is a theater designed for children; youngsters can take part in lectures, and browse in shops concerned with toys, ships' models and games with a nautical bent.

Observation decks ◁€

Empire State Building (*350 5th Ave., near 34th St. ☎ 736-3100; open daily 9.30am-midnight; closed Christmas and New Year's Day; children under 12 half-price*); there are two decks, on the 86th and 102nd floors.

World Trade Center (*2 World Trade Center, Lower Manhattan ☎ 466-7377; open daily 9.30am-9.30pm; children 6-12 about half-price ▣ under 6*). An enclosed deck is on the 107th floor, an open deck on the 110th. On a clear day, it is easy to imagine that you can see the curvature of the earth.

Closer to sea-level (and free) are the pedestrian walkways of the **Brooklyn Bridge** and the **George Washington Bridge**, as well as the **Brooklyn Heights** promenade.

In addition, there are several restaurants with excellent views, sky-high or from the ground. As long as one does not inspect the check and/or what appears on the plate too critically, the following can be pleasant: **The River Café** (*1 Water St., Brooklyn*), **The Water Club** (*500 E 30th St*), Giando (*400 Kent Ave., Brooklyn*), **The Hors d'Oeuvrerie** (*1 World Trade Center*), **Rainbow Promenade** (*GE Building*), **The Terrace** (*Butler Hall, Columbia University*), **Windows on the World** (*1 World Trade Center*).

Parades

For youngsters, the big one is the **Macy's Thanksgiving Day Parade** (*last Thurs in Nov*), with its huge floating balloons of comic-book heroes. The longest and most eagerly anticipated is the **St Patrick's Day Parade** (*Mar 17*), but that can be rowdy, with its roving bands of intoxicated teenagers. Most months have a parade of some kind in some part of the city, but 5th Ave. has several events in fall.

See *Calendar of events* on page 34.

Playgrounds

Numerous conventional playgrounds dot New York. But the ones suggested below are described as adventure playgrounds, with stacked wooden blocks, rope nets, sections of concrete tubes, and comparable combinations of imagination-firing shapes and materials.

Central Park ‡ Central Park West and 68th St. ‡ Central Park West, near 85th St. ‡ 5th Ave. and 85th St. ‡ 5th Ave. and 71st St.
Gramercy Park ‡ 2nd Ave. and 19th St.
Greenwich Village ‡ Washington Square Park, between 5th Ave. and University Pl. ‡ Abingdon Square Park at Hudson St. and Bleecker St.
Upper East Side ‡ 1st Ave. near 67th St. ‡ East End Ave. and 84th St.
Upper West Side ‡ W 45th St. near 10th Ave. ‡ W 90th St. near Columbus Ave.

Puppets and marionettes

The famous toy store **F.A.O. Schwarz** (*5th Ave. and 58th St.* ☎ *644-9400*) has free puppet shows (*Mon-Fri at 2.30pm*).
Heckscher Puppet House (*Central Park, 59th St.* ☎ *397-3162*) has two performances Mon-Fri, for elementary-school children and their younger siblings. Reservations essential; ask about suitable age group when calling. **Museum of the City of New York** (*1220 5th Ave. at 103rd St.* ☎ *534-1672. Shows Oct-Apr, Sat at 1.30pm.*): inexpensive. **Puppet Playhouse** (*555 E 90th St.* ☎ *369-8890; Oct-May, two shows each Sat and Sun.*): past performances have brought Winnie the Pooh and other favorites to life. The stage is occupied by visiting puppeteers of considerable skill. Inexpensive; reserve ahead. **South Street Seaport Museum** (*16 Fulton St. at South St.* ☎ *766-9020*): shipboard puppet shows and related entertainments on Sun at 2pm. **Swedish Cottage Marionette Theater** (*81st St. and Central Park West* ☎ *988-9093; performances Sat, Sun, some weekdays; call ahead for times.*): Inexpensive entry; reservations required. **Papageno Puppet Theater** (*173 W 81st St.* ☎ *874-3297*): the long-established group usually has two shows Sat and Sun, but its schedule varies and it has appeared at other locations, so call first. Inexpensive; reserve ahead.

Restaurants

Apart from their prohibitive cost, the shrines of *haute cuisine* set children to squirming and are unlikely to have available the simple fare they prefer. There are many moderately-priced restaurants catering to families, however, with special children's menus, high-chairs, and speedy service. The following tend to be large and rather touristy, but they go to considerable lengths to amuse young patrons.

America (*E 18th St.* ☎ *505-2110*). In a room the size of an aircraft hangar and with the noise level of a 747 starting up, there is ample opportunity for audiovisual diversion. Up to 400 people mill about beneath its neon canopy, ordering from a 200-plus-item menu of fast food and yuppie drinks. Portions are large, prices relatively low, the clientele a vivacious cross-section of tourists and the striving classes.

Benihana (*47 W 56th St.* ☎ *581-0930 and 120 E 56th St.* ☎ *593-1627*). Diners sit in groups of 6-8 around a horseshoe counter that encloses a sizzling grill. A cook in *toque blanche* arrives and, with a showy clatter, swoops over piles of shrimp, zucchini and beef, slicing, flipping, sautéing, serving. It may not be Japanese, but it is theatrical.

Caribe (*117 Perry St.* ☎ *255-9191, no cards*). This West Indian outpost in far west Greenwich Village hops around the islands for its culinary inspirations, from Martinique to Cuba to Jamaica. Kids will find some of the preparations "icky" — oxtail stew, perhaps — but others quite to their liking — deviled turkey leg, say. Ask about the degree of spiciness before ordering. There are so many potted plants that a native guide is almost required to find a table. Go early, since it can get a little raucous as the evening wears on.

Hamburger Harry's (*145 W 45th St.* ☎ *840-2756*). Designer 'burgers are the obvious fare, in variations unseen elsewhere and usually satisfying to adults as well as youngsters. A counter around the open grill adds to the fun. Menu alternatives include *fajitas*, chicken and chili. It's a good choice for a quick meal before the theater. The original branch is in TriBeCa (*157 Chambers St.* ☎ *267-4446*).

Hard Rock Café (*221 W 57th St.* ☎ *459-9320*). Parents are almost obligated to take their progeny, aged 6-16, to this New World version of the London original. The wait is long, under the "awning" of the rear end of a finned 1950s Cadillac, the noise level comparable to that of a departing jumbo jet. Rock memorabilia decorates the walls; good burgers and chocolate malts adorn the tables. A Hard Rock T-shirt will be a teenager's proudest memento of the trip to New York.

John's Pizzeria (*278 Bleecker St.* ☎ *243-1680 and 408 E 64th St.* ☎ *935-2895*) All arguments about New York pizza start over who is in *second* place, for most everyone agrees that John's is number one. Beware of imitators and assorted frauds with similar names, and if possible, get to the Greenwich Village branch. Expect a wait.

Sports and other activities

See *Sports and activities* on pages 190-94 for information on **Bicycling**, **Boating**, **Horseback riding**, **Iceskating** and **Swimming**.

Model boats

Miniature boats both humble and elaborate, radio-controlled or sail-powered, are seen nearly every day of the year on the **Conservatory Pond** (*in Central Park, near 5th Ave./72nd St.*).

Television shows
A number of game shows and variety specials originate in New York. Children between the ages of 6-18 must be accompanied by an adult. Tickets are free, and sources are:
American Broadcasting Company (*1330 6th Ave.* ☎ *581-7777*); **Columbia Broadcasting System** (*51 W 52nd St.* ☎ *581-4321*); **National Broadcasting Company** (*30 Rockefeller Plaza,* ☎ *664-3055*); **New York Convention and Visitors Bureau** (*2 Columbus Circle,* ☎ *397-8222*).

Zoos and aquarium
For addresses and opening times, see individual entries in *Sights and places of interest*.
Bronx Zoo: the new Children's Zoo, within the larger park (*open Apr-Oct*), has gentle animals for petting, and camels and pony carts for riding. Kids also enjoy the monorail that circles the "Wild Asia" preserve, the aerial tram that glides over the re-created "African Plains," and the tractor train that tours the entire park.
Central Park Zoo: (*open 7 days a week, all year round*) next to the 64th St. entrance is a merry-go-round, and inside are pony rides. The hub is the seal pool. To the N is the **Children's Zoo**, on a triangle of land on 5th Ave. between 65th St. and 66th St.
New York Aquarium: there are performances (*May-Oct*) by dolphins, whales and sea-lions. Most winter in Florida, but there are still indoor tanks featuring fish that resemble floating flowers and others, even stranger, that inspire shudders.
Prospect Park Zoo: this compact zoo also features pony rides, and a section of small farm animals set aside for children.
Staten Island Zoo: the comprehensive reptile collection is the big attraction, supplemented by a children's zoo and pony rides. Admission free on Wed.

Excursions

Unlike the capitals of Europe, New York has no medieval cathedrals or ancient university towns within easy reach. Beyond the inner ring of bleak smaller cities, however, the countryside is dotted with hamlets of Colonial serenity, inviting inns, dairy farms, and a surprising number of stately homes. These places are found in a great variety of natural settings, from hushed valleys to surf-pounded shores. For the following tours a car is essential.

A taste of New England
105 miles round trip NE. One day, preferably with an overnight stop.
Leave the city via the West Side Highway, which goes through several name changes and two toll booths. After the second toll, take the first exit onto the Cross Country Expressway. This merges eventually with the Hutchinson River Parkway, heading toward Connecticut. Leave it at Exit 27, turning left, N, on Route 120 (*Purchase St.*).
  At the next traffic signal, turn right, E, on Anderson Hill Rd. and follow it to the next intersection, Route 120A (*King St.*). Turn left, N. Continue past the entrance to the Westchester County Airport on the left. Keep a sharp look-out for Cliffdale Rd. on the right and turn into it. It winds down a steep hill into a bosky gorge with a tumbling brook, and leads on through a neighborhood of

luxurious estates. After a mile, Cliffdale Rd. ends at Route 433 (*Riversville Rd.*). Turn left, N.

At the intersection with John St., about a mile farther on, is the tall, chunky steeple of the **N Greenwich Congregational Church**, erected in 1896. On the opposite corner is an **Audubon Center**, with nature trails open to the public. Continue N on Route 433 to the first traffic signal, and turn right on Route 22. Just beyond a large modern furniture store is **Smith's Tavern** (*open Wed-Sat 1-3.30pm*). Built at the time of the Revolutionary War, it is now a modest museum of such items as antique dollhouses and quilts.

Route 22 rolls on, across undulating hills, past country clubs and examples of residential architecture dating back 300yrs. Eventually there is **Bedford Village**, settled in 1680 by pioneers from New England. At the fork in the road, park near the tiny schoolhouse (1829), which is now a museum of local history (*open Wed-Sun 2-5pm, often closed from Christmas to mid-Feb*). Across the street is a white clapboard Methodist Church (1806), now headquarters of the Bedford Historical Society (**☎** *914-234-9328*). The adjacent burial ground was established in 1681.

Bedford deserves an exploratory stroll. Around the triangular village green are the **Bedford Free Library** (1807), the **Courthouse and Museum** (1787), and **Post Office** (1838). Side streets have homes of the Dutch Colonial and Greek Revival styles. Most date from after 1779, when a British commander burned all but one of the then existing houses, in retribution for rebel resistance. Some of the historic buildings are open to the public (*usually open Wed-Sun 2-5pm*), but they are dependent upon volunteers, so they might be closed at unpredictable times.

You will soon have an opportunity to picnic, and good wholesome fare can be purchased at the delicatessen next to the Post Office, or at the **Bedford Gourmet** take-out store, opposite the movie theater. Return to the car and continue through the village on Route 22. Just beyond, bear right at the junction on Route 121, N. If a picnic does not strike your fancy, there is **Nino's** (**☎** *914-234-3374*), with good if unremarkable veal, pastas and mussels. Continue on Route 121, which eventually passes the Cross River Reservoir, part of New York City's water system.

Just before the junction with Route 35 is the entrance to the **Ward Pound Ridge Reservation** — 4,750 acres of hiking trails and campgrounds. If you did decide on a picnic, this is the place, but drive around to choose a spot. There are tables, stone barbecues, and fields in which to fling Frisbees. In cooler months, deer and racoon are often sighted, and cross-country skiing is popular. Return then to Route 35. After about 2 miles, look for the "State Police" sign and turn left into **South Salem** (settled 1731). Although the hamlet is of mild interest, the primary reason for the detour is to note for future reference the **Horse and Hound** restaurant (*dinner only* **☎** *914-763-3108*), where the chef-owner specializes in game dishes. Follow the street through town, turning left back onto Route 35.

Soon, this crosses into Connecticut and the town of Ridgefield. On the left is the **Inn at Ridgefield**, which offers lodgings, and lunch and dinner (*Wed-Sun*). Turn left on Main St., an avenue of majestic trees and splendid 19thC homes. On the right is the **Aldrich Museum of Contemporary Art** (*open Sat, Sun, Wed 1-5pm*). Sculptures monumental and whimsical are placed about the lawn and are on view every day. They, and the works within, are primarily by Americans since 1945. There are frequent special shows, but opening is sometimes haphazard. Should it happen to be open, a visit is a must. Continue N through the village on Main St. About 2 miles farther on, at the flashing traffic signal, turn right on Haviland Rd. At the next traffic signal, turn right again on Route 7. After half a mile, make a sharp right turn for **Stonehenge** (☎ 203-438-6511) — not a megalithic monument, but the finest restaurant in the area. It serves imaginative game dishes and quick-poached trout taken straight from the kitchen's own holding tank. Reservations are essential for weekend dinners, and necessary if you want to stay in one of the eight cozy bedrooms overlooking the inn's geese-filled pond. Should they be fully reserved, or if time is limited, return to New York via Route 7 and Interstate 95.

The Hudson River Valley
150 miles round trip N. Minimum one long day, preferably two days.

Travel N on the West Side Highway, which becomes the Henry Hudson Parkway and then the Saw Mill River Parkway after it crosses the city line into Westchester County. It is designated Route 9A all the way. Continue through the city of Yonkers and the town of Hastings-on-Hudson, taking exit 17 in Dobbs Ferry, W on Ashford Ave. until it joins with Broadway (*Route 9*). Turn right, N, and drive on past the commercial district of the village of Irvington. Four blocks beyond Main St., turn left, W, on Sunnyside Lane. At the end, just before the railroad tracks and the Hudson, is **Sunnyside** (🆒 *open daily 10am-5pm Apr-Dec, Sat, Sun only Jan-Mar*), the home of Washington Irving (1783-1859), an author, diplomat and scholar, who always returned to this region, which he called "Sleepy Hollow" in his novels and stories. The house, gardens and outbuildings have been scrupulously restored, with guides dressed in appropriate 19thC garb. This is part of the Historic Hudson Valley restorations, a group of historic buildings that includes **Philipsburg Manor** and **Van Cortlandt Manor** (see below). Combination tickets can be purchased for all three, at a substantial saving.

Return to Route 9 (*S. Broadway*) and go N, to reach a Gothic Revival mansion called **Lyndhurst** (☎ 914-631-0046 🆒 *open May-Oct, Wed-Sun 10am-5pm*), constructed in 1838 by a mayor of New York, and purchased by the railroad tycoon Jay Gould in 1880. Many of Gould's furnishings are in place, complementing the vaulted ceilings and stained-glass windows. There are popular summer concerts on the grounds. Picnicking is permitted.

Back on Route 9, proceed N 2 miles beyond the Dewey Thruway, watching for signs to **Philipsburg Manor** (🆒 *open as Sunnyside, above*). Frederick Philipse, a late 17thC Dutch immigrant, was clearly a businessman and entrepreneur of exceptional acumen. This bustling complex of dam, gristmill, granary, bakery, stockyards, shipping wharf and farmland was only part of his holdings, which at one time totaled 90,000 acres on both banks of the Hudson. Costumed attendants give demonstrations of Colonial cooking, millwork, weaving, and agricultural trades and crafts. There is a guided tour, beginning with a short film and then visiting the farmhouse, mill and barn. The **Old Dutch Church** across the street was built by Philipse in 1697. Washington Irving is buried in the nearby cemetery.

Route 9 passes N through Ossining and arrives after 8 miles in Croton-on-Hudson. Turn right at Croton Point Ave., continue to the first traffic signal, and turn right again on S. Riverside Ave. **Van Cortlandt Manor** (*open as Sunnyside, above*), another part of the Historic Hudson Valley organization, is about 100yds down the road. The main house began as a modest lodge erected in the late 1600s and was expanded to its present size by subsequent generations of the wealthy Van Cortlandt family, who lived on this land for more than 260yrs. The original 86,000 acres have now vastly shrunk, but they are well-tended, and the manor has been restored to its 18thC splendor.

Down by the river, past flourishing gardens and fruit trees, is the **Ferry House**, an inn of the same period, which served passengers of the ferry operated by the Van Cortlandts. George Washington stopped by frequently, as did many other prominent figures of the Revolutionary War period. As at the other Historic Hudson Valley restorations, appropriately attired guides and craftspeople give demonstrations of home and farm skills. Frequent special events include a Christmas Candlelight Tour and the Fall Crafts and Tasks Festival.

Return to Route 9 and continue N. Beyond the city of Peekskill, turn W on Route 6. The road ascends, curling around the mountain face, with an excellent outlook at the top, on the left. Continue down toward the Bear Mountain Bridge, now in view. But instead of crossing the bridge, drive N on Route 9D. After the town of **Garrison**, turn left at the traffic light on Main St., into **Cold Spring**. The street, with many 19thC houses, descends to the edge of the river. Opposite looms **Storm King Mountain**, the tallest peak in these "Hudson Highlands." Down to the left (S) is seen the fortress-like **US Military Academy**, the officers' training college better known as **West Point**.

There are several places to eat in the village, the best-known being **Hudson House** (*open all year*), opposite the bandstand at river's edge. If you decide to stay the night, the inn has a number of plain but comfortable rooms. Afterwards, return to Route 9D and drive N, joining with Route 9 again a mile N of Wappingers Falls. This leads into the river port town of Poughkeepsie. If time and interest permit, turn E on Route 55 to the **Vassar College** campus. One of the first institutions of higher education for women (opened 1865) and a member of the prestigious "Seven Sisters" group, it turned co-educational in 1968. For evening refreshment at the end of a full day, drive about 16 miles on, to Rhinebeck, and stop at the **Beekman Arms** (*open all year; meals and room rates moderate*), dating from 1700 and claiming to be the oldest inn in continuous operation in the United States.

Should the next day be a Sat or Sun (*May-Oct only*), you can see an airshow featuring vintage planes at the **Old Rhinebeck Aerodrome** (☎ 914-758-8610 *to check times*), reached by driving N on Route 9. On other days (or in addition), there are the historic sites in Hyde Park, to the S on Route 9. Near the center of that sleepy village is the 1898 **Vanderbilt Mansion** (☎ 914-229-9115, *open June-Aug 9am-6pm, Sept-May 9am-5pm*). Most of the works of art and furnishings in it are original. A mile or two S on Route 9 is the entrance to **the home of Franklin Delano Roosevelt** (*times as Vanderbilt Mansion; see above*). Parts of the house date from 1826; F.D.R. was born there in 1882, and he and his wife are buried in the rose garden.

Two miles farther S on Route 9 is an unusual educational institution sometimes called "the other CIA," **The Culinary Institute of America** (☎ 914-471-6608). The student-chefs operate several restaurants, all open to the public. Advance reservations are essential.

Continue s on Route 9 to Poughkeepsie and take the Mid-Hudson Bridge, picking up Route 9W on the opposite side of the river. Turn s. Just beyond Newburgh, pick up Route 218 through Cornwall, a winding but especially scenic drive high above the Hudson. This road ends at the Washington Gate of the **US Military Academy**, seen before from Cold Spring. The campus is open to the public all year. Ask for directions at the **Visitors' Information Center** (*open Apr-Nov daily 8.30am-4.30pm, Dec-Mar Wed-Sun 8.30am-4.30pm*). There is an interesting **Military Museum** on the grounds, but be sure to stop at the belvedere overlooking the Hudson.

Exit from the main gate at the s end of the reservation, driving through the village of **Highland Falls** and on to Route 9W once again. This passes **High Tor State Park** (▧ *open June-Sept*) in Haverstraw, with hiking trails, swimming, and picnic facilities. After about 3 miles, watch for the right turn onto Route 303. If it is mealtime, take that road to the **Bully Boy Chop House** (☎ *914-268-6555, open for lunch Mon-Fri, and dinner daily*), for generous portions of non-gimmicky American food. Alternatively, continue s on 9W, detouring into the business district of Nyack, with its many antique and bric-a-brac stores.

Pick up Route 87 (*the Dewey Thruway*) at the edge of town, driving E across the Tappan Zee Bridge and s into the city.

Shakers and Berkshires
290 miles NE. Minimum two days.
There are numerous opportunities for swimming, hiking, and picnicking along this route, so dress and pack accordingly.

Leave Manhattan via the West Side Highway. This becomes the Henry Hudson Parkway, which joins the Saw Mill River Parkway. Follow the latter to Hawthorne Interchange, transferring to the Taconic State Parkway, N, which passes through a sparsely settled countryside of meadows, groves, and green and tawny land with folds like a rumpled blanket. Leave the Parkway at the Route 44 exit, following signs E toward **Millbrook**. Watch for the junction with Route 82. Just beyond is Tyrrell Rd. Turn right, s, and follow signs to **Innisfree Garden** (▧ ☎ *914-677-8000, open May-Oct Wed-Sun 10am-4pm*), the creation of a painter by the name of Walter Beck. A gallery contains a selection of Beck's paintings.

Return to Route 44 and turn right, E, into the small, pleasant village of **Millbrook**. In recent years, it has become more and more an antique hunter's heaven. Continue about 10 miles to Amenia, there picking up Route 363 E. Off this road is **Troutbeck** (◪ ☎ *914-373-8581*), an exemplary inn that serves as a conference center during the week, with tennis courts and pool. Private guests are accepted from Fri afternoon-Sun evening. Weekend packages are expensive, but include all meals. Reservations are essential. Continue on Route 363 into **Sharon**, a charming Connecticut town with white clapboard frame houses beneath sheltering elms and maples. Two miles SE on Route 4 is an **Audubon Center** (▧ ☎ *203-364-5826, open Wed-Sat 9am-5pm, Sun 1-5pm*), a wildlife sanctuary with miles of nature walks, a museum, and a herb garden. When you leave, return to the center of Sharon and pick up Route 41, N, to Lakeville. Once there, turn left, w, on Route 44, crossing once again into New York State and arriving in Millerton. Look for **McArthur's Smokehouse**, by the railroad tracks, where superior sausages and other smoked meats are sold. With supplementary supplies from the nearby grocery store, the ingredients of a memorable

Excursions

picnic can be assembled; and the perfect place to eat it is nearby.

To find the spot, take Route 22, N, and after about 8 miles look for the inconspicuous sign directing you to **Boston Corners**, then look for signs to **Bash Bish Falls Reservation**. From the designated parking lot, a woodland path rises toward the gap between two peaks, a brook tumbling by on the right. After less than a mile, a slender waterfall plunges 50ft into a large clear pool, spilling into a series of smaller rock clefts and crevices. Man-made intrusions do not detract from the primitive grandeur of the place.

The road leading from the parking lot up to a vantage above the falls is a worthwhile detour. Afterward, return to Route 22 and drive N to **Hillsdale**. At the juncture with Route 23 is **L'Hostellerie Bressane** (*information and reservations* ☎ *518-325- 3412*), an ambitious (and costly) inn of classical Provençal leanings. Only dinner is served, and it is closed at unpredictable times. Turn right, E, on Route 23. This leads back to Massachusetts, through the pretty hamlet of South Egremont, eventually connecting with Route 7. Turn left, N, through Great Barrington and on to **Stockbridge**, 8 miles farther on.

On most counts a quintessential New England village, Stockbridge stops short of touristy clutter. Turn right, E, into Main St. (*Route 102*). At that corner is the **Red Lion Inn** (☎ *413-298-5545* 🏨 *108 rms, advance reservations essential*). The dining room serves three meals daily, and there is a convivial tap room downstairs with live music most weekend evenings. The revered illustrator Norman Rockwell lived in Stockbridge much of his life, and many of his paintings are on view at the 18thC **Corner House** (🏛 *open June-Oct daily, closed Tues Nov-May*), just down the street. Two blocks in the other direction, W, is the **Mission House** (☎ *413-298-3383* 🏛 *open late May-early Oct, Tues-Sat 10am-5pm*), built in 1739 and maintained as a museum of domestic Colonial life. The **Chesterwood** estate of the sculptor Daniel Chester French is 2 miles away, N on Route 102, then S on Route 183. French created the moving sculpture of Abraham Lincoln in Washington, DC's Lincoln Memorial. There are daily guided tours of the house and studio (🏛 *open late May-early Oct 10am-5pm*).

The southern Berkshires host a multitude of cultural activities every summer. In Stockbridge, the **Berkshire Playhouse** presents classics and some pre-Broadway try-outs (*June-Oct*). The **Boston Symphony Orchestra** and other musical ensembles perform at **Tanglewood**, an open-sided "shed" on spacious grounds in nearby Lenox. The town of **Lee** is known for the annual **Jacob's Pillow Dance Festival**, in a theater created by Martha Graham and Ted Shawn. In winter, there are several popular ski resorts, including Bousquet, Brodie, and Jiminy Peak near Pittsfield and Butternut Basin near Great Barrington.

When ready to leave for New York, drive N on Route 7 to Pittsfield, then W on Route 20. Five miles from the center of Pittsfield is **Hancock Shaker Village** (☎ *413-443-0188, open June-Oct 9.30am-5pm*), one of the former settlements of the celibate religious sect founded as an offshoot of the Quakers in the 18thC. In accordance with their beliefs, their houses and furnishings were crisp and exquisitely simple. This painstakingly restored village illustrates their crafts and trades, from cookery to "spirit painting," with admirable clarity. Don't miss it.

Drive W on Route 20, then turn left, S, on Route 22. At Hillsdale, take Route 23 right, W, to the Taconic State Parkway for the return to New York.

Index

Individual hotels, restaurants and shops have not been indexed, because they appear in alphabetical order within their appropriate sections. The sections themselves, however, are indexed. Streets are indexed separately in the *List of street names* on page 215.

Page numbers in **bold** type refer to main entries. Ordinary *italic* page numbers refer to the illustrations and plans. Page numbers in larger *sans serif italics* refer only to the British edition: for the first 16 pages, some index entries *not* in this special type may not apply to the British edition.

Index

Index

Index

List of street names

All streets mentioned in the book that fall within the area covered by our maps are listed here. Each street name is followed by a map reference to one or more of the maps that follow this list. Map numbers are printed in **bold** type.

It was not possible to label every street drawn on the maps, although of course all major streets and most smaller ones are named. Those streets that are not named on the maps are still given map references in this list, because this serves as an approximate location that will nearly always be sufficient for you to find your way.

An explanation of the Manhattan street grid system can be found on page 13.

Street names

N
Nassau St., **2**U4

O
Ocean Parkway, **12**E3
Orange St., **3**U6
Orchard St., **3**S5

P
Park Ave., **5**M-Q4, **7**J-N4,
  9H-J4
Park Drive, **7**L4
Park Pl., **2**T4
Park Row, **2**T4
Pearl St., **2**U4
Peck Slip, **3**U5
Pell St., **3**T5
Perry St., **2**R3
Pierrepont St., **3**U6
Prince St., **2**S4

Q
Queensboro Bridge, Map
  5N5
Queens-Midtown
  Tunnel, Map **5**O5

R
Remsen St., **3**V6
Richmond Terrace, **12**F2
River Ave., **11**F4
Riverside Drive, **8**I2
Rockaway Boulevard,
  13E5
Rockefeller Plaza, **5**O4
Roosevelt Drive (FDR
  Drive), **5**P-Q5

S
St Luke's Pl., **2**S3
St Marks Pl., **2**R5
Schermerhorn Row, **3**V6

Sniffen Court, **5**P4
South St., **3**U5
Southern Boulevard,
  13B-C4
Spring St., **2**S3-4
State St., **2**U4
Stone St., **2**U4
Sullivan St., **2**S4
Surf Ave., **12**F3
Sutton Pl., **5**N5
Sylvan Terrace, **8**F3

T
Thompson St., **2**S4
Times Sq., **4**O3
Transverse Road, **6**M3-4
Triborough Bridge, **9**H5

U
Union Sq., **5**Q4
United Nations Plaza,
  5O5
University Pl., **2**R4

V
Van Cortlandt Park
  (Bronx), **13**B4
Vandam St., **2**S3
Vanderbilt Ave., **5**O4
Varick St., **2**S3-4
Verrazano Narrows
  Bridge, **12**E2-3
Vesey St., **2**T4

W
Wall St., **2**U4
Washington Ave., **12**E3
Washington Mews,
  2R4
Washington Pl., **2**R3-4
Washington Sq., N and S,
  2R4

Washington St.,
  2R3
Water St., **3**T5
Water St. (Brooklyn),
  3T6
Waverly Pl., **2**R4
West St., **2**T3
West End Ave., **6**I-M2
White St., **2**T4
Whitehall St., **2**U4
William St., **2**U4
Willow St., **3**U6
Wooster St., **2**S4
Worth St., **2**T4

Y
York Ave., **7**K-L5

Numbered
avenues
1st Ave., **3**Q-R5, **5**M-R5,
  7I-N5, **9**I-J5
2nd Ave., **3**R5, **5**N-Q5,
  7K-L4-5, **9**I-J5
3rd Ave., **2**Q-R4, **5**N-Q5,
  7L-M5
4th Ave., **2**, **5**R4
5th Ave., **2**R4, **5**M-R4,
  7J-N4
6th Ave. (Ave. of the
  Americas), **2**R-S4,
  5P-R4
7th Ave., **2**Q-R3, **4**N-Q3,
  6I3, **8**E-I3
8th Ave., **2**Q-R3, **4**N-Q3,
  6I3, **8**E-I3
9th Ave., **2**Q3, **4**N-R3
10th Ave., **4**N-O2
11th Ave., **4**N-O2
12th Ave., **4**P2
15th Ave., **2**R4
45th Ave. (Queens), **13**D4

Numbered streets
Numbered steets in Manhattan run from E-W across the island.
Above 14th St. streets are called W to the left of 5th Ave. and E to
the right. 5th Ave. runs from N-S, along the right hand edge of
Central Park. Above 136th St., streets called E are across the
Harlem River, in The Bronx.

1st-9th St., **2**R4-**3**R6	99th-110th St., **6**J2-**7**J5	E 161st-168th St.,
10th-13th St., **2**R3-**3**R6	111th-123rd St., **8**I2-9I5	**11**E4-6
13th-25th St., **4**Q2-**5**Q5	124th-135th St., **8**H2-9H4	W 173rd-184th St.,
26th-37th St., **4**P2-**5**P5	126th St. (Queens), **13**D4	**10**D2-3
38th-49th St., **4**O2-**5**O5	136th-147th St., **8**G2-9G4	E 169th-172nd St.,
50th-62nd St., **4**N2-**5**N5	W 148th-159th St., **8**F2-3	**11**D4-6
63rd-74th St., **6**M2-**7**M5	E 148th-160th St., 94-6	W 185th-193rd St., **10**C2-3
75th-86th St., **6**L2-7L5	W 160th-172nd St.,	E 172nd-177th St., **11**C4-6
87th-98th St., **6**K2-**7**K5	**10**E2-3	E178th-183rd St., **11**B4-6

NEW YORK

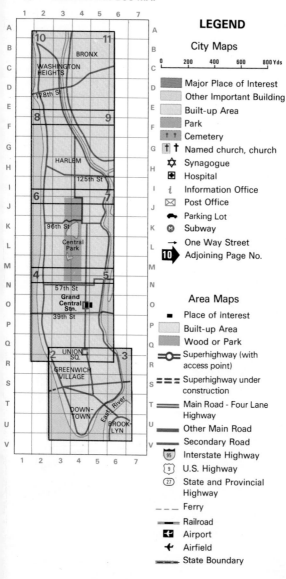

LEGEND

City Maps

0   200   400   600   800 Yds

	Major Place of Interest
	Other Important Building
	Built-up Area
	Park
† †	Cemetery
† †	Named church, church
✡	Synagogue
✚	Hospital
i	Information Office
⊠	Post Office
☎	Parking Lot
Ⓜ	Subway
→	One Way Street
10	Adjoining Page No.

Area Maps

▪	Place of Interest
	Built-up Area
	Wood or Park
=○=	Superhighway (with access point)
= = =	Superhighway under construction
═══	Main Road - Four Lane Highway
───	Other Main Road
──	Secondary Road
95	Interstate Highway
9	U.S. Highway
27	State and Provincial Highway
– – –	Ferry
══	Railroad
✈	Airport
✦	Airfield
▬▬	State Boundary

Map labels: BRONX, WASHINGTON HEIGHTS, 178th St, HARLEM, 125th St, 96th St, Central Park, 57th St, Grand Central Stn., 39th St, UNION SQ., GREENWICH VILLAGE, DOWN-TOWN, BROOKLYN, East River

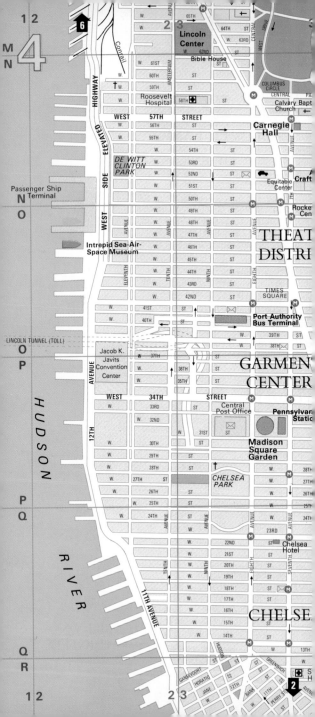

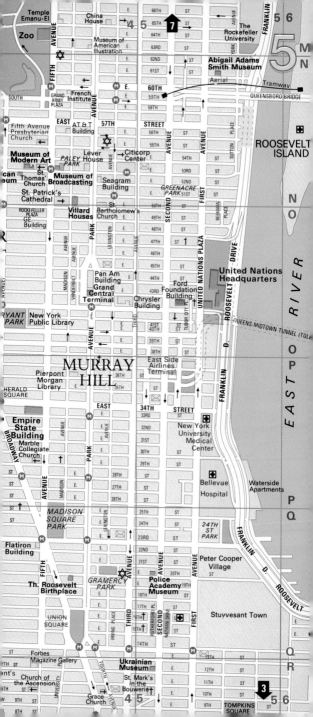

6

I J

J K

K L

L M

M N

1 2

W 114TH ST
W 113TH **2 3** ST
W 112TH ST
W 111TH ST Cathedral of St John the Divine

W 114TH ST

8

HUDSON PARKWAY

W 109TH CATHEDRAL ST
W 108TH PARKWAY ST
W 107TH ST
W 106TH ST
W 105TH ST
W 104TH ST
W 103RD ST
W 102ND ST
W 101ST ST
W 100TH ST
W 99TH ST
W 98TH ST
W 97TH ST
W 96TH ST

EIGHTH AVENUE

CENTRAL

HA
N

WEST END AVENUE

AMSTERDAM AVENUE

COLUMBUS AVENUE

MANHATTAN AVENUE

CENTRAL PARK WEST

CE

F

UPPER
WEST
SIDE

95TH ST
94TH ST
93RD ST
92ND ST
91ST ST
90TH ST
89TH ST
88TH ST
87TH ST

RI

Soldiers and Sailors Monument

86TH ST
85TH ST
84TH ST
83RD ST

RIVERSIDE DRIVE

Children's Museum of Manhattan

American Museum of Natural History and Hayden Planetarium

Met
Muse

Cle
Ne

W 82ND ST
W 81ST ST
W 80TH ST
W 79TH ST
W 78TH ST
W 77TH ST

AMSTERDAM AVENUE

76TH ST
75TH ST New-York Historical Society

THE LAKE

74TH ST
73RD ST
72ND ST
W 71ST ST Dakota Apartments
W 70TH ST
W 69TH ST
W 68TH ST
W 67TH ST

COLUMBUS AVENUE

CENTRA

PARK

HUDSON PARKWAY

HENRY HUDSON PARKWAY

FREEDOM PLACE

WEST END AVENUE

BROADWAY

Museum of American Folk Art

W 66TH ST
W 65TH ST

Lincoln Center

W 64TH ST
W 63RD ST

COLUMBUS
CIRCLE

CENTRAL

PARK

W 62ND ST
Bible House

Conrail

4

W 61ST ST
W 60TH ST
W 59TH ST Roosevelt Hospital **2 3**
W 58TH ST

HUDSON RIVER

1 2

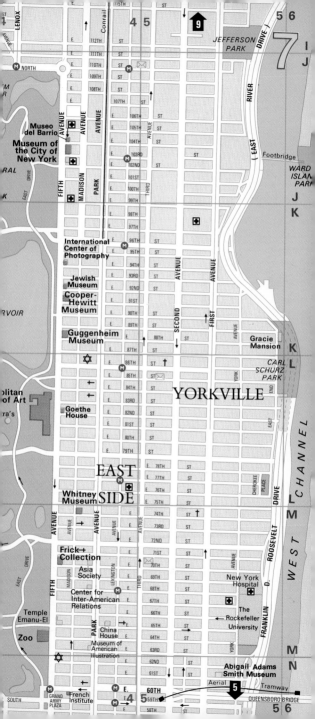

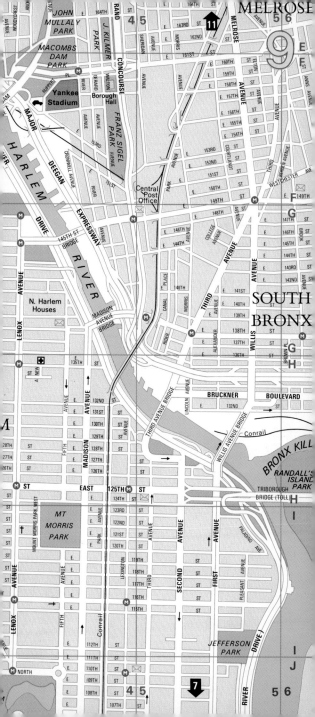

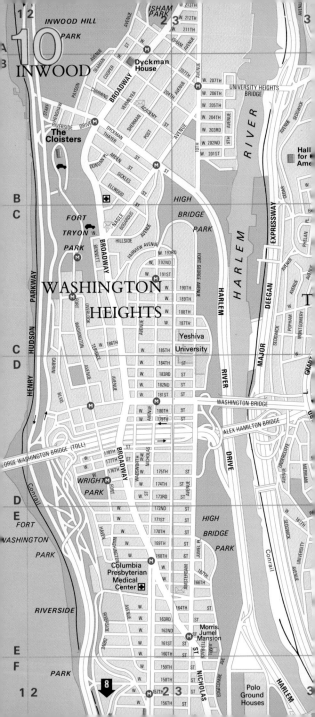

NEW YORK ENVIRONS

0   1   2   3   4 Miles

Oradell
Reservoir

Fair Lawn
Paramus
208
Bergenfield
Passaic River
Paterson
Bergenville
Paramus
4
Garden State Parkway
Bergenfield
80
Passaic
17
Hackensack
Englewood
46
Garfield
Teaneck
Clifton
Expressway
80
Fort Lee
Passaic
21
46
TETERBORO
AIRPORT
3
Bloomfield
17
MEADOWLANDS
SPORTS COMPLEX
Jersey Turnpike
North Bergen
Hudson Park
State Parkway
Garden State
NEW JERSEY
HACKENSACK
New
RIVER
Jersey
West New York
Hand
Central Park
95
3
MANHATTAN
NEW JERSEY
HISTORICAL
SOCIETY
21
Kearny
New
95
Union City
Lincoln Tunnel (TOLL)
Queensboro Bridge
Passaic River
1-9
501
Hoboken
EAST
Pulaski Skyway
478
QUEENS MIDTOWN TUNNEL (TOLL)
NEW YORK
NEWARK
1-9
N.J. Turnpike
ROOSEVELT STADIUM
440
JERSEY CITY
78
HOLLAND TUNNEL (TOLL)
CITY HALL
MANHATTAN BRIDGE
WILLIAMSBURG BRIDGE
Ellis Is.
BROOKLYN BRIDGE
278
Brooklyn
NEWARK INTERNATIONAL AIRPORT
95
New Jersey
Turnpike Ext.
STATUE OF LIBERTY
BROOKLYN-BATTERY TUNNEL (TOLL)
Brooklyn Heights
Liberty Is.
Governors Is.
Elizabeth
UPPER BAY
BROOKLYN ZOO AND BG GARD
NEWARK BAY
Bayonne
NEW JERSEY
NEW YORK
BROOKLYN ZOO
Prospect Park
27
BAYONNE BRIDGE
440
SNUG HARBOR CULTURAL CENTER
STATEN ISLAND ZOO
Queens Expressway
BROOKLYN
278
Bay Ridge
278
Ocean Parkway
Staten Island Expressway
STATEN ISLAND
Shore Expressway
VERRAZANO NARROWS BRIDGE (TOLL)
J.M. CENTER OF TIBETAN ART
RICHMONDTOWN RESTORATION
GATEWAY NATIONAL RECREATION AREA
LOWER BAY
Coney Island
AQUARIUM

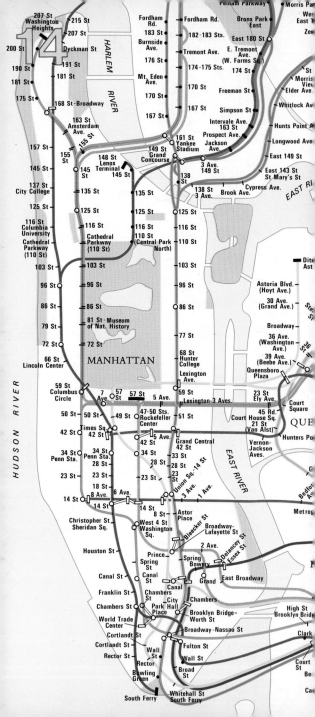

NEW YORK SUBWAY SYSTEM

ROUTES

Broadway - 7th Ave.
(Local/Express/Shuttle)

Lexington Ave.
(Express/Local/Local Pelham Express)

Flushing
(Local/Express)

Broadway
(Local/Express/Shuttle/ Nassau St Local)

8th Ave.
(Local/Express/Rockaway Shuttle)

Ave. of Americas (6th Ave.)
(Local/Express/Shuttle)

Brooklyn/Queens
(Crosstown)

Nassau St
(Local/Shuttle)

14 St - Canarsie
(Local)

Terminal

Local Stop

Express Stop

Express & Local Stop

Free Transfers

Special Rush Hour
Express Service

THE BRONX

east 177 St
Parkchester
wrence Ave.
Sound
es.

Castle Hill Ave.

ter Sq.
unt Ave.
Ave.

Blvd.

---

103 St-Corona Plaza

Junction Blvd.

82 St
74 St-Broadway
Jackson Heights
65 St
46 St
Northern Blvd.

90 St-Elmhurst Ave.

Grand Ave.
Newtown
Elmhurst
Ave.

Woodhaven Blvd.
Slattery Plaza

63 Drive
Rego Park

67 Ave.

71-Continental Aves.
Forest Hills

75 Ave.

Roosevelt Ave.
69 St Jackson Heights
61 St (Fisk Ave.)
52 St (Lincoln Ave.)
46 St (Bliss St)
40 St (Lowery St)
Rawson St)

ns

Forest
Parkway

Metropolitan Ave.

Fresh Pond Rd.

Forest Ave.

Seneca
Ave.

Halsey St

Elderts Lane

Cypress
Hills

Crescent
St

Jefferson St
DeKalb Ave.
Myrtle
Ave.

Wilson Ave.

Bushwick Ave.
Aberdeen St
Broadway Junction
Eastern Parkway

Norwood
Ave.
Cleveland St
Van Siclen Av

Knickerbocker
Ave.
Wyckoff
Ave.

Central Ave.

Chauncey
St

Halsey
St

oint Ave.

Grand
St
Lorimer St
Graham Ave.
Montrose Ave.
Morgan Ave.
Broadway
Lorimer St
Flushing Ave.

assau
Ave.

Gates
Ave.

Kosciusko St

Alabama Ave.

Atlantic
Ave.
Broadway
East New
York
Rockaway Ave.

Liberty
Ave.

Van
Siclen
Ave.

n Ave.
nd St
Marcy
Ave.
Hewes
St

Flushing Ave.

Myrtle Ave.

Ralph Ave.

Sutter
Ave.

Livonia
Ave.

OOKLYN

Myrtle-
Willoughby
Aves.

Bedford-
Nostrand Aves.

Clinton-
Washington Aves.

Classon Ave.

Nostrand-
Franklin
Aves.

Utica Ave.

Kingston-
Throop Aves.

Junius
St

Rockaway Ave.
Saratoga Ave.

k St

Borough Hall
Jay St
Lawrence St
DeKalb
Fulton

Clinton-
Washington Aves.

Lafayette Ave.

Franklin Ave.

Utica Ave.

Sutter Ave.
Rutland Rd.

Hoyt St

Nevins
St
Pacific
St
Hoyt-
Schermerhorn
Sts.

Atlantic Ave.

Nostrand Ave.
President St

Kingston Ave.

ugh

Bergen
St

Union
St

Smith-
9 Sts.

7 Ave.

Grand Army
Plaza

Eastern Pkwy.
Brooklyn Museum

Sterling St

Sterling St

Prospect
Park

Winthrop St

Church Ave.

St
9 St
4 Ave.
7 Ave.

MANHATTAN BUS MAP

16

A selection of crosstown
and uptown routes

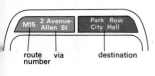

route   via   destination
number

UPTOWN

M1 5th & Madison Aves
(8 St/4 Ave & 146 St/Lenox Ave)

M4 5th & Madison Aves
(32 St/7 Ave & 193 St/Ft Washington Ave)

M5 5th Ave & 6th Ave
(Houston St/W.B'way & 178 St/B'way)

M6 7th Ave/B'way & 6 Ave
(59 St/6 Ave & South Ferry)

M10 7th & 8th Aves
(Houston St/7 Ave & 159 St/8 Ave)

M11 9th & 10th Aves
(12 St/Hudson St & 133 St/B'way)

M15 1st & 2nd Aves
(South Ferry & 126 St/2 Ave)

M101 3rd & Lexington Aves
(6 St/3 Ave & †93 St/Amsterdam Ave)

M104 Broadway
(42 St/1 Ave & 129 St/Amsterdam Ave)

CROSSTOWN

M19 96th St
(1 Ave/96 St & West End Ave/96 St)

M18 86th St
(York Ave/91 St & West End Ave/86 St)

M17 79th St
(East End Ave/79 St & West End Ave/79 St)

M103 59th St
(York Ave/61 St & B'way/72 St)

M28 57th St
(Sutton Place/55 St & 12 Ave/55 St)

M27 49th & 50th Streets
(1 Ave/47 St & 12 Ave/42 St)

M106 42nd St
(1 Ave/42 St & 12 Ave/42 St)

M16 34th St
(1 Ave/34 St & 12 Ave/42 St)

M14 14th St
(FDR Drive/Delancey St & 10 Ave/15 St)

M13 8th St
(Ave D/10 St & West St/Christopher St)

M21 Houston St
(1 Ave/27 St & Hudson St/Van Dam St)

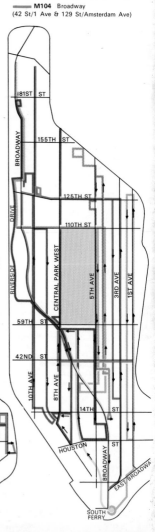